I0199871

After Saturday Comes Sunday

After Saturday Comes Sunday

Susan Adelman

GORGIAS PRESS

2018

Gorgias Press LLC, 954 River Road, Piscataway, NJ, 08854, USA

www.gorgiaspress.com

Copyright © 2018 by Gorgias Press LLC

All rights reserved under International and Pan-American Copyright Conventions. No part of this publication may be reproduced, stored in a retrieval system or transmitted in any form or by any means, electronic, mechanical, photocopying, recording, scanning or otherwise without the prior written permission of Gorgias Press LLC.

2018 ܐ

ISBN 978-1-4632-3904-6

Library of Congress Cataloging-in-Publication Data

A Cataloging-in-Publication Record is available from the Library of Congress.

Printed in the United States of America

To Norma Hakeem, who has been a loving mother to me for
forty years, and to the memory of Karim Hakim,
her husband, who in every way lived up to the meaning of his
name – generous.

TABLE OF CONTENTS

ACKNOWLEDGEMENTS

Many people helped bring this book to fruition. First I must thank Norma Hakim, my strength and inspiration for over forty years. Indeed, her entire extended family has helped me in countless ways, in particular feeding me innumerable meals when I came home from work exhausted; they truly are family. While assuring everyone in the family of my appreciation for all they do, in connection with this book I must mention Julie Hakim, Azucena Hakim, and her father, Dr. Ulises Casab-Rueda in partiular. I also would like to thank another member of the Chaldean community of southeast Michigan, Joseph Kassab, who gave of his time and shared copies of many of his publications.

Beyond my Chaldean family, I have received assistance from Profs. Shalom Sabar of Hebrew University, Yona Sabar of UCLA, and Yona's son Ariel Sabar, the author of the wonderful book *My Father's Paradise*. I also want to single out out Professors Geoffrey Khan of Cambridge University and Christopher Rollston of George Washingon University, who both have both been of enormous help. Whenever I needed that extra bit of help, Professor Khan was there to ease me past the problem. In Israel, Batia Aloni was gracious enough to share her story at great length, and this became a crucial chapter of the book. George Mammen shared his considerable expertise on the St. Thomas Christians, and I am grateful to him for that. For attracting us to India over the last forty years, and for teaching us an inestimable amount about his world, I must thank our friend, the eminent lawyer and politician, Ram Jethalani. Similarly, for years of teaching me about China, for helping to arrange our many trips there and for putting me in contact with Prof. Jender Lee to review the chapter on Christians in China, I must thank my friend Taymin Liu and her husband Paul

Liu. For organizing our trip to Thessaloniki and for our contacts within Hebrew University, I must thank Judith Shenkman, the cousin that everyone should have.

Ella Moskowitz, a Hebrew teacher, native Israeli and friend, helped with Hebrew translations and with arcane points of biblical history. My Arabic teacher and friend, Fatima Fawaz, helped with translations of Arabic words. And Norma Hakim, as usual, helped with the Chaldean translations. The prolific author Edwin Black was kind enough to read the manuscript, to comment, and to offer a cover blurb. My editor, Melonie Schmierer-Lee and her colleagues at Gorgias Press have been of inestimable assistance, and I cannot thank them enough. I would also like to thank Melissa Sung for her work on the cover design. David Waldshan, a Holocaust survivor himself and all too familiar with persecution, had the patience to listen as I read him the entire text. And his wife Sarah also listened to most of it, then insisted on serving me dinner after each reading session. Last but not least, my husband, Prof. Martin J. Adelman of George Washington University, has been my sounding board, my cheering squad and my constant support throughout this entire project.

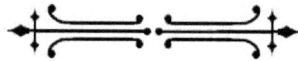

INTRODUCTION

'If we close our eyes, prayers in Western Syriac or Eastern Syriac in a Church in the Middle East will soon only be a distant memory – nothing more than a breath of hot wind in the desert.' In the original French : 'Si nous fermons les yeux, les prières exprimées en syriaque occidental ou en syriaque oriental dans une église du moyen orient ne ser ont bientôt plus qu'un lointain souvenir – rien de plus qu'un souffle de vent chaud dans le désert.'[1] Christophe Neff.

Christians could soon become extinct in the Middle East. And with them, the Aramaic language is dying, after three thousand years. The Christians and Jews who still speak it soon will be dead or vanished into the Diaspora. In the late nineteenth and early twentieth century the Christians of the Ottoman Empire suffered murder and mutilation. Now in the twenty-first century, fanatics on the warpath are decimating the villages that survived, villages that housed Assyrians, Chaldeans, and Kurdish Jews, the heirs of the Babylonian Exile and the children of the Ten Lost Tribes of Israel.

What the indigenous Christians of the Middle East and the Jews have in common is the Aramaic language. It is the language that Jesus spoke, the language of the Jewish Talmud, the language which Maronite Christians use to pray in Lebanon, the vernacular of the Chaldean Church in Southfield Michigan and the liturgical language of the St. Thomas Christians in southern India. But of all those who have fled the pogroms and the beheadings, of those who escaped a command to convert or die, how many of their grandchildren will speak anything but English, one of the European languages, Arabic or Hebrew? What is the world losing? *Who* are we losing?

1

First we will learn about the language, one so old that inscriptions chiseled on stone steles have been effaced by time. Then we will meet the biblical peoples who speak it today. Amazingly, most belong to the Church of the East, once the most far-flung church in the world. The only people of greater antiquity are the Kurdish Jews who the Assyrians brought to Mesopotamia in 722 BCE, and who lived there until they moved to Israel.

Americans hardly know anything about the ancient Church of the East. This is not the Roman Church, not the Greek Church, but a church that once stretched from Mesopotamia through Mongolia to eastern China, a church whose women married into the tribe of Genghis Khan, whose language influenced scripts in India and Asia, and a church that has contracted back to a single triangle of land in the Middle East, where they now are under vicious assault.

Why should we care? Why do I care enough to write this book? As a young pediatric surgeon, I operated on a little Chaldean boy from northern Iraq who was dying of a rare parasitic disease. The aunts who translated at his bedside were Norma Hakim and Julie Hakim. In the course of a prolonged series of operations, the Hakims gathered me into their family. Since then, for over forty years I have experienced their warmth and love. This family would have been lost had the Ottomans massacred them as they did so many other Christians a hundred years ago. Now I shudder to think how many other Chaldean families in the Middle East are about to succumb to today's radical forces of death.

The reasons are not just personal. I also learned their history. In Norma's kitchen years ago, I asked one man about their village in Iraq. He said their native town was Telkaif. "So do you have a tell?" I asked, knowing that a tell is a hill that once was an ancient city or fortress. "Certainly," he smiled. "Does anyone know what city it was?" I persisted. Proudly, he answered, "Nineveh."

Startled, I recognized the name from the Bible, but what popped into my head first was a song from the Broadway show Kismet, "Not since Nineveh, not since Tyre, Not since Babylon turned to mire..." I rushed home to look it up. Nineveh was the fabled capital of the ancient Assyrian Empire!

After years of listening to the Chaldean language in the Hakim kitchen, dancing to Chaldean music at weddings, eating redolent Chaldean home cooking and experiencing enveloping hospitality

for all these years, now I watch the destruction of their heartland in
Iraq with disbelief.

After I first met the Hakim family I studied Arabic, more recently Hebrew. Now I see how much their Chaldean language, a
latter-day version of Aramaic, shares with both Hebrew and Arabic. Once though, Aramaic was the most wide-spread of all.

As I prepared to tell this story, I realized that, just as I had to
find out who these ancient people were, where they lived, and what
language they spoke, other Americans need to learn this history, or
they will never know what is at stake. The harsh truth is that the
survival of Christians in the Middle East may depend on western
intervention. Moreover, if we all knew the horrendous history of
the Christians in the Ottoman Empire during the early twentieth
century, we might not be so sanguine about their future when we
read about them seeking refuge in Kurdistan today.

What I hope to do is identify the people, the issues and the
problem. After that I would like to suggest some solutions. Ah, if
only it were so simple. When Turks and Kurds massacred Greeks
during World War I, the Greeks had a country to advocate for
them. That country may have hurt their cause as much as it helped,
but it did try. When Armenians were massacred, they had no country, but now they have one. The Jews escaped massacre in 1915,
only to suffer a Holocaust during World War II, but later when
pan-Arab sentiment threatened them in the Middle East, the Jews
had a country.

When the Assyrians were massacred during World War I, they
had no country to defend them, and they still have none. Moreover, there is little realistic prospect of their having one in the near
future. To their misfortune, their historical heartland in northern
Iraq overlaps the land the Kurds are defending today against ISIS,
its successors and competitors, and the probability of establishing a
country called Kurdistan is far greater than that of creating an Assyrian or Chaldean protected territory, to say nothing of a state.

Before we begin, we must remember that Mesopotamia has
been Assyrian, Babylonian, Persian, Ottoman and Arab, and all
these peoples have left behind names that reflect their gods and
their languages. On our journey, we will encounter multiple different names and spellings of the same places, and we will provide
alternate spellings and names in parentheses. In turn, towns and
cities have passed from king to caliph over the centuries, and we

will try to help the reader by identifying the country they are in now. In the source material, many western missionaries and historians spelled names phonetically, used quaint terms or cited outdated religious designations, but we will retain their terms when quoting them, for the sake of fidelity to the text. In fairness, we must remember that this is the history of the cradle of western civilization, and it spans several thousand years.

One more point. Unfortunately, in order to grasp the enormity of this story, we need to stop periodically to tot up numbers of people killed and numbers of survivors. Between confusing place names, inconsistent religious categories and the conflicting stories told by victims and perpetrators, we have to recognize that all these statistics are estimates. Imagine trying to obtain reliable population statistics between wars, massive population transfers, large scale conversions, periods of starvation, sales of women and children into slavery and wholesale massacres. Still, we will do our best at least to give ranges, while begging the reader to understand that various sources have widely differing numbers. Finally, this book has grown out of my love for my Chaldean mother, Norma Hakim, her warm, welcoming family, and my Chaldean father, Karim Hakim, who is no longer with us. In the midst of the ancient and modern history, we will tell their story too.

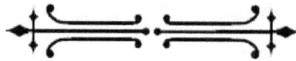

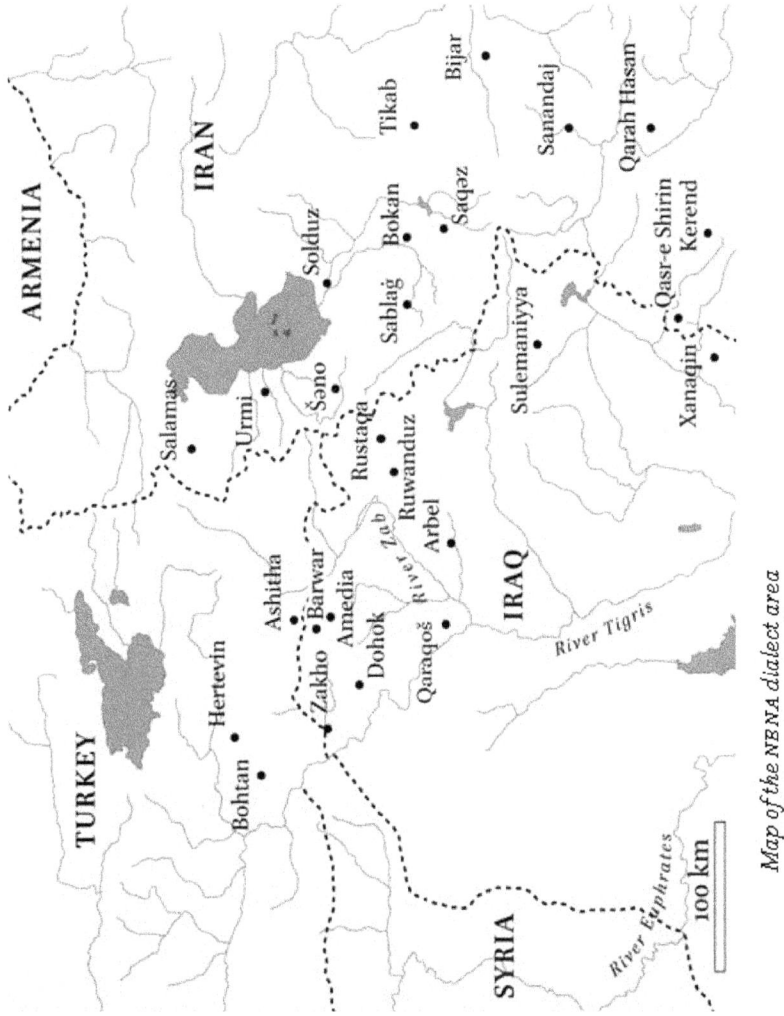

Map of the NBNA dialect area

[From Geoffrey Khan, *The Neo-Aramaic Dialect of the Assyrian Christians of Urmi*, vol. 1 (Leiden: Brill, 2016), p. 22]

Map 2: TUR ABDIN AND SURROUNDING REGIONS (Turkish names are shown

[From Khalid S. Dinno, *The Syrian Orthodox Christians in the Late Ottoman Period and Beyond: Crisis then Revival* (Piscataway: Gorgias Press, 2017), pp. 96–97]

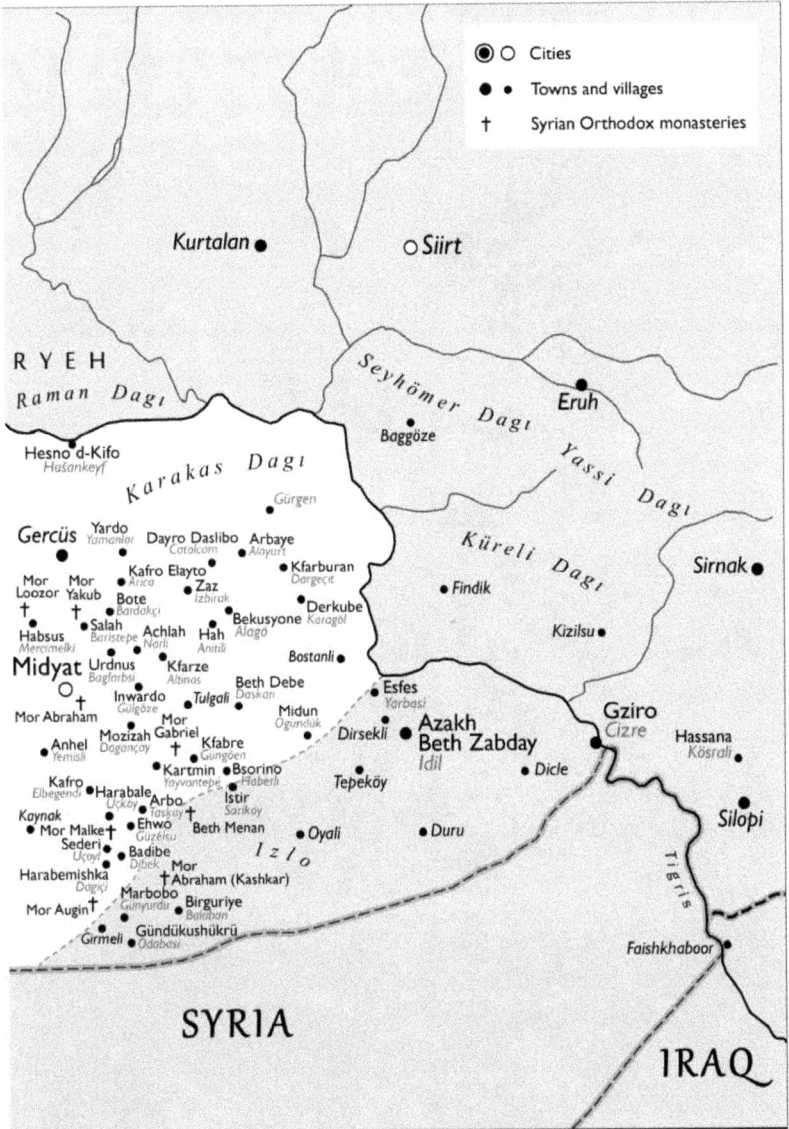

Cities
Towns and villages
Syrian Orthodox monasteries

Kurtalan

Siirt

R Y E H

Raman Dağı

Seyhömer Dağı

Eruh

Baggöze

Hesno d-Kifo
Haşankeyf

Karakas Dağı

Yassı Dağı

Gürgen

Gercüs Yardo Dayro Daslibo Arbaye
Yamanlar Catalcam Alayurt

Küreli Dağı

Sirnak

Mor Mor Kafro Elayto Kfarburan
Loozor Yakub Arıca Zaz Dargeçe
Bote Izbırak Derkube
Bardakçı Karagöl

Findik

Salah Bekusyone Alago
Habsus Baristepe Achlah Hah
Mercimelki Narlı Anıtlı Bostanli

Kizilsu

Midyat Urdnus Kfarze
Baglarbsi Altınbaş Beth Debe

Gziro
Cizre

Inwardo Tulgali Daskan Esfes
Mor Gülgöze Midun Yarbası
Mor Abraham Oğundük Azakh Hassana
Anhel Mozizah Gabriel Dirsekli Beth Zabday Kösrali
Yemişli Dağançay Kfabre Idil
Kartmin Bsorino Güngöen Dicle
Kafro Yayvantepe Haberli Tepeköy
Elbegendi Harabale Uçköy Arbo Istir
Kaynak Taşkay Sarıköy
Mor Malke Ehwo Beth Menan Oyali Duru
Sederi Güzelsu
Uçoyl Badibe
Harabemishka Dibek Mor
Dağçı Abraham (Kashkar)
Mor Augin Marbobo Birguriye
Günyurdu Balaban
Girmeli Gündükushükrü
Odabaşı

Silopi

Tigris

Faishkhaboor

SYRIA

IRAQ

in italics)

WHAT IS AT STAKE

After over 3,000 years, will the Aramaic language last beyond the life of 90 year-old Norma Hakim? Will the Christians who speak it survive in the Middle East? To be blunt, now that the Jews are gone, will the Christians be next? My Christian friends from the Middle East have told me for years that Muslims used to warn them: "After Saturday comes Sunday." That meant: after we kill the Jews, we kill you, the Christians.

Now that Saturday has left, is today Sunday? If it is, the death of Christians in the Middle East will doom one of the world's most ancient living languages to the dustpan of history.

Reports from the Middle East today describe how ISIS or other similar groups force Christians to convert or be killed, unless they can run away. Fast. Far. Attractive women are assaulted in ways we cannot even believe. Children are sold in the marketplace. Towns and villages are emptied. Some of the world's most storied monuments are pulverized.

A thousand years ago, perhaps a million Christians lived in Mesopotamia. Five hundred years later, Christians still were in the majority in northern Mesopotamia. Before World War I, they numbered perhaps a quarter million. By 2015 the numbers that have been lost were shocking, and we will give the most recent ones when we go through the countries individually.

Here is a preview from the press. 'Before Syria was engulfed by war, its Christian population was around 1.8 million, or 10% of the total,'[1] according to *The Economist*. *Newsweek*[2] has reported that 'Christians are believed to have constituted about 30% of the Syrian population as recently as the 1920s.'

Syria was approximately 5.2% Christian in early 2015. By mid-2015, some 10,000 Christians had either left or had been displaced from the area around Homs. By then in Aleppo, an estimated 30,000 had fled. Now that the city has been attacked by barrel bombs and cluster bombs in one of the most intense battles of the Syrian Civil War, the number killed and fled surely is much higher. The once peaceful little town of Maaloula almost has been emptied of its 3,000 Christians. Perhaps 500,000 Christians were left in the country by 2015.[3]

Iraq lost thousands of Christians during World War I. Then perhaps 1,000 Assyrians disappeared in the 1970s and 1980s. Hundreds of thousands fled Saddam Hussein. After he fell, perhaps another million emigrated – two-thirds of Iraq's Christians. According to *The Economist*, 'in Iraq, the pre-2003 Christian population may have been as high as 1.5 million, or 5% of the population; it has probably fallen to under 400,000.'[4] You will note that these numbers differ.

The Knights of Columbus prepared a highly detailed 278–page report for submission to U.S. Secretary of State John Kerry. This provides extensive documentation that the Islamic State is committing genocide in the Middle East. Right after receiving this report, in March 2015, the U.S. House of Representatives unanimously condemned ISIS (ISIL, or IS) for genocide. The body of the report contains a Genocide Memorandum dated March 2016,[5] prepared by legal counsel Ewelina Ochab of the Alliance Defending Freedom (ADF) International. She wrote that in Syria 'The population of Christians dropped from 1.25 million in 2011 to as few as 500,000 today.' Also, 'It is estimated that in 2015 alone, over 700,000 Christians in Syria sought refuge.' Among the many horrifying Syrian statistics: 'In February 2015, IS seized 35 Assyrian Christian villages, kidnapping over 300 Christians. IS released 23 people in March 2015 and demanded £15 million for the release of 230 remaining people.'

The ADF Memorandum next turns to Iraq: 'In 2003, the Christian population in Iraq was estimated at 1.4 million. Currently the Iraqi Christian population is estimated at 275,000.' Mosul had been the largest Christian community of northern Iraq. 'In June 2014, IS took over Mosul, giving an ultimatum to Christians living there (then over 30,000) to convert to Islam, pay a tax, leave Mosul or face death. Thousands of Christians fled to the Nineveh Plains.'

The Knights of Columbus report[6] that on one day, August 6, 2015, over 200,000 inhabitants, mostly Christian, of towns and cit-

ies in the Nineveh Plain fled just before ISIS, or IS, arrived; among
them were 50,000 who had previously been displaced from Mosul.
A table lists 1,131 Christians killed, by name, in the Nineveh Plain
between 2003 and the summer of 2014. Another names 125
churches and monasteries attacked in Iraq from 2003 to 2014.[7]

In 2014, Mosul was almost emptied of Christians for the first
time since the time of Jesus. In the Nineveh Plain to the north of
Mosul, many of the Christian villages of Qaraqosh, Karemlesh,
Bartella, Bashiqa, Batnaya, Tesqopa, Alqōsh, Sharafiya, and Tel
Keppe (Telkaif) were deserted. The Chaldeans in Southfield Michi-
gan put it quite simply: they are all gone.

Here are the key premises of a resolution the European Parliament passed on March 11, 2015:[8]

'whereas Christians in particular have been deliberately targeted by various extremist or jihadist groups for many years, forc-
ing more than 70 % of Iraqi Christians and more than 700 000
Syrian Christians to flee their countries;

'Whereas in Iraq the 250 000 Chaldeans/Assyrians/Syriacs
comprise a distinct ethno-religious group and it is estimated
that up to 40 000 Assyrians lived in Syria before the country's
civil war broke out in 2011;

'whereas on 23 February 2015 an estimated 220 Assyrians were
abducted by ISIS/Da'esh near Tell Tamer on the southern
Khabur River bank in north-east Syria; whereas during the
same campaign the extremists also destroyed properties and
holy places of the Christians; whereas dozens of Assyrians
were killed during the IS assault; whereas IS reportedly issued a
declaration in February 2015 requesting Assyrian villages in the
Syrian Hasaka Province to pay the jizya, a tax on non-Muslims
dating to early Islamic rule and abolished in 1856 across the
Ottoman empire, to convert to Islam or else be killed; whereas
major ISIS/Da'esh attacks have been reported on Assyrian
Christian towns in the Khabur River area since 9 March 2015;

'whereas since 1 March 2015 ISIS/Da'esh has released several
dozen Assyrians, mostly infants and elderly people, following
negotiations with tribal leaders, but most Assyrians are still
held captive and the terrorists have threatened to kill them if
the coalition bombings do not stop;

'Whereas… IS has reportedly destroyed more than 100 churches in Iraq, and at least 6 churches in Syria, as well as a number of Shiite mosques in Iraq;

'whereas in February 2015, IS fighters deliberately publicized their destruction of statues and other artifacts in the Mosul Museum dating back to the ancient Assyrian and Akkadian empires;

'Whereas IS subsequently bulldozed the ancient Assyrian city of Nimrud and, most recently, it reportedly destroyed the UNESCO World Heritage site of Hatra;

'Whereas the Syrian regime has reportedly shelled churches in opposition neighbourhoods, for example in Homs in 2012 and Idlib in 2013…'

In conclusion, the European Parliament 'Strongly condemns ISIS/Da'esh and its egregious human rights abuses that amount to crimes against humanity and war crimes according to the Rome Statute of the International Criminal Court (ICC), and which could be called genocide…[and]… Supports the international efforts against ISIS/Da'esh, including the military actions of the international coalition, coordinated by the United States, and encourages the EU Member States who have not already done so to consider ways of contributing to these efforts…'

The EU also lists 16 other recommended actions. None of these creates a protected area in Iraq or Syria for these persecuted communities. None of them would offer them any practical help at all. It all amounts to a collective, 'Tsk, tsk.'

The cultural heritage of Iraq has literally been turned to dust. In July 2014, ISIS dynamited the tomb of Jonah – the prophet who, according to legend, was swallowed by a whale. Then they bragged about blowing up the tomb of Daniel – the prophet sent into the lion's den. Now ISIS has defiantly made priceless monuments in Palmyra, Syria into rubble.

The human part of this catastrophe sounds eerily familiar. The ancestors of Sephardic Jews were given two choices – convert or leave – in fifteenth century Spain. Armenians had three choices: convert, leave or die – if these are choices – in the Ottoman Empire during World War I. Perhaps the reader will be surprised to know that, along with the 1.5 million Armenians, at least 250,000 Assyrians and Chaldeans were murdered in Turkey at that time – perhaps two or three times as many as that – in addition to similar numbers of Greeks, and hardly anyone outside of their communities even knows. We will tell the story.

THE PEOPLE AND THE LANGUAGE

Today's onslaught against the Christians of the Middle East is a humanitarian crisis, a linguistic disaster, and the end of a rich, irreplaceable tradition. These last living speakers of Aramaic come as close as anyone alive today to speaking the language of Jesus and the language of the great collection of Jewish books known as the Talmud. Some religious groups still use Aramaic today to study or to pray, but that is not the same as using it to ask for a cup of coffee. Hebrew, for instance, is the language of the Jewish Torah, read every week for over 2,000 years in synagogue services, but it remained virtually frozen after the Romans expelled the Jews from Jerusalem in the second century. Only when Eliezer Ben Yehuda began to revive the language at the turn of the twentieth century were children born learning Hebrew as their first language. It moved from being a language of the synagogue to a *living language* in which one could make reservations for a train or an airplane. Aramaic developed differently. As the Chaldean villages of Iraq came into contact with the modern world, Aramaic evolved naturally, and villagers developed their language so they could speak of telephones and railroads. At the same time, they maintained a centuries-old oral tradition of songs and sayings.

While there have been, and still are, other small groups who have spoken Aramaic until recently, those who have actually spoken Aramaic into the twenty-first century are mainly Kurdish Jews, Assyrians and Chaldeans.

Kurdish Jews

Ironically, in the era of ISIS, IS and their successors, the Jews of Syria and Iraq are safer than the Christians, because they were forced to leave for Israel years ago.

Approximately 30,000 Jews lived in Syria in 1948. Until November 1954, the Syrian government banned Jewish emigration, but most Jews managed to get out by the end of the 1973 October War, leaving something over 2,000. In 1992, the government of Syria began granting exit visas to all Jews who wanted to leave, unless they admitted they were planning to go to Israel. Judy Feld Carr, a music teacher from Toronto, has smuggled 3,228 Jews out of Syria. By 2012 she believed that only 16 were left.[9]

We will discuss the Jews of Iraq in two subsequent chapters. In brief, about 150,000 Jews lived in Iraq in 1948. After a series of bombings in Baghdad, over 120,000 Jews left the country in 1950–51. By the end of 1951, almost all the Aramaic speaking Jews of Kurdistan had left for Israel. By 2013, an estimated five Jews remained. Saturday was over. Now it was time for Sunday.

Assyrians

The Hebrew Bible describes the Assyrians as a fearsome people who invaded, conquered, exacted tribute and paraded ten massive tribes of Jewish captives back to Assyria. This terrifying reputation greatly overshadowed very real contributions that they made to the arts, sciences and culture.

Sumerians and Akkadians ruled the region from 3000–2000 BCE (Before the Common Era). The Sumerians lived in southern Mesopotamia and spoke a language that was not Semitic. Akkadian speakers – Assyrians and Babylonians – came later, speaking a Semitic lauguage that gradually replaced Sumerian. Modern Semitic languages, as we shall see, inherited many words from Addadian.

Assyria was ascendant from 1521–911 BCE. From 911 to 612 BCE, when Nineveh was sacked by the Babylonians, the Assyrian Empire reached its zenith. Even the prophet Ezekiel (31:3–9) extolled its wonders.

The land of Assyria lay between the Tigris and Euphrates rivers in northern Mesopotamia, now Iraq. Nineveh, the capital, was just across the Tigris River from present day Mosul. Some of its thick crenulated walls are still standing, but its spectacular palaces and the magnificent library of King Ashurbanipal (668–627 BCE) are history. Archaeologists have found remains of a fine aqueduct that brought water to its gardens.

Fortunately, the Assyrian royal archives have preserved three centuries of history, almost all of them tales of war. In 247 BCE the Parthians came from east of the Caspian Sea to conquer Nineveh, and in 224 CE the Sassinids overran them, establishing a vast empire across the entire Middle East and part of Asia. By then, Rome had become Christian. When the Assyrians converted to Christianity, suspicious Sassanid rulers claimed that these Christian Assyrians had dual loyalties – to their country and to their country's arch-enemy, Rome. That may not have been the first time, but it surely was not the last time that accusations of divided loyalty were made against Christians or Jews in the Middle East.

Until the mid-nineteenth century, most Mesopotamian Christians generally did not call themselves Assyrians. That changed in the nineteenth century, perhaps in part because archeological excavations of Nineveh unearthed monumental sculptures, wall-sized alabaster bas reliefs, and other astonishing Assyrian findings. M. Botta, the French Consul at Mosul in the 1840s, discovered the vast palace of Emperor Sargon at Khorsabad, just northeast of Nineveh. The British explorer Sir Austin Henry Layard[10] and the Assyrian Christian explorer Hormuzd Rassam unearthed some of the vast ruins of Nineveh. Given the grandeur of these findings and the waves of nationalism that swept from Europe to the Middle East in the nineteenth century, many local Christians now take pride in calling themselves Assyrian.

All historians do not buy it, but Warda[11] among others puts forward many arguments to show that his community did descend from the Assyrians of Nineveh. He starts with the obvious: they lived exactly where archeologists have dug up Assyrian sculptures and structures, in the ruins of the city of Nineveh, on the Plains of Nineveh. The tomb of Jonah is located right where the Book of Jonah tells us that a reluctant prophet Jonah warned the Assyrians of Nineveh to reform their ways. The names of many villages, towns and cities are of Assyrian origin. The names of ancient Assyrian gods are preserved as part of many Christian family names throughout the Plains of Nineveh.

Then there is their name. The Greek name for Assyrian is *Assurioi*. The Armenian name is *Asori*, and the Kurds call them *Asuri*. Until recently, Mesopotamian Christians called themselves *Suryaye* or *Suraye*. Now some say that *Assuraye* include Chaldeans, Jacobites and Syrian Catholics. Most Chaldeans disagree. While some scholars might say that these twentieth century villagers simply want to identify with the glories of ancient Assyria, many in the west simply take the easy path of calling all the Christians of northern Mesopotamia by the name Assyrian.

Chaldeans

In ancient times, Chaldeans were known as magicians, astronomers and astrologers, probably coming from a priestly caste of Medes who advised rulers through their powers of divination. Lamsa[12] writes that in his Assyrian tradition, the Magi who visited the infant Jesus were Aramaic-speaking, and that there were twelve, not three. Others described them as Assyrian-Babylonian practitioners of magic, astrologers, probably Chaldean, not the kings from Persia, India and Arabia of popular legend. The book of Daniel 2:2, groups Chaldeans with magicians: 'Then the king commanded that the magicians, the enchanters, the sorcerers, and the Chaldeans be summoned to tell the king his dreams.'

Chaldeans first appear in Assyrian records in about 883 BCE. Their cities, including Ur, were located downriver from Babylon, extending down to the swamps of the lower Tigris and Euphrates. That is south of the Nineveh Plain, where the Assyrians lived. Chaldeans allied themselves against the Assyrians with the Medes of northwest Iran, the Elamites of southwest Iran, the Arameans and the Babylonians. After a siege that started in 626 BCE, the Medes, Babylonians and Chaldeans sacked Nineveh in 612 BCE, and they finally burned it down in 606 BCE. Scholars call the regime they established the Neo-Babylonian Empire. The people of the Nineveh Plain called it the Chaldean Empire, and the most famous king was a Chaldean – Nebuchadnezzar.

The Bible says that Nebuchadnezzar destroyed the Jewish Temple in Jerusalem, and historians date that destruction to 587 BCE. From there, he carried off thousands of Jewish captives to Babylon. In Babylon he built the famous hanging gardens, and he made it the greatest city of Mesopotamia, a city Isaiah (Isaiah 13:19) called 'Babylon, glory of kingdoms.' Jeremiah (Jer 51:7) called it, 'a golden cup in the Lord's hand.' Today the Ishtar Gate and Nebuchadnezzar's throne room are in the Pergamon Museum in Berlin, and their blue tiles dazzle as if they were brand new. They are so shiny that walking through them feels like walking through a Disneyworld reproduction.

Nebuchadnezzar presided over Babylonia at its peak, but disaster was not far off. The capital fell to Cyrus the Persian in 539 BCE, just as the prophet Daniel (Dan 5:27) had predicted. Babylon was conquered next by Alexander the Great of Greece, the Roman Emperor Trajan; then in turn by the Parthians, the Sassanid dynasty and the Arabs. The Greeks called it Seleucia. The Parthians called it Ctesiphon. This is worth remembering, because many historians refer to Babylon by the combined name Seleucia-Ctesiphon. The Muslim Abbasid Caliphate built a new city close by, and they called it Baghdad. This would become the seat of the Patriarchs of Babylon in the Church of the East.

That was the thumbnail history. Now we will see how the name Chaldean became attached to the Chaldean Church, but first, before learning about any of the Churches of the East, and before we get to the Sunday of the title, the reader should meet a Chaldean family. Let us introduce Norma.

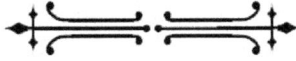

NORMA

Norma's story begins in a northern Iraqi Chaldean village in the early twentieth century, and it takes us into the twenty-first century.

Over 40 years ago, while performing a long operation on a nine-year old boy from Iraq, I discovered that I was dealing with special people. I broke scrub to come out and reassure the family that everything was going well, and my patient's aunt Norma asked, "Doctor, have you eaten?" Of course I had not. She immediately began stuffing me with Middle Eastern delicacies. "It is a long operation. You have to eat doctor, to keep up your strength."

It did not take long before I became part of the Hakim family, One day a brother asked Norma in Chaldean for my name, saying *Meela shima*? To my surprise, from my scanty knowledge of Hebrew at the time, I understood. In Hebrew the question would be *Ma shma*? Later when I really studied Hebrew, I discovered even more striking similarities.

For almost all of her married life, Norma cooked for 30–50 people every day, not just her sons and daughters, but also in-laws, miscellaneous relatives, and hangers-on, often including me when I came home exhausted from work. That would be when she would feed me and send me home with a doggie bag for my husband. Sitting around Norma's kitchen table with her daughters and sisters-in-law and helping them make kibbe (*kuppi* in Chaldean) or *dolma* would refresh my spirit when my surgery practice left me completely depleted.

Incidentally, *dolma* (also called *yaprah*) may be one of the great culinary achievements of the Middle East, probably originating in Turkey, but reaching its apogee in Norma's kitchen. A savory mixture of meat, rice and spices rolled inside cabbage, onion, egg plant, squash or green pepper, Norma cooks it to perfection with just the

19

right amount of tomato sauce. I can assure you that no Greek, Persian, Armenian, Lebanese, or even Turkish version – and I have tried them all – comes close. ("Do I have to give them my recipe?" Norma asks.)

In the kitchen cooking, the women would take turns exchanging stories. Maybe they would laugh about some Chaldeans who rented expensive cars and fancy clothes for a party, and Norma would assure me that the whole Chaldean community always 'bragged about' how the Karim Hakim family was the best; they would never do anything so tasteless. She and her daughters then would put out plates and plates of food, plop a small child in my lap, clap hands with a baby to the ditty *ishy ishy Ba Ba*, laugh, eat, take turns going in and out of the room, and be a family like none I had ever experienced.

TELKAIF

When Norma was born over ninety years ago, the villagers of Telkaif still lived as they had for centuries, although they were on the verge of modernization. As far as Norma remembers though, at the time she left, nothing had really changed.

The ancient town of Telkaif (Tele-Keppe in Chaldean, meaning mound of stones) is less than eight miles northeast of Mosul in the Nineveh Plain. Until ISIS emptied it of Christians, Mosul was the largest Chaldean city of Nineveh Province, sitting opposite the ruins of Nineveh, 250 miles north of Baghdad. Telkaif's namesake mound of stones is all that remains of a fortress that once was part of Nineveh's outer ring of defense. Excavations have revealed ancient vases and the remains of irrigation ditches from the time of the Assyrian King Sennacherib (705–681 BCE). Some of these are connected to a seventh century BCE Assyrian well that is on the top of the hill.

Eighth through sixteenth century manuscripts describe visits from monks and priests, and they describe efforts to renovate a nearby monastery. Telkaif suffered raids by Mongol invaders in the fifteenth and sixteenth centuries, by the Persian King Nader Shah in 1743, and by the Kurds in 1833. Whenever there were massacres in adjacent towns, Telkaif filled with immigrants. In Norma's time, the town had between 7,000 and 10,000 Christians, but today all of them are gone.

The father of Naima Dalaly Hakim, as she was called at birth, was Hana Hanoush. Dalaly, his last name when he came to America, was a nickname. In a playground one day a child asked whose little boy he was, and someone said he was Bir Dalaly, son of Dalala. Dalala actually was his mother's name, but the name stuck. When he grew up he become a merchant, traveling from town to town on a horse, his saddlebags laden with dates, figs, almonds, raisons and pistachios, trading them for cash, wheat or other barter. Merchants like him were unarmed, and their biggest fear was of encountering Kurdish thieves on the road. Telkaif is on the border of Kurdish territory.

The family lived in a mud brick house, as far as Norma's daughters remember. Norma remembers the house as cement. Norma's brother remembers walls of foot-wide stones, and he remembers that the house had two stories. It was the tallest in town. It had a basement suitable for keeping his horse and a roof that was perfect for sleeping on hot summer nights. The house had a door, but no windows. The entire extended family lived in the house – parents, children, husbands, wives and grandchildren. The family conducted their daily lives on the first floor, and they used an outdoor stairway without handrails to go up to the second floor. There they slept on carpets or blankets spread on the floor. The toilet was on the roof. Norma's brother tells me that the newer houses built their spanking new bathrooms out from the front wall of their houses, just to show off.

Their life style was typical of that part of the world, at that time. We must remember that even in America many rural houses did not have in-door plumbing or electricity until well after the turn of the century. After dark the family used kerosene lamps. The cook stove burned wood, and the furnace burned coal. Meals were eaten sitting on the floor. Some families spread a cloth on the floor for eating, but nobody remembers any such cloth in their house. When you ask about chairs, Norma says, "There weren't any."

They took their tea from teacups, called *ystikan*. They did not use individual dishes for food; family members picked up their food from common platters with thin pieces of bread, even using bread to scoop up soup from a pot. When her grandson asks if there were platters on the table, she answers, "What table?"

Water came from a nearby lake, and the women had to fetch it daily, unless their family had access to a well. There were no hoses, no grass and no flower gardens. Nobody had a telephone. Norma does not remember seeing roads or railroads for transporting foodstuff or any other goods. There were no automobiles. Traffic lights? "Well," she points out, "there were no paved roads."

According to time-honored rituals, cleaning day was Saturday; Sunday was for church and Monday was laundry day. The butcher came to Telkaif once a week, and people preserved their meat with salt in a big clay pot, much as Jews would kosher meat. Families worked their own plots of land and grew their own fruits and vegetables. Anything else they bought in the souk. Village farms just produced enough food for the family's consumption. The father was firmly in charge of all farm activities, and he was succeeded by the oldest son in the family.

When Norma came to America, she still was a child. She had spent more time on the playground than in the kitchen, but she still remembers the labor-intensive food preparation. They made the classic *kibbe* by wrapping a layer of meat and cracked wheat around spicy *heshway*, a coarse meat stuffing. It is cooked in a variety of ways; sometimes in a delicious lemon-flavored soup, *kibbe hamuth*. *Patcho* requires repeatedly cleaning pieces of intestine or stomach and stuffing them with rice and spices. The more women there were in the family, the more hands were available to sit and stuff these delicacies.

Harissa is a savory porridge of barley and meat, indescribably good. *Caddy* is probably the easiest dish, meat and potatoes cooked in a spicy curry sauce, served over rice. The ubiquitous *gurgur*, cracked wheat flavored with meat and spices, *burgul* in Arabic, is boiled and often eaten with a meat and vegetable sauce. In Telkaif, the women cracked the wheat at home.

Masguf is a spicy fish that men traditionally cooked in a pit in the ground, amid great laughing and ceremony. In America Norma would cook another fish in the oven, in case the men's fish did not come out. The women made yogurt at home, and when they drained yogurt, chives and salt in a cheesecloth bag, it produced a cheese that was wonderful on bread. To this day Norma's daughters say her special talent is in cooking this paper-thin bread. Cookies made with nut flavoring, *kuleche*, were a typical desert.

The women made their own clothes, except for certain items they bought in Mosul. Daily clothing was simple. Men wore a long robe, a *dishdasha*, and a belt. For special occasions they wore fine embroidered materials, the men decked out in turbans, a shirt, a long dark wrapped robe with a belt, loose trousers and a short jacket. Sometimes they put on Arab headdress; in some villages they wore a conical felt cap with a cloth wound around it. The women wore a patterned gown that reached to the knees, colorful pants and sometimes a robe draped over their shoulders like a cape. Married women wore a headdress over their hair and ears, called a *kuchma*. The younger women often sewed coins on it; older women left it plain.

Norma remembers no doctors, nurses, lawyers, police or firemen. Her son's father-in-law, Dr. Ulises Casab Rueda,[1] remembers seeing a doctor, who had a little clinic. There were farmers, stonecutters, masons, bricklayers, shoemakers, dyers and tailors. Some villagers raised sheep; others did a bit of weaving. The farmers grew grain, and the village had its own mill. A barber, a clinic and a shop that sold cheap jewelry were next to the tea shop. Adjoining the tea shop was a large room for social events.

In 1925 her mother became pregnant with her seventh child, and her father told his business partner, Tobia Hakim, that if it was a girl she would be for his son Karim, already 13 years old. The name Karim means generous, and he was. They sealed the promise with a handshake. Karim was one of two surviving boys after his mother had delivered 14 babies; later in America there were two more girls. In those days, the midwife sported rusty scissors hanging from her belt, to be used for cutting the cord. Norma remembers that seven days after a baby was born if the umbilical cord would 'fill up with air,' the baby would die.

The family name, Hakim, which means wise man, also means doctor. In their case, it came from Karim's grandmother, a midwife, perhaps the one with the rusty scissors.

Little Naima was born into a family of four girls and four boys. The name Naima means good, and it was prophetic. Tobia Hakim and his family emigrated when Karim was eleven. The British made the arrangements for him in gratitude for services he had rendered to them. Karim showed me his passport one day; it listed his place of birth as Mesopotamia. Because it was difficult to enter America directly, first the family went to Mexico, where they built a business. They sold it three years later, and with that money they made their way to New York, finally to Detroit.

One New Year's Eve when Naima was seven years old, a cra-
zy neighbor, probably drunk, stabbed and killed her father at a party, for no reason. Both her family and his family agreed he was
daft. When the authorities asked her mother if she wanted him sentenced to death, she said no, because he would eventually go blind
anyhow. And he did.

I asked Norma about village burial traditions, and just as I had
expected, she described many that are the same as Jewish customs.
Burial had to be within 24 hours of the death; the deceased was
wrapped in a white winding cloth, not put in a coffin. They sat in
mourning for seven days, commemorated 40 days and held another
ceremony at one year. At the funeral, professional mourners on the
women's side of the room keened mournful dirges. Everyone wore
black, the women usually remaining in black for the rest of their
lives.

Once Naima approached marriageable age, about ten years
old, Tobia Hakim, known as Big Baba, heard all the way from
America that other families were interested in her, so he asked a
friend in Mosul to go to Telkaif, take her picture and send it to
him. When he saw the photo, he said "Grab her."

As part of the engagement, the Hakim family paid her family
the *urtha*, the bride price, but there was no wedding contract. Nobody would have been able to sign one anyhow. Big Baba supervised all the arrangements for the engagement party from Detroit.
His sisters and relatives in Telkaif represented the Hakims as prox-
ies. The party was in the social hall adjacent to the tea shop, the
same place where the men would sit in a circle of an evening to
talk, smoke and drink Turkish coffee.

Karim and Baba arrived in Telkaif for the wedding in 1937,
one year after the engagement. This was the first time Naima met
her fiancé. One of his eyes had a blue spot, because a chicken had
pecked his eye when he was six months old, playing on the floor,
but Naima did not care. She was going to get married and move to
America. A blond, blue-eyed niece of hers, while admiring herself
in a mirror, said, "Look at you. You're going to go to America and
I'm going to stay here?"

Karim and his father came to Telkaif with a big 1937 Buick,
which they drove all over town before the wedding, to everyone's
excitement. After the wedding they sold it to pay for the trip home.
Their entire stay in Telkaif lasted less than a week.

The wedding was a grand affair, in the only church she ever knew, Mother of God. Travelers have reported seeing five churches in town, but Naima only knew of one. Naima was 11 and a half years old. Karim was 25. Baba wanted everything western style, because they were going to America. The one exception was that women could have henna applied to their hands, according to custom. A seamstress in Mosul sewed the trousseau, with a western wedding dress, suitable for a bride who was going to America. Because she was going to America, she was spared the *kuchma* that Chaldean brides normally put on their heads on the day of their wedding and wear for the rest of their lives. Naima also rejected other traditions. She refused to be paraded around the town on a horse followed by an entourage of dancing and singing celebrants. She also refused to sit in a corner of a room in her husband's house for a week after the wedding, receiving visitors. She says that in many families the bride ate dinner at her parents' house for her first month of marriage, still on approval perhaps, but Naima would leave for America.

Naima's wedding reception was in the same hall as the engagement party. There was no other place. The whole town was invited; she remembers seeing everyone dressed in their very best. All of these arrangements were unusual; normally the party would be at home. For Naima's wedding the women cooked the food and brought it in, and Baba had them bring ice for the drinks from Mosul, which caused a sensation. They even brought silver tableware from Mosul. People had never seen it before; some stole the silver and took it home.

Karim used to tell me stories from his childhood. One day as a young boy he hiked up a hill and realized that he had strayed into Kurdish land. "You don't know the Kurds," he said. Realizing he could be killed on sight for trespassing, he ran all the way home. Another day he rode to Mosul on a donkey, and the donkey ran into a little girl. The family screamed that he had killed their daughter and called the police. After a suitable amount of money changed hands, they calmed down. Incidentally, the girl was just fine.

DETROIT

Naima and Karim travelled back to Detroit on the *SS Escambia*, sharing a stateroom, but as if they were brother and sister, because she was pre-pubertal. The boat ride took 30 days, but it was very exciting. They dressed up for dinner every night and even stopped over in Paris, although Norma was not used to American food and subsisted on hard-boiled eggs and potatoes. On arrival she was detained overnight at Ellis Island, because the authorities questioned how she could be married at her age.

Now Naima became Norma; Baba wanted his family to be American. Nevertheless, she entered his family as a traditional Chaldean new wife. Her mother-in-law trained her to clean the house, taught her the family recipes and trained her to cook for the whole family. Still, she says the only time she cried was when she missed the other little girls who she used to play with on the village playground. Her husband's sisters were like sisters to her. They all slept in the same bedroom together for two years until her first pregnancy.

Norma attended public school regularly for her first years. Shortly after she delivered, a truant officer came to the house to inquire about young Norma Hakim; his records showed she had not been attending school. Karim called up to her in Chaldean, "Norma, come on down and bring the baby."

When the truant officer saw her standing on the landing holding the baby, he turned to leave, "Oh, never mind."

Norma's first child arrived when she was age 14. All together she had eight children. At this writing, so far she has 19 grandchildren and 17 great grandchildren.

A book of pictures from Chaldean families in Detroit contains one from 1951 when Aziz Ghaziz, the governor of Mosul, stayed in the house of the Tobias Hakim family for two weeks. Two weeks after he went home, he was killed. Another important guest, Abdul Karim al-Shaikhly, one of the founders of the Ba'ath Party and its first foreign minister, also stayed in the Hakim house in 1970, where they entertained him lavishly. He was so grateful that when he returned to Iraq he paid a courtesy visit to Norma's mother in Telkaif. Soon afterward, he was hanged; his last words were "I'm going to my G-d and you're all under my feet."

The third important guest was the 17 year-old King Faisal II of Iraq, who visited Detroit in 1952 on his first official trip to the U.S. At the last moment he was instructed not to stay at a private house because of security concerns, but the Hakims did entertain him in their house. One of Norma's daughters, Patsy, remembers presenting him a big bouquet. In 1958 during the July 14 revolution he was killed, Norma says by his own uncle.

In 1968 Norma brought two of her daughters, a sister-in-law and brother-in-law to visit Telkaif. The girls still talk about how they visited all the relatives' houses, where every family killed a lamb, the last word in hospitality, and served it undercooked with bits and pieces of blood and fur stuck to the meat. The girls did not want to touch it, but they assumed it was safe since their mother seemed to be eating it. At least it was disappearing from her plate, which adoring relatives refilled every time it went empty. Later the girls discovered that their mother had been slipping the lamb into a sac hidden in her purse. Nobody in the family has ever eaten lamb since.

Norma's daughters Patsy and Dale also remember that every morning when they woke up a line of young men was waiting outside the house waiting to see them. As they saw it, Norma had brought two daughters of marriageable age, and they even were pretty. Every boy was hoping to score an American wife, whatever she looked like, as long as she came with an American green card.

When Norma came, there were no more than ten Chaldean families living in the area, all from Telkaif, and each new arrival would be incorporated into a community that grew into a sprawling Chaldean extended family. Now there are over 120,000 Chaldeans in the Detroit area. The first Chaldean church in Michigan was named Mother of God, just like the church in Telkaif. When we get into the religious controversies that have involved the Chaldean Church, the reason will become clear. One day their priest, Father George Garmo, told me that their spoken Aramaic was the same as the Aramaic of the Babylonian Talmud and that he had written this in his theological dissertation. To his regret, in the early 1980s, the pope assigned him to return to Iraq as an archbishop, even though he had lived in Southfield, Michigan for years.

One year an Assyrian shot a Californian priest in the leg, Norma says because he had refused money that Saddam Hussein had offered for a new church. The priest survived, but Jim Bannon, the Executive Deputy Chief of Police of Detroit and Norma's brother-in-law, brought the priest to Detroit and put him under secret 24-hour guard in Detroit's Sinai Hospital, to keep the assailant from finishing the job!

Norma has other close Jewish friends, and just before the First Iraq War, the son of some very special friends of hers brought home a Yemenite fiancée from Israel. Norma was the one who helped the American family communicate with the Yemeni-Israeli family on the telephone. When the war started, the young Israeli was terrified for her parents' safety in Tel Aviv, and it fell to Norma to calm her, even while America was bombing Norma's native country. In another only-in-Detroit story, when I called my Shiite Muslim Arabic teacher to tell her that scuds were landing on Riyadh where some of her in-laws lived, she inquired anxiously whether the family of my friend Norma was okay in Iraq.

Today the Hakim family is so Americanized that they discourage women from trilling the traditional ululation at weddings. They have, however, restarted an old tradition, the *zeffa*, a joyous send-off for a bride from her home amid a deafening mixture of drums and wind instruments, the *tubel* and *snuja*, while everyone sings and dances. Later after the wedding, everyone joins a *dubki*, a traditional Middle Eastern circle dance like the Jewish *hora*.

Norma has taught her daughters to make great *dolma*, but what about all the other Chaldean dishes they have not learned? Will they pass on all the other recipes that generations of Chaldean women have handed down to their mothers? What about the traditional Chaldean sayings Norma knows, the nursery rhymes, the folk wisdom that has been passed down in the Aramaic/Chaldean language? Will her daughters teach all this to their granddaughters? Norma's oldest three children can speak fluent Chaldean, but will her great grandchildren understand Chaldean at all? Her father-in-law predicted that once the Chaldeans left for America their language would be doomed. If the Christians of Iraq and Syria leave their homelands today, *all* of this heritage will be doomed. If they do not, *they* will be doomed.

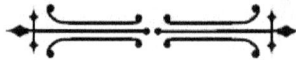

ARAMEANS AND ARAMAIC

'My father was a wandering Aramean' it says in the Jewish Passover Haggadah. These words from Deuteronomy 26:5 describe the patriarch Jacob. (*Arami obed avi vyrad mitzrayim vygar sham* – ארמי אבד אבי וירד מצרימה ויגר שם) The usual full translation of this passage today is: 'A wandering Aramean was my father. And he went down into Egypt and sojourned there…' Oddly, an alternate meaning for the word, *obed*, would make the phrase say that an Aramean ruined my father. Such are the perils of translation.

At the Passover Seder, each person at the table reads a passage. Often someone misreads this one as 'My father was a wandering Armenian.' Then a family member scolds, "No, Aramean." Rarely does anyone ask *why* the Bible calls the patriarch an Aramean.

The Bible says that Abraham comes from *Ur Kasdim*, normally translated as 'Ur of the Chaldees.'" So where was Abraham's homeland? Ur is in southern Mesopotamia, but the site shows no evidence that Chaldeans were there before the seventh to sixth centuries, which were well after the time of the patriarchs. And in any case, the Arameans originated from northern Mesopotamia. Maybe there was more than one Ur? In the words of one biblical commentator, '…the Ur of our text may be one of the sites in Upper Mesopotamia, founded by citizens of the famous city in the south and named after it. An Upper Mesopotamian Ur would have been much closer to Haran, a city crucial to patriarchal narratives.'[1] Complicating things further, the city of Sanliurfa in southeast Turkey maintains an oral tradition that it actually was the biblical Ur Kasdim, home of Abraham.

Haran is where Abraham moved with his family after he left the home of his father. It is usually identified with Paddan Aram, in

Aramean territory. At any rate the Bible presents Abraham and his family as close relatives of Arameans. The Book of Genesis says that Abraham, Nahor and Haran are brothers, and that a grandson of Nahor was named Aram. Abraham's son Isaac marries Nahor's granddaughter, who is called 'daughter of Bethuel the Aramean and sister of Laban the Aramean' (Gen. 25:20). Isaac's son Jacob marries Leah and Rachel, both daughters of 'Laban the Aramean.' Aram the grandson of Nahor has been called the ancestor of the Arameans, also of the Syrians, since the city-state of Damascus was known in ancient times as Aram-Damascus.

The generations of men who descended from Noah after the Flood are said to have repopulated the world. Noah's sons were Shem, Ham and Japheth. Shem – from whom comes the word *Semitic* – had sons named Elam, Ashur, Arpachshad, Lud and Aram. According to tradition, the descendants of Elam are the Elamites, a people of southwest Iran, and from Ashur come the Assyrians. One grandson of Arpachshad was Eber, the ancestor of Abraham. (Gen. 10:21). The apocryphal Book of Jasher repeats the tradition that from Arpachshad come the Ammonites, Moabites, Midianites, Edomites, and Ishmaelites.

To continue the story, among Ham's descendants are the people of Egypt, Cush, and Canaan. From Canaan came the Canaanites. We could keep going, but the point seems to be that the entire family of nations is related – everyone is at least a distant cousin.

Despite the lack of any objective documentation for them, these traditions remain powerful. Writers in the eighteenth century were still speculating about which people descended from which grandson of Noah.

In the annals of history, Arameans first appear as mountain people, nomads, eventually settling down by the end of the eleventh century BCE. Aram means *height*, and Arameans came from the mountains of the northern Euphrates River, from the portions of Mesopotamia that now are northern Syria and Iraq. The earliest written record of them is an inscription from 1150 BCE announcing that the Assyrian King Tiglath-pileser I had smote the Arameans. The Aramaic tribes in Syria were a significant irritation to the Assyrian rulers, and by the ninth century they were established as a regional power in Damascus, able to exert authority over neighboring states. In the ninth century, a king of Aram-Damascus left a stone stele in what is now Tel Dan in northern Israel announcing his great victory over the 'house of David'.

The biblical version of the story may be in II Kings 9–10, where the upstart Jehu overthrows King Joram, son of King Ahab, a putative descendant of King David. In II Kings 9:15, "...King Joram had gone back to Jezreel to recover from the wounds which the Aramaens had inflicted on him in his battle with King Hazael of Aram." We further read in II Kings 10:32 "In those days the Lord began to reduce Israel; and Hazrael harassed them throughout the territory of Israel east of the Jordan..." Scholars debate whether the Tel Dan inscription and this biblical account describe the same historical events, and they also differ on the important question of whether the inscription is a rare written reference to the House of David. Nevertheless, there is no doubt that Aram-Damascus, Israel and Judah fought often during this period.

WHO FIRST SPOKE THE ANCIENT SEMITIC LANGUAGES?

As children we might have imagined the first man in history. He probably would have been a shepherd in sandals and white robe, carrying a staff, leading his flocks over rocky hills. Right? But who and where was this first man? In truth, most of us have no idea, nor do we know where he lived or what language he spoke.

Among the earliest to populate Mesopotamia were the Sumerians, perhaps as far back as 5500 BCE. They may have been the first to write, pressing cut reeds into wet clay to create a series of wedge shapes that stood for first simple and then increasingly complex meanings. They were the first astronomers and astrologers, the first mathematicians and the first to irrigate the land. In the early third millennium BCE new arrivals conquered the region and unified northern Mesopotamia. The language of these new arrivals – Akkadian – was unrelated to Sumerian, but the Akkadian speakers adopted the cuneiform ('wedge-shaped') writing system of the Sumerians to write their own language and administer their growing empire. By the early second millennium BCE Akkadian had become the common language, the *lingua franca*, of the entire Middle East. The famous Code of Hammurabi was in Akkadian, written in cuneiform.

Many nations make an appearance in the Bible. We read that the Canaanites lived in the land that now is Israel. North of them, Phoenicians lived on the coast of Lebanon and dominated the

Mediterranean as sailors and traders. Amorites moved from west of the Euphrates to settle further south between the rivers of Mesopotamia. The biblical Ruth came from the Moabite people, living in the hills of Jordan, east of the Dead Sea. Edomites were desert people, living just south of Moab. Ammonites lived in the area around Amman, Jordan. Today, of all these nations and languages, only scattered words live on in modern tongues. Other people – Eblaites and Ugarites – left inscriptions, but they too were forgotten. How do we know who they were or what languages they used? The only evidence comes from their writings.

HOW DID THEY WRITE?

The earliest writing was based on pictures. Around the same time that the Sumerians were inventing the cuneiform system of wedge shapes stamped in clay, the Egyptians developed a system of carved designs with a similar principle – hieroglyphs ('sacred carvings'). Sumerian/Akkadian cuneiform and Egyptian hieroglyphs were not alphabets – rather, a sign might stand for a whole word, for a part of a word, or for a single sound. In the first half of the second millennium, speakers of Semitic languages began to modify and simplify Egyptian hieroglyphs, creating a system in which a limited number of signs stood for individual sounds and could be combined to represent any word. The wavy line that had been the Egyptian hieroglyph for 'water' would now stand for a letter 'm', because the Semitic word for 'water' was *may*. The sign for 'house' – would now stand for a letter 'b' because the Semitic word for 'house' was *bayt*. The simplified writing system – an alphabet of consonants – was easier to learn and quicker to write. By the end of the second millennium BCE different Semitic speaking peoples had taken the Semitic consonant-alphabet invention, standardized it, and developed their own versions.

The Phoenicians – seafaring traders who expanded from the coasts of Lebanon over the Mediterranean and North Africa – passed on their 22-letter version of the Semitic consonant-alphabet to the Greeks, who felt it would be more useful if vowels could be similarly represented. The Greek alphabet passed to the Romans, and from there it became the ancestor of all Western alphabets.

The early scripts evolved, influenced by the writing material on which they were written, by fashions, and by local variations. When the Akkadian-speaking Assyrians conquered and incorporated Aramean tribes into the Assyrian empire, Aramaic rapidly became the language of this empire. Early Aramaic inscriptions show regional differences in grammar and spelling, but these became standardized after Assyrian kings deported Aramean tribes from the western shores of the Euphrates back to Assyria. Called *Eber-Nari* in Akkadian, *Abar-Nahara* in Aramaic and *Ever HaNahar* in Hebrew, their name meant 'across the river.' In their new homes they intermingled with the locals, who adopted the language of the newcomers, a testament to the usefulness of Aramaic. It became the language of administration and commerce, and it was more often written with ink on scrolls or potsherds than carved in stone on monuments. Many letters that were angular in Phoenician became more curved when written quickly by an Aramaic scribe. In ancient Israel a script similar to Phoenician had been used – paleo-Hebrew – but after the Babylonian exile the returned captives brought back Aramaic letter-shapes, and these developed into the square Hebrew letters that are used today. After the Assyrians came the Babylonians and then the Persians, but Aramaic maintained its place as the international language of communication and administration. When the tide of empire retreated, patches of Aramaic were left behind like stranded rock pools on a shore, developing local characteristics in relative isolation.

Aramaic cursive script spawned regional scripts, not only in the Middle East, but all across Asia. Archeologists have found related scripts in the Syrian Desert, which they call Palmyrene, in Turkey, which they call Sam'alian and near Hatra, Iraq, which they have named Hatran. Aramaic cursive script is used to write Syriac and to write Mandaic in southern Iraq. The Nabateans who carved the red-striped caves of Petra used it, and from that version Arabic script evolved.

Between the fifth and tenth centuries of the Common Era, scholars of three religions, in three areas of the Middle East, developed systems of dots and dashes to represent vowels. In the fifth century at the School of Nisibis, Turkey, scholars of Aramaic introduced dots. Between the sixth and tenth centuries, Masoretic scholars in Tiberius and in Babylon did the same for Hebrew, and in the sixth century, Arabic scholars created a system of dots, dashes and commas to indicate Arabic vowels. Since these cities are not far apart, the notation invented by scholars of one language clearly inspired scholars of the others. Dots and dashes must have been in the air.

Christian missionaries brought Aramaic deep into Asia, where it influenced the script of Sogdians in Samarkand and Uyghurs in the Mongolian steppes. Going even farther afield, Syriac script can be traced through Persian Pahlavi and Sogdian to Mongolian and Manchurian. It even left its mark on the Brahmi and Kharosthi scripts of India. Moving East, the Uyghur script was derived from the Syriac alphabet, though it is written from top to bottom, and when Genghis Khan decreed that his Mongolian Empire would adopt an official writing system, his first scribe was Uyghur.

The Samarians in their closed communities in the hills north of Jerusalem spoke a dialect of Aramaic until they transitioned to Arabic in the tenth to twelfth centuries CE. They also were the very last people to continue using the ancient paleo-Hebrew script for sacred, literary and secular purposes, both to write Aramaic and Arabic. The name Samarian, or Samaritan, is related to the Hebrew word for guardian, *shomer*, and they consider themselves to be the last faithful guardians of old Jewish tradition.

The local Aramaic dialect spoken in the great city of Edessa, now Sanliurfa, Turkey, became known as Syriac. It was written with an Aramaic script known as Estrangela, which remained in general use to the thirteenth century. Syriac was used over a large part of the Middle East, and eventually evolved local variations. Two new scripts developed around the eighth century. The East Syriac script, also known as Chaldean, Assyrian or Nestorian, uses dots above or below certain consonants to indicate vowels. The West Syriac script, also called Serta, Psita, or Jacobite, is the script used by the Syrian Orthodox and the Maronites. Simpler and more cursive than Estrangela, it uses small Greek letters above consonants to represent vowels. This is the script that gave rise to Nabatean, and Arabic.

IS THAT STUDENT A TALMID, TALMITHU, TALMIDU OR TALIB?

Aramaic and Hebrew are language siblings, close relatives in the Semitic language family, and Arabic is their cousin. Which is older? Scholars have advanced claims for both Aramaic and Hebrew, based on archeological and literary sources, but it is not necessary for us to solve that question here. Let us simply recognize the extreme antiquity of both. Akkadian, another ancient language that we discussed earlier, is a more distant relative, and it also is Semitic.

The strong similarities between the Semitic languages point to a common ancestor. Names of Akkadian gods live on in Arabic, Aramaic and Hebrew today. In Hebrew, to the annoyance of some wives, a husband is called a *baal* – 'lord' or 'master', after the ancient Semitic god *Baal* or *Bel*. The words for sun, sky, water, many items of daily life and parts of the body hardly require translation between Semitic languages. Tooth is *shen* in Hebrew, *san* in Arabic. Question: which is which? Is hair *sha'ar* or *se'ar*? Is the number ten *a'sher* or *eser*? Answer: in both cases the first is Hebrew, the second Arabic. The resemblances are like those of Spanish and Italian, perhaps Spanish and Portuguese.

Kol Nidre, a Jewish prayer with a haunting melody, is in Aramaic. The Kaddish, the Jewish prayer for the dead, also is Aramaic, with a few phrases in Hebrew. In this prayer, my husband has challenged me to distinguish between the Aramaic and the Hebrew words. It is not that easy, because the same alphabet is used for both languages.

One year a neighbor of my Arabic teacher complemented me fulsomely on my Arabic, saying that I really must visit his home village in Lebanon. Snapping my fingers as if I were thinking, I answered, "I would love to, but... what is the Arabic word for 'hostage?'" Since then, when I mix up Hebrew words with Arabic, my teacher says, "Oh no honey. Don't do that. You are going to be a hostage."

Semitic languages all have a similar structure. A typical verb has a three letter root, and it adds prefixes and suffixes to denote past or future. Other added letters indicate singular or plural, masculine or feminine. Hebrew, Arabic and Aramaic use many of the same prefixes and suffixes. When I began studying Hebrew, my Arabic teacher looked at my grammar book and showed me immediately how the personal pronoun was tacked on the end of the verb in the Hebrew past tense, just as it is in Arabic.

Linguists identify certain patterns that help them differentiate between Aramaic and Hebrew. Many Aramaic plurals end with an 'on' sound, as contrasted with an 'im' sound in Hebrew. In Aramaic *bar* means 'son of' and son is *ben* in Hebrew.

We can find striking similarities between Semitic languages. Aramaic uses *Allaha* for god, *Mshiha* for Christ and *Ruha d'qudsha* for the Holy Spirit. Hebrew uses *El* for god, *mashiach* for savior, and *ruah kodesh* for the Holy Spirit. Arabic uses *Allah*, *msiah*, and *ruah kudos*. If you try to pronounce these words, you will see their similarities, despite their different spelling.

The Aramaic word for teacher is *rabban*; the Hebrew word for rabbi is *rav*. Ancient Akkadian used *rabu* for great. In Aramaic, *raba* is great.[2]

Over 4,000 years ago, Akkadian used the word *talmidu* for apprentice or student,[3] *targumanu* for interpreter, and *tinuru* for oven. In Aramaic, *talmitho* is a student, *tarzhuman* an interpreter, and *tanoor* an oven. In Hebrew, a *talmid* is a student, *metargem* an interpreter and *tanoor* an oven. Arabic uses *talib* for student, *targiman* for interpreter and *tanoor* for oven.[4]

One last group of words: in Akkadian, *kalab* was dog. It is *kelba* in Aramaic, *kelev* in Hebrew, and *keleb* in Arabic. Akaddian used *dayyānum* for judge; it is *dayanu* in Aramaic, *dayan* for a religious judge in Hebrew, and *alqadi alddini* for a religious judge in Arabic, all of them derived from *din*, which means either law or religion. *Lamādu* meant learn in Akkadian. To learn is *ilapa*[5] in Aramaic; *lamad* means he learned in Hebrew and it is *liyita'llim* in Arabic. *Išme* in Akaddian meant he heard. Listen is *shmale* in Aramaic, *shma* in Hebrew, and *semia* in Arabic. These transliterations cannot convey the exact pronunciation of these words, but they make the point.

Biblical Hebrew adapted words, personal names and months from Akkadian, Aramaic, and Assyrian, and all of them borrowed from each other. Most Akkadian loan words in Hebrew came by way of Aramaic, since Akkad was near Babylon. Prof. Geoffrey Khan of Cambridge University's Faculty of Asian and Middle Eastern Studies has told me that some people would have spoken both Akkadian and Aramaic, mixing them up just as I mix up Arabic and Hebrew.

An Israeli friend of mine is a Hebrew teacher and a Bible scholar. When I show her an Aramaic text, she can identify most of the words, but she is hard put to suss out the meaning of all the sentences. One can visualize Jesus speaking Aramaic, reading Hebrew and teaching in both languages. Fitzmyer writes that Jesus probably spoke a fused language that combined Aramaic and Hebrew,[6] and Greek would have been in common use too at the time. Simple farmers or craftsmen probably continued to speak Hebrew even after the intelligentsia switched to Aramaic or Greek. Some documents from that time contain passages in combinations of Hebrew, Aramaic and Greek.

Experts can cross-walk between languages, but how? Some commemorative stones were inscribed in two or more languages, the most famous being the Rosetta Stone. Books, especially the Bible, have been translated into multiple languages, thus acting as literary Rosetta Stones. It is particularly helpful when inscriptions are discovered that present one language transliterated into another script, thus shedding light on how the original language was pronounced. Many texts contain recognizable names of gods, personal or geographic names. Kings in the Middle East used standard legal formulae to proclaim their victories, as did magicians writing their spells. Commercial lists of trade goods followed certain conventions. We also know that over time languages tend to simplify sounds and grammar in similar ways, dropping endings and awkward syllables. Letters, conjugations, and word order change in predictable patterns. Thus, scholars not only can distinguish between most languages in inscriptions, they also can map their relationships and time-lines.

OLD, IMPERIAL, MIDDLE AND LATE ARAMAIC

At least 3,000 years old, Aramaic has evolved over time. The earliest known form of the language, **Old Aramaic,** dates back to between 925 and 700 BCE. Even then it had dialects, which linguists name after the places where inscriptions were found: Standard Syrian, Samalian in southeast Turkey and Mesopotamian.

Official Aramaic was the Imperial Aramaic of the Persian Empire. This became the standard form, the *lingua franca,* used across the entire Middle East from 700 BCE to 200 BCE. The script has been documented widely, from the 500 BCE Jewish Elephantine Papyri found on an island in Egypt to fourth century deeds of sale squirreled away in a cave near Jericho.

Middle Aramaic is the form that originated in the great city of Edessa, Turkey, now called Sanliurfa, and it was used between 200 BCE to 250 CE. Middle Aramaic inscriptions have been found in the archeological sites of Palmyra, Syria; Hatra, Iraq and Petra, Jordan. Others came from the ancient religious centers in Tur Abdin, Turkey, and in Georgia. This Aramaic also appears on some of the Dead Sea Scrolls. Middle Aramaic is what the Christians spoke in the eastern Roman Empire and in Persia, although they called it Syriac.

Late or **Classical Aramaic**, the main dialect of which is called Syriac, was used from 250 CE to 700 CE, possibly up to 1250.

After the breakup of the Persian Empire, Imperial Aramaic fragmented into regional dialects: Babylonian, Jewish Babylonian, Judean, Jewish East Jordanian, Samarian, Galilean, Damascene, Jewish Palestinian, later Christian Palestinian, Mandaic and Syrian.

EASTERN AND WESTERN NEO-ARAMAIC

The Aramaic spoken today, to the linguist, is classified as Neo-Aramaic; its popular name – for Christians – is Syriac. It survives in Eastern and Western varieties, though the speakers of the Western dialects are badly threatened. Western Neo-Aramaic once was the language of the Jews, Christians and Samaritans in Palestine. By the twentieth century, it was confined to three Syrian villages. The only Christian one today is Maaloula, which was cruelly attacked in April, 2014. The other two villages became Muslim, perhaps the only Muslims in the world today who speak dialects of Aramaic.

Eastern Neo-Aramaic once was spoken from Edessa, Turkey across Iraq, Syria and northwestern Iran. One version, Turoyo, was specific to Tur Abdin in the Mardin province of Turkey. Unfortunately, despite its historical importance, Turoyo barely survived World War I. For practical purposes, it is gone. Another Eastern Neo-Aramaic language is Mandaic, now spoken by only a handful of Mandaeans.

Northeastern Neo-Aramaic dialects (also known by the acronym NENA) are the descendants of Targumic Aramaic, the language of the Jews in Babylonia. Today these dialects are the languages of certain Jews, Chaldeans and Assyrian Christians of Kurdistan. The NENA dialects are the largest surviving group of modern Aramaic dialects; in the words of Jastrow the group comprises 'an amazing variety of languages and dialects, many of which are still unexplored or even undiscovered…some of the NENA subgroups should perhaps be set up as different languages.'[7] Until ISIS appeared, these regional NENA dialects were spoken in many small northern Iraqi communities, even in cities, such as Mosul, Irbil, Kirkuk and Dohuk.

DIALECTS

Modern local dialects of Aramaic struggle to stay alive. Many vanished in the twentieth century when waves of relocations mingled refugees from different locales. Because regional dialects are so severely endangered, Prof. Geoffrey Khan has dedicated the past 20 years to locating remote villagers, recording their speech, and building an archive of their words and accents before they are gone forever. He told me about how he sat one day with a frail little old lady who clutched him by the wrist and begged him to ask her anything he could. And she kept holding on for over two hours. Both Prof. Khan and his subject knew that her dialect would die with her.

Christian and Jewish dialects often were mutually intelligible, but not always. Kurdish Jews who traded with outside communities often incorporated words of Kurdish, Turkish, Arabic, Azeri, Persian and Hebrew into their Aramaic. These borrowed words would have been unintelligible to their neighbors.

In contrast, many Christian villagers lived in isolation, surrounded by mountains, and retained very archaic dialects. When Norma was a girl in Telkaif, the villagers never even came in contact with other Chaldeans from neighboring villages. Thus her Chaldean endured as a relatively pure dialect of what linguists would call Northeastern Neo-Aramaic. Norma just calls it Soureth, and hers could be the last generation to speak it.

CAN A LANGUAGE DIE?

Over the vast sweep of history, not only do civilizations rise and fall, so do languages. Still, who would think that a 3,000 year old language could disappear in our time without an outcry? Just think about what that means. In how many other ancient Semitic languages does a mother today tell her child to go to bed?

How do we decide whether a language is living? We might ask whether the ancient version of the language would still be intelligible today. Must it have been spoken continuously? What if it is only used for study or worship? What do we know about languages that never were written?

How many languages are endangered? Some 6,703 languages[8] were spoken in the world in 1996. Not surprisingly, the languages of native, tribal and aboriginal peoples are at the greatest risk, along with those of marginalized Europeans. Experts estimate that at least 50% (2500–3000), perhaps 80%, of these languages will disappear before the end of this century.

'The application of the Language Endangerment Scale to all known languages has revealed that a total of 3,176 can be considered endangered. This is about 46% of all living languages...Today 457 or 9.2% of the living languages have fewer than 10 speakers and are very likely to die out soon if no revitalization efforts are made. Of the languages known to have existed, 639 are already extinct – 10% of all languages,' according to The Rosetta Project.[9] The National Science Foundation[10] and UNESCO[11] have published comparable numbers.

As an endangered language, Aramaic has plenty of company, but this is far from a simple tribal or aboriginal language. Aramaic once was the common language of the entire Middle East. It is the language of the Jewish Talmud and the Targum (expanded translation) of the Bible. Every Jewish marriage contract (*ketuba*) in the world uses it today. In it, Jewish and Christian scholars have written some of their greatest works. It still is the liturgical language of the Maronite Church in Lebanon, the Chaldean Catholic Church, the Syrian Catholic Church and the Assyrian Church of the East. In India it is used by the Indian Orthodox Church, the Malankara Syrian Orthodox Church, the Syro-Malabar Church and the Syro-Malankara Catholic Church.

Spoken Hebrew too was threatened with extinction. When the Jews brought Aramaic back from Babylonia in the fifth century BCE, it replaced Hebrew, and Hebrew only enjoyed a brief resurgence during a nationalistic rebellion in 132–135 CE. After about 200 CE, it was only used for liturgical or scholarly purposes. Hebrew was not reborn as a colloquial language until the turn of the twentieth century, when scholars resurrected it from the dusty shelves of old libraries, borrowing or creating new words, and updating the grammar. Theoretically Aramaic could be resurrected again in the future too, but its rich linguistic heritage of regional dialects will have been irretrievably lost. If it dies, so does a part of the rich tapestry of our Judeo-Christian heritage.

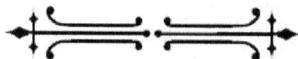

THE JEWS AND THE CHURCH

In the first two decades of the twenty-first century, newspapers announced the killing of Christians in Iraq and Syria by ISIS. We read that the Christians have three choices: convert, die or pay an onerous tax, which probably will not do them any good. Jewish readers find these stories to be all too familiar, because they are reminded of the year 1492 in Spain, when the Jews of Spain had almost the same stark choices: convert, die or leave Spain. At that time, the Inquisition reserved its worst tortures and death penalties for those who pretended to convert while secretly maintaining Jewish practices. For many centuries after the Inquisition, Jews faced a vicious cycle of pogroms, perilous escapes and forced conversions in many European countries. In Muslim lands, both Jews and Christians, called *dhimmis*, were subjected to a special tax, the *jizya*, designed to extract as much money as possible for the benefit of the shake-down operators who collected it.

We will expand upon the subject of *dhimmis* in a subsequent chapter, but here it may be instructive to sample a few of the ways in which Jews and Christians have suffered comparable persecution, ranging from being relegated to second class status to being forced to flee life-threatening danger. An eighth century Muslim caliph required Christians to sew a special patch on their outer clothing. Medieval Europe took a page from this book, requiring Jews to wear a silly pointed hat, distinctive clothing and a yellow patch on their clothes. In 850 CE the Abbasid caliph al-Mutawakkil ordered both Christians and Jews to wear a sash (*zunnah*), a special shawl or headscarf, and little bells in the public bath.

Coming to more serious threats, a Turk in the Ottoman Empire had the right to test the sharpness of his sword on the neck of a Christian. Under some caliphs, if a Muslim beat up a *dhimmi*, he

41

was not punished; if a *dhimmi* beat a Muslim, punishment was severe. Provincial governors closed their eyes to pogroms. In some villages, both Christians and Jews were treated as serfs, subject to being sold by one Muslim notable to another. As the Ottoman Empire broke down at the turn of the century, Christians were treated as foreigners, essentially losing their citizenship.

JEWISH BACKGROUND

The Babylonian Captivity attracted the earliest Christians to Babylon.

The first group of Jews to reach Mesopotamia had been taken captive by the Assyrian king Sennacherib, who invaded the Northern Kingdom of Israel, besieged Jerusalem and deported many Israelites back to Assyria in 722 BCE. This is known as the Assyrian Exile, and the deportees have become known as the Ten Lost Tribes. Josephus, while not always reliable, reported in Roman times that the Ten Lost Tribes of Israel were 'an immense multitude' living beyond the Euphrates. Since then, travelers have claimed to find them in strange locations all over the world, places as far flung as South America, Asia or England.

The British explorer, Sir Austin Henry Layard, found graphic depictions of such deportations. In the mid-nineteenth century he carried out extensive excavations in the ruins of ancient Nineveh. Lining the palace halls were huge slabs of alabaster with bas-relief sculptures that depict Assyrian conquests. Prominently featured are horsemen, chariots, swords, fires, processions of captives and bodies being tossed over walls. In front, soldiers pile severed heads in front of an assessor, who enters the numbers into a book. So it goes in the Middle East until today.

The Book of Kings (II Kings 17:6) says that the king of Assyria captured Samaria, deported the inhabitants to Assyria, and 'settled them in Halah, at the [River] Habor. At the River Gozen, and in the towns of Media.' We know that the river that encircles the city of Zakho in northern Iraq is called the Khabur River, and Zakho was the home of a large population of Kurdish Jews before they moved to Israel. So are the Kurdish Jews descended from the Ten Lost Tribes? They think so, but the answer remains shrouded in the mists of time.

The Babylonian Jewish Heritage Museum in Or Yehuda is built close to a site where Iraqi Jews once started new lives in Israeli refugee camps. In the museum are examples of a Babylonian Jewish house, synagogue and a commercial street lined with shops. In one exhibit, a placard estimates that 200,150 Israelites were carried off in the Assyrian Exile alone. In the basement is a large Hebrew archive, with a librarian who will bring out books on the subject – in Hebrew – upon request.

Nebuchadnezzar of Babylon, King of the Chaldeans, invaded the southern kingdom of Judah in 597 BCE. The Book of Kings (II Kings 24 and 25) describes how he conquered Jerusalem at the head of an army of 'Chaldeans, Arameans, Moabites and Ammonites,' forced the Jewish king to surrender and placed King Zedekiah on the throne as a puppet. After an attempted rebellion, 'the Chaldean troops' subsequently captured Zedekiah, put him on trial and put out his eyes. In 587 BCE they burned the palace and principal houses, tore down the walls, destroyed the Temple in Jerusalem and carried off its riches. They then transported 40,000 captive Judeans to Babylonia.

The aristocrats, warriors and priests of the Judean community in that Babylonian Exile created a vibrant center of religious and communal activity 'by the rivers of Babylon.' Jehoiachim, a Judaen king who found favor with the Babylonians, is said to have incorporated ashes from the Temple into the foundation of the great synagogue of Babylon.

Cyrus the Great of Persia conquered Babylon in 539 BCE. The Cyrus Cylinder, now in the British Museum, was inscribed in 539 BCE, and on it Cyrus recounts how he returned statues to sanctuaries, restored those ruined by war, and 'gathered all their inhabitants and returned to them their dwellings'. These benign policies are reflected in the biblical account of the exiled Jews given permission to return to Jerusalem and rebuild their Temple. It was when these elite Judean Jews returned that they brought the Imperial Aramaic of the Persian Empire back to Jerusalem. According to The Book of Ezra, 42,360 Jews returned, and they completed the Second Temple in 515 BCE.

While the Second Temple was not as lavish as the first, Ezra the Scribe writes that, before they left Babylon, Cyrus did generously give back the spoils and gold that Nebuchadnezzar had stolen from the First Temple. An article on the website of the Iran Chamber Society[1] grandly quotes the verses in full, footnoting the Hebrew Bible.

The Jews remember Cyrus fondly as Cyrus the Great. In the Book of Isaiah (Isaiah 44:28) it is written that the Lord says of Cyrus, 'He is my shepherd' because he orders Jerusalem to be rebuilt and the Temple founded again. Isaiah 45:1 writes that the Lord spoke 'to Cyrus, His anointed one.' The Iranians have a right to be proud.

The Babylonian Exile was not over after those Judeans returned to Jerusalem. More Jews still moved to Babylonia. At the time Jesus was born, Jerusalem had fallen into the hands of the Romans and their vassal, the half-mad King Herod. This was the beginning of the end. Under the Roman Emperor Hadrian the situation became intolerable. In 132 CE, Shimon Bar-Kochba and his sons began a full-scale Jewish revolt, but in 135 CE the Romans thoroughly defeated him, plowed Jerusalem under and expelled all the Jews.

Refugees left in droves, but many, fearing the jaws of the Roman lion, preferred to go east to Babylonia or north to Antioch, a major Roman colony now in Turkey. The disciples Paul and Peter are believed to have gone to Antioch. Winkler[2] writes that it was from Antioch that the gospel traveled through Edessa to Mesopotamia. That is how the Syriac dialect of Edessa became the liturgical language of eastern Christianity.

This was not the first time Jewish refugees had fled to the Jewish communities of Babylon, Adiabene, Edessa or Nisibis. They also came when the Seleucid emperor, Antiochus IV, destroyed the Second Temple in 70 CE. Their choice of destination was logical. They spoke the same Aramaic as the Babylonian Jews, and the Jewish community would have received them warmly. In the second century though, among this wave of refugees from Jerusalem there were Judeo-Christian evangelists, who would be welcomed in Babylon as teachers from Jerusalem. After all, tradition taught that someday a Messiah would come from Palestine.

ADIABENE AND BEYOND

A curious event occurred in 30 CE. Queen Helena of Adiabene, both the wife and the sister of King Monobaz I, converted to Judaism along with her son Izates, members of her royal family and several members of her court. Adiabene was a region in Assyria whose capital was Arbela, one of the world's oldest cities. Arbela rose in importance after Nineveh fell, and it is mentioned in the

Talmud. Variously called Erbil, Arbel, Arbil or Irbil, in Akkadian it was Arba-Illu, in Assyrian *Arbael*, all of which meant the same thing – 'Four Gods.' Once a place is sacred, it remains sacred, even if the religion changes.

After her conversion, Helena made many pilgrimages to Jerusalem bearing gifts of gold, and she generously fed the starving during a famine in 45 CE. One of her sons even was reprimanded for squandering large sums on Jewish charities. Her family participated prominently in the first Jewish revolt against Rome in 66 CE, perhaps partly motivated by the thought that, if the revolt had succeeded, they would have been well positioned to claim the throne of King David. Queen Helena even built a palace in Jerusalem, and she spent many of her last years there as a Nazarite, an ascetic. She was buried in a mausoleum just north of Jerusalem, among the Tombs of the Kings. Thanks to her, Adiabene became a significant Jewish center. This may have facilitated a later movement of Christian missionaries into Adiabene, which became an important Christian community. Oddly, we will read later about a very similar conversion story that took place there, this time to Christianity.

In 50 CE, the Apostolic Decree of the Council of Jerusalem abrogated the requirement of circumcision for gentiles who wished to convert to Christianity. It did not take long before Christianity spread beyond the Aramaic speaking Jewish communities of Edessa (Urfa, Sanliurfa) and Nisibis, Turkey. Since many Jewish traders traveled the Silk Route, the new religion moved along with the traders all the way to the capital of China. Before that though, it went to Babylon.

JEWS IN BABYLONIA

The greatest Jewish community of the ancient world was in Babylonia. A million Jews may have lived in Babylonia in 70 CE, possibly two million by the third to sixth centuries, though the population fluctuated.[3] During the fourth century under the Sassanid Empire, Shapur II transferred 7,000 Jews from Babylonia to the interior of Persia.[4]

Two groups of Jews coexisted in Mesopotamia until the twentieth century. The Jews in the north had been there for over 2,700 years, since the Assyrian Exile. They became the Kurdish Jews, who continued to speak Aramaic in villages of northern Iraq. We will dedicate a later chapter to their story. The Jews of the Babylonian Exile became the Baghdadi Jews, cultured, educated, affluent, and eventually Arabic-speaking. While they no longer speak Aramaic in their daily life, the literature they created in Aramaic lives on today as the basis of all Jewish learning. More Jews came to Baghdad later. Ladino-speaking Sephardic Jews came from Spain, and Ashkenazi Jews came too, but their history is beyond our purview.

From the Parthian Empire (247 BCE – 224 CE) through most of the Sassanid Empire (224–651 CE), the Jews enjoyed a relatively stable political, intellectual and economic environment. Thus it was in Babylonia that Jewish scholars would create the greatest body of commentary ever written on Jewish law and the Bible. As Middle Eastern history has demonstrated repeatedly, when rulers are not threatened by external or internal forces, they often adopt a benevolent attitude toward their Jews and Christians. In contrast, turbulent times and menacing enemies make governments turn paranoid, suspicious and repressive. We will see this in the Ottoman Empire and in its successor nations.

For twelve centuries, the Babylonian Jews were led by the Exilarch, the Head of the Exile, by tradition chosen from the House of David. He appointed judges and high officials, confirmed appointments in the academies, acted as a final court of appeal and supervised a Jewish prison. He collected taxes for the government, and in return he was allowed to keep half the tax money for community use. Thus it was said that the House of David ruled the Jews for more than two thousand years.

One of the greatest scholars and teachers of all time was Hillel, born in Babylon. Hillel went to Jerusalem in 70 BCE at the age of 40, and he is famous for his teachings. One of the most beloved is his celebrated response to the man who challenged him to teach the whole Jewish religion while standing on one foot. His answer is known as the Golden Rule: 'That which is hateful to you, do not do to your fellow. That is the whole Torah; the rest is the explanation; go and learn.'

Another revered figure was Rabbi Abba Arika, known as Rab (Rav), who came to Babylonia in 219 CE from Jerusalem and founded a religious academy in Sura. At about the same time, a Babylonian scholar named Samuel founded another famous academy, this one in Nehardea, which was later destroyed and relocated in Pumbeditha. Pumbeditha today is Fallujah. These two important academies deserve much of the credit for the Babylonian Talmud. Aptly, the name is related to the Hebrew verb 'to learn,' and to the Hebrew word for student, *talmid.*

Two hundred years earlier, a Jerusalem Talmud had been compiled in the Galilee, but by the mid-fourth century Christian persecution forced the most important Jewish scholars to flee to the great Talmudic schools of Babylonia. There, students listened to lectures, memorized passages of the Bible, and engaged in spirited dispute, just as students in religious schools do today. The records of these early debates were compiled by the end of the fifth century BCE into the monumental, multi-volume Babylonian Talmud, second only to the Bible as a repository of Jewish civil law, religious law, and folk wisdom. Babylonian Aramaic is the medium in which Jewish scholars still study this literature all across the world today.

Many major Jewish scholars moved to Baghdad by the end of the third century, and through the eleventh century, rabbis from as far away as northern Europe directed their legal questions to them. The responses travelled back to Europe from the leading academics of Babylonia, moving along established trade routes, either through the Balkans and the Alps to Germany or up the eastern shore of the Caspian Sea to Kiev, Prague and points north.

In 928, a great scholar and writer from Egypt, Saadya ben Joseph, became the head of the academy at Sura. His title was *Gaon,* from the Hebrew word meaning splendor. Now it is virtually synonymous with genius. The brilliant period of scholarship from the seventh to the eleventh century is known as the Gaonic Period. Saadya wrote works on philosophy, biblical commentary, even a book of poetry, but in Arabic.

During the ninth century Abbasid caliphate Muslim scholars became interested in the major works of the Roman Empire. Jews and Christians had previously translated many of these works into Syriac (Aramaic), and now they were engaged to translate these important books of medicine, astronomy, physics, mathematics and philosophy from Greek and Syriac to Arabic, thus preserving ancient knowledge and culture. Centuries later, these texts would be translated from Arabic into Latin, restoring scientific knowledge back to Christian Europe where it had been lost. The translation movement under the Abbasids sparked interest in the original texts themselves, and Jewish, Muslim and Christian translators who encountered difficult points exchanged letters freely. In the twelfth century the Jewish traveler Benjamin of Tudela[5] reported that even caliphs studied the Bible in Hebrew.

Next door, the Persian Jews had a different story, and there were fewer of them. For example, Ottoman Empire records from 1520–30 show 1,647 Jewish households in Constantinople and 2,645 in Salonika (Thessaloniki), representing over two-thirds of the city. Contemporary figures for Persian cities were: Tabriz – 54 Jewish households, Hamadan – 132 and Kermanshah – 53.[6]

Before we discuss the origins of Christianity in the Middle East, it is important to remember that the Greeks and Romans could not understand why these strange people did not worship their emperors and did not honor the sacred rites of their gods. They resented what they saw as a double standard whereby Christians, and some Jews, lived in separate communities but also wanted the rights of regular citizens. Antiochus IV resorted to similar anti-Jewish propaganda to justify looting the Jewish Temple.

In the fourth century, the Roman Empire shifted its center of gravity to Constantinople (modern day Istanbul), also known as Byzantium, and the Roman emperor Constantine converted to Christianity. Shortly after that, Byzantium issued severe laws that discriminated against the Jews. The western portion of the Roman Empire lingered on in Rome until it collapsed in the fifth century. By that time the Church of the East had appeared.

JEWISH ASPECTS OF THE CHURCH OF THE EAST

Members of the congregation and clergy cheerfully agree that the Church of the East has Judeo-Christian roots.[7] That becomes even more obvious when we learn about the liturgical elements it has in common with Judaism, when we learn the names of some ceremonies and we hear what titles are given to the clergy.

Lamsa,[8] a Christian Assyrian, remembers going with his mother when she sacrificed an ox at an ancient shrine. This is reminiscent of sacrifices in the ancient Jewish Temple. The practice is not unique to Assyrians though. A Christian Palestinian friend of mine has shown me where his mother used to sacrifice a goat every May 1 in their village of Taybeh in Samaria (the West Bank). The village priest told us that the Taybeh tradition was to split up the meat of the animal sacrifice between the family, the clergy and the poor. Lamsa writes that his family strictly observed Jewish holidays and never ate pork.

The East Syrian Rite maintains many recognizable Jewish liturgical practices. The church layout resembles a typical Sephardic synagogue, with a raised platform in the middle for the clergy. In front is an area called the holy of holies, reminiscent of the ancient Jewish Temple. The church has no graven images. Many of these churches date back to the second and third centuries.

The Syriac Eucharistic Prayer of the Apostles resembles the Jewish blessing after meals, the *birkat hamazon*. The Eucharist is called the Holy *Qurbana* in East Syriac, *qurbono qadisho* in West Syriac. In Jerusalem, sacrifices at the Jewish Temple were called *korban*. During celebration of the Eucharist they read two selections from the Old Testament, just as the Jews read a portion of the Torah three times a week. Before the readings, they sing certain Syriac hymns, called *Turgama*, which means 'translation' in both Syriac and Hebrew. The psalms sung before the gospel are called *Zumara*. *Zemer* means 'song' in Hebrew.

Holy rituals are called *kudasha*, similar to the Hebrew word *kedusha*. A deacon is a *shamasha*, almost the same as the *shamas* in the Jewish synagogue. When the priest performs sacerdotal functions, he is called a *Khana*. The Jewish priest was a *Cohen*. As Chief of the Priests, a bishop is called *Rab khani*, equivalent in Hebrew to *Rav* (Rabbi) *Cohen*. The word *Khanutha*, 'priesthood' (*Cohanim* in Hebrew), applies to the deacon, priest, and bishop. The ordination formula for a priest says that the newly ordained clergyman has been consecrated '...to the work of... the Levitical and Stephanite Office... [for the office of the Aaronic priesthood]'. The Levites were a Jewish priestly tribe and Aaron was the brother of the biblical Moses.

The traditional Assyrian Patriarch[9] was a Nazarite, the Jewish term for a man committed from childhood to holiness, forbidden to eat meat, shave or marry. The office was hereditary, typically passed on to a nephew, reminiscent of the priests of the Jewish Temple, who were part of a hereditary priestly caste. A regular Assyrian priest may eat meat and marry, just as the Jewish rabbi does. In battle, the Nestorian Patriarch marches in front of his people, like a Levitical priest.

In Judaism, the *Shekhina* is the Divine Presence. In the Syrian Orthodox ordination rite, the Lord is asked to cause the *Shekhina* to reside in the new clergyman. In a West Syriac hymnal, the Virgin Mary is described as the *Shekhina* of the Lord.[10]

The Church of the East, the Chaldean church and some other Syriac traditions observe the yearly Fast of the Ninevites, also called the Fast of Rogation. This commemorates Jonah's prophecies in Nineveh and the repentance of the people. The Tomb of Jonah was venerated on a hill, Nebi Yunis, close to Mosul in the Nineveh Plain, for centuries, until ISIS blew it up.

Lamsa[11] writes that in Assyrian tradition the Assyrian Jilu Tribe in Hakkari, Turkey was one of the lost tribes of Israel. The Aramaic word *jilu* means captivity. Who knows? It certainly is in the right location.

Moving on a few centuries, we remember that the Essenes were an ascetic Jewish community that lived a monastic life in the desert at the time of Jesus, although they were not hermits. In the fourth century CE, a bizarre form of asceticism arose in Syria. Christian holy men lived, preached and fasted on the tops of pillars, often for years or for a whole lifetime, in plain view. Called *Stylites* from the Greek word for pillar, many of these holy men achieved great local renown, attracted throngs of admiring pilgrims and were worshiped as saints. The tradition even spread beyond Syria and lasted beyond the Middle Ages. Dalrymple[12] writes of one church that was seeking a Stylite in the twentieth century.

Bar Hebraeus, one of the most respected church historians of the thirteenth century, was a Jacobite bishop. His father was a Jewish physician from the village of Ebra (meaning Hebrew), and his name meant 'son of the Hebrew.' As a prelate of the Syriac Orthodox Church of Antioch, he took the Christian name Gregory. He has been called 'one of the most learned and versatile men that Syria ever produced.' A student of mathematics, medicine, philosophy, and law, he published a lengthy three-part historical *Chronicle* in Syriac, with a summary in Arabic. He also wrote an important commentary on the Bible, basing it on the original Hebrew, as well as the Greek, Oriental, Armenian and Syriac translations. His enormous body of work summarizes all the known literature to date on science, history, theology, ethics, monasticism and grammar, even on jokes.

Bar Hebraeus also enjoyed an odd tale or two. His *Chronicle* relates the tribulations of 90–year old Israel of Kashkar, who sought to become bishop in 872. According to Wilmshurst,[13] quoting Bar

Hebraeus, he had a rival, who was supported by the emir of Baghdad. At the end of a lengthy conflict, a fan of his rival assaulted him in church and castrated him, causing his death.

Another famous writer was a Nestorian priest, Giwargis, called son of Israel, from the Shikwana family of Alqosh, Iraq.[14] Between 1676 and 1727 he is said to have copied at least 48 manuscripts into Soureth, the common name for vernacular Aramaic. Along with Joseph of Telkaif, he helped revive the Syriac literary tradition.

For years the Muslims, Christians, Jews, Sufis, Bahais and Yazidis of rural Mesopotamia lived in similar houses, dressed much the same, shared festivals, dances and songs, farmed and cooked in similar ways. Together they coped with draught, floods, locusts and petty wars. On Passover, Christians and Muslims sent sweets to their Jewish neighbors. This blended culture survived for centuries, and within it the Church of the East flourished, fought, divided, reunited and just tried to stay alive.

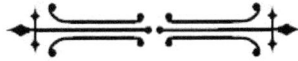

THE CHURCHES OF THE EAST

The saga of the Church of the East is indeed Byzantine. Although it once extended from the Middle East all across Asia, many in the west have never heard of it. It has been split by heresies, excommunications and schisms, its parishioners divided by conflicting loyalties to competing patriarchs, sometimes approaching Rome and other times stubbornly independent. The history of this church – or these churches – mirrors the political chaos of the Middle East over the last two millennia. To its detriment, these fractures have prevented it from standing united against plunderers, pogroms and political pressures.

Before we start, here is a short primer, with membership numbers pre-ISIS:

The modern **Chaldean Catholic Church** is an Eastern Syriac Church that has unified with Rome. Pope Eugene IV chose the name Chaldean in 1445 when a patriarch joined the Latin Church. After multiple schisms, starts and stops, in 1830 the Vatican designated the patriarch of Mosul as the Patriarch of Babylon. The church now became the **Chaldean Uniate Church**, with its own liturgical traditions but in union with the Catholic Church. The U.S. Conference of Catholic Bishops estimated its membership was close to 500,000 in 2010. Of these, some 310,000[1] were in the Middle East. Services are in the vernacular, meaning Chaldean. Patriarchs have been in Diyarbakir (Amida), Turkey, Mosul and Baghdad, Iraq.

The **Syriac Orthodox Church**, sometimes known as the **Church of Antioch** or the **Western Syriac Church**, is also called the **Jacobite Church**, after its great church father, Jacob Baradaeus. This church developed a separate identity during a century of theological controversy. Its heartland covered northern Syria, northern Iraq and southeastern Turkey. Most of the Jacobite churches in the U.S. changed their name from the Assyrian Apostolic Church of Antioch to the Syrian (Syriac) Orthodox Church of Antioch. The official website provides no numbers,[2] but the *New Advent Encyclopedia*[3] quotes a current membership of 80,000 in the Middle East, probably on the low side. Patriarchs have sat in Damascus; in Mardin, Turkey and in the Deir Al-Zaafaran monastery, Turkey. The most recent patriarch was consecrated in Damascus, Syria.

The **Syriac (Syrian) Catholic Church** united with Rome in 1782 and now is also called the **Uniate Syrian Church**. In 2010 there were an estimated 140,000 members in the Middle East and several thousand more in the Diaspora. Patriarchs have sat in Aleppo, Mardin, Turkey, more recently in Beirut.

The **Holy Apostolic Catholic Assyrian Church of the East** is also known as the **Assyrian Church of the East**, the **Syrian Church of the East**, the **Apostolic Church of the East** or the **East Syriac Church**. Since it developed in the Persian Empire, it often was called the Persian Church. In the fifth century it became known as the **Nestorian Church**, because its members supported Nestorius, a patriarch from Antioch. As we soon will see, this became its traditional name, and we will use it frequently. In 2010, this church had an estimated 130,000–150,000 members in the Middle East and as many or more in the Diaspora.[4] On the website of the World Council of Churches, the church posted 323,300 for its worldwide membership in 2016.[5] The Patriarchs once sat in Salmas, northern Iran, and then moved to Kochanes (Konak), Turkey, remaining there until 1915, when they moved to San Francisco, and now to Chicago.

In a 1968 schism within the Assyrian Church of the East, another church split off, to be called the **Ancient Church of the East**. Patriarch Shimun XXI Eshai, then in exile in Cyprus, had changed the church calendar to the Gregorian calendar, among other suggested reforms, but an opponent of that change, Thomas Darmo, became patriarch of this break-away church. The current patriarch is seated in Baghdad, and discussions about future unification with the Assyrian Church of the East are ongoing.

The **Syro-Malabar Catholic Church** originated on the Malabar Coast of southwest India. Its members call themselves Assyrian Christians, or St. Thomas Christians, in honor of the apostle whom they believe established their church. The website indicates a membership of 4.5 million, mostly in India, but also abroad.[6]

The **Syriac Maronite Church of Antioch** is a Lebanese church that is fully unified with the Roman Catholic Church. Services are in Aramaic, but the liturgy is Latinized. In 2010 this church had an estimated 1,661,800 members in the Middle East and about the same number in the Diaspora.[7] The seat of the Maronite Patriarch of Antioch is in Bkerke, north of Beirut.

The **Melkite Catholic Church** is another church of the Middle East. The Melkites consider themselves the original Christians. The name Melkite signified that they were loyal to the Roman Emperor; the Syriac word for king is *melk*, similar to the Hebrew *melek* and the Arabic *malik*. This church was first established in Antioch, and it later spread to Jerusalem and Alexandria. The liturgical language changed to Greek, then mixed with Arabic, but many still call the church Syriani. The church also has been called Greco-Melkite, Greek, Syriac, or Syro-Melkite. In 2010 it was estimated to have over 755,200 members in the Middle East, with even more in the Diaspora.[8]

I hope that was perfectly clear.

Keep in the mind that many of these estimated numbers were from 2010. Since then many of these numbers may have dropped drastically. This book will explain.

THE SPREAD OF CHRISTIANITY IN THE EAST

According to legend, King Abgar V of Edessa was a leper, or maybe he just had gout; in any case, none of the wise men of his kingdom could heal him. Desperate, he sent a plea to Jesus. According to the *Doctrine of Addai* and other Syriac chronicles, Jesus is said to have written him a letter, promising to send one of his disciples. The disciple he sent was Addai (also known as Addaeus or Thaddeus), one of a circle of Seventy Apostles. Some elaborate on the story to say he arrived in Edessa with a miraculous portrait of Jesus. As any Jew would have done, he stayed at the home of a Jew, Tobias. Miraculously, perhaps through the merit of the painting or else purely through the apostle himself, the king was cured, and the whole city of Edessa converted to Christianity. This would have been in 37–65 CE. The occasionally fanciful *Chronicle of Erbil* adds that Addai preached in Mosul, in Beth Garmai and went on to found the diocese of Erbil.

If any part of the legend of Abgar sounds familiar, it should. Queen Helena of Adiabene, whose conversion to Judaism we read about earlier, was King Abgar's chief wife, and his sister. Moreover, she was queen of both Adiabene and Edessa. In the Armenian tradition, she went to Jerusalem after King Abgar died. Sources differ.

In another tradition, it was St. Thomas, one of the original twelve apostles, who sent Addai to Edessa. As an aside, in Aramaic, *Teome* – from which the name 'Thomas' comes – means *twin*. Some have wondered if this means Thomas was the twin of Jesus, though most Christians would be astonished at the idea.[9]

Apostolic stories of Addai and Mari are revered in the East Syrian Rite. Thus, St. Thomas is supposed to have travelled through Palmyra and Babylon to India. Addai is said to have consecrated Mari, a next generation apostle whose mission took him to Nineveh, Nisibis and along the Euphrates River. Mari is credited with establishing the patriarchal see at Seleucia-Ctesiphon, which would make him the founder of the Church of the East. Aggai, another disciple of Addai, may have preached in Beth Huzaye, Media and Khuzestan, now Iran. Much of this history is in the Acts of Thomas (*Acta Thomae*), which Emhardt and Lamsa call 'one of the most remarkable apocryphal writings of the Christian Church,' and which contains the lovely poem, *The Hymn of the Soul*.

These stories have been so embroidered over the ages that many skeptics regard them as folklore. The church cherishes them as a demonstration of its apostolic origin, yet there are discrepancies. Confusingly, a tomb of St. Thomas is worshipped in Mylapore (Meliapur), India, and another is in Edessa, now Sanliurfa, Turkey. No aspect of the tale has gone unchallenged.

Mar Soro[10] recounts a traditional church history, beginning with the original apostles. Following them were supposed to be three Judeo-Christian apostles, considered to be relatives of Mary, James and Joseph, but he says they must be apocryphal. He names them because 'the mere mention of their names and relation to Jesus' immediate family members... indicates this church's self-understanding.' Next he lists three bishops of Adiabene, none of whom are documented in the historical record, but he explains that the Church of the East wants to show that its birthplace is Adiabene, the land of Queen Helena, adjacent to Edessa.

Many Judeo-Christian missionaries did travel from Jerusalem to Babylonia, passing through Damascus, Palmyra, Antioch, Arbela

(Erbil), possibly even Nisibis and Nineveh. In the second century, Christianity followed the Persian 'Royal Road' through Adiabene, Babylon, and Elam. By the early third century, Christian communities had spread across Mesopotamia to Persia, the western shore of the Caspian Sea and the Hindu Kush. From Persia they sailed to the Malabar Coast of southern India.

Christianity was not alone. A great flowering of religions and sects grew out of Persia and its indigenous Zoroastrian religion: Mandaeans, Manicheans, Elkasaites, Gnostics, and Bahais. Manichaeism in particular competed directly with Christianity, though both Catholics and Zoroastrians considered it to be a heresy. Founded by the Persian holy man Mani (216–277 CE), a self-styled apostle of Jesus Christ, the religion blends ideas from Christianity and Zoroastrianism, with a focus on the battle of good against evil. The Manichaean apostles were Addai, Mari and Thomas. For nine or ten years, St. Augustine was a practicing Manichaean, and this religion is said to have influenced his theology.

The beliefs of Manichaeism are said to be Gnostic. The dictionary defines Gnosticism as 'distinguished by the conviction that matter is evil and that emancipation comes through gnosis.'[11] Gnosis is defined as 'esoteric knowledge of spiritual truth held... to be essential to salvation.' In the fourth century Manichaeism spread rapidly across Europe, largely disappearing by the sixth century. By the end of the seventh century it had all but vanished in Mesopotamia. It spread to India and reached China by the seventh century, but by the ninth century, it was officially banned in China.

In contrast, the Mandaeans are a small, closed sect of southern Iraq and Iran, though some have moved to the U.S. Many of the words in their liturgy strongly resemble Hebrew and the Chaldean dialect of Aramaic. The word for light is *nhora*, similar to *or* in Hebrew and *behora* in Chaldean. The word *hshoka* means dark, again resembling the words *khoshekh* in Hebrew and *khoshka* in Chaldean.[12] A few Mandaeans still speak Neo-Mandaic, a modern form of Classical Mandaic, derived from Aramaic. Since Islam does not consider them to be People of the Book, they are severely oppressed today. Perhaps 10,000 remained in Iraq in 2013.[13] Their website estimates a world-wide membership of no more than 100,000.

NESTORIANS AND JACOBITES

The fourth century was an era of great Christological wars between the Catholic Church and the Church of the East. At the same time, the Persian Empire and Roman Empire were at actual war. These wars were interrupted by at least one period of peace in the fourth century, but they broke out again in the beginning of the sixth century, not ending until Persia and Byzantium signed a treaty in 628.

The Church of the East found itself caught in the middle. Once Rome became Christian in the early fourth century, its Emperors regarded heretical Christian sects with suspicion. In 338–363 CE, during the Roman-Persian wars, the Roman Emperor Constantine wrote to the Persian Emperor Shapur II, urging him to be lenient toward the Christians. This only confirmed the suspicions of Shapur that the Christians were in sympathy with Christian Rome, and he blamed the Persian Christians for his early losses. On an infamous Good Friday in 339, he began what was known as the 'forty-year persecution.' Indulging in beheadings, heinous atrocities and crucifixions, his troops reputedly murdered 16,000 Christians. After this, the liturgical wars heated up.

The religious doctrinal battles of the fourth century began with the First Council of Nicaea (now in Turkey) in 325 CE. This Council formalized the canon, established a common understanding of which books had been authentically inspired by the Holy Spirit and published the Nicene Creed, still the official Catholic profession of faith today. In addition to doctrinal matters though, church politics played a major role. Up to 381, the First Council of Constantinople, the Roman church had five patriarchates: Rome, Alexandria, Constantinople, Antioch, and Jerusalem, in that order. The Council of Constantinople confirmed the Nicene Creed with some modifications, but it created a firestorm when it promulgated a third canon: 'The Bishop of Constantinople, however, shall have the prerogative of honour after the Bishop of Rome because Constantinople is New Rome.' This dropped Alexandria to third place in the rankings.

Archbishop Cyril, the Patriarch of Alexandria, was thereby demoted to a position less important than that of Mar Nestorius, the Patriarch of Constantinople. Nestorius, a Greek born in the Byzantine Empire and educated in Antioch, was known as 'a great scholar, lecturer, and an eloquent speaker,'[14] but the aggrieved Cyril now accused him of heresy for refusing to call the Virgin Mary by the title Theotokos, meaning Mother of God. Instead he called her Christotokos, meaning Mother of Christ. Cyril claimed that Nestorius denied that the divinity and humanity of Christ existed in one nature because he taught that Christ was born a man, and the Holy Spirit entered him after he was born. Looking back, many have described this disagreement as a failure of the Greek world of Alexandria and the Semitic world of Antioch to understand one other, since in Greece and Egypt, gods could have spouses and children, but in the Semitic world of Mesopotamia, only pagan gods had sons.

Cyril convened the First Council of Ephesus in 431 for the express purpose of condemning Nestorius. Questionably, he presided personally over the synod, argued his own case and served as the judge. Nestorius was detained by travel problems, or perhaps he deliberately stayed away; in any event, he was not present to defend himself. The Council confirmed a modified version of the Nicene Creed, and, *in absentio*, it deposed Nestorius, exiling him to Egypt.

So, what was the disagreement about? The Nicene Creed that Catholics recite today describes Christ as 'the Only Begotten Son of God, born of the Father before all ages. God from God, Light from light, true God from true God, begotten, not made, consubstantial with the Father; through him all things were made. For us men and for our salvation he came down from heaven.' This is an abridgement of the full length version. While the word order varies in different sources, the full translation in the Papal Encyclicals[15] helps explain:

> 'We believe in one God the Father all powerful, maker of all things both seen and unseen. And in one Lord Jesus Christ, the Son of God, the only-begotten from the Father, **that is from the substance** [Gr. ousias] **of the Father, God from God, light from light, true God from true God, begotten not made,** <u>consubstantial</u>, with the Father, through whom all things came to be, both those in heaven and those in earth; for us humans and for our salvation he came down and became incarnate, became human, suffered and rose up on the third day, went up into the heavens, is coming to judge the living and the dead. And in the Holy Spirit.

'And those who say "there once was when he was not", and "before he was begotten he was not", and that he came to be from things that were not, or from another hypostasis or substance [Gr. ousias], affirming that the Son of God is subject to change or alteration these the catholic and apostolic church *anathematises.*'

What did Nestorius say to get himself in so much trouble? According to Mar Soro, the first principle[16] of Nestorius was 'The union of divinity and of humanity in Christ is voluntary; however this union is neither moral nor spiritual; it is the result of joining two persons together.' Principle 7 was: 'The principle of this union is to be found in the combined *prosopa* of divinity and of humanity, namely, in the revealed *prosopon* of Christ incarnate, the Person of the Union;' and 8 was: 'The incarnation is real; both natures in Christ are true and complete; his humanity is not "imaginary" nor is his divinity "unsubstantial."'

Soro argues that Nestorius did affirm the oneness of Christ, rejected 'a duality of sons in Christ' and believed that the two natures came together in the person of Christ. So far, so good. Two Greek words caused much of this confusion: *prosopon* and *hypostasis*. *Prosopon* may be translated as person, but another Greek word used in the Nicene Creed, *hypostasis*, also can mean person. Nestorius used the Aramaic word *konoma* for person. Each word is important to this argument, and these Greek words were almost impossible for the protagonists to agree upon. As they translated these words back and forth, it would appear that neither side understood what the other was talking about.

In 449, Emperor Theodosius II convened the Second Council of Ephesus, in the name of Pope Dioscorus I of Alexandria. The Council condemned Nestorius for saying that there were two persons in Christ, but because of procedural improprieties it was discredited as the 'Robber Council of Ephesus.'

In 451, Emperor Marcian convened the Council of Chalcedon. The Pope weighed in from Rome. The Council of Chalcedon ruled that Christ had two natures 'a divine nature and a human nature, united in one person (*hypostasis*).' This became the accepted orthodoxy. Nestorius later said that the creed of the Council of Chalcedon had expressed exactly what he believed, even though the Council condemned him. Many bishops called the Council a poorly attended cabal of enemies. Moreover, they claimed that the doctrine of Cyril – that Mary was the Mother of God – had neither appeared in the Gospels nor in the writings of the early fathers.

Ironically, in his work, *The Bazaar of Heracleides*,[17] Nestorius said that an erroneous translation of the word *hypostasis* had implied his supposed heresy. Nestorius showed that even *he* did not believe in Nestorianism as defined by his enemies. Mar Soro argues that the Nestorian Church was not even Nestorian when it came to doctrine. The Syriac churches of Antioch, though called Nestorian, simply believed that Nestorius had been treated unfairly. They did not necessarily agree with the ideas attributed to him; they just thought he had been misrepresented. By now the reader has thrown up his hands in exasperation, but because of these arcane Greek words, a schism developed that would last over a thousand years.

Under Theodosius I (379–395), Christianity became the state religion of the Roman Empire. By the end of his reign, the city of Antioch was almost entirely Christian. In the second through fifth centuries, Syriac churches formed their own monasteries and institutions of learning, the most famous of which was the famous Antioch School. This became a center of intellectual ferment, starring such famous theologians and scholars as Diodorus of Tarsus, John Chrysostom, and Theodorus of Mopsuestia, who influenced Nestorius.

Mar Ephrem the Syrian has been credited with founding the great School of the Persians, also called the School of Edessa, though it opened in the late fourth century, and he died in 373. Ephrem is famous for writing thousands of lines of Syriac poetry filled with parables, similes and symbolism; a high point in early Christian literature, despite the inherent anti-Semitism. Emperor Zeno condemned the School of Edessa as a Nestorian outpost, and he closed it in 489.

The Persian scholar, Narsai[18] of Ma'altha, the 'Harp of the Holy Spirit,' began as the head of the School of Edessa, but then he started the great School of Nisibis (Nusaybin), modeled after Edessa. Narsai also was a prolific writer of homilies and important commentaries on the Hebrew Bible. While Narsai showed great respect for Nestorius in his writing, he disagreed with the idea of 'two *prosopa* (persons) in Christ,' the supposed heresy of Nestorius. Even so, as founder of the school of Nisibis and a Persian, he was held responsible for introducing Nestorianism into the Persian Church.

Despite a series of fifth century Catholic synods in Persia, the Church of the East defiantly asserted its independence, rejecting any supervision by Rome. It reiterated its support for clergical marriage, and it stubbornly adopted a version of Nestorianism taught by Theodore of Mopsuestia: '...let our faith in the dispensation of Christ be in the confession of the two natures, of the divinity and of the humanity, while none of us shall dare to introduce mixture, mingling or confusion into the differences of these two natures; rather, while the divinity remains preserved in what belongs to it, and humanity in what belongs to it, it is to a single Lordship and to a single (object of) worship that we gather together the exemplars of these two natures, because of the perfect and inseparable conjunction that has occurred for the divinity with respect to the humanity.'[19]

Bar Sawma, a metropolitan (archbishop) of Nisibis and a strong supporter of Theodore of Mopsuestia, convened the Synod of Beth Lapat in 484. Persian soldiers assailed the Syrian Orthodox Church for refusing to accept the dual nature of Christ (Dyophysitism). According to Bar Hebraeus, Bar Sawma pushed his friend the Persian king into this rampage, which put to death one metropolitan, ninety priests and 7,700 laymen.

Even though the Church of the East had broken away from Rome, the controversies did not stop. Next a bewildering series of internal disputes and schisms ensued. Just to give the flavor of the time, we will select a few examples.

The next Persian king passed over Bar Sawma and appointed a more peaceable churchman, Acacius (485–96), as patriarch. This did not go well. The two rivals excommunicated each other. Another version of this story holds that the pope excommunicated Acacius, and Acacius excommunicated the pope. In the end Bar Sawma was mobbed in church by a group of monks and murdered. The resulting schism lasted into the early sixth century. The next patriarch, the elderly Babai, held a synod at Seleucia-Ctesiphon in 497. It endorsed clergical marriage, a hotly contested subject, and Wilmshurst writes that this synod cut any remaining ties with Rome.

In 523[20] a lawyer, Narsai, and a physician, Elisha, both were consecrated as patriarchs. The problem was that Silas, the previous patriarch, appointed his son-in-law Elisha to succeed him. Opponents of hereditary succession wanted Narsai instead. To preempt that, a handful of bishops and the metropolitan David of Merv quietly consecrated Elisha. The metropolitan Giwargis of Nisibis now consecrated Narsai. The two patriarchs both assumed office, and they promptly set up a lucrative competitive bidding system for bishoprics. Because he had exceeded even the lax standards of the time for covetousness, Narsai found himself in jail. After his release he died. Either right after his death or at a synod in 539, Elisha was deposed and excommunicated. The next appointee died soon after, but the schism lasted for 15 years.

Now a new heresy had cropped up, Monophysitism. This taught that 'Christ has a single inseparable nature that is at once divine and human rather than having two distinct but unified natures.' Monophysites said that, because he was fully human, Christ's death overcame the original sin of Adam, the first man. Though both Rome and the Nestorian Church rejected the Monophysite heresy, it found a powerful sponsor with the empress, and a vigorous proponent in Jacob Baradaeus, the Bishop of Edessa from 543 to 578.

Born just east of Edessa, Jacob started his career as an ascetic. Later he left his beloved monastery, was consecrated as a bishop with the authority of a metropolitan, and devoted his life to building a Monophysite church. The wife of Roman Emperor Justinian (527–565), Empress Theodora had been an actress, strip dancer, and woman about town. Later, she followed a group of Christian ascetics. She actively encouraged Jacob and supported the Monophysites, even while the Emperor brutally suppressed them as heretics.

Jacob travelled for years across Mesopotamia, Syria and Asia Minor camouflaged in the robes of a beggar, ordaining Monophysite clergy – two patriarchs, multiple bishops and reportedly 80,000–100,000 priests. Thus the West Syriac church became known as the Jacobite Church, and many, especially the French, still use that designation, the preferred name today is the Syrian Orthodox Church. This church considers itself to be the true heir of the Church of Antioch, and it still elects its own patriarch.

The East Syriac Christians, called Nestorians, enjoyed a series of outstanding patriarchs, all trained at the School of Nisibis. One was Mar Aba I, a converted Zoroastrian who wrote biblical commentaries, translated Greek texts into Syriac and founded a school of theology in Seleucia-Ctesiphon. A smooth and effective leader, he helped heal the hurt feelings that lingered after the schism of Narsai and Elisha.

The greatest figure of the East Syriac church at the turn of the seventh century was Babai the Great (551–628), and he was not even a patriarch. He studied medicine and theology in Nisibis, then he became the superior of the Monastery of Mar Abraham of Kashkar on Mount Izla, Turkey. He led the Nestorians against the growing Jacobite Church, and he found the time to write at least eighty-three books.[21]

The names of these scholars are obscure today, but we need to know that the church enjoyed such a glorious period, so we do not define it by the depressing picture that nineteenth century missionaries sent home – of clergy reduced to deplorable ignorance. This early literature also remains of great historical interest, and will continue to be, as long as future scholars still can understand their Aramaic.

During the Roman-Persian wars, the border between the two empires shifted back and forth between Mardin on the Roman side and Nisibis on the Persian side, both in Turkey today. When the Persians captured Antioch they deported a large number of Jacobites into Persia, right next to the Nestorians. The friction between them did not cease until the advent of Islam overshadowed their differences.

By the seventh century, the Christian population of the Persian Empire had reached its peak. Now it would decline.

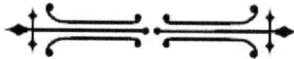

ISLAM ARRIVES

History changed when a man named Muhammad was born to the Quraysh tribe of Mecca near the end of the sixth century CE. As his fortieth year approached, Muhammad received the call to prophecy. In 622 CE, he led his followers out to a pilgrimage, a *Hijira*, to a city he would call Medina, 'The City.' Here he created a new religion called Islam, the Arabic word for surrender. The related Hebrew word, *shalem*, means complete. Islam connotes surrender to a complete system of religion, law and tradition.

Muhammad had expected local Jewish tribes to welcome him, but Jews who interviewed him believed his education to be wanting. While early Suras of the Koran show respect for the Jews, later teachings take a darker tone. However, as Bernard Lewis writes, later Suras (verses) preempt early ones. Historians write of a falling out between Muhammad and the Qurayza tribe of Jews, after which his enraged followers attacked them, looted their property, decapitated 600–700 men and enslaved their women.[1] According to one contemporary Muslim writer, this is a myth,[2] but many believe that Koran 33:26 refers to this event: 'And He brought down those who supported them among the People of the Scripture from their fortresses and cast terror into their hearts [so that] a party you killed, and you took captive a party.'[3] If it really happened in that way, this was a bad precedent.

After Muhammad's death in 632, the mantle of leadership passed to a series of four caliphs, a word derived from the Arabic *khalifa*, a successor or deputy. For Islam this was a time of blossoming, a time of expansion, optimism, and rapidly growing power. Some called it part of a golden age. Fundamentalists today still long for its pure promise.

65

Abu Bakr was chosen from the inner circle of Muhammad to be the first caliph in 632. Abu Bakr chose Umar ibn al-Khattab to succeed him, and Umar became the second caliph in 634, with the added honorific 'Commander of the Faithful.' Umar greatly expanded the reach of Islam, and under him it conquered the Persian Empire. He was killed by a Persian captive at age 53. Uthman became caliph in 644, and he was the one who formed the committee that standardized the written Koran. In 656, he was assassinated by Egyptian mutineers, who installed the fourth caliph, Ali ibn Abi Talib. A key figure in the history of Islam, Ali was Muhammad's cousin and the husband of his daughter Fatima.

In 661 Ali was murdered in Kufa and buried in Najaf. This split the community of Islam. Many of the faithful insisted that the position of caliph could not leave the Prophet's family. Among them, one large group became the Shiatu Ali (party of Ali), also called Shi'a or Shiites.

The governor of Syria, Muawiya ibn Abi Sufyah, founded the Umayyad (or Omayyad) caliphate in 661, with a capital in Damascus. The Shiites regarded the Umayyads as usurpers. In 680 CE, Hussein (Husayn or Husain), the brother of Hasan (Hassan), son of Ali and grandson of Muhammad, challenged the Umayyads at the Battle of Karbala, Iraq. Hussein was killed, along with seventy of his men, and he was buried at Karbala. Although Ali's son Hasan eventually recognized Muawiya and renounced any claim to the caliphate, the division between Shi'a and Sunni became permanent.

Shiites commemorate this tragedy yearly, often with public displays of self-flagellation. The Shiite succession now passed down through a series of descendents of Ali, called imams. Several Shiite branches have developed, differentiated by the number of imams who they venerate. Typical of the Fivers (Zaydi) are the Houthis of Yemen, and prominent among the Seveners are the Ismailis, led by the Aga Khan. The majority of the Shiites today are Twelvers, the official religion of the Persian Safavid Empire (1501–1736) and of modern day Iran.

In 750, a revolution deposed the nearly 90 year-old Umayyad Caliphate and replaced it with the descendents of Muhammad's uncle al-Abbas. This began the second great hereditary caliphate, the Abbasids. The Abbasid Caliphate moved in 762–3 to Baghdad, a new city next to Ctesiphon. Abbasid power grew through the reign of Harun al-Rashid (786–809,) and it subsequently diminished until 1258, when the Mongols destroyed Baghdad. This ended a caliphate that had lasted for over 500 years.

Meanwhile, another center of power emerged. During the early tenth century, a group of Turkish slaves from the military founded the Ismaili dynasty, whose capital became Cairo. This was the Fatimid Caliphate, named after Fatima, the daughter of Muhammad. This caliphate expanded from North Africa to rule Palestine, Syria and western Arabia, in direct competition with the Abbasids, until it ended in 1171 with the rise of Saladin.

The third great hereditary caliphate of Islam, the Ottomans, began with the Oghuz Turks in 1299. By 1453, they were able to conquer Constantinople and replace the Byzantine Empire with the Ottoman caliphate, 900 years after the death of Muhammad. In 1517 they conquered the Mamluk Sultanate of Cairo, beginning their empire. In short, from 632 CE to the end of World War I, three caliphates dominated the Middle East.

As the Muslims advanced across the Middle East and North Africa, the majority of all Nestorians and Jacobites – in 300 Christian dioceses – became subject to the Koran (sometimes spelled Quran), a compilation of Muhammad's teachings. While Islam may have matured in an urban setting, it mirrors many of the harsh customs of the surrounding desert. The sands of Arabia are scorching during the day but freezing at night. In their tents, Arabian tribes entertain each other by day with obsequious hospitality, and raid each other's settlements at night, carrying off sheep and women. Many sins, small and large, are punished by death. This culture is reflected in the verses of the Koran.

THE KORAN

In order to understand the history of the Muslim Middle East, we need to look at the Koran and the verses (*Suras*) that refer to Christians and Jews. We will look at these again in the context of modern Islamic fundamentalism.

Koran 5:73 declares 'They have certainly disbelieved who say, "Allah is the third of three." And there is no god except one God. And if they do not desist from what they are saying, there will surely afflict the disbelievers among them a painful punishment.' This is one of several that singles out Christians.

Again, in Koran 5:17 'They have certainly disbelieved who say that Allah is Christ, the son of Mary. Say, "Then who could prevent

Allah at all if He had intended to destroy Christ, the son of Mary, or his mother or everyone on the earth?"…'

Koran 9:29 says 'Fight those who do not believe in Allah or in the Last Day and who do not consider unlawful what Allah and His Messenger have made unlawful and who do not adopt the religion of truth from those who were given the Scripture – [fight] until they give the jizyah willingly while they are humbled.'

The word humbled means abased, humiliated, shamed, made to feel the power of Islam. This verse means that Christians must be forced to convert to Islam under pain of death, unless they pay the *jizya*. Even though it often was confiscatory, this was not the only tax under Islam. Another was the *kharaj*, a feudal land tax that the Umayyads levied on Christians and Jews who had converted to Islam. Another tax, the *avariz*, was pure protection money – giving new resonance to the word avaricious and collected at the pleasure of the Ottoman tax collector. Thus, impecunious rulers could, and did, raise or impose new taxes at will, treating their vassals, by their own admission, as rich sources of revenue. In effect, these taxes subjected Jews and Christians to the whims of caliphs, viziers and tax-collectors, who controlled their fate.

Koran 9:29 restricts the freedom of Christians to proselytize Muslims, and it restricts Muslims from committing apostasy, meaning conversion from Islam to Christianity. Raymond Ibrahim,[4] a Coptic Christian from Egypt, explains that this means that they also are not to engage in blasphemy, and that blasphemy means any criticism or offense toward Muhammad. The penalty for any of these offenses was, and still is, death.

This penalty is spelled out unsparingly in Koran 5:33 'Indeed, the penalty for those who wage war against Allah and His Messenger and strive upon earth [to cause] corruption is none but that they be killed or crucified or that their hands and feet be cut off from opposite sides or that they be exiled from the land. That is for them a disgrace in this world; and for them in the Hereafter is a great punishment.'

Koran 5:51 warns 'O you who have believed, do not take the Jews and Christians as allies. They are [in fact] allies of one another. And whoever is an ally to them among you – then indeed, he is [one] of them. Indeed, Allah guides not the wrongdoing people.' Muslims often have assumed that Christians living among them are a fifth column, believing they sided with Crusaders, Mongols, British, French or Russians. Of course, this was sometimes true.

The Koran explicitly sanctions the taking of women as spoils of war in Koran 4:3 'And if you fear that you will not deal justly with the orphan girls, then marry those that please you of [other] women, two or three or four. But if you fear that you will not be just, the [marry only] one or those your right hand possesses. That is more suitable that you may not incline [to injustice].' Ibrahim[5] interprets the phrase 'those your right hand possesses' as meaning women who have been captured in war, saying that this sanctions the use of captured women as sex slaves.

The Koran does have a number of verses that are not adverse to Jews, especially early ones. Koran 2:47 is quite friendly: 'O Children of Israel, remember My favor that I have bestowed upon you and that I preferred you over the worlds.' Koran 5:60 takes a different view: 'Say: Shall I inform you of [what is] worse than that as penalty from Allah? [It is that of] those whom Allah has cursed and with whom He became angry and made of them apes and pigs and slaves of Taghut. Those are worse in position and further astray from the sound way.' Both Ibrahim and Bernard Lewis caution that when verses disagree, the later verse takes precedence.

Seventh century *dhimmis* had to defend themselves against the decrees of the Koran, and Christians in the Middle East today confront them with renewed urgency.

THE PACT OF OMAR

Muslims call Christians and Jews the People of the Book, but the Arab word for them is *dhimmi*. By tradition the Pact of Omar (Umar), also called Conditions of Omar, was an agreement between the Christian community and Caliph Omar I in 637 (or possibly Omar II a hundred years or more after that). This was supposed to guarantee that the Muslims would protect *dhimmis*, as long as the *dhimmis* kept a long list of promises. Ever since, it has remained the blueprint for relations between Muslims and Christians, by implication Jews, and sometimes Samaritans, Sabaeans, Zoroastrians, even Hindus.

Bernard Lewis explains[6] that the document can hardly have been authentic, even though its clauses have become enshrined over the years in Muslim practice. For one thing, the Christians were supposed to have submitted it to Omar, but it was written in Arabic, which the Syrian Christians did not even know.

The edicts of the Koran and the Pact of Omar were the plainest possible expressions of Muslim attitudes toward Christians, even if in practice there was a certain pragmatic accommodation. Interpretation could be variable, and enforcement depended on the caliph.

Ibrahim has translated the pact, listing 22 points.[7] We will look at a number of these. The reader will note that these are phrased as assurances from the Christian community that, among other things, they will not do any of the following:

'Not to build a church in our city – nor a monastery, convent, or monk's cell in the surrounding areas – and not to repair those that fall in ruins or are in Muslim quarters;

'Not to prevent Muslims from lodging in our churches, by day or night, and to keep their doors wide open for [Muslim] passersby and travelers;

'Not to harbor in them [churches, monasteries] or our homes a spy, nor conceal any deceits from Muslims;

'Not to display a cross on them [churches], not raise our voices during prayer or readings in our churches anywhere near Muslims;

'to produce a cross or [Christian] book in the markets of the Muslims;

'Not to congregate in the open for Easter or Palm Sunday, nor lift our voices [in lamentation] for our dead…;

'Not to display any signs of polytheism, nor make our religion appealing, nor call or proselytize anyone to it;'

The Christians further promised

'…To honor the Muslims, show them the way and rise up from our seats if they wish to sit down; [and]

'…None of us shall do business with a Muslim unless the Muslim commands it…'

There was more. Christians, Jews, even Samarians and Zoroastrians, could not ride a horse or carry swords, and they had to wear special clothes, shoes, hats or turbans. Some caliphs specified the color. Green, the color of Islam, was always forbidden. Christians had to wear black. Under one caliph it was yellow for Jews. *Dhimmis* had to cut their hair in a certain way, to distinguish them from Muslims. It was a ninth century caliph in Baghdad who had the bright idea that Jews should wear a yellow badge on their outer clothes. The Nazis picked that up during World War II when they required Jews to wear a yellow patch. A male *dhimmi* could not marry a Muslim woman, although a Muslim man could marry a *dhimmi* woman. A *dhimmi* could not present evidence against a Muslim in a court of law. A *dhimmi* could not inherit from a Muslim nor could a Muslim inherit from a *dhimmi*.

In the pact, the Christians guaranteed these conditions 'upon ourselves, our descendents, our spouses, and our neighbors,' and they agreed that if they fail to keep them, [we] 'forfeit our *dhimma* [covenant], and we become liable to the same treatment you inflict upon the people who resist and cause sedition.' The treatment this referred to would be death or enslavement.

Persecutions were not confined to breaches of the pact. Slavery was common. While non-Muslim men could be bought and sold, it was the women who suffered the brunt of slavery. Conquering Muslim warriors traveled without women, knowing that they would have their pick of women in their raids. Christian children were not safe either. Infidel children of both sexes were enslaved for a variety of purposes, but the Turks had another use for Christian boys who were the cream of the crop.

Ottoman Empire, Balkan and Anatolian Christian boys were routinely kidnapped, forcibly converted and pressed into service as Janissaries, an elite infantry corps that the Ottoman Sultan Murad I created in the fourteenth century. Initially Janissaries were rigorously trained slaves, celibate, forbidden to own property or marry, lodged like monks in cells. Absolutely loyal to their Sultan and hand-picked for intelligence and strength, they gradually reached a high status both in the Ottoman military and in civilian affairs. Eventually they obtained the right to marry and learned to accumulate power. By the seventeenth century, the Janissaries ceased to recruit more slaves, branched out into nonmilitary professions and become a rich hereditary ruling class.

Ironically, Sultan Murad I created a system that used slaves of Christian origin to rule the largely Christian subjects of his empire.

As Lord Kinross puts it, 'It meant in effect rule through the conquered in the interests of the conqueror.'[8] In later years their strength became a threat to the sultan. The Janissary corps was abolished for corruption and abuse of power in the nineteenth century.

Why does the Koran single out Christians?

The Koran and the Pact of Omar seem to focus a singular opprobrium on Christians. Jews lived in the east too, along with Zoroastrians, Mandaens and Hindus. From a political standpoint though, Jews and most of their fellow minorities appeared relatively harmless because no western country had shown an interest in protecting them. On the other hand, Christians were protected by the European states with which Islam had been at war for generations.

Ibrahim points out that Christianity was the largest religion in the Middle East, that it proselytizes and that it 'is the quintessential religion of martyrdom.' The Christian Trinity offended the monotheistic Muslims; crosses and icons were considered idolatry by a Muslim religion that strictly forbade worship of images.

Especially ominous today, consistent with a concept of collective punishment, if a Christian anywhere offends them, some Muslims feel entitled to punish any other Christian, anywhere, including in the Christian states of the west. That puts a lot of Christians at risk.

Until the advent of Islam, about half the population of Mesopotamia had been Christian; now Christians were pressured to convert. Many of them did too, either to improve their position in society, for business purposes, or to avoid the *jizya*. As conversions to Christianity decreased and conversions to Islam rose, the Christian population of the Middle East declined.

The patriarchate of Jerusalem collapsed, as did those of Damascus, Alexandria, Mesopotamia, Edessa, Nisibis and even Persia. Adopting the administrative techniques of the Persians, from 650 to 1050, the Muslims appointed twelve out of the thirty Catholicoi who took office. These usually were Nestorian patriarchs, slighting the Jacobites, still, both Nestorians and Jacobites denounced the Christians who adhered to the Council of Chalcedon. They suggested to the ruling caliphs that these were traitors, loyal to (the king of) Rome, thus called Melkites. The Christians and the Arabs were learning to speak in terms that both could understand.

The Pact of Omar had much to deplore, but it did have another side. It perpetuated the inferior status of *dhimmis*, but it provided them with a series of rights and protections that, for the time, were relatively enlightened. *Dhimmis* had guarantees of security, property rights, freedom to practice their religion and a certain amount of autonomy. Of considerable importance, they were allowed into any profession. In practical terms, they often benefited from a religious prohibition against Muslims dealings with the non-Muslim public. Thus, not just Janissaries, but also many other Christians were government officials.

Islam also provided an umbrella of relief for the Jews, as contrasted with their persecution in Christian lands. It united the eastern world, its culture, economics, and politics. Jews flourished in the Muslim world. In the Middle Ages, the greatest flowering of Jewish creativity, culture and literature was in the Middle East, not in the Europe of Christendom. Jews learned from the Babylonians, later the Greeks, and both Jews and Christians learned techniques from Arab skilled traders. From the early years of Islam, Jews and Christians engaged in philosophical discussions, shared scientific knowledge and even traded poetry with their Muslim colleagues. Often they rose to wealth and high position as administrators or politicians.

Muslims could justify this reversal of roles by claiming these *dhimmis* were only executing the orders of Muslims. Notwithstanding the prohibitions against associating with *dhimmis*, the Arabs respected educated Christians, called *Salabi*, from the Arabic word for cross. *Salab* came to mean a learned man. As we will see, the Arabs relied heavily on the sophisticated people who they had subjugated, especially the Persians, who often served as their bureaucrats and scribes. Since the Arabs came from a less urban culture, they had to learn quickly how to take advantage of their more educated subjects.

Jews, Assyrians and various European adventurers translated for the Empire, but Greeks, Armenians, Syriac Christians and Jews were competing for the same positions. Jews who migrated from Spain to Constantinople in the fifteenth and sixteenth century had the advantage of superior education and skills. They often were preferred for high positions because they were unlikely to present a challenge to their Muslim masters.

By the seventeenth and eighteenth centuries, Greeks and Syriac Catholics had displaced the Jews. The Greeks in particular were
interpreters, essentially ambassadors, sometimes actually governors.
In the seventeenth century the position of chief translator, the
Grand Dragoman, was created; that became a Greek monopoly, a
link to embassies and businesses across Europe. After the Greeks
began agitating for independence, their loyalty became suspect and
Armenians eventually displaced them. A 1912 document from the
Ottoman Empire[9] listed forty bankers and 34 stock brokers in
Constantinople (Istanbul), all *dhimmis*, the majority of them Greek
and Armenian.

Over the centuries, caliphs favored Christian doctors, administrators, teachers, scribes and accountants, just as they did Jewish
doctors and professionals. Many Jews were printers, tax collectors
or officials at the mint. Both Jews and Christians were able to establish successful careers in diplomacy, commerce, banking and
finance. From the sixth to the ninth century, a series of outstanding
doctors studied in the Nestorian Christian academy of
Gundeshapur in Persia. Many of them also advised the caliph, and,
fluent in Persian, Turkish and Greek, they translated documents
into Syriac or Arabic. Their positions enabled them to defend
Christian interests, but they also conspired, interfered in church
matters, and aspired to become patriarchs.

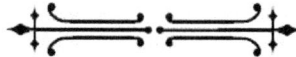

LEARNED MEN, PATRIARCHS AND SCHISMS

There is something fissile about the hot sun of the Middle East. Religious groups fracture, and they fight. Worse, old disputes never die. The memory of old empires never vanishes, and rulers always plot a return to their old days of greatest glory. The word compromise is seldom heard.

Under the Arabs, Nestorian patriarchs acquired exceptional power. One of the most consequential was Ishoyahb III of Adiabene (650–8), famous for returning the cross of Christ to the Roman Emperor Heraclius in 650. A scholar, he founded a major theological school in Adiabene, and he wrote many major theological works. He supervised a codification of church rites, called the *Taksha*, that divided the church year into a fixed number of liturgical seasons, and he was responsible for a compilation of major church hymns, the *Hudra*.

Despite the restrictions in the Pact of Omar, Ishoyahb III managed to build a new church, and he preserved the monastery of Beth Abe. In fact, Christians were able to build new monasteries in the seventh century, and they could maintain the Rabban Hormizd Monastery near Mosul – the site of nine patriarchal graves. In his energetic eight-year patriarchate he suppressed dissidents, opposed the efforts of Jacobites to build a church in Mosul or Nisibis and fought to deter the Christian Arabs of Oman and Bahrain from converting to Islam.

The most celebrated translator of the time was Hunain b. Ishaq, a ninth century Assyrian physician fluent in Arabic, Persian, Syriac and Greek. Through the reign of ten caliphs, he translated works on agriculture, astronomy, mathematics, linguistics, pharmaceuticals, and medicine. His contributions to ophthalmology alone were immense. Besides writing many original works, he translated the Greek version of the Old Testament, called the Septuagint, into Arabic. Along with his son and nephew, he translated works by Aristotle, Euclid, Archimedes, Ptolemy and Galen, reportedly translating 129 works by Galen alone. He has been called the 'Erasmus of the Islamic Renaissance.'[1]

In the eighth through tenth centuries other Syriac translators and theologians translated, annotated and provided commentary for Greek texts. Several original seventh century works have survived, though some are of questionable authenticity. Among these, whether reliably factual or not, the *Chronicle of Arbela*, *Chronicle of Edessa* and *Chronicle of Seert* preserve a rich tapestry of religious culture and traditions from the earliest days of the church.

SCHISMS

We will not write about all the church schisms of the seventh through the seventeenth centuries, but we must acknowledge that, even when it came under existential threat, the church never ceased its rivalries. The pressures of Islam were great. Church treasuries were under regular assault by greedy taxmen who confiscated precious resources on the authority of the Koran, but the church never could maintain a solid front. The wonder was that it survived these external attacks at all. Of the many disputes we will select a few of the more outlandish.

One rift occurred in 691 following the election of Patriarch Hnanisho I. Bar Hebraeus wrote that one day Hnanisho I offended the reigning caliph with a tactless remark during a theological dispute, and the caliph accused him of insulting Islam. Taking advantage of this opportunity, one Yohannan the Leper (!) dexterously contrived to get himself consecrated instead of Hnanisho, splitting the church. The caliph cheerfully stoked the fires of dissention. It all ended when Hnanisho went to prison, and there he died. Or, according to another version, Yohannan's supporters threw him off a cliff. Then again, maybe they left him to starve in a cave. Elsewhere, we read that he was found by shepherds, nursed back to life and ultimately came back to depose Yohannan in 693. In the end, Yohannan was imprisoned for debt,[2] where he died – or so they say.

Elections of Nestorian patriarchs remained turbulent up to the time of the Crusaders, and contenders often went to the caliph

to settle their disputes. In the mid-eighth century Patriarch Yaqob
II (Jacob II) (754–75) and a rival, Surin (Sourin), fought so publicly
that an exasperated Caliph al-Mansur threw them both in prison.[3]
Soon after, the caliph sent an annoying bishop, Shlemun of Hdatta,
to the same prison. An ambitious court doctor, Isa bar Shahlafa,
was appointed as interim head of the church, and it went to his
head. He convinced the caliph to imprison the Jacobite Patriarch
Giwargis and the Melkite Patriarch Theodoret. The three patriarchs
languished in the same prison for seven years. Finally, the doctor
solicited the metropolitan of Nisibis for a bribe that was unseemly
even for those times, and that was too much. He was arrested and
sent into exile. The caliph released the patriarchs, but Yaqob died
soon after.

The Nestorian Patriarch Timotheos I (780–823) had a colorful
ascent to the office of Patriarch.[4] He is said to have bought his
election by distributing bags of gold – which turned out to be filled
with stones. He openly curried favor with the Muslim governor of
Mosul and his court physician. One of his rivals died under unclear
circumstances, and he bought off another. A group of opposition
bishops excommunicated him, and he excommunicated one of
them. Now supporters of a rival metropolitan, Ephrem of Elam,
excommunicated him, and Timotheos returned the favor. After
several more plots against him failed, he settled into his job, proving to be a prolific scholar as well as a superb and wily administrator.

Timotheos I went down in church history for a notable theological Christian-Muslim debate with al-Mahdi, the Abbasid Caliph,
in 780 or 781. He also rebuilt churches, imposed celibacy on bishops and monks, brought the dissident Persian province of Fars
under control, created six new ecclesiastical provinces, and expanded the missionary activities of the church. He appointed metropolitans for Damascus, Samarkand, Armenia, India, China, a province
on the Caspian Sea and possibly Tibet, and he established six new
dioceses and a bishopric in Jerusalem. During his 43-year term of
office, the church is said to have expanded to 230 dioceses, with
twenty-seven metropolitans, but many of these dioceses would be
short-lived.

During his time, Baghdad became the new seat of the Abbasid
caliph Al-Mansur, and it was becoming one of the most important
centers of learning in the Middle East. In 775, Timotheos I

shrewdly moved the seat of the Nestorian patriarchate from Seleucia-Ctesiphon to Baghdad, where it remained for almost 500 years. Some call this the golden age of the Nestorian Church. Certainly the church was wealthy and powerful, but it also became corrupt and urbane, and the patriarchs flaunted scandalous, opulent lifestyles.

PATRIARCHS AND CALIPHS

Timotheos I had excellent relations with four caliphs, but official attitudes toward Christians would swing back and forth, depending on the caliph. Generally the Umayyads were favorably disposed. The first caliph, Muawiya, had a Christian wife, a Christian court poet and a Christian physician, but his successor imposed many restrictions on Christians. The beginning of the Abbasid caliphate was promising, and Nestorian doctors, poets, philosophers and theologians flourished. In time, this caliphate too slid downhill into widespread persecution of the Christians and their churches.

In Egypt, the Fatimid Caliph al-Hakim (996–1021) persecuted both Jews and Christians. Thousands were given two choices: either convert or be expelled from Egypt, Syria and Palestine. Sometimes known as the Mad Caliph, in 1009 he destroyed the Church of the Holy Sepulchre in Jerusalem. Reportedly, he forced Christians to wear a four pound wooden cross around their necks or they would be put to death.

The Seljuk Turks seized Fatimid territories, including Jerusalem, but their heirs fell to quarreling among themselves, leaving the door open to the Crusades. The Fatimids were able to recapture Jerusalem in 1098, but the city's defences were in poor repair and the armies of the First Crusade captured the holy city in 1099. Less than a hundred years later, a new Muslim champion, Saladin, won the decisive Battle of Hattin, near Tiberias, on the Sea of Galilee, in 1187. Jerusalem was back under Muslim control.

This pushed the Crusaders back to the Mediterranean coast. More crusades swept through Europe and the Middle East throughout the thirteenth century. The Crusader states in the Middle East were relatively short-lived, but gory tales of their massacres, pillage and barbarism have lasted longer. The western world has forgotten them, but the memory of the Crusades still is painful in the Muslim world. Today, radical organizations such as ISIS identify all Christians with Crusaders, holding them up as a source of Muslim humiliation until today, and the inspiration for a battle cry of vengeance.

The Persian church gradually retreated through the eleventh century, until the Christian populations of Media and Fars were almost gone, and no Christians were left in Qum. By the twelfth century, Christianity had disappeared in Arabia, Oman and Qatar. By the thirteenth century, few Christians remained in the Persian province of Elam. The Iraqi dioceses of Maishan and Basra closed in the thirteenth century. In contrast, the populations of Nisibis and the Plains of Nineveh ballooned with displaced Christians.

Empires and caliphates come and go. Conquering nations develop internal weaknesses. Early on, Christianity overcame paganism. Later, Islam would dominate Christianity, but before that, both would face an invasion from the steppes of Asia.

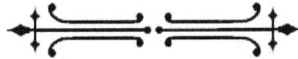

MONGOLS AND TURKS

Waves of tribesmen migrated from the steppes of Mongolia toward the west in the sixth century. First were Khazars, then Seljuks, their names redolent with romance and legend. The Oghuz Turks came to Anatolia from Central Asia in the ninth century, becoming known as the Turkmen. Genghis Khan burst out of Asia with his men in the thirteenth century, and the western world called them Mongol hordes. Finally the distinction between Turks and Mongols would blur, and the Turks would rule the Middle East for a thousand years.

The Mongols earned a reputation for extraordinary bloodthirstiness, a nightmare still vivid in the Arab memory, but their story was more complex. Jack Weatherford writes: 'In twenty-five years, the Mongol army subjugated more lands and people than the Romans had conquered in four hundred years... Genghis Khan conquered more than twice as much as any other man in history..."[1]

Weatherford says that at its greatest extent the Mongol empire "covered between 11 and 12 million contiguous square miles, an area about the size of the African continent and considerably larger than North America". Today, that would "include thirty countries with well over 3 billion people." And this was accomplished with a force of some one hundred thousand warriors recruited from a Mongol tribe of around a million.

Moving west along the Silk Route, in 1220 the horsemen of Genghis Khan swept across Bukhara and Samarkand. They eventually went on to Peshawar (now in Pakistan), Hamadan (now in Iran), Tabriz (in Iran), and Tbilisi (now in Georgia), then through Russia, Hungary and Poland toward Vienna. The slaughter in Merv was one of the most devastating. Merv, now in Turkmenistan, was once the capital of the entire eastern Islamic world. One of the great cities of Asia, it had been a Nestorian metropolitan province since the sixth century. In 1221, the army of Tolui, a son of Genghis Khan, killed the entire population, said to be over a million. After that, the bloody conquest of Nishapur and Herat brought the large Iranian province of Khurasan under Mongol control.

In the city of Nishapur, Khan's son-in-law was killed, and his widow was allowed to choose the punishment. She ordered the death of all its inhabitants. The Mongols are said to have piled the heads of men, women and children in three separate pyramids. However, the Mongols are known to have inflated the numbers of their victims. As Weatherford writes, 'The Mongols operated a virtual propaganda machine that consistently inflated the number of people killed in battle and spread fear wherever its words carried.'[2] For example, 1,747,000 are said to have been killed in Nishapur, 1,600,000 in Herat, and a total of 15 million murdered in Central Asia in five years. That would mean that every Mongol soldier had slaughtered 350 people, and the total number would have exceeded the pre-war population.

In any event, the numbers surely were high, and Genghis Khan's death in 1227 brought little respite. In 1235 the Mongols took Erbil. The Russian Principalities and parts of Eastern Europe fell in the late 1230s. Isfahan fell in 1237. After the Mongols conquered western Iran and the Caucasus they crossed Anatolia. They were swashbuckling their way across the Balkans and Poland when the great Khan Ogodai died in 1241. Miraculously, they went home. A papal envoy was sent to the Mongol court, and he was amazed to find that the acting regent was the widow of the Khan, a Nestorian Christian.

A Franciscan monk, William of Rubrick, visited the Mongol court in 1253. To his astonishment, he found that they celebrated Christmas, attended mass in church, and distributed Christmas presents. In his opinion of course, they were heretics. Assyrians, Armenians and Orthodox Christians, he sniffily dismissed as Nestorians. When he finally received an audience at court, he proceeded to lecture Mongke Khan, who challenged him to debate the offending Christians and the Muslims before three judges: a Christian, a Muslim and a Buddhist. As drinks flowed freely between rounds, the debate deteriorated. In the end, Rubrick took to singing; the Muslims loudly read the Koran and the Buddhist meditated.[3]

The Mongols were partial to Christians. Ong Khan, the adopted father of Genghis Khan, belonged to a Christian tribe. Ogodei, the son of Genghis Khan, married Christian wives, and his favorite grandson, Shiremun (Mongolian for Solomon) was Christian. Sorghaghtani Beki, the mother of Kublai, Mongke and Hulagu Khan, was a Nestorian Christian. With Genghis Khan and his sons away from home waging war for months or years at a time, these wives were the effective rulers, most of them Christian.

When Hulagu, the grandson of Genghis Khan, returned to Mesopotamia with his army, he brought Nestorian advisors, and Christians often were spared the worst of his massacres.

The great prize of Mesopotamia was Baghdad, the richest city in the Abbasid caliphate, the seat of the Christian patriarch and the seat of the caliphate. The Abbasid caliph ruled there as the head of the entire Muslim world, as powerful as an emperor and pope combined. Hulagu first made secret contact with Christian leaders, including the patriarch, to offer them protection in return for their willingness to negotiate with the caliph to surrender. When the caliph held out, in 1258 Hulagu destroyed Baghdad. He did leave the Christian churches alone, even presenting one of the caliph's palaces to the patriarch, but the slaughter was immense. History records that at least 90,000 Jews and Muslims were murdered. Hulagu bragged that he killed two million. What he clearly did was destroy the city and its political importance, end the 500 year old Abbasid dynasty, and end the caliphate itself for centuries.

The Christians and Jews had been oppressed under the Muslims for years, and at the fall of Baghdad, they celebrated. The King of Armenia, a prince of Antioch and Hulagu mounted their horses and thus became the famed three Christian kings who rode into Baghdad. Even more humiliating for the Muslims, Hulagu married Dokhuz-Khan, a Nestorian Christian, and she conferred regularly with her advisor, an Armenian monk. Her son, Abaqa, married the Byzantine Emperor's daughter.

Arab historians described Hulagu's conquest of Aleppo and Damascus in 1260 as victories of the cross over Islam, even though he killed many Christians in Baghdad, Nineveh and Arbil. Mercifully, his brother the Great Khan Monke died, and Hulagu returned home with the bulk of his warriors. That was the only way the Mongol advance could have been halted. In a battle with dramatic consequences, at Ayn Jalut, Israel, in 1260, Mamluk warriors soundly defeated the small force that Hulagu had left behind.

Hulagu's heirs ruled Persia, Iraq and eastern Anatolia for generations. The kingdom was known as the Ilkhanate, one of the four khanates Genghis Khan created when he apportioned his empire among two sons and two grandsons. The four khanates used similar managerial styles. After the Khan of the Golden Horde in Eastern Europe and the Ilkhan of Persia converted to Islam at the end of the thirteenth century, the khanates fused Mongol culture with Islamic culture. The bureaucrats who made the system work were educated vassals, usually sophisticated Persians. This became the common administrative culture of Turkey, the Middle East, Russia, China and most of Asia. When Tamerlane took over, he simply had to refresh this system in order to govern.

The great historian of this time was Rashi al-Din (1247–1318). Born a Jew and named for the famous Jewish scholar Rashi, he converted to Islam at age 30. He already was a doctor and scholar when Ilkhan Ghazan, Hulagu's great-grandson, appointed him vizier. He documented the Ilkhanate, but he also wrote histories of the Middle East, Asia, the Franks, the Jews of Europe and India. Writing in Persian and in Arabic, he has been called 'the first world historian.' We cannot assess his accuracy, but certainly he knew the history of Persia and the Mongols intimately; as for the rest, he probably preserved faithfully what was known at the time.[4]

Overconfident Christians tried to promote a Mongol-Christian alliance. They even prayed ostentatiously in a Baghdad mosque, flaunting their sense of privilege. The Muslims were resentful, but after the Mamluk victory at Ayn Jalut they felt free to retaliate. They celebrated by lynching Christians in Damascus.

Dokuz Khatun, the widow of Hulagu, appointed the Nestorian Patriarch Denha I (1265–81). It was a difficult time. Muslims were seething. They were shocked that the Mongols preferred Christians and Jews and angry that the Ilkhan openly protected Christians against Muslim rioters. Faced by heavy Muslim hostility, Denha moved his patriarchal seat away from Baghdad to the protection of the Ilkhan's encampment. This backwater location dramatically decreased the power of the patriarchate.

That was not Denha's worst problem. One day he imprisoned a freshly consecrated metropolitan in a monastery and shortly after that the metropolitan and his entourage were discovered dead.

Denha went down in history as the murderer of Shem'on bar Qal-
agh, whether true or not.[5]

Another notable event occurred when two Asian Nestorian
monks, Rabban Bar Sawma and Mark, came to visit. Members of a
tribe of Christian allies of Genghis Khan, Onguts, they came from
north of the Yellow River. The Chinese called them white Tartars.
Denha consecrated Mark as a metropolitan of a Chinese province,
naming him Yahballaha, but before Yahballaha could leave for
China, Denha died. Believing that he had influence with Kublai
Khan, the bishops consecrated him patriarch. Thus Yahballaha III
became the Ongut patriarch, commonly known as Yahballaha the
Turk. Later, when the Ilkhan Arghun needed an envoy to the pope,
Yahballaha put forward his associate and teacher, Rabban Bar
Sawma. This was how Bar Sawma came to visit Constantinople, the
College of Cardinals in Rome, the king of France and the king of
England. He never did meet the pope, but his accounts of these
travels gave the world a delightful window into those times, written
as innocently as if he had just dropped down from Mars.[6]

Yahballaha was committed to amity between Jacobites, Nestorians, Armenians and all other Christians. An outsider himself, he
was not bothered about the niceties of their doctrinal disputes.
Yahballaha pacified one visiting Dominican missionary by assuring
him that he was not a Nestorian, and he did not subscribe to the
teachings of Nestorius. In 1304, he sent a letter[7] pledging his obe-
dience to Pope Benedict XI – at the same time that his flock remained faithful to their Nestorian practices.

After Hulagu, the Mongols became Buddhist, but, tragically,
Ilkhan Ghazan converted to Islam in 1295. After that, he began
persecuting Christians, destroying churches and at one juncture
brutally tortured Yahballaha. In 1310, Ghazan's successor, another
converted Christian, perpetrated a bloody massacre at Arbil, laying
siege to a citadel that sheltered a large number of Christians.
Yahballaha bribed the troops to secure safe passage for the trapped
Christians, but, in a massive double-cross, they released one hundred and fifty unarmed men and their families, only to kill them
immediately. The next group to be let out also was killed. In the
end, those who remained inside were either starved to death, murdered in cold blood or sold into slavery.[8]

Tamerlane (Timur the Lame) came from Central Asia. A Ta-
tar, he was not related to Genghis Khan, nor was he a Mongol.

Members of his family did marry descendents of Genghis Khan, but that was to acquire the status of being part of his family. As contrasted with Genghis Khan, Tamerlane became infamous not only for murder, but also for torture, tarnishing the name of the Mongol in-laws forever. More germane to our story, the Church of the East never fully recovered from its losses of people and property.

Tamerlane and his hordes streamed out of their capital, Samarkand, for a full-scale Muslim invasion of Persia in 1393. In Isfahan[9] according to most reports, Tamerlane built 28 pyramids out of 70,000 Christian heads – or maybe it was 42,000 heads and he killed 100,000. Perhaps he killed 200,000. Then again, maybe it was not in Isfahan, but another Persian city. After all, much of this is myth and legend. He conquered Baghdad in 1401, killing thousands and piling up severed heads into 120 towers. When he moved into Kurdistan, his army of thousands besieged the Christian city Tikrit and demolished it. He then continued through Diyarbakir, and in 1402 he defeated the Ottomans near Ankara. In 1403 he leveled churches in Georgia. Antioch fell. Everywhere he went, he slaughtered Armenians, Georgians, Jacobites and Nestorians, but many Nestorian villages in Kurdistan and Hakkari escaped. In the following years, Tamerlane conquered Delhi, finally dying as he turned toward Ming China.

The Turks had taken over Mongolia in the sixth century, arriving in Samarkand in the eighth century. The Abbasids initially hired these Turkish warriors as mercenaries, but by the ninth century, the Turks had converted to Islam. Now they dominated the Abbasid military. Slowly they accumulated political power. By the eleventh century, a Turkish dynasty, the Seljuk Turks, had displaced the Abbasids as the rulers of Persia. With Greek Byzantium crumbling, the Seljuk Turks beat the Greeks in the Battle of Manzizkert in 1071.

The most important Turkish dynasty was founded by a tribal chieftain, and his son Osman gave his name to its empire – the Ottoman Empire.

The Black Death came in 1346, decimating both Europe and Asia. Half of all Europeans died within seven years. Without enough workers to till the fields, the peasants in the Balkans chafed under the rigid feudalism of their Christian overlords. Byzantium (Constantinople) was ripe for the Ottomans to take over, and it fell on May 29, 1453. Now living in a Muslim environment, many Byzantine Greeks married Turks and converted in order to escape the *jizya*. This class became the mercantile, administrative and military backbone of the Ottoman Empire as it spread over Palestine, Egypt, the North African coast, and Mesopotamia.

In their advance, the Turks had taken advantage of the extreme disunity of the Christians. The Catholics opposed the Orthodox, and both of them opposed the Church of the East. Bishop contended against bishop, patriarch against patriarch. In the fourteenth century, European Catholic Crusaders attacked Orthodox Greeks in Byzantium. Warring Christians in the Balkans even invited Turkish troops to intervene in their internecine disputes.

The Churches of the East clearly had external existential threats during this time, but they never ceased to indulge in internal doctrinal disputes. One of these was the unsolved matter of unification with Rome.

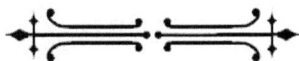

Unification with the Catholic Church

After the Crusades, after the Black Death, after Byzantium fell, the Christians of the Middle East were under threat as never before. This should have been a time for unity, to come together in a common front against outside threats. So it would seem, but unification was not going to be easy.

The Struggle for Survival

The Black Death began what historians call the 'dark centuries,' a time of wars, bloodshed and plague. From the fourteenth through the sixteenth centuries, survival was the dominant concern of Nestorian Christians. To escape from Tamerlane, or perhaps even before his time, the Nestorian communities of Mesopotamia and Asia literally headed for the hills, scaling the forbidding Hakkari Mountains of Turkey to join a smaller Nestorian community that had been there since the thirteenth century. Their chosen sanctuary was Tur Abdin, once the easternmost point of the Roman Empire, with its great fortress that Constantine had rebuilt in 348. Adjacent areas remained fortified, and a rich network of monasteries covered the mountains.

So high and impregnable were these mountains that neither Alexander the Great nor the Roman Emperor Trajan ever tried to invade them. Persians and Parthians had fought in the lowlands, but east of Tur Abdin between Lake Van and Lake Urmia, the land was riven by sheer cliffs and almost impassable – except by the most intrepid of bandits. This would be a haven of refuge in the coming centuries, and its small Christian villages would remain isolated guardians of their ancient language, customs and heritage.

In the fifteenth century, warring Turkmen tribes raided any Christian villages they could reach. The sixteenth century found the Christians caught in wars between the Ottomans and central Asian tribes who were on the move after the dissolution of the Mongol Empire. All across Anatolia, Iran, and Azerbaijan, Turkish tribes destroyed churches and monasteries, pillaged villages, killed priests, enslaved children, murdered men, and raped women. The Christians scrambled to stay ahead of them. Those living in the plains fled to the Nestorian and Jacobite villages clustered north of Mosul.

By the sixteenth century the Church of the East had contracted from a great missionary church extending all the way across Asia down to a small triangle of land, which they shared with Kurds, Persians and Turks. To the west was Mardin and to the north was Lake Van, both in Turkey. To the east was Lake Urmia, now in Iran. To the south were the Plains of Nineveh, where the Chaldean Patriarch sat nestled in the Rabban Hormizd Monastery. The Nestorian Patriarch was perched in Kochanes (now Konak), in the Hakkari Mountains. There too lived most of the Nestorians, later called Assyrians, and there they raised their sons to be formidable mountain fighters.

AND SCHISM AGAIN

Parishioners of the Church of the East have always been intensely loyal to their own ways. Patriarchs may make a show of reconciling with Rome, but the people act like the bobbing toy that, when pushed over, rights itself again.

Several popes attempted to bring the Nestorian church into mainstream Catholicism. In 1247 Pope Innocent IV sent a Dominican monk, Andrew of Longjumeau, as an envoy, and the Nestorian patriarch received him with great courtesy. He even signed an orthodox profession of faith and sent back an encouraging letter to the pope, but nothing came of it. Though the envoy might not have realized it, this may just have been middle-eastern hospitality. In another version of the story, Andrew never did contact the patriarch personally,[1] because he reached the Mongol camp right after the khan died. It would be another 250 years before the Nestorian Patriarch Yohannan Sulaqa converted his flock to Catholicism in 1553, and even then the conversion was tenuous. But we are getting ahead of the story.

Again in 1340 and in 1304, Nestorian patriarchs made moves toward the Catholic Church, but their congregations did not. In 1445, Pope Eugene IV sent the Archbishop of Colossai to approach Timothy, the Archbishop of Tarsus and Nestorian metropolitan, who was confined to Cyprus at the time. Timothy professed loyalty to the Catholic Church at that time, and so did the Maronite Bishop Elias, as recorded in the papal encyclical entitled 'Council of Basil (1431–45).'[2] In August 1445, the Bull of Union with the Chaldeans and the Maronites of Cyprus records that the pope accepted union with the Chaldeans, and the pope forbade members of the church to treat either of them as heretics any longer. This appears to be the first time on record that a pope used the word Chaldean for this church, possibly choosing it because this was their name in the Syriac language. In fact, this encyclical uses the name Chaldean as if it already were well established, so it is difficult to verify whether this really was the first time a pope used it. As their forbearers had in the past, these newly accepted Catholics gradually slid back to their old Nestorian ways.

In the same encyclical, the November 1444 Bull of Union with the Syrians records that Abdala, archbishop of Edessa and legate of Ignatius, the patriarch of the Syrians, made a profession of faith in Rome, and the pope accepted union with the Assyrians. This must have been a time of great optimism in Rome. The very same encyclical records that Rome approved professions of faith and desire for union expressed by Greeks, Copts, Jacobites and Armenians. We hear nothing about the success of these other promises of union.

The most lasting attempt at union was in 1552, but here begins a rollercoaster ride. The Nestorian patriarch Shimun VI Ishoyahab was succeeded by his brother, Shimun VII Ishoyahab, who chose his 12-year-old nephew, Hnanisho, as his successor.[3] Hnanisho died, and Shimon VII Ishoyahab chose another teenage nephew, Eliya. Rebelling against the principle of hereditary succession and also reacting against the patriarch's flamboyant lifestyle, a group of bishops countered by electing John Sulaqa, a monk from the monastery of Rabban Hormizd. For his consecration, Sulaqa went to Rome, made a formal profession of the Catholic creed, and gave the pope a letter 'from his supporters in Mosul.' In the most oft-repeated version of this story, this letter said, *inter alia*, that a person called 'Shimun Bar Mama' was dead and that Sulaqa had been elected after his death. In 1553, Pope Julius III consecrated Sulaqa, proclaiming him Patriarch of Mosul and Athura. When Sulaqa returned to the patriarchal see in Amida (now Diyarbakir, Turkey), he began to consecrate metropolitan bishops.

Meanwhile Shimun VII Ishoyahab was consecrating his own metropolitan bishops, which alerted the pope to the fact that he was alive. Consequently the pope designated Shimun's line as the Patriarchs of Babylon, and he renamed Sulaqa's line the Patriarchs of the Eastern Assyrians. Shimun took his grievances to the governor of Amida, and the governor arrested Sulaqa. Sulaqa was murdered in 1555. The line that started with Shimun VII Ishoyah continued through his nephew, Eliya VII, becoming known as the Mar Eliya line. The schism that resulted would last for four centuries.

Just an aside. My last doctor retired. Coincidentally, my new doctor is a Dr. Sulaka, and he says that his family honors Sulaqa as a martyr. In the Middle East, memories linger.

The uniate church that started with Sulaqa in 1553 has hardly been unswerving in its allegiance to Rome. As patriarch, Sulaqa was known as Mar Shimun VIII Yohannan Sulaqa. His line of patriarchs moved to Amida, then on to Salmas, Iran. By the 1600s, they had moved their seat back to Kochanes in the Hakkari Mountains. Though the patriarchal seal still read "Patriarch of the Chaldeans," effectively their church had become Nestorian again.

The Abuna family was the oldest patriarchal line of the independent Church of the East, with a seat and traditional burial site at the monastery of Rabban Hormizd, near Alqosh in the north of the Mosul patriarchate. They were called the Eliya line, since all the patriarchs took the name Eliya.

In 1672, the Archbishop of Amida, Mar Joseph I, left the Eliya line and united with Rome, creating a uniate patriarchy in Amida, the Josephite line. The pope, at a loss for titles, dubbed him 'Patriarch of the Chaldeans deprived of its patriarch.'

Meanwhile another patriarch of the Eliya line split off to form a second uniate church. After a complex series of events there now were four: two uniate patriarchs in Amida and Mardin, and two non-uniate patriarchs, one in Kochanes and the other the Mosul patriarchate in Alqosh.[4] This may appear confusing, but in fact a complete discussion of this whole dispute could go on for pages. The road to unification was bumpy.

In the early nineteenth century, a man named Gabriel Dambo became the lay superior of the Rabban Hormizd Monastery, reviving a monastery that had fallen into disuse. Soon he fell into conflict with Patriarch Yohannan Hormizd of Mosul, the last of the Eliya line in Alqosh. After many accusations by Dambo's supporters, the pope suspended Yohannan. He also appointed an 'apostolic delegate for the affairs of the patriarchate of Babylon' in place of a patriarch who had just died. Meanwhile Yohannan convinced the pope that he had made a sincere Catholic profession of faith. Finally the apostolic delegate died, making it possible for Pope Pius VIII to consolidate the remaining Amida patriarchate with the Mosul patriarchate. In July 1830 he did so and announced his new appointment, Yohannan VIII Hormizd Patriarch of Babylon, of the Chaldeans. This was the year the modern Chaldean Church was born.[5]

Soon a bitter schism developed between Yohannan VIII Hormizd and a papal administrator, Joseph Audo. Eventually Yohannan died, and Audo became the Patriarch Joseph VI Audo (1848–79). Audo built a new monastery and seminary near Alqosh, called Notre Dame des Semences, but he also clashed bitterly with the Vatican, earning an unusually sharp papal rebuke. Undaunted, he zealously pursued his missionary activities to convert the Nestorians of Hakkari to Catholicism, and so did his successors, right up to World War I. Nero fiddled while Rome burned.

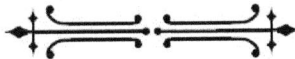

THE CHURCH SPREADS ACROSS ASIA

The remarkable successes of Nestorian missionaries in Asia are forgotten today. In fact, at one time theirs was the most far-flung church in the world. In the seventh through the thirteenth centuries, Nestorian Christians sailed to India and travelled to the farthest reaches of Asia. They brought their religion, their language and their script east as far as China, possibly even further, and they reached as far south as the tip of India. Some of these exploits may be legends, but some are – literally – written in stone.

CHINA

According to archives in Beijing 'The followers of Jesus came to the east 65 years after the slaughter of Christians by the Roman emperor Nero and 69 years after the destruction of Jerusalem. Just at that time the Buddhist religion was introduced into China.'[1] This occurred during the Eastern Han Dynasty, in the first and second centuries CE. Other Chinese records document the arrival of Jews, mostly from Persia, during several dynasties: Chou (1046 BCE – 256 BCE), Western Han (206 BCE – 7 CE), the reign of Emperor Han Yung-ping (70 CE), Tang (618–907 CE) and Northern Sung (960–1127 CE). Chinese records mark time by dynasty, and so do Chinese writers. Many of the dates we quote are difficult to correlate precisely with western records.

Legend has it that St. Thomas carried the gospel down to India and east to China, but this cannot be verified by the historical record. St. Bartholomew may have reached China, but this story too is hazy. Yang writes that Nestorianism was taught in China during the seventh century, but that much of the evidence for this is 'not very trustworthy.' The first undisputed evidence of a Christian presence is the marble stele of Xian.

The Silk Route led to Xian, the capital of China, and that is where Christians came during the Tang Dynasty (618–905). In 1621, a stone stele was found at Xian with the title 'The Popularity of Roman Empire Nestorianism.' The Chinese call this the marble stele of Si-Ngan-Fu. Western scholars call it the stele of Xian. It was erected in 781 CE, with inscriptions in both Chinese and Syriac, accompanied by Nestorian religious writings. It tells of nine missionaries who arrived from 627 to 649 under the leadership of a Nestorian who the Chinese called Alopen (possibly A-to-pen, or Abraham). The stele lists 87 priests and a bishop, demonstrating that the Nestorian Church already had a hierarchal organization by the end of the eighth century. When the stele was found, some Chinese questioned its authenticity, but their problem was that, while Chinese language experts of the time could translate Latin, Greek and Hebrew, they did not know Syriac, so it was difficult for them to be certain of the translation.

This was a continuing problem with inscriptions found in China, especially since certain Chinese characters were ambiguous and could refer to Muslims, Buddhists, Zoroastrians, Manichaeans or Nestorians. Perhaps for that reason, for a while the Chinese regarded the Jews, Christians and Muslims as practicing variations of one single religion. Based on the customary color of their hats, in the tenth century the Chinese called Jews 'blue hat Muslims;' Muslims were 'white hat Muslims,' and Christians, who wore a cross, were called 'Cross Muslims.' Adding to the confusion, some Nestorian temples were used by both Nestorians and Jews.[2]

Here and there along the Silk Route in northwestern China one finds cave temples and huge statues of Buddha carved into cliffs. One impressive example that I visited over twenty years ago featured a massive Buddha reclining in a grotto in the middle of a large carved complex in the Dazu County of Sichuan Province. Archeologists have made a major find in the Caves of Tunhwang,[3] Gansu Province. The caves held a rich lode of fifth to eleventh century Buddhist manuscripts, classic eighth century Nestorian writings and a silk painting of Christ, again confirming that Christians were indeed in China at the time of the Xian stele. In southwest Korea too, seventh century caves have been found with an entrance 'said to be in the pattern of the Christian cave-churches of Syria.'[4]

Bernard Lewis writes: 'in 552 CE two Nestorian monks succeeded in smuggling silkworm eggs from China to Byzantium
(Constantinople), and by the early seventh century sericulture was
well established in Asia Minor.'[5] This was of great importance. It
ended the Chinese monopoly on silk production and the commercial importance of the Silk Route.

One Chinese emperor invited representatives of three Persian
religions, called the 'three foreign temples' in Chinese, to explain
their beliefs: Zoroastrianism, Manichaeism and Nestorianism. Ultimately all were expelled. The Manichaeans left China after the
rule of Empress Wu ended in 732 CE, and the Tang Dynasty expelled them in 843. North of Tibet the Uyghurs adopted Manichaeism as their state religion in the eighth century. By 900 there were
still Nestorians, Manichaeans and Buddhists among the Uyghurs.
Manichaeans built monasteries as far east as the Yangtze River,
only to be persecuted in the ninth century. By the eleventh century,
just a few isolated communities remained in Asia, mostly in the
Uyghur capital. Only in the far eastern Fujian province of China
did some persist to the end of the nineteenth century.[6]

Nestorian missionaries, mostly from Persia, had proselytized
actively in China since 635 CE. Because of their origin, the Chinese
called their temples 'Persian', sometimes 'Roman'. During the Tang
Dynasty, Chinese records show the presence of Nestorian 'temples'
in 100 cities[7] and they list 17 priests, although these numbers may
be high. Monasteries were documented in two northern capitals
along the Silk Route, and churches were found as far east as the
port city of Canton.

Nestorianism influenced six generations of the Tang Dynasty
imperial court, but when Empress Wu (618–907) shifted her support to Buddhism, she discriminated against Nestorians. It was
about 845 when Emperor Wu Tsung, probably under the influence
of his Taoist priests, persecuted Buddhists, Zoroastrians, Nestorians and Muslims. He expelled Christians and Zoroastrians from
China, destroyed temples and monasteries, and forced nuns and
priests to return to secular life. Numbers vary, but an Arab merchant wrote in 879 CE that the Tang Dynasty had killed 200,000
Muslims, Nestorians, Jews and Persians.[8] An Arab merchant, possibly the same one, reported in 877 that thousands of Christians
were killed during a rebellion in Canton. By the end of the Tang

Dynasty, travel along the Silk Route had stopped. A Nestorian monk reported in 987 that Christianity was nearly extinct in China.[9]

Turkish tribes in central Asia had Nestorian communities by the fifth century CE. Timotheos I (780–832) had sent monks to Persia, Azerbaijan, Afghanistan, Turkey, Mongolia, China, Tibet, and India. Patriarch Ishoyahb II founded metropolitanates in Hulwan (now Iran), Herat (Afghanistan) and Samarkand (Uzbekistan). A tenth century traveler found a Nestorian monastery near Samarkand. Conversions are said to have taken place on the shores of the Yellow River. Nestorian missionaries may have made it to Indonesia, possibly Java.

During the eleventh century, Nestorians converted several Mongol and Tartar tribes near Lake Baikal, deep in Asia. We already have mentioned the Uyghur tribe, and a ruined Nestorian monastery has been found in their land. Another tribe was the Ongut, one of whose emissaries became Patriarch Yahballaha III, Patriarch of the Church of the East, in 1281.

The name of the Kerait tribe of Mongols may come from the way they pronounced Christ, if Marco Polo is to be believed. He says that they converted as early as the eighth century; scholars say 1009. One Christian Kerait prince was an early ally of Genghis Khan, and their families intermarried. Therein lies a tale.

Medieval legend tells that a Christian King, Prester John (Priest John), would come one day from Asia to rescue the Crusaders. Stories about Prester John made their way to Rome in 1145, and Pope Alexander III actually wrote to him in 1177[10] offering to send an envoy to instruct him in proper Catholic doctrine. Marco Polo wrote in the 1280s that the story of Prester John was well known in Asia, adding that Genghis Khan had asked for the hand of John's daughter, but when he refused, Khan fought a great battle to win her, during which John was killed. No proof of any of this ever was found, but the tales have long been staples of travel books and historical fiction, with increasingly elaborate embroidery.

The annotations to Marco Polo[11] go on at length about Prester John's name and origin, recounting medieval beliefs that a powerful Christian prince once ruled over vast lands in Asia, travelled west to Jerusalem, made war on the Persians and Medes, captured Ecbatana in Media, and stopped at the Tigris River. According to one version, he ruled 40 kingdoms. Some said he came from Armenia, others from Georgia, maybe Azerbaijan, although Marco

Polo says it was northern China. Another legend says he hails from the ancient race of the Three Wise Men. Yet another calls him the man who carried the relics of St. Thomas to India. Some enthusiasts speculated that he was the forerunner of the second coming. Further confabulation created a great-grandson David, who captured Samarkand and Bukhara and marched almost to Baghdad. So much for European fantasies about Asia.

In 1237 Pope Gregory IX sent a delegation to him, regarding him as the 'archbishop of the Nestorians in the Orient.'[12] In the thirteenth century Pope Innocent IV also reached out to Asian Nestorians – and Jacobites – without success. Pope Innocent IV sent the Franciscan John of Piano Carpin to Mongolia, and there he found Nestorian Uyghurs. In 1247 a Nestorian confessor to Genghis Khan's niece presented his credentials to the pope, with a request for union with Rome. The pope neither understood nor trusted him, and this came to naught.

When Marco Polo returned to Europe, he caused a sensation by reporting that a son of Genghis Khan had converted to Christianity. Remembered largely as an advertising slogan today, Marco Polo once was the most famous European traveler ever to visit Asia. Born in Venice in the thirteenth century to an adventurous family, his father and uncle had travelled to the magnificent palace of the great Kublai Khan, situated across a river from Peking, now Beijing. It was their description, or that of Marco, that inspired Samuel Coleridge to write in an opium-laced haze 'In Xanadu did Kublai Khan/A stately pleasure dome decree/Where Alph, the sacred river, ran/Through caverns measureless to man, down to a sunless sea.'

When the father and uncle returned to Venice in 1269 they met 15 year old Marco (!). Two years later, the three of them set out for the court of Kublai Khan, where Marco would serve with honor for 21 years. During that time Kublai Khan sent him on lengthy missions all over Asia, and Marco delighted him by bringing back captivating mixtures of strange facts and marvelous yarns. After returning to Venice, Marco was captured in a naval battle and jailed in Genoa. To our great fortune, in the jail Marco met a writer, to whom he dictated his adventures. Thus they are preserved for the enjoyment and edification of posterity. Marco Polo's impish melange of fact and fiction leaves the serious historian in a quandary, but subsequent travelers have substantiated many of his routes and descriptions.

Throughout the Sung Dynasty (960–1279) no Christians were to be found in China, but they returned during the reign of Kublai Khan (1271–1368). The importance of Kublai Khan in China cannot be overstated. Through his political, diplomatic and military skill, he combined the realm of the Sung Dynasty with parts of Manchuria, Tibet, the Tangut Kingdom, and the Uyghur territories to create the China of today.[13] He also invented a Chinese identity for himself and his family. The efficient, orderly administrative system that he built easily overthrew the tired Sung Dynasty bureaucracy, helping him come to power at the end of the thirteenth century. His new capital, now called Beijing, had quarters designated for Catholics, Nestorians, Buddhists and Muslims, a place for all who had something to contribute.

Remember that Kublai Khan's brother was Christian, as were his court physician, many advisors and one of his generals. His sons had Christian Kerait wives, and his granddaughter married a Christian king. His favorite wife was influenced by Nestorianism, and his politically powerful daughter-in-law was Nestorian. His grandson Mongke appointed a Kerait as chancellor, and his uncle married a Kerait. His mother was proclaimed Empress posthumously in a Nestorian ceremony.

Kublai Khan sent out his father and uncle with letters to the pope, asking him to send a hundred men of learning 'who would be capable of "proving to the learned of his dominions by just and fair argument that the faith professed by Christians is superior to and founded on more evident truth than any other."'[14] The annotations to Marco Polo's book say that Kublai Khan would summon all the Christians in the realm to his court on their festival days,[15] and he would honor their holy books. Other European travelers complained that Nestorian priests had adopted a Mongol lifestyle, with multiple wives, a predilection for bribery, and a great fondness for drink. They also lamented that priests chanted the Syriac liturgy, but they did not understand it.

In the thirteenth century, the Mongols appointed a Nestorian monk as commissioner for Christian affairs in Azerbaijan, and Beijing had a Nestorian bishopric. Nestorian churches enjoyed many privileges, and individual Nestorians and Catholics held prominent positions in the Mongol Yuan Dynasty (1260–1368). In 1275, Polo found Nestorians and Jacobites all the way to Tangut and he saw Nestorian churches in 11 Chinese cities. One Yuan Dynasty edict listed 72 dioceses. One traveler found over 30,000 Nestorians in Beijing in 1330.[16] In May 2016, the University Museum and Art Gallery (UMAG) of the University of Hong Kong exhibited[17] 700 artifacts from its extensive collection of Yuan Dynasty (1272–1368) Nestorian iron crosses, many of them originally found in southern Mongolia. Inscriptions, gravestones and sarcophagi from the Yuan Dynasty have been found as far east as Quanzhou, across from Taiwan. Many are in Syriac script, written in a mixture of Syriac and Old Turkish, though some are in Phags-pa, the Mongol script. This may be evidence that the Mongol Khans employed Christians as civil servants in Quanzhou.

Archeologists can document the path of early Christians across Central Asia. A large cast-iron Christian cross from the Three Kingdom period (221–280 CE) was found in Kiangsi Province, China.[18] A fifth or sixth century clay jar was found in Kazakhstan, and a seventh or eighth century clay fragment was found in Tajikistan,[19] decorated with psalms written in Aramaic. In 1885, two Nestorian graveyards were discovered close to the border of Uzbekistan and Tajikistan. Also, at the same location there were 610 Nestorian tombs that had crosses and Syriac inscriptions, dating from 858 to 1342.[20] In the early eighth century,[21] an Indian scholar and a Persian monk translated over 500 texts – including the New Testament and parts of the Old Testament – from Syriac or Uyghur into Chinese.

Christian texts have been discovered in the land of the Uyghurs, in a ruined Nestorian monastery. These were written in Syriac, Middle Persian, Parthian, Khotanese Saka, Sogdian and Turkic. Near Lake Balkhash in Kazakhstan there were bilingual Syriac-Sogdian texts. Early ninth century inscriptions were discovered en route to Lhasa, Tibet. Gravestones in southern China bore scripts in Syriac and Uyghur. Scholars claim that Syriac influenced Sogdian (in Afghanistan), Mongolian, Manchurian and Uyghur scripts.

In the mid-thirteenth century, intrepid Nestorian missionaries plodded for weeks across the harsh Gobi Desert, a land of few oases, no animals to catch along the way and forbidding conditions, finally reaching the Korean border, according to Marco Polo.

The Black Death began in China in the early fourteenth century, killing half to two-thirds of the Chinese population, resulting in the virtual breakdown of society and the demise of the Yuan Dynasty by 1358. Monasteries were shut down and turned into Buddhist shrines. Trade routes closed for fear of the plague, and the Mongols turned inward; Christian influence ebbed away. By the close of the fourteenth century almost all the Nestorian Christian communities had disappeared from Central Asia and Mongolia.

As their empire collapsed around them, the Mongols resorted to repression and primitive superstition. When the Ming Dynasty replaced the Yuan Dynasty, it outlawed all Mongol customs or dress and expelled all the Christians, Muslims, Buddhists and Jews. The next successful Christian missionaries in China would be the Jesuits, over two centuries later.

INDIA

It is an article of faith for the St. Thomas Christians of India that their church was founded by St. Thomas. The third century *Acts of Thomas* tells the story. Apocryphal in the eyes of the Catholic Church, it was written in Syriac, probably in Edessa. It recounts how Jesus sent the apostle Thomas to take the gospel to India and how Thomas travelled there with a wealthy Indian merchant in search of someone who could build a great palace for his king. According to the *Acts* and to popular tradition, Thomas landed with the merchant on the Island of Malanka, just north of Cochin, in 52 CE. The king gave him a large sum of money for the palace and left town. Looking about him, Thomas was overwhelmed by the poverty, and he spent the money on the poor. When the king returned to find no palace, he threw Thomas in prison. Thomas was about to be executed when the king's brother died and went to heaven. There he saw that a great palace had been built in honor of the king. He came back to earth to tell the tale, and the king, accompanied by his entire entourage, converted to Christianity.[22]

In addition to performing many miraculous cures, Thomas is said to have sailed around the southern tip of India, on to China and back to the Malabar Coast. According to tradition he established congregations in seven cities: Malanka, Chayal, Kotamamgalam, Niranam, Parvur, Palayur, and Quilon. After that he traveled to Mylapore, near Chennai (Madras) on the eastern coast of India, where he was martyred in 73 CE. A basilica with his tomb is still venerated in Mylapore, even though many believe that in the third century his relics were returned and buried in a tomb in Edessa.

The state on the southwestern coast of India is Kerala. The ancient Dravidian name was Malanad, the land of mountains. The Arabs transformed this word to Malabar, and this was translated to Malankara in the local language.[23] All these names will appear in this discussion.

While it is hard to know if Thomas really travelled in India, he could have, since a community of Aramaic speaking Jews already lived in Cochin. Multiple gold coins found there are inscribed with the name of the king who is believed to have commissioned the palace from St. Thomas, and crosses dating from the second century have been found in at least six locations along the Malabar Coast, many of them attributed to Thomas. A 1601 composition, *The Songs of Thomas* (*Thomma Parvam*), tells how Thomas arrived at Malanka, and how he converted several thousand Hindus, 40 Jews and a rabbi.

Several travelers discovered Christians in Ceylon (Sri Lanka), just off the southeastern coast of India. According to one tradition, St. Thomas preached there too. A fifth century granite cross was found at the ancient Sinhalese capital Anuradhapura, and in the twelfth century, an Arab learned that the king of Ceylon had four St. Thomas Christian viziers, out of a total of 16.[24]

Boats from the Persian Gulf that sail east with the monsoon winds eventually will reach the Malabar Coast. This was the sea route to Cochin that Jewish traders used, and this is one way that many Jewish refugees came to Cochin after the First Temple was destroyed. These may have been the ancestors of the Beni Israel tribes of India. Jews also came by way of Yemen. More Jewish refugees came after the destruction of the Second Temple and again in 136 CE. Roman, Persian and Syrian Christian merchants came later, either by sea or by land from Persia. In the sixteenth century, Jews came from Spain and Portugal, by way of Jerusalem, Aleppo and Constantinople. And just as the Jews came, so did apostles, bishops, and other historic Christian communities of the Middle East.

The middle easterners who first set foot on the beaches of the Malabar Coast must have thought they landed in heaven. A broad swath of pure white sandy beach extended as far as the eye could see, edged by palm trees.[25] Behind the palms were lush, tropical backwaters where village women squatted on their haunches pounding coconut husks into fiber. Floating gently along these backwaters were green crops growing on tiny islands of coconut fiber. The city of Cochin now sprawls across several large islands, and fishing nets curve gracefully over the sea channels between them. As fishermen tug their nets of fish to the beach even today, their deep male voices chant timeless melodies. So the scene was on our first visit in 1973, and so it would have been millenia ago. Even though the beach has lost much of its rustic charm in recent years, these early refugees from Jerusalem would have marveled at its primal state.

The Hindus of India called the early middle easterners by the name *Mappila*. Muslims were *Mappila*, Cochin Jews *Yuda Mappila*, and Christians *Nasrani Mappila*. The Syriac word for a person from Nazareth is *Nasrani*.[26] What does the word *Mappila* mean? Husband. Of course they married local girls, and that was a natural way for a church to spread!

Christians in India were influenced by the culture of the surrounding Hindus, even adopting a caste system. While castes are characteristic of Hinduism, virtually all religions in India have some type of caste. This is the way the subcontinent organizes itself. The earliest Christians were merchants; thus they became identified with the merchant caste of India. In recent years, many low-caste Hindus have become Christians in order to improve their social position.

The first immigrants from the Church of the East were Persian. From the third to the ninth century, Kerala's Christian population grew through waves of immigration and through natural growth, quietly becoming indigenous to India. Then, somewhere between 345 and 795 CE, members of seventy-two Syriac-speaking 'royal' 'Christian Jewish' families came from Seleucia-Ctesiphon, near Babylon. They were led by a merchant warrior, Bishop Mar Yusuf, also called Thomas of Cana, and four pastors. The maharaja presented special copper plates to these elite newcomers,[27] signifying a land grant and special privileges. They became identified with the Brahman and Nayar castes, were allowed to sit on carpets and to ride on elephants, and, most important, they were given 'a monopoly over weights and measures and administration over the king's seal.' The Jewish community too had a set of copper plates, kept in the Mattancheri Synagogue that we visited in Cochin.

Now the Christians were divided. Some considered themselves to be descendents of the original St. Thomas Christians and others of the congregation that came with Thomas of Cana. Both claimed high status, in this country where caste is everything. The Thomas of Cana 'Jewish Christians' later became known as Malankara Nazaranis, proudly identifying themselves as descendents of Jews. Many believed they descended from the house of King David, and still today they marry only among themselves to avoid polluting their genealogical line. They call themselves Knanites or Knanaya, which some say means Canaanite, and they continue to be a distinct group of Christians in Kerala. A sizable group has settled today in Chicago, where they still maintain their tradition of endogamous arranged marriages.

From the fourth through the sixth century, few clergymen from Egypt or the Middle East visited India and few Indian Christians visited the Middle East. In the eighth century, Patriarch Timotheos I sent a Nestorian 'Metropolitan-Bishop of the Seat of Saint Thomas and the Whole Christian Church of India,' intending him to come under the authority of the patriarch of Seleucia-Ctesiphon. Previous metropolitans were under the control of Persia. The local Christians objected, insisting that their church was independent of Antioch; they were disciples of St. Thomas. Baum sees this as the 'earliest reliable evidence that the Indian Christians portrayed themselves as Thomas Christians.'[28] In 823, two Syrian monks visited the St. Thomas tomb at Mylapore. A Franciscan missionary came in 1203, and Marco Polo in 1295. A body of historic research that was completed and finally published in 1936 references several Franciscans who visited in the fourteenth and fifteenth centuries, and it also describes a number of crosses found at Mylapore. The author recounts that travelers found these and other relics when they visited in 1000 CE.[29]

Over the years, Christian traditions began merging with the Hindu culture of Kerala. Catholic missionaries discovered coastal fishing communities who, while nominally Christian, worshipped the Virgin Mary in the form of an Indian goddess, parading her in a Rath Yatra (a typical Hindu ceremonial procession) once a year.[30] St. Thomas has been pictured on a peacock with a spear in his hand, like the Dravidian god Murukan.[31] Still today he is worshipped as 'The Old Man of the Golden Mountain' at a church on Malayattoor Mountain. When the Christian pilgrims climb the mountain to pay respects to the large St. Thomas cross on top, they wear saffron robes, the costume of all Indian pilgrims.

Artifacts of early Nestorians are scant. A sixth to ninth century East Syriac stone cross inscribed with Pahlavi script was found near Mylapore.[32] Syriac crosses of that era were found in Kottayam and Travancore in Kerala, and gravestones in a churchyard near Kottayam have early tenth century inscriptions in Malay and Tamil.

In the eleventh through fifteenth centuries, formal contacts between India and the Middle East ceased. A Franciscan missionary noted in 1347 that Christians in Quilon (Kollam), Kerala, controlled the pepper trade, and that they no longer had a bishop. The two facts are probably unrelated.

Another traveler, likely a Venetian, encountered 1000 Nestorians when he visited the Basilica of St. Thomas in Mylapore in 1447. In 1490, Antioch regarded southern China and India as a single diocese. By then no Christians remained in northern India, and barely any remained on the eastern coast, except in Mylapore. In the early sixteenth century there were reports of more than 30,000 Christians[33] in Cranganore (Kodungallur), 25,000 Christians in Quilon, and 300 churches in India. By 1503 south India had four Syrian Christian bishops. One, Mar Jacob, met several times with the Portuguese when they came in 1498.

The Portuguese were at the forefront of western colonialism in India, but they were strict Roman Catholics, as contrasted with the St. Thomas Christians. Initial meetings between the two were courteous, especially once the Portuguese found out that the 60 Christian towns on the Malabar Coast could put up a force of 50,000 skilled riflemen.[34] Once the Portuguese learned about the heretical practices of the Syrian Christians though, they turned to proselytizing.

In the 1550s, the status of the St. Thomas Christians was in dispute. The question was whether they were under the king of Portugal or answerable to Rome through the Chaldean patriarch. In 1553, they were placed under the Chaldean patriarch Sulaqa. When he died, his successor sent two Chaldean bishops to India, Mar Eliya and Mar Joseph Sulaqa. Unfortunately, by now the Inquisition had begun in Goa. The Portuguese arrested Mar Joseph and shipped him to Cochin, then on to Goa and Lisbon for indoctrination.[35] Thus forewarned, Mar Eliya left India. As it happened,

Mar Joseph made a good impression on the Inquisition in Lisbon, and he was sent back to India.

By the time he returned, he had competition. In his absence, the Syrian Catholicos had consecrated a Mar Abraham in 1557 and sent him to India. A Nestorian bishop came too, Mar Shimon. Now there were Nestorian and Chaldean bishops in India, along with the Latin hierarchy. Mar Abraham denounced Mar Shimon to the Portuguese, who arrested him and sent him to Rome. From there he was shipped to Lisbon, where he died under house arrest.

When Mar Joseph Sulaqa returned, he found Bishop Abraham had firmly asserted his authority, and Mar Joseph complained to the Portuguese that Abraham had usurped his office. Meanwhile the St. Thomas Christians suspected that the Portuguese had co-opted Mar Joseph. Finally the Portuguese packed both Mar Joseph and Mar Abraham off to Rome. In 1569 Mar Joseph inexplicably died en route, and he was buried in Rome.

Mar Abraham escaped the ship and managed to get to Rome on his own. There he convinced the pope that his beliefs were orthodox. In the end, the pope confirmed him as bishop, and he returned to Goa. The Portuguese arrested him again, but he slipped back safely to the Malabar Coast. Thus Mar Abraham ended up the sole survivor, and he remained a bishop until the Inquisition came to Kerala in 1597.

As one would imagine, there are several different versions of this story. The point is though that the Chaldean Church and the Nestorian Church competed to lead the St. Thomas Christians while the Portuguese exerted their power high-handedly. Meanwhile, most of the people remained stubbornly opposed to the threatening colonial power. They were truly Indian. Their governance system synthesized caste, guild and church in a very Indian manner. The church hierarchy was uniquely Indian, and its Indian subdivisions could not be directly translated into Latin concepts of dioceses or clergical categories. The Portuguese had their Inquisition, but it was the total integration of the St. Thomas Christians into the fabric of India that ultimately determined their unprecedented success.

The St. Thomas Christians were transferred to the aegis of the Portuguese church in 1599, and Goa became a Latin archdiocese. Even so, the 1562 prayer book was written in Syriac. So was the Nestorian prayer book in the seventeenth century, but the Syriac tradition was in serious jeopardy. After Mar Abraham died in 1595, an aggressive Catholic Archbishop of Goa, Aleixo de Menezes, started a serious fight for the Latin rite. Mar Abraham's successor, Archdeacon Geevarugese, tried unsuccessfully to resist Menezes. Mar Thoma I, his successor in 1653, was more successful.

In 1599 Menezes, with the support of the Maharaja of Cochin, convened the Synod of Djamper (Udayamperur) to force the St. Thomas Christians into conformance with Rome. The synod ruled that clergy could not marry, required already married priests to divorce their wives and strong-armed the St. Thomas Christians into accepting the Creed of Ephesus. A hundred and fifty priests and 660 laymen were forced to sign a document subjecting them to the pope. One of the big issues was language. The Portuguese did not understand the Syriac liturgy, and they were suspicious of it. By fiat, they changed the liturgy to Latin. They also did not understand the Indian system of local rule, and they sought to impose their Catholic system of dioceses and bishops. As a side benefit, they knew that bringing the St. Thomas Christians under the control of the Portuguese hierarchy would help keep the spice trade in the hands of Portugal. To their great discredit, the Portuguese burned almost all of the precious medieval Syriac Christian manuscripts of India.[36] Somehow, the church preserved over 80 Syriac manuscripts. One surviving text dates to 1290.

Wherever possible, the local St. Thomas Christians disregarded the Portuguese rules. In 1650, they sent letters to patriarch Eliya IX Shimon in Mosul, patriarch Shimon XI in Kochanes, the Jacobite patriarch in Antioch and the Coptic patriarch in Alexandria, pleading for a Syrian bishop. Metropolitan Mar Cyril Ahatallah arrived two years later, with the title 'Patriarch of All India and China.' The Portuguese promptly arrested him, claiming they were deporting him to Lisbon. Somehow he seems to have died, allegedly in Paris in 1659. When they realized he was dead, the St. Thomas Christians were convinced the Inquisition had burned him to death in Goa. The official word was that he drowned at sea.

In 1653 a group of St. Thomas Christians, led by Mar Thoma, gathered in a churchyard of Mattancheri, near Cochin, to swear an angry oath on a large granite cross. The Oath of the Coonan Cross proclaimed that they never would submit to Roman domination.[37] After that, a native-born Metropolitan of Kerala was appointed, and a Carmelite vicar promptly excommunicated him. At first,

most remained faithful to their ancestral rites, and only a small
number went over to the Catholics. After Catholic missionaries
mounted a major effort, more converted to Catholicism, becoming
the Syro-Malabar Church (the Chaldean Church of India). Still,
many continued to push for native bishops, the Syriac liturgy, and
local control.

A Jacobite bishop arrived in 1665, and the local Metropolitan
pragmatically joined forces with him, wielding temporal power
while the Jacobite bishop held religious authority. The two coexisted for twenty years in the Jacobite Malankara Church, also called
the Malankara Jacobite Syrian Orthodox Church. The St. Thomas
Christians now split again. Most of the Knanaya Christians joined
the Syro-Malankara Church, also called the Malabar Independent
Syrian Church. Most of the Catholics joined the Syro-Malabar
Catholic Church, also called the Assyrian Church of the East.

When the British came to India, they set up an Anglican seminary, and by 1836 there was another schism. Just like the quarreling Mesopotamian churches, competing churches fell into a complex series of jurisdictional, territorial, political, and property disputes. But this was India; the two sides did not assassinate their
rivals, they sued. The St. Thomas Christians who followed the Anglicans now found themselves in court fighting the church that was
loyal to Antioch. The resulting lawsuit reached the Travancore
High Court in 1852, and it eventually went to London.

Finally, the Patriarch of Antioch came to Travancore to sort it
all out, and he promulgated a series of edicts that made matters
worse. Blessedly, he returned to Antioch. Soon afterward one of
the two contending clergymen died. After his death, the Catholic
Church and the Jacobite patriarchate of Antioch continued to battle over succession within the Malankara Church. They eventually
went back to court, on to another schism, and an excommunica-
tion.

By the turn of the century, resistance to colonialism was growing in India. In 1923, the local Catholics persuaded Rome to let
them have indigenous bishops. In 1934 the pope allowed St.
Thomas Christians to restore their original Syriac liturgy, although
numerous Latin elements remained. Once they were freed from
Roman domination, the population of Catholic St. Thomas Christians ballooned from 200,000 to at least four million.

Now there are a dizzying number of Syrian churches in India: the Malankara Jacobite Syrian Christian Church, the Malankara Orthodox Syrian Church, the Malabar Independent Syrian (Thozhiyur Sabha) Church, the Syro-Malankara Catholic Church and the Syro-Malabar Catholic Church, which alone has 3,677,000 Catholic Thomas Christians.[38] There also is the Malankara Mar Thoma Syrian Church,[39] which reports 1.5 million members, and a Syriac Orthodox Church of Antioch.[40]

Wilmshurst agrees that the largest eastern rite uniate church in India is the Syro-Malabar Church, which he identifies as the Chaldean Church of India. He divides the Malankara Church into five separate categories: three Syrian Orthodox, one reformed Syrian Orthodox and one Syrian Catholic. He wrote in 2011 that there were 4.3 million Syrian Orthodox and 150,000 Syrian Catholics.[41] Discrepancies between the numbers are inevitable, given the bewildering complexity of all the churches, but clearly the Indian branches of the Church of the East are among the largest in the world.

Anyone who knows the people of India realizes that they are at the same time deeply respectful of tradition, litigious, spiritual, and clamorous. St. Thomas Christians are fully integrated into the country, and widely respected. In China, Nestorian Christianity was foreign. It spread widely, but it was forced to retreat almost completely, just leaving traces among the languages and monuments of Asia. In India, Christians may have fought among themselves, but the country embraced them, just as they embraced India.

The St. Thomas Christians have earned the reputation of being highly educated, and the state where they are most numerous, Kerala, has always been famous as the most educated state in India. After World War I, one Syriac scholar founded the Mar Narsai Press in Trichur. The fonts from this press later travelled from India back to a printing press in Mosul. The Mar Narsai Press printed the daily prayer book, called the *Hudra*, in Syriac, even though most worshippers do not speak or understand Syriac. Usually today the liturgy is in a local language.

The churches that grew from St. Thomas and from Thomas of Cana are vigorous. The St. Thomas Christians of India are living evidence of the missionary success of the Church of the East, and they are more numerous than the congregants of their mother church.

THE JEWS OF KURDISTAN

Jews have lived in Kurdistan since the seventh century BCE, the time of the Assyrian Exile, well before the destruction of the First Temple in Jerusalem and the Babylonian Exile. There they spoke, taught their children the Jewish law and composed poems in praise of the Lord, in Aramaic, for over 3,000 years. Over time their Aramaic incorporated words from Kurdish Kurmanji, from Hebrew, Arabic, Persian and Turkish. Jews in Azerbaijan called their language *lishan didan*, meaning 'our language', and they wrote it in Hebrew script. Jews living in the plains of Kurdistan called their language Targumic; in the mountains they called it Jabali, from the Arabic word for mountain. Some of these languages were not written. The names of their cities came from Arabic, Kurdish or Iranian. They called one city Nusaybin, Nesibin, Nisibis or Nisebi, another Arbil, Arbela, Erbil, or Irbil. Travelers used all these names, spelling them as they sounded.

THEIR HISTORY

The Jews of Kurdistan lived mostly in the mountains of today's northern Iraq; a few were scattered in northeast Syria, southeast Turkey and northwestern Iran. To thwart potential assailants, they kept a low profile. Surprisingly few ever found them. The world knew them as the Ten Lost Tribes.

Ezekiel was one of their greatest prophets. The Book of Ezekiel says he lived along the Chebar Canal in the land of the Chaldeans. This might be the Habur River, or Khabur River, now in northern Iraq. Five years after King Jehoiachin and the Judeans were deported from Jerusalem, Ezekiel saw the first of his magnificent visions. There he prophesized that worship in the Temple of Jerusalem would be restored some day, and he set rules for the

113

priestly code of ritual behavior. Over the centuries, Jews, Christians and Muslims have revered him. Muslims pay their respects at the tomb of the Koranic prophet Dhu l-Kifl, whom they identify with Ezekiel. This tomb is located between Najaf and Al Hillah in southern Iraq, but there also is a Jewish tale.

Jewish legend locates Ezekiel's cave just outside of Betanura in Dohuk Province, northern Iraq, where a synagogue and shrine are said to have been built according to instructions from the prophet himself. One day, workmen started building a synagogue in the town of Betanura, but the next day they found that the wall they had built had moved to just outside Ezekiel's cave. Since this was not where they wanted their synagogue, they kept trying, but each time they began another wall, the next day it would be beside Ezekiel's cave. Finally Ezekiel appeared to a local leader in a dream to tell him that if they built anywhere but at his cave, he would destroy the whole community. The synagogue was built outside his cave.[1]

The twelfth century Jewish traveler Benjamin of Tudela[2] reported finding Jewish communities of 7,000 in Ashur (also called New Nineveh, now Mosul), 50,000 in Chaibar (possibly Chabur), 2,000 in Rehoboth, 1,000 in Nisibin, 4,000 in Jezira, 2,000 in Pumbeditha, 70,000 in Kufa, 15,000 in Hardah, 10,000 in Hillah and 5,000 in Ras al Ain. These numbers seem inflated, since he only reported 1,000 in Baghdad and 3,000 in Damascus. He also found the graves of many famous rabbis, scholars and prophets, including Ezekiel in Kefil (Al-Kifl), Nahum in Alqosh and Ezra the Scribe in al-Uzair, near Basra. There were many more he could have seen: Prophet Daniel near Kirkuk, Joshua the high priest in Baghdad, Jonah and Obadiah near Mosul and the tombs of Queen Esther and Mordechai in Hamadan, Iran. Among the few Jewish visitors to the Jews of Kurdistan there were eighteenth century emissaries from Palestine, who gave legal opinions and collected money to take back to Palestine. In the nineteenth century, Christian missionaries, some of them former Jews, came to the Nestorians in Urmia, and they attempted to convert the Kurdish Jews.

Many rulers reigned over the land of Kurdistan: Parthians, Sassanids, Arabs, and Mongols. As these regimes exerted pressure on the Jews, false messiahs appeared. Benjamin of Tudela told the story of David Alroy.[3] A Baghdad trained scholar, Alroy came from Amadiya, Iraq. He claimed to speak seventy languages in addition to being a magician, an expert in both Jewish and Muslim law, oh, and the Messiah. His mistake was that he fomented a Jewish rebellion against the king of Persia. Legend has it that he was arrested, made a miraculous escape, was arrested again, disappeared, was caught, and walked to safety across a river on a shawl. The angry king pressured the caliph of Baghdad to force the Jewish Exilarch to do something about him. The pressure was transmitted to Mosul, and David ended up dead.

The Ottoman Empire welcomed the Jews who came from Spain after 1492, happy to have them bring their money and education. Many of the Jews who went first to Baghdad would run to Kurdistan when cholera hit Baghdad in 1773 and 1831. From the sixteenth century on, Jews lived in many villages of the Amadiya region. The village of Betanura once had 1,500 families,[4] most of them gone by the twentieth century.

The Ottomans divided Kurdistan into the *vilayets* of Mosul, Baghdad and Kirkuk, and Kurdish chieftains were the local rulers. Iraq became a separate nation under King Feisal in 1921. Though it was under a 25-year British Mandate, apprehensive Jews began to emigrate. When British troops entered Baghdad in 1917, 80,000 Jews lived in the city, over a third of its population of 200,000. By one estimate, when the mandate ended in 1932 after eleven years, about 25,000 Jews were in Kurdistan.[5] By 1952, virtually all of Iraq's Jews had left for Israel.

Why did they leave? After all, they were doing well. Baghdadi Jews had attained prominent positions in the import-export business, in government, and in law. There were four Jewish judges. All this would end in a cacophony of calls for pan-Arab unity. Meanwhile, the Kurds had been promised a state of their own, and they began to harbor nationalist aspirations. When an Iraqi-Turkish border dispute broke out over oil-rich territories, both Assyrian Christians and Jews were in the middle. Wisely, the Kurdish Jews remained quiet. They were not attacked, but after the border was drawn, most of the Jews on the Turkish side emigrated to Mosul or Jerusalem.

In a more ominous development, Nazis moved in, and with them the notorious Haj Amin al-Husseini, the Grand Mufti of Jerusalem. Norma's husband Karim always told us that the Jews "were fine in Iraq until the Germans came". So, how did they live?

THEIR LIVES

The lifestyles of Jews in Kurdistan were remarkably similar to those of the Chaldean villagers we already have met. Jews in Kurdistan lived much the same way for 3,000 years, farming, raising cattle and making wine. Jewish peddlers often were paid in barter. Dodging bandits regularly, they could not afford to be weaker than the Kurds. One picture of two Jewish smugglers shows them in colorful Kurdish-style garb, sporting formidable mustaches, swords and ammunition belts, holding rifles.[6]

The local Kurdish chiefs, *aghas*, usually protected their Jews, but the Jews remained at their mercy since the *agha* could reduce them to vassalage. On Jewish and Muslim feast days, his Jews brought him gifts. Normally he took a third of each bride price, sometimes all of it. Jewish peddlers had to turn over a percentage of their earnings to the *agha*. The *agha* could, and sometimes did, sell his Jews. On the other hand, when the Jews left Zahko, the police chief, Abdul Karim Agha, personally escorted them to safety. Then he dropped dead of grief.[7]

Jewish houses were similar to those in Telkaif. Stacked up like steps along a hillside, one could go uphill by climbing from roof to roof. They resembled the ancient Jewish houses of Babylonia,[8] complete with an outside ladder to the second floor. Since the oldest son, and sometimes others, stayed in the patriarchal home with his wife and family, the house often held over thirty people.

The center of the Jewish village was the synagogue. There they prayed and sang *piyutim*, poetic prayers set to Arabic or Kurdish music. Kurdish Jews refined these to a fine art form. They accompanied them with the *baz* and *baglama* – both of them stringed instruments; the *zonra* – an instrument like an oboe – and the *dahol* – a drum. The rabbi, or at least the most literate man in the village, would read the Torah in Hebrew, and he would retell it in Aramaic, perhaps also Kermanji (Kurdish), to be sure that everyone had understood.

The synagogue had to be near a body of running water, so Jewish women could take their required monthly ritual bath for purity, a *mikve*. Zahko's synagogue was next to a river, but in some towns the synagogue was outside the town center. One synagogue had a spring flowing in two streams through the building and out beneath the courtyard.[9]

Brauer tells a marvelous tale. The Jews in Kurdistan were respected for their success in praying for rain. If the Muslims and Christians failed to produce rain using their rituals, they turned to the Jews, who followed their own special rites. In Arbil, the Jews made donations in the synagogue on Wednesday night; on Thursday they fasted, prayed, and blew the ram's horn (*shofar*). After that they walked to the cemetery, led several animals around the tombs seven times, blew the shofar, and ritually slaughtered them. The meat went to the poor. Witnesses swore that as soon as the ritual slaughterer grasped his knife, the rain would fall.

Their dress was typical of Kurdistan. Jewish men wore conical hats wrapped with cloth, similar to Christian hats and to the Assyrian hats depicted on the walls of Nineveh. Kurdish style, they wore baggy trousers, a jacket, a wide-sleeved tucked-in shirt, a vest, a short embroidered jacket, a colorful folded sash and a sheepskin coat in the winter.[10] Jewish men added a small ritual Jewish prayer vest (*tallith*) over the shirt and an embroidered skullcap. Unusual for Jews in Muslim countries, they were allowed to bear arms.

The women also dressed the Kurdish way, in a colorful vest, an embroidered hat wrapped or topped with a scarf, a long dress, baggy trousers, a flowing outer garment tapered at the waist, and as much jewelry as possible. Travelers found Jewish men in elaborate embroidered turbans and Jewish women with tattoos, often adorned with nose-rings. Some Jewish and Christian women wore a large cloth square wrapped around their bodies, fastened on the left shoulder. Brides wore a headdress similar to the Chaldean *kuchma*. The Jews of Persian Kurdistan preferred costumes in a more Persian style.

Jews ate beef or mutton at dinner if they could afford it, and they prized chicken, partridge or sparrow on holidays. They too served *kubea* (*kibbe*), the special meat and cracked wheat dish of Kurdistan. Norma recognizes all their dishes, such as the *masguf* fish, and their stuffed grape leaves, *yiprach*, which she calls *dolma*. Allowing for dietary rules, Kurdish Jews, Muslims and Christians enjoyed the same food. The local drink for everyone was homemade arak.

Jewish girls married at puberty; Christian and Muslim girls often married younger. The grandmother of one of our friends was 16 when she married; her husband was 35. Intricate rules and rituals governed the bride-price, the feasts and all the rituals of Jewish marriage. Like all Kurdish women and girls though, they had henna applied to their hair and hands before the wedding. On a Jewish wedding day, the bride was accompanied to the home of the groom by music, singing, dancing and rejoicing. After the marriage, the Jewish couple accepted congratulations together, side-by-side, for seven days, a more congenial custom than the one in Telkaif, where the new Chaldean wife sat alone in a corner receiving guests for seven days.

The burial customs of Christians and Jews were similar. Both buried their dead within 24 hours. It is hot in the Middle East. Both Christians and Jews wrapped the body in a shroud, without using a coffin. Muslims used a coffin. My Muslim Arabic teacher says that her grandfather once appeared to be dead and they buried him. Later in the day, villagers heard knocking from inside the coffin. Apparently the burial was premature. Fortunately they dug him up in time, or she would not be here today!

Jewish mourners received callers for seven days after the burial, as did Christians. All observed mourning for a year. The women dressed in black, wore no jewelry, and avoided all celebrations. In the Diaspora, both communities often shorten their period of mourning and relax some of the traditional rules.

In Jewish villages, 90% were illiterate, but they still kept kosher, kept the Sabbath, celebrated the holidays and observed the rituals. Town boys achieved up to 80% literacy, at least enough to read the Bible and to do some arithmetic. At thirteen, most boys went to work. Girls normally were not educated.

However, Jewish women of Kurdistan point proudly to the daughter of one seventeenth century rabbi, Samuel Barzani. Since he had no son, he educated his daughter, Asenath Barzani, and he made her husband promise to allow her to continue her studies. After her father died, it was Asenath who succeeded him as leader of his Talmudic school (*yeshivah*). That must have made her the first woman in history, maybe the only one, to become a *Rosh Yeshivah*. Not only was she a formidable scholar of Bible, Talmud, Midrash and Kabbalah, she wrote many beautiful *piyutim*. She was the very model of a learned woman.

IN ZAKHO

Where exactly did the Ten Tribes of Israel go? There are two identical passages in Kings. We already quoted II Kings 17:6. II Kings

18:11 says the same thing: *Then the king of Assyria carried Israel away into exile to Assyria, and put them in Halah and on the Habor, the river of Gozan, and in the cities of the Medes.* The modern city of Zakho lies on the Khabur River, north of Nineveh, the ancient capital of Assyria. And Kings mentions this river twice.

Zakho has been called the Jerusalem of Kurdistan.[11] Two excellent Hebrew texts describe Jewish Kurdistan. Ben Yaakov describes the most important centers of Kurdish Jewry, including Mosul, Erbil, Sulaymaniyah[12] and Kirkuk in Iraq. Urmia was in Persia, and Urfa (Sanliurfa), Adana, Diyarbakir (Amida), Mardin and Nisibin were in Turkey. These cities also were important to Assyrians and Chaldeans. Mordechai Yona profiles Amadiya, Aqrah, Sandor, and Dohuk and then he comes to Zakho, his birthplace.

Mosul was the largest. Travelers found widely differing numbers of Jews there, depending on the century. Twelfth century travelers reported anywhere from 1,000 to 6,000 Jews in Mosul over a span of twenty years. In 1827, a visitor found 600 Jewish families. In the 1920s, there were 13,800 Jews. By 1947, there were 7,000, until they all left for Israel.

Arbil and Diyarbakir once were the main centers of Jewish life in Kurdistan, but it is Zakho that best fits the biblical description of Israel's settlement on the Habor River. Yona Sabar is a professor of Aramaic in California, and he comes from Zakho. His son, Ariel Sabar, wrote a powerful book, *My Father's Paradise*, about a trip, both actual and spiritual, that he took with his father to visit Zakho. He describes Zakho nostalgically, bringing it to life with stories remembered from his father.[13] Zahko is strategically located on the northern border of Iraq, eight kilometers from the border of Turkey and 20 from the border of Syria. That made it convenient for smuggling out Jews before World War I and during the Mandate. Far to the north, the snow melt from Mount Ararat flows into the Khabur River. Immediately to the north and south, mountains surround the city.

The center of the city is on an island between two branches of the Little Khabur River. Its houses were of traditional clay and mud brick, separated by narrow dusty alleys. On the island were the market, municipal buildings, and an old castle. Each housing bloc was named for its most prominent family. The two large synagogues were of hewn stone. Jews used to constitute the majority of the island population, adjacent to a small Christian quarter.

The island was connected by three bridges to Muslim neighborhoods and to small Christian areas. The Christians in town generally were intellectuals, teachers, doctors, salesmen and municipal workers. Muslims often were shopkeepers, tinsmiths, shoemakers, weavers, peddlers and farmers. The Jews worked as shopkeepers, butchers, weavers, dyers, tailors, carpenters, porters, woodsmen, stable keepers, shoemakers, goldsmiths and tailors. Some worked the fields for Muslims. Some island Jews of Zakho had a unique occupation – river rafting. They were experts in making the special buoyant sheepskin pouches that float Mesopotamian river rafts. In Zakho, occupations passed from father to son. Once they arrived in Israel, how could a father pass this skill on to his son who wants to design software?

The river was the center of town life. The synagogue was there. The women did their laundry; children played; young people promenaded and families picnicked. It was the place for celebrating rituals and holidays, for dancing and for singing. Businessmen rafted their merchandise from there downstream to Mosul. When there was a flood, water ran into the streets and eroded the clay houses.

One important tradition was the yearly pilgrimage to the tomb of prophet Nahum of Alqosh, held on the holiday of Shavuot. Of the seventeen tombs of Jewish holy men in Iraqi, his was the most important to Zakho. It was Nahum who came from Jerusalem to Assyria expressly to prophesy that Nineveh would be destroyed but that the Jewish people would be redeemed.

Jews, Muslims and Christians all revered the tomb of Nahum, located in the Christian village of Alqosh. They brought sick children, barren women, the mentally disturbed and the physically ill to the tomb to be cured. Situated on a hill they called Mount Sinai, the synagogue had a courtyard big enough to accommodate 1,000. During the pilgrimage, Kurdish police would guard them against marauding bandits. The trip required expensive preparations and food, and the women wore their best clothing. They believed that the more money they spent on the pilgrimage, the more benefit would accrue to them. In the nineteenth century, a Muslim woman kept the key to the tomb and tended an eternal flame. The most recent guardian was a Chaldean man.[14] Several reports have suggested that it is in danger of destruction today, either from ISIS or just from extreme disrepair.[15]

In 1827 Zakho had 600 Jewish families. Before World War II its Jewish population swelled, possibly to as high as 2,400. Mordechai Yona writes that in 1950 there were 315 families, or 1800 people, 10% of all Kurdistan's Jews. By 1961, 45% of Zakho had become Christian, and there were five churches. Now they are in peril.

The Jews of Zahko emigrated out of a deep desire to live in Jerusalem, out of pure piety. They were especially affected when they heard that Britain had appointed a man named Herbert Samuel to be the High Commissioner of Jerusalem. In their minds, the arrival of a Samuel in Jerusalem fulfilled a biblical prophecy; a Messiah had arrived. That would have shocked Mr. Samuel, an exceedingly secular Jew. But a messiah was what the Jews of Iraq needed. Things had just turned ugly.

SATURDAY IN IRAQ

In 1941, the tranquil life of Kurdish Jews was about to come to an end because of events over which they had no control. Starting in the early 1930s, German agents and anti-Semitic propaganda were pouring into Baghdad. In the mid-1930s, a large number of Jews were fired from government jobs, and quotas were set to limit the number of Jews who could attend universities.[16] At first the Jews thought this just reflected Arab opposition to Jewish settlement in Palestine, but soon it became apparent that it was part of a series of measures that copied those of the Nazis in Germany. Soon a new Iraqi organization, *Futuwwa*, arose, a clone of Hitler youth. The German envoy to Baghdad, Dr. Fritz Grobba, actively stirred up resentment against Jewish domination of commerce in Baghdad. By 1939 it became clear that a Nazi-style pogram was not far off. One did occur in Basra in May, 1941, but this just was a forerunner of the catastrophe in Baghdad the next month.

It all started with a pro-Nazi coup to drive the British out of Iraq, led by Prime Minister Rashid Ali al-Gaylani. The king was just a child at the time, and the Regent was his uncle Abdullah. In the spring of 1941, learning of a German-influenced plot to kill him, Abdullah fled to Transjordan. Fighting back against the coup, the British were able to retake their vital base of Habbaniya, which guarded their vital shipping routes to India and the oil fields of northern Iraq. In May it was Rashid Ali al-Gaylani's turn to flee, and he went to Berlin. Grobba fled as well. Once the British were back in control, Abdullah reentered Baghdad in June 1941. It was the Jewish holiday of Shavuot, and Jews in their festive clothes ran to the street to greet him.

Many Iraqis claimed later that the mobs attacked because they were enraged at the sight of Jews apparently celebrating a British victory, but in fact, the environment already was hostile to Jews. In fact, lists of Jews were drawn up; Jewish homes were marked with a bloody handprint, and the date and time of a massive attack already was set for May 29.[17] Under pressure, this was cancelled at the last minute, but on Shavuot the pogrom, called the *farhud*, broke out.[18] The mayhem began on June 1, and it continued unchecked until the end of the day on June 2. The police, the military and the municipal authorities looked the other way. The *farhud* was responsible for the murder of at least 146 Jews, for countless rapes and for serious injury to at least 800. Of the various estimates, the highest was 600 murdered. Mobs ransacked 911 houses, containing 3,395 families, and between 586 and 1,500 shops. The property damage has been valued at over three hundred million dollars in today's currency, since this was a wealthy community. This combination of Arab nationalism and German incitement created the most lethal and costly prologue to the expulsion of 850,000 Jews from Arab lands, most of them moving to Israel.

This was the first pogrom in Mesopotamia since the so-called Damascus affair in 1840. At that time Jews were arrested and killed because of a rumor that they were responsible for the disappearance of a Capuchin monk.[19] A hundred years later in Baghdad, the scale of the attack was vastly greater. Baghdadi Jews were integrated in Iraqi culture and politics, affluent, well-educated, many of them prominent intellectuals. Up to then they had looked to the British for their safety. Now they formed underground Zionist organizations and self-defense units that aroused the paranoia of the Iraqi government. In 1948 during Israel's War of Independence, Iraq sent some 15,000 troops to join the Arab nations in fighting Israel, but they experienced a resounding defeat. When they came home, they whipped up sentiment against their own Jews, accusing them of disloyalty, the usual canard.

In 1948 the Iraqi Parliament declared Zionism to be a political crime. At the same time, they began a Nazi-style campaign against the Jews, with boycotts of Jewish businesses, arrests, confiscation of property and executions. By now, thousands of Jews had found their way out. Still, in 1949, 'Jewish firms transacted 45 percent of the exports and nearly 75 percent of the imports. A quarter of Iraqi Jews worked in transportation, such as the railways and port administration. The controller of the budget was Jewish; a director of the Iraqi National Bank was Jewish; the Currency Office board was all Jewish; the Foreign Currency Committee was about 95 percent Jewish.'[20]

In March 1950 the Iraqi government tried to stem the tide of departing Jews by passing a Denaturalization Law, modeled on similar laws in Germany. It allowed Jews to leave, but only if they forfeited their citizenship, which theoretically could be regained if they returned within one year. In March 1951, the state formally froze the assets of all the Jews who had been denaturalized by the 1950 law. At the same time it shut down the telephones and closed the banks for three days. 'Estimates of the value of Iraqi Jewry's blocked assets ranged from 6 million to 12 million dinars or, at its highest valuation, some $300 million in 21st century money.'[21] Eighty percent of Iraqi Jews now were destitute.

From April, 1950 to June, 1951, bombs exploded in Baghdad at the popular American Cultural Center in Baghdad, in cafes next to tables of Jews, at the sites of Jewish companies and at a synagogue. The official line was that the Zionist underground had planted them to scare Jews into emigrating. This would seem unnecessary after the *farhud*. Moreover, Israel already was hard put to absorb all the Jews coming from Iraq.

At least now Iraqi Jews were free to emigrate legally. And they did, after 2,600 years of life in Iraq. From May, 1951 through June 1952, Israel organized great airlifts, called Operation Ezra and Operation Nehemiah. By 1951, 124,000 of the 135,000 Iraqi Jews had left for Israel.[22] The family of an Israeli friend of mine left Iraq in 1947. Her parents always told her that Christians in Baghdad had said, 'When the Jews leave Iraq, Iraq's luck will leave with them.'

Patai counts 187 Kurdish Jewish communities before 1948:[23] 146 in Iraq, 19 in Iran, 11 in Turkey, and 11 in Syria or elsewhere, with a total population estimated at 25,000–30,000. This estimate may be low. He says two early migrations to Israel took place in 1900–1926 and 1935, before the final migration in 1950–51.

Grandchildren of the Jews from Kurdistan will never speak
Aramaic again on a daily basis in their own homes. Those days are
gone. Fortunately, many first and second generation immigrants are
still with us to tell their stories.

BATIA

Batia Aloni was born in Jerusalem, the daughter of a distinguished
family of devout Kurdish Jews.[24] She was named for pharoah's
daughter – the one who found Moses in the bulrushes. *Batia* means
daughter of God. Her grandfather was Rabbi Shabbetai Alwan, a
revered figure in Zakho. Shabbetai Alwan commanded such respect that even the Kurds kissed his hand, and they brought their
disputes to him to adjudicate. Her father, Rabbi Haviv Alwan, was
born in 1906. By the time he was thirteen his father had trained
him in all the traditional rabbinic occupations: performing circumcision, ritual slaughter, the art of tying ritual knots on prayer shawls
and the calligraphy used for Hebrew documents. When Rabbi
Shmuel Baruch and his brother in law Yaakov Shalom came to
Zakho from Israel to collect donations, Haviv seized a cherished
opportunity to leave for Israel. Haviv was thirteen. Shabbetai presided over his Bar Mitzvah, and that same day, Haviv performed a
circumcision. After that he left for Israel, the only unaccompanied
boy with two Israeli emissaries and several families.

Rabbi Shabbetai Alwan wanted to go with him, but his congregation begged him not to. What would they ever do without
him? After his son left he did try repeatedly to come to Israel, but
events prevented him from leaving Zahko. Three times he reached
Mosul, and three times something happened, an accident, a passport problem, a sick relative. On the fourth try, the mysterious
forces that had caused the delay finally allowed him to leave.

Haviv, now called Haviv Aloni, had an uncle in Israel, but it
was the *mukhtar* of the Kurdish community, known as Mamo Falo,
who took care of him. In Israel, the education he had received in
Zakho was hardly unusual, and his skills were not in great demand.
To survive, he and two other Kurdish youths set up in business as
carpenters. When his cousin Murad (Mordechai) came to Israel,
they founded a religious school for Kurdish Jewish children and a
yeshiva for adults in Jerusalem. This way they could support themselves, but when Israel instituted free education, the school closed.
Fortunately, another Iraqi, Moshe Sofer, heard that he was a

trained *sofer*, a writer of religious documents, and he asked him to write a sample *mezuzah* – the prayer that Jews affix to the doorpost of a house. That began his career writing *mezuzot*, *ketubot* (marriage contracts), Torah scrolls and the *tefillin* that observant Jews wear for their morning prayer. Batia shows me a picture of him sitting cross-legged on a floor pillow, inscribing a document with a sharpened bamboo branch, the same way they used to write Torahs in Kurdistan.

In 1940, Haviv brought his father Shabbetai, his stepmother and their two children to Israel. (His mother died when he was born.) During the 1967 war, Haviv was put in charge of water distribution in Jerusalem, because they needed a man of impeccable honesty who would be impervious to bribes. After the war Arabs would kiss his hand, as Kurds might in Zakho. The street where Rabbi Shabbetai lived still bears his name.

In time, Haviv dedicated so much time to the absorption of Kurdish Jews that people called him a one-man immigration service. Batia says he never was a businessman. While many Kurdish Jews started out as construction workers, went on to become investors, later building owners, he had no interest in any of that. Before he died he was awarded the honor *Yakir Yerushalayim* – Worthy of Jerusalem. A picture taken that day shows him standing next to President Chaim Herzog.

Batia's mother, Esther, was born in Israel after quite an odyssey. Esther's mother, Farha, was born in Dohuk, Iraq to a wealthy family. Her family left Kurdistan for Israel at the turn of the century, but they found life there difficult. They moved to Egypt, and after a few years, they returned to Israel. Soon after, Farha's husband died in Israel. They had no children, and, typical of the Middle East, everyone blamed her.

Since Farha was rich and independent, she resisted remarriage, until she was wooed by a charming man named Saleh. Saleh had a son from a previous marriage, and he told Farha it did not matter to him if she could not have children. They had his son.

As it turns out, Saleh would become Batia's grandfather, and he had a story of his own. Born in Zakho, his mother was named Sitoona (Aramaic for Esther) and his father was Yechezkal (known as Chasko), an extremely handsome man. They already had a family of two sons when the woman next door fell madly in love with Chasko, and she threatened her family that if they did not let her marry him, she would marry an Arab. Chasko was pressured to marry her, which he did. Sitoona was talented and spunky, not about to tolerate this situation very long. She never divorced him, but soon she set out with her sons for Israel. We should explain that taking a second wife was perfectly acceptable among Kurdish Jews. Many Kurdish Jews came to Israel with two wives. They were allowed to keep them, but the practice was not allowed to continue in Israel.

Sitoona and her sons stopped just across the border in Qamishli, Syria, waiting for a group of Jews who they were supposed to travel with to Israel. Qamishli today is the capital of the Syrian Kurdish enclave known as Rohava. While she waited, Sitoona began to take in stitching. In the end, she stayed in Syria, and so did her older son Baslo. The younger son, Saleh, left with a son for Israel. That was where he met Farha. Baslo visited Israel once for their wedding, and returned to Syria. To the day Saleh died in 2007, he never saw his mother again.

This was a second marriage for both; Farha was over 40 and Saleh was over 50, but soon, to their surprise, she gave birth to a girl. Thrilled, they named her after his mother, Sitoona (Esther). There was no ultrasound, no genetic testing; they simply thanked G-d for the healthy daughter. This was a domestic victory for Farha. In the Middle East the wife is always blamed for infertility, but with the arrival of her daughter, Farha was vindicated. It clearly was the fault of the first husband.

Esther, the daughter of Farha and Saleh, was talented and beautiful. Anxious to avoid trouble, they wanted to marry her off safely at a young age. She was 11 when they made her marry Haviv, 13 years her senior. For the rest of her life she resented being forced to marry so young, because she had always wanted a higher education. Esther had her first child at 17, not that young by the standards of the time. In all, she had four daughters and four sons, all educated, all either professionals or married to professionals.

Esther was an exceptionally brilliant woman, often compared to the legendary female *Rosh Yeshiva* Asenath Barzani. The whole community came to her to mediate disputes, solve problems, mediate divorces and answer questions of Jewish law; in effect she acted as a rabbi. She died in 2014. Batia earned a B.A. in economics and an M.A. in sociology, becoming a social worker who would carry on the work of her mother, but as a modern woman. Her son maintains the family's love for their culture and language. He earned a degree in Aramaic at Cambridge with Prof. Geoffrey Khan, and did post-graduate work in England, a modern version of his studious rabbinical forbearers.

Batia emphasizes how kind her father was. Not a conventional authoritarian patriarch, he acted more like a big brother to his children. She says that everyone who came to her father for something would receive something. Her love and respect for her father and her learned mother shines through her words.

After we finished our conversation, she urged me to enjoy one of the Kurdish dances that are held in her neighborhood each week. In the Kurdish tradition, men and women dance together, hand in hand.

Batia called for her friend Batya Mazor Hoffman to join us. Batya told me her mother was married at age 13, and there are seven generations of rabbis on her father's side.

IN ISRAEL

Kurdish Jews always dreamed of moving to Jerusalem. The first to come settled in Safed during the sixteenth century. More came to Israel in the 1920s and 1930s, the rest in 1950–52. Batya emphasizes that they started out in tent camps outside the industrial development Talpiot, or in an area designated for Kurdish and Moroccan immigrants, Katamonim. Some were marooned in an abandoned Arab village, Qastel, which later became the upscale Mevaseret Zion suburb. Many were placed in quite charming areas of Jerusalem: Katamon, Nachlaot, Zichron Yosef, and the village of Sheikh Badr, near a Jewish cemetery at that time, now part of Givat Ram, which is right next to Hebrew University. Katamon, where Batia lives, is a leafy neighborhood of former Christian Arab homes.

In the Tel Aviv area, Kurdish Jews lived in Ramat-Gan, Or-Yehuda and in Kiriyat-Ono, which once had an immigrant transit camp. Today Bar Ilan University is in Ramat Gan. Some were placed in another deserted Arab village, Lifta, and later they were transferred to Yardena in the scorching Beit She'an Valley. Regardless of how they started, members of the Kurdish community have prospered and contributed a great deal to Israel. Former Israeli Defense Minister Yitzchak Mordechai is a Kurdish Jew, as are the former Commander of the Air force Dan Halutz and the former Defense Minister Benjamin Elazar.

Holon is the home of a movement to preserve the Aramaic language and culture of Kurdish Jews. The "unofficial chief rabbi" of Holon, Haim Yeshurun, born in 1919, is a twelfth generation rabbi. He came to Israel in 1950[25] fully trained as a ritual scribe, ritual slaughterer, *mohel* (one who performs circumcision) and a scholar conversant in five languages. He has translated the Bible and many other works into contemporary Aramaic. In 2008, an interviewer found him to be remarkably sharp at age 89 and easily able to discern whether a specific bird they brought to him was kosher. It was. Holon also hosts a radio program in Aramaic, and a program to preserve the Aramaic language.

In 2005, the head of the National Organization of Kurdish Jews in Israel, Abraham Simantov, told an interviewer that some Kurdish synagogues in agricultural areas today still maintain the tradition of reading the Torah twice in front of the congregation, once in Hebrew and once in Aramaic, to be sure that everyone understands.[26]

An estimated 150,000–200,000 Kurdish Jews are in Israel today, half of them in Jerusalem.

One music group, Nash Didan, performs in Aramaic. The name means 'our people.' These are Persian Jews who hail from Azerbaijan and also from Urmia, Salmas, Bashkale and Gavur in adjacent parta of Iran and Turkey. Nissan Aviv is their most outstanding composer and orchestrator. His Aramaic translation of the song 'Jerusalem of Gold' is especially moving. The station not only broadcasts to Holon, Givatayim and Jerusalem, but also to Australia, Canada and Sweden. In 2005, 14,000 Persian Jews lived in Israel. Fewer than half spoke their language.[27]

Kurdish Jews brought Saharana (Seharane) to Israel. This is a holiday that traditionally celebrated nature, the end of winter, the beginning of spring and the Passover (Pesach) holiday. Brauer describes the Saharana celebration in Zakho. On the third day of Passover,[28] boys and girls enjoyed an excursion out of town, danced the *deranga* together, and had a rare opportunity to meet. Girls who found boys hiding in the hills were supposed to beat them with boughs. Kurdish men and women danced the *chopi* together, a circle dance like the debke, accompanied by the drum, *dahul* or *dumbuk*, and the *zurna* (*zonra*).

Since the Moroccan holiday of Mimoona is celebrated at the end of Passover, when they came to Israel the Kurdish Jews moved the Saharana, first to the end of Sukkot, then to Tu b'Av. Ever hospitable, they want to share their three festive days of dancing, singing, drinking, and Kurdish picnicking with the whole country. The Saharana is held now in Jerusalem, Yokneam, Mevasseret Zion and Yardena in Beit Shean. Yardena also hosts a Center for Kurdistan Cultural Heritage.

The Kurdish Jews of Israel maintain strong ties with the Muslims of Kurdistan, despite official travel restrictions. Kurdish Jews have performed Kurdish music for Kurds living abroad to an ecstatic reception. Press reports describe businessmen who travel between Israel and Iraqi Kurdistan. In 2013, Bakhteyar Ibrahim came from Germany to attend the Saharana in Jerusalem.[29] The founder of a Kurdistan Israel Friendship Association in Germany, he says they have branches in Australia, England, Belgium, Syria, Iraq and Iran.

Tel Aviv Prof. Ofra Bengio, Senior Research Fellow at the Moshe Dayan Center for Middle Eastern and African Studies and head of the Kurdish studies program,[30] told the *Times of Israel* that her Syrian Kurdish contacts would be willing to have relations with Israel. The *Financial Times* reported[31] that Israeli refineries and oil companies purchased 19 million barrels of Iraqi Kurdish oil – three quarters of its imported oil supplies – worth roughly $1 billion, between May and August of 2015. Prof. Bengio tells me that this number has to be inflated. Still, it does crop up repeatedly.

On November 30, 2015, the Kurds of Arbil, in the autonomous Kurdish area of Iraq, commemorated the departure of Kurdish Jews to Israel 70 years ago. The event was organized by the first Jewish member of Kurdistan's religious affairs ministry, Sherzad Omar Mamsani. Mamsani says[32] there are several hundred families in Kurdistan who identify as Jews but register as Muslims, and 'thousands' who identify as Muslims but are Jewish in origin. To his surprise, over 400 people of all religions, 'including an important imam,' attended the event. From that day on he and a number of the Jews who remain in Kurdistan have worn their Jewish skullcaps in public. He says some older Kurds have been moved to tears by the sight, remembering the days when Jews used to walk openly among them. When asked if there have been any problems, he answered 'A fruitful tree will always be stoned by children.'[33]

Mamsani says that the rise of ISIS has caused Kurds to withdraw from attending mosques, and has encouraged everyone to freely proclaim their own religion. He says he wrote 'a plan to bolster religious tolerance and help religions defend themselves. We first presented the plan to the communication and co-existence minister... Every parliamentary bloc, including the PDK (Kurdish Democratic Party) and PUK (Patriotic Union of Kurdistan) supported the law, which was adopted on May 5, 2014, under the title of *The Law for Minorities in Kurdistan*...Under this law, any Jew who emigrated can request what is rightfully his from the government, including lands, buildings and farms. He can even get compensation from the Kurdish government. Additionally, any man is free to practice his religion.' All political parties supported the legislation, even the Islamist parties.

Geneticists[34] from Hebrew University have studied the Y chromosomes of Jewish men and concluded that 'Jews were found to be more closely related to groups in the north of the Fertile Crescent (Kurds, Turks, and Armenians) than to their Arab neighbors.' This was true even though there was no evidence of 'admixture between Kurdish Jews and Muslim Kurds.' The researchers conclude that these groups had a common ancestor. The newspapers immediately blared that Kurds are the Jews' closest relatives.

Kurdish Jews in Israel certainly are sympathetic to the Kurds in Kurdistan, and Israel has given them quiet military support[35] since 1964, when Mullah Mustafa Barzani sent a representative to Israel to talk, among others, with defense minister Shimon Peres.[36] After first holding joint defense meetings, in 1965 a training course was created for Peshmerga officers. Soon after, the Israelis assisted the Kurds with a field hospital. Military connections between the Kurds and the Israelis have continued ever since.

An Israeli of Kurdish descent[37] explains that 'The late Haviv Shimoni, who founded the National Association of Kurdish Jews in Israel, held a close personal relationship with Barzani and made sure that Israel helped the Kurds in their struggle for independence.'

At this writing, Shimoni's nephew Yehuda Ben Yosef heads the National Organization of the Jews from Kurdistan in Israel, which publishes an annual magazine, *hitHadshut*, in Jerusalem. The magazine features many young Israelis of Kurdish descent who have posted clamorous entries on Facebook and passionate songs on YouTube in support of Kurdish independence.

On September 25, 2017, a referendum was held in Iraqi Kurdistan to gauge support for Kurdistan to become an independent country, and over 90% voted for independence. In the rallies that preceded the vote, Israeli flags were prominent. In fact, the only country that visibly supported Kurdish independence was Israel. Not surprisingly, some of the surrounding population complained that they did not want a second Israel in the Middle East.

After living for almost 3,000 years among a people who also want to have their own country, it is little wonder that Jews feel a kinship with the Kurds, and vice-versa.

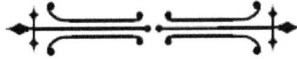

THE NINETEENTH CENTURY AND PERSECUTIONS

Until the nineteenth century, Christians in the Middle East largely eluded discovery by the Europeans. In retrospect, this was their best possible strategy for survival. Unfortunately, well-meaning missionaries discovered them, and they did not approve of the religious practices they found. The Churches of the East had their own ways. Some had joined the Catholic Church; some appeared to have; some never did. The more the western emissaries and missionaries did for them, the more they aroused the jealousy of the surrounding Muslims. Soon all of these communities were buffeted by the pressures and dislocations of a world marching toward war. As nations jockeyed for influence and built coalitions, the hapless Christian communities were caught in the middle, fractured and vulnerable.

The French arrived first. Less than a hundred years after the Turks conquered Constantinople, Francis I of France and Sultan Suleiman the Magnificent signed the landmark Franco-Ottoman Alliance of 1535. This put the Christians of the Ottoman Empire under the protection of France, and for two and a half centuries the French traded on this relationship. The French Dominicans in particular actively helped establish a French sphere of influence. This is what the Germans would challenge as World War I approached.

In the nineteenth century, French Dominican, Capuchin, Lazarist and Jesuit missions all flocked to Tur Abdin in southeast Turkey, hoping to convert Nestorians to Catholicism, but these Christians were disappearing. Tur Abdin once had been home to three quarters of the Assyrians in the Ottoman Empire, spread among 70 to 140 Jacobite, Chaldean and Nestorian villages. By the end of the century only half of these remained, and Arabic had largely replaced the Turoyo language that had evolved from Aramaic. By then, only 450 Orthodox Syriac families still lived in the Tur Abdin town of Midyat and Nusaybin (Nisibis) was abandoned.[1] Soon we will see why.

British Protestants also came in the early nineteenth century. One of the earliest missionary groups was the English Euphrates Expedition, but other British adventurers worked there too. A nineteenth century geologist and geographer with the British Geographical Society, William Francis Ainsworth, travelled to Hakkari, and he published a book on his travels and researches.[2] The Anglican theologian, George Percy Badger, spent years in the Middle East, and wrote about his discoveries in *The Nestorians and Their Rituals with a Narrative of a Mission to Mesopatamia and Coordistan in 1842 to 1844*.[3] Some of the most richly detailed descriptions are found in the fascinating books of Sir Austin Henry Layard,[4] the archeologist of Nineveh and later an English ambassador. Layard hired a local Assyrian, Hormuzd Christian Rassam, to supervise his excavations, and he sponsored his education at Oxford. Rassum later became the British Vice-Consul at Mosul and was instrumental in pushing England to reach out to Chaldeans and Nestorians. All this scientific, religious and political effort improved Britain's position in competition with other western nations.

The job of a missionary is to convert, but attempts to convert Muslims are risky. Under the strictures of the Koran, both the life of the missionary and the life of any Muslim who converts are in jeopardy. Hence the actual market of potential converts was confined to members of the 'heretical' Church of the East, and the occasional Jew. This set the Catholic Church and the Chaldean Catholics against the Assyrian churches that were not unified with Rome. The more converts, the more tension between the two sides. From a geopolitical standpoint though, the more success the French Catholics enjoyed, the fewer inroads the British Anglicans could make.

In 1856 during the Crimean War, Syriac Christians appealed for help directly to the Archbishop of Canterbury, complaining that 'the Christians of the West had forgotten them.' Westerners actually had done very little for them. Baum writes that 'after thirty-five years of missionary activity, not one of the "converted" was in a position to read the biblical writings and offer commentary.'[5] The

Archbishop of Canterbury publicized his mission to Hakkari as a mission to Assyrians.[6] His calculation apparently was that the more exotic and biblical-sounding the name, the more attractive the mission would sound to potential participants, since the British were in awe of Christians who 'spoke the language of Jesus.' By the end of the war, England had donned the mantle of 'guardian of the Christians of Kurdistan.' And they called them Assyrians, not Nestorians.

The most important rivalries played out in the Nineveh Plain and the Urmia district of Persia. Capuchin fathers and Italian missionaries reached Mosul in the eighteenth century. The Archbishop of Canterbury Mission to Assyrian Christians, the Swedish Lutheran missionaries, and German missionaries all worked solicitously among the Christians of Urmia. The German Orientalist Eduard Sachau returned home with 250 Syriac manuscripts – some dating back to the sixth century – and 50 missionary publications, the basis of the Sachau collection now in the Berlin library. Many others collected information that had the side benefit of helping the German war effort.

The French Dominicans established a major mission and seminary in Mosul in the nineteenth century. They also founded a mission, school and hospital in Urmia, later a life-saving shelter for refugees during the Assyrian Genocide of 1915. The Dominicans had other successes. Several Christian merchant families converted to Catholicism in order to improve their trading opportunities with France.

America was not far behind. The American Board of Missionaries ran the highly respected Urmia College and Fiske Seminar of the American Mission from 1830 to 1914. Justin Perkins, considered the first American missionary to the Church of East, led this mission for 36 years. Under him it became known as the 'Assyrian Evangelical Church with certain Nestorian characteristics.' Its printing press produced a psalter, the Old and New Testaments, and the magazine *Zahire d-Bahre*, all in Syriac. In 1915 the mission would play a dramatic role in saving thousands of Christian refugees from genocide.

A Russian Orthodox mission in Urmia had extra political significance, because its location was so close to the Russian border and the Assyrian community that had lived across the border in Georgia since the sixth century. West of the Russian border, the easternmost region of the Ottoman Empire was heavily Christian. At the turn of the eighteenth century, Peter the Great of Russia had sought to expand his empire toward the west, and he began a series of border wars that kept the area in turmoil. At least the Russians did exact a guarantee from the Ottoman Empire that their Christians would have freedom of worship, and Russia played the role of Orthodox defender of the faith until it was preoccupied with its own revolution. That gave the Christians three defenders, French, British and Russian, all acting in their own self-interest.

A war between Russia and Persia raged back and forth across Urmia from 1826 to 1828, frightening thousands of Christians into running to Russia. The surrounding Muslims were angry when Christians crossed the border to Russia, and they suspected them of assisting foreigners to invade their country. They further resented the fact that western nations pressured Constantinople to treat Christians fairly. This gave the Christians an advantage, one which they would not have needed had Muslims treated them as equals. Another provocation was that missionaries educated Christians, not Kurds or Turks, which raised the Christian standard of living. The Muslims became ominously envious. Reprisals would not be long in coming.

UNDER ATTACK BUT STILL NOT UNITED

Nestorians and Chaldeans had suffered persecution for centuries. During the Ottoman-Persian War of 1743, the Persian Nader Shah captured Kirkuk and Erbil, besieged Mosul for 40 days, assailed nearby towns, and destroyed churches.[7] Villagers of all confessions huddled together in the monastery of Rabban Hormizd, but finally the Persians stormed and destroyed it, killed many, took captives and demolished countless rare books. The Persians also laid siege to Mosul, but there the Christian and Muslim townspeople united and fought them off together. The grateful Muslims of Mosul allowed the Chaldeans to rebuild their churches, but the Nestorians chose to shutter their monastery. At least Christians were not fighting each other. Not yet.

By the mid-nineteenth century Christian churches were divided by jealousies and dissent, and devastated by constant attacks. Provincial governors had taxed local dioceses to the point of impoverishment, and they either ignored or encouraged the mercenaries who plundered villages. Layard writes at length[8] about priests in the Nineveh Plain who cried to him that bandits had ridden off with all their church and monastery valuables, including ancient, precious manuscripts. Surely some of their sacred books were hidden, but as priests were killed, the secret of their hiding places died with them. Many of the books that the brigands found were burned, their yellowed pages used to tamp down rifles. On his visits, priests tried to host Layard with their traditional hospitality, but they had barely anything to put on the table. The only villages that could defend themselves were the ones high in the craggy mountains.

In these mountains lived four main tribes of 40,000 Nestorian Christians: the Tiyar, Tikhuma, Baz and Jilu, and each tribe had a hereditary leader, the *malek*. Their patriarch had brought them into the Hakkari Mountains in order to maintain their independence and for pure survival. Patriarchs wielded both temporal and ecclesiastical authority. Hereditary chieftains, they designated nephews as their successors. They held court, bribed authorities, and amassed riches like oriental potentates, even when their people lived in poverty. Like the biblical Moses, the patriarch's most critical job was to lead his people in war.

American missionaries who ascended these mountains to reach the Nestorian patriarchs in Kochanes were horrified by the absence of active monasteries, liturgical texts or learned clergy. The harried Nestorians in Hakkari were poorer and less educated than the Chaldeans of the plains. Their priests only had to be able to read Syriac. Still, many were illiterate or unable to comprehend what they read. Assigned to a village for life, priests were allowed to marry and have a family. Many were dedicated, but others seemed more interested in the income from their fields and the tithes villagers paid them. Most missionary efforts to build churches and establish schools were met with polite indifference.

Back down on the Nineveh Plain, from 1828 to 1840, the governors of Amida and of Rowanduz repeatedly savaged Alqosh and nearby Christian landmarks. They set the great seventh century Chaldean Rabban Hormizd monastery on fire, destroyed its irreplaceable books and manuscripts, and stole over 500 of them.[9] They demolished the tomb of the prophet Nahum and assaulted the clergy of nearby villages. The Kurds followed, rounding up and killing nearly four hundred men and selling vulnerable young village girls into slavery.[10]

The Church of the East once gloried in the priceless libraries of its most famous monasteries, but by the twentieth century, these had been devastated. By 1890 the Rabban Hormizd monastery, the home of patriarchs for centuries, sat all but abandoned. The monastery of Mar Yaqob in Dohuk was only opened for the occasional summer program. The monastery of Mar Yaqob the Recluse near Seert was barely in use. On the border of Syria and Turkey, the great Nestorian monastery on Mount Izla, Abraham of Kashkar, was ceded to the Syrian Orthodox Church. No more than fifteen of the hundreds of medieval monasteries that once dotted Tur Abdin remained open, limping along with elderly caretakers. Only 200 years before, the sixth century monastery of Deir el-Zafaran (the Monastery of Saffron) was one of 300 Syrian Orthodox monasteries in the area and held 700 monks. When Dalrymple[11] visited in 1977, he found two.

The missionaries had visions of liturgical education, but local priests could only see clouds on the horizon.

STORM CLOUDS GATHER

Some of these clouds were caused by the missionaries. First the French and the Russians, then the nineteenth century British missionaries to Kochanes and the American missionaries in Urmia disrupted the delicate relationship between Christians and Kurds. In some cases their missions were virtual fortresses, and the more the Christians looked to them for protection, the more the Kurds concluded that the Christians must be enemies.

Kurds play a complicated role in this story, since they are the majority population in the area that most Assyrians and Chaldeans call home. In 2000, at least 10,000 Kurds lived in southeast Turkey, 6,000 in northern Iran, 3,000 in the Nineveh Plain of Iraq, and several thousand in northeast Syria. Marco Polo wrote that their 'delight it is to plunder merchants.'[12] A footnote claims their name is derived from a Persian or Turkish word for 'wolves' and lists their vices as 'murder, robbery and treachery.' Yet today Kurds are seen sympathetically as one of the largest peoples in the world not to have a country of their own.

In contrast to the mountain Kurds, many of the Kurds in the plains of northern Iraq lived a quiet life side by side with the Christians and Jews. At the time of World War I relationships between the Kurds and Christians disintegrated disastrously, but twenty-first century Kurdistan has become a refuge for minorities. Article 6 of the Draft Constitution of the Iraqi Kurdistan Region says that it 'upholds and respects all the religious rights of Christians, Yazidis, and others.'[13] It also guarantees freedom for all to practice their own religious rites and rituals. Article 14 says, 'This Constitution guarantees the right of the citizens of the Kurdistan Region to educate their children in their mother tongue, including Turkmen, Assyrian, and Armenian.' Also, 'Along with Kurdish and Arabic, Turkmen and Assyrian shall be official languages in administrative districts that are densely populated by speakers of Turkmen and Assyrian. This shall be regulated by law.' Is this just pie in the sky?

In the early nineteenth century the Kurds were less enlightened. Patriarch Mar Shimun XIV Abraham made a costly mistake when he intervened in a power struggle between Kurds and Ottomans.[14] Unwisely, he promised his support to the Kurds, then turned around and disclosed their plans to the Ottomans. To make things worse, the Kurds wanted a state of their own, and the Christians were in the way. A further complication was that this whole conflict was part of a larger Kurdish battle of hereditary succession in which two fierce leaders – Badr Khan and Nurallah Bey – were allied with the side that the patriarch had double-crossed. Local missionaries made it all worse when they blundered in, trying to help. The Kurds swore revenge.

In 1842, Badr Khan Bey and Nurallah Bey ransacked the Rabban Hormizd monastery and launched into a wholesale massacre[15] of the Bohtan and Tiyari tribes in the Hakkari region, allegedly wiping out 10,000, one-fifth of the Assyrian population. The massacre has been described as genocidal. They murdered all the men and sold the women and children into slavery. The patriarch's aged mother was raped, beheaded and thrown into a well. In 1846 Badr Khan went after the Tkhuma tribe, destroying churches, killing clergy, shooting all the men on sight, and again selling the women and children. Neither the Americans nor the British intervened during the massacre. At the end, British protests stimulated the Porte to capture Nurallah and Badr Khan and send them into exile.

The *London Times* observed: 'No sooner had their country been exploited by missionaries, and the interest of learned and scientific men been awakened with respect to them, than this terrible visitation befell them.' It went on to say 'It was the impudent zeal of rival missionaries that first excited the jealous apprehensions of the Pasha of Mosul, and caused him to "let slip the dogs of war" on the unfortunate Nestorians.'[16]

ALL NUMBERS ARE GUESSES

Before we begin our interlocking tales of disaster, it would be useful to know how many Christians were in Mesopotamia and the Ottoman Empire, both before, during and after the momentous events of World War I. The problem is that population shifts took place on such a massive scale that all numbers are probably wildly inaccurate. Imagine a time of massive deportations, widespread starvation and disease, community-wide forced conversions, masses of refugees fleeing to asylum, and whole villages of women and children sold into slavery. How could anyone keep track of how many had died?

The Middle East has additional complications. Categories of people, geography and languages change over time. In 1915 for instance, many Syriac families also spoke Armenian, and they would have been counted as Armenian.

Some missionaries report population statistics by religion, such as Chaldeans, Jacobites, Nestorians and East Syriacs. French missionaries categorized these same people as Jacobites, Orthodox Syriacs, Monophysite Syriacs, Syrians, Old Syrians and Suryani. English and Germans used different designations. In the nineteenth century, the name Assyrian commonly replaced Nestorian; sometimes this also included Chaldeans. Others referred to Chaldeans as East Syriacs; the Nestorian Church later was called the Assyrian Church of the East. We will quote most sources using the terms they used, in order to avoid making incorrect assumptions about their data.

Problems of geography come next. The Ottoman Empire was divided into *villayets*, or provinces, and each of these was divided into *sanjaks*, or districts. Provinces, districts and place names change too. The Ottomans reported their census numbers in terms of ethnic groups, asking local *aghas* to guess how many were in their village. Some records list numbers of families; others list individuals, generally assuming that a family had five people, probably more in rural areas. Counts of villages assumed 434 people per village.

In the wake of catastrophe, the traumatized survivors and their advocates tend to inflate the number killed. In contrast, the perpetrators and their apologists often admit to only the lowest possible numbers. Bias is inevitable. Researchers who depend on Ottoman archives may have another unconscious bias. If they offend, they risk being cut off from future access, and in some cases their lives could be in danger.

Having assured the reader that we are well aware of how inconsistent many of these estimates are, we will try now to give some of the numbers that seem the most authoritative. Wilmshurst is one of the most qualified experts on the whole subject of the Church of the East. He quotes numbers from the 1830s, which estimated that 60,000 Nestorians (about 10,000 families) lived in the Hakkari Mountains and 25,000–40,000 Nestorians and Chaldeans lived in the Urmia and Salmas regions of northern Persia.[17] In 1850, the English theologian Badger estimated that 40,000–70,000 Nestorians (11,378 families) lived in Kochanes (a city in Hakkari), and other estimates went as high as 100,000–120,000. In 1900, one source counted over 97,000 Syrian Christians in the *sanjak* of Hakkari. These numbers are fairly consistent.

De Courtois[18] quotes one count of 68,210 Assyro-Chaldean, Orthodox and Christian Syriacs in the Mardin *sanjak* of Tur Abdin at the end of the nineteenth century. Again, this is the Hakkari region. Wilmshurst comes in much lower, writing that only 70,000–79,000 Chaldeans lived in the entire Ottoman Empire before the twentieth century and that in 1913, a Chaldean priest counted 101,610 Chaldeans (East Syriacs). Along with his estimate of 120,000 Assyrians (Nestorians), Wilmshurst's working total of both Chaldeans and Assyrians was 220,000. Since the number killed in the entire Assyrian Genocide usually is quoted as at least 250,000, perhaps even two to three times that, Wilmshurst's numbers raise questions. Some of the numbers below may be closer to the mark.

Donabed is an expert on Assyrian history, and in *Reforging a Forgotten History: Iraq and the Assyrians in the Twentieth Century* he gives a count of 126,000–140,000 Assyrians living in Hakkari in 1902, close to agreeing with Wilmshurst. He also quotes Travis, a law professor whose pre-war numbers have '80,000 Assyrians in the Tigris valley from Mosul to the villages of the Bohtan region,' plus '35,000 in 70 villages in Urmia and Salmas, and 100,000 in Hakkari.'[19] This would add up to 215,000, and Travis writes that one normally would expect a 25% increase every 20 years.[20] Stafford, who was the British Administrative Inspector in Mosul in 1933, gives the lowest numbers of all – only 40,000 Assyrians in Hakkari before the war[21] and 15,000–20,000 in the Urmia region. It may have been in the interests of the British to give a low number.

Gaunt too has devoted a career to the subject. In one set of data[22] he quotes from the 1919 Paris Peace Conference, the As-syro-Chaldean delegation claimed that before the war there were 620,000 Christians – including 18,200 Armenians and 485,000 As-syro-Chaldeans. The Armenian Patriarchate claimed even more: 1,018,000 Armenians, plus 123,000 Nestorians, Jacobites and Chaldeans.

Gaunt also quotes the Agha Petros submission[23] on behalf of the Syriac Orthodox delegation to the 1922 peace conference in Lausanne. Tables of data appear to show that in 1914, 563,000 As-syro-Chaldeans lived in Mosul, Diyarbakir, Aleppo, Urfa, Hakkari, Urmia, Salmas and adjacent regions. Clearly these are the highest numbers of all, exceeding many estimates of the total mortality during the 1915 genocide.

THE HAMIDIAN MASSACRES

Before everything went wrong, the Ottoman Empire appeared to be on the verge of reform. Starting in 1789, Sultan Selim III tried to institute the New Order, a modernization program for the military, educational system and the economy. It all fell flat because of bureaucratic inertia and cupidity. Many in government just profited too much from selling offices, tax farming, and other corrupt practices. The *Tanzimat* reforms of 1839 gave minorities new rights, abolished tax abuses, and fixed the terms of the military. In 1876, the first Ottoman Constitution was written, and for the first time it gave full citizenship to all subjects. It was suspended after two years. None of these reforms took root.

Sultan Mahmud II, The Reformer, destroyed the Janissaries and set their quarters on fire. Now he needed to reorganize his military. In the 1830s he asked Britain and France to help, but he was rebuffed. After that, at his request Lieutenant Helmuth von Moltke arrived, beginning a fateful German military influence on the Porte.[24]

The Crimean War of 1853–1856 gave the western nations leverage to pressure the Ottomans for real reform. The result was the Ottoman Reform Decree of February 1856, also stillborn. Meanwhile, the Porte, with no clue how to finance a modern country or a modern war, was borrowing money to pay off debts from the last time they borrowed money. The Ottomans had neither the will nor the cash to fulfill their grandiose promises of reform, but restive minorities across the country were beginning to dream of autonomy. In 1865, an idealistic group, the Young Ottomans, formed in the Balkans.

The Bible says, *Now there arose a new king over Egypt who knew not Joseph.* We might follow suit by saying that now there arose Abdul Aziz in the Ottoman Empire, who became the paranoid Sultan Abdul Hamid II. Known as the Murderous Sultan, he ascended to power in 1876 following two well-timed assassinations of his kinsmen. His reign started ominously with drought, flooding, locusts, a severe famine and the financial collapse of the Empire. The winter of 1873 was the coldest on record. The Ottoman Empire was becoming known as 'the Sick Man of Europe.' In 1875 the Empire defaulted on its loans, and revolution was not far away.

When the Russo-Turkish War of 1877 broke out, the Ottomans accused the Christians of siding with the Russians. There was some truth in that, and the surrounding Kurds resented it. Adding to their indignation, the post-war Congress of San Stefano and the Congress of Berlin in 1878 were disasters for the Porte. Bismarck carved up the Ottoman lands in the Balkans, and the Turks lost almost all of their European territory.

At this point, the Porte was unable to transport the armaments and supplies that a modern military requires. Government financial affairs were delegated to Christians, and the Muslim leadership did not understand how to coordinate them with the needs of the state. Education was parochial. Trade guilds and artisans resisted change, and an oriental fatalism had sapped the Ottoman spirit. In the 1880s Sultan Abdul Hamid II again turned to Germany, who obligingly sent Marshall von der Goltz and another group of German officers to train the Ottoman army.[25]

At the end of the nineteenth century, an estimated two and a half million Armenians lived in Turkey, over half of them on the Russian border. Frequently raided by marauding Kurdish chieftains, the Armenians formed self-defense organizations. Already suspicious of Armenians, the sultan exploited this provocation to kill them. To be clear, they did not make careful distinctions between Armenians and Assyrians, because, 'in the cities of Diyarbakir and of Urfa, all Christians used Armenian to communicate, as they did wherever there was a high Armenian concentration.'[26] Some Assyrians even added an Armenian ending to their names.

The French vice-consul in Diyarbakir[27] reported the first signs of an Armenian insurrection in 1894. That was all the Turks and Kurds needed. In 1894–96, Abdul Hamid created a Kurdish force similar to the Cossacks, called the Hamidiye, and this became the core of an Ottoman army cavalry force of thousands. In the ensuing massacre the Kurds and Turks together murdered hundreds of thousands of Armenians, Assyrians, Jacobites and Nestorians alike. These were the Hamidian Massacres. Drunk with blood-lust, the attackers committed heinous atrocities.

One ship captain on the Black Sea off the coast of Trebizond watched as Armenian fugitives swam toward his ship only to be deliberately drowned by Muslim boat men, after nearly a thousand had been massacred in town.[28]

The French reported 1,500 deaths in the first villages attacked, 7,500 in several others, and a three-day bloodbath in Diyarbakir that killed 1,000 Armenians and over 180 other Christians. Another 2,000 were reported missing. Some of the regional numbers reported may be exaggerated, but they were: 3,000 killed in one village, 3,000 in another, 300 in another and 4,000 in another ten villages. The daughters of one priest were raped and killed before his eyes, and he went insane.[29]

Near Mardin, the Kurdish leader Ibrahim Pasha and his two sons pillaged, burned, and completely destroyed surrounding villages. One group of Syriac Christians defended themselves for five days in the monastery of Deir al-Zafaran, ultimately to lose 70–80 people. In 1896 a Kurdish sheik in Urmia entertained the Nestorian bishop Mar Gabriel and fourteen priests in his home. When they walked out they were ambushed and slaughtered.

In Urfa, a pogrom burned the city cathedral, murdering 3,000 women and children inside. Outside the cathedral, Kurdish forces slaughtered 13,000 more.[30] In both Diyarbakir and Urfa, the perpetrators blamed the victims. They accused the Armenians of conspiracy and treason, and they had the nerve to ask other Christian communities to sign a complaint against them. In 1896, a Jacobite patriarch and a Syrian Catholic bishop reportedly buckled, signing a document with multiple complaints against the Armenians. Divide and conquer.

The French vice-consul for Diyarbakir[31] said that the 1895 campaign of terror against Armenians and Assyrians foreshadowed the Kristallnacht of Nazi Germany. Christians were murdered, shops looted, homes ransacked and burned. Warda quotes an estimate that 300,000 Christians were killed between 1894 and 1896,[32] but that number may be high.

During the 1890s Christians were pressured to convert to Islam under pain of death, but converts remained suspect – shades of the Jewish *conversos* of fourteenth century Spain! The French complained to Constantinople in 1895 that 7,500 Christians of Diyarbakir had been forced to convert and that captured Christian women and girls were being sold into slavery. In the six worst-hit provinces (including Diyarbakir) they listed 36,200 deaths, with 5,482 more in four outlying provinces.[33]

The actual number murdered in 1895 probably was 50,000–100,000.[34] Then in 1896, a group of Armenian patriots invaded a Constantinople bank, sparking a massacre that left some six thousand corpses. American Ambassador Henry Morgenthau wrote that two million men, women and children were destroyed in the thirty years of massacres under Sultan Abdul Hamid II. Yet in 1898 Kaiser Wilhelm II went to Constantinople, pinned a decoration on Abdul Hamid, and kissed him on both cheeks.[35]

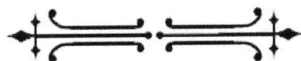

THE TWENTIETH CENTURY AND GENOCIDE

At the turn of the century, Muslim persecution of Christians built up steadily to the earthquake of 1915, and that was followed by aftershocks of varying magnitude over the next decade.

After the massacres of the 1890s, armed Hamidiye fighters and Kurdish chieftains brutalized the pastoral villages of Armenians, Jacobites, Chaldeans, Assyrians and even other Kurds. They seized land with impunity and literally engaged in highway robbery. The Kurdish Ibrahim Pasha was out of control. Complaints to Ottoman authorities were fruitless. Horrified French diplomats sent dispatches predicting that Christians would disappear entirely. It was anarchy.

In Persia, the year 1907 was one of poverty, famine, pestilence and a freezing winter. Kurds reacted by stealing village sheep, laying waste to homes and destroying villages. Crowds of destitute refugees ran to the Russian consul in Urmia, pleading for the Tsar's protection, but soon the Tsar himself would be history.

Before we go on, we should review where the Christians lived in the Ottoman Empire at that time:

- Assyrians (Nestorians) lived in the Hakkari Mountains, primarily in the towns of Barwar, Tyari, Tkhooma, Baz, Jilu and Gavar. Kochanes, now abandoned, was their traditional patriarchal seat.

- Chaldeans predominated in the province of Mosul and in the Nineveh Plains to its north. Mosul was their patriarchal seat.

- Jacobites lived in the Turkish province of Diyarbakir, in Syria and in adjacent areas. The city of Mardin was their patriarchal seat.

- Persian Assyro-Chaldeans lived mostly in the districts of Urmia (7,800) and Salmas (10,000). Their pre-war total population was 78,000 in Persia.[1]

The genocides of World War I generally affected two border areas: 1.) Diyarbakir, Mardin and the Hakkari Mountains in southeastern Turkey; 2.) Urmia and Salmas in northern Persia, just east of the Turkish border. The Chaldeans further south were relatively safe. The Assyrians lived high in the perilous Hakkari Mountains, but that did not help. The Kurds lived there too. It should not be a surprise that neighboring Kurds and Turks viewed Assyrian mountaineers with suspicion and some fear. It is very surprising to see what they did.

THE POLITICAL ISSUES

The Young Turks plotted revolt in the cafes of Paris, London and Thessaloniki (Salonika), unveiling their Committee of Union and Progress (CUP) in 1905. In 1908, Enver Pasha gave a resounding speech in Thessaloniki saying, "We are all brothers. There are no longer in Turkey Bulgarians, Greeks, Serbians, Rumanians, Mussulmans, Jews. Under the same blue sky we are all proud to be Ottomans."[2] All the minorities threw up their hats and cheered.

Why was there a revolution? The Young Turks were enraged at Sultan Abdul Hamid's obvious contempt for the first Ottoman constitution and his move to dissolve the first parliament after it only had met for three months. All attempts to reform the Ottoman Empire had failed. The war with Russia failed. Revolutionary ideas of nationalism were in the air, and a world war was looming.

The Young Turks dreamed of creating an Ottoman confederation that would give all nations and religions equal rights. Under the banner of 'Unity and Progress,' the CUP captured Constantinople, and it deposed the 'bloody' Sultan Abdul Hamid II. They also proclaimed a second constitution and convened Turkey's second Parliament. When they entered Constantinople, Muslims, Jews and Christians met them with raucous joy.

Anyone could have predicted that this euphoria would not last. As Lorieux, a reporter for the respected French newspaper

Figaro,[3] described the situation, 'Ainsi naquit une reciproque hos-
tilite. Le Turc envia la richess qu'il avait dedaigne d'acquerir; le
chretien et le juif envierent le pouvoir qu'on leur refusait.' In English: 'And so there was born a reciprocal hostility. The Turk envied
the riches that he distained to acquire; the Christian and the Jew
envied the power that they were refused.'

The first challenge for the CUP was the Persian-Turkish border war of 1907–8. While Russian and Turkish troops fought, England and Russia agreed to partition northern Persia and eastern
Turkey. And, as the Turks knew, Russia's long-term goal was to
acquire a port on the Mediterranean.

The CUP also wanted to eliminate the despised capitulations.
These consisted of a special extraterritorial status that France, Britain, the Netherlands, Russia, and Germany enjoyed in Turkey.
They conferred such privileges as special financial access, unrestricted entry and the right to bring in tariff-free imports. Foreign
nationals lived in special *khans* or *funduqs*, locked at night for their
protection. Foreign consuls had special courts, prisons and post
offices. They obtained protection certificates for their own nationals, and they also could buy them for minority merchants who were
citizens of the Ottoman Empire. Jews bought protection too, many
becoming protégés of the same Christian nations. Viziers, pashas
and army officials profited nicely from the *baksheesh*. The Porte was
open for business. The CUP abolished these abuses as soon as it
came to power.

In 1909, Abdul Hamid attempted a comeback. According to
the official report, in the town of Adana alone, 2,093 Armenians,
133 Chaldeans, and 481 Syriacs were killed in the riots in his support. Contemporary observers believed that up to 20,000 Christians
were killed in the entire province, including 850 Syriacs and 422
Chaldeans.[4] None of this carnage helped him. In the end, the CUP
did not back down, and they put his brother, Sultan Mehmed V, in
his place as a figurehead. The first CUP cabinet had an Arab-
Christian, a Dohme (a Muslim of Jewish ancestry), a Circassian, an
Armenian and an Egyptian. In this first flush of democracy, a
number of ethnic groups, including the Armenians, formed political societies. The Assyrians were quiet, but the Turks remained
suspicious. All this nascent liberalization would vanish.

October 1911 was the month when the Italians landed in
Tripoli, the Ottoman Empire's last province in Africa, setting the

conditions for the 1912 First Balkan War. In it, Bulgaria, Serbia, Albania and Greece, encouraged by Russia, united against Turkey, winning territory and gaining independence for Albania. In the 1913 Second Balkan War, the Greeks took Thessaloniki, one of the last Ottoman territories in Europe. Turkey turned again to Germany for help retrieving the land they lost in the Balkans and for future protection. Meanwhile, Muslim refugees flooded across the Greek border into Turkey, and Turkey had to make room for them. It did not take long before they decided to clear out the land on their eastern border, the home of the Christians. This chapter tells what happened.

The Young Turks completely rejected the settlement at the end of the Second Balkan War in 1913, and a triumvirate staged a coup d'etat. Ismail Enver became Minister of War. Mehmet Talaat became Minister of the Interior, later Grand Vizier. Ahmed Djemal became Minister of the Navy and commander of the Turkish army. None of these three pashas had the experience or skills to govern or to command a military. Enver once had been a military attaché in Berlin, and his first move as Minister of War was to bring forty German officers under the command of major-general Liman von Sanders to reorganize the war ministry, the army and the general staff.[5] It is worth remembering that German officers already had been training the Ottoman army for five years when Kaiser Wilhelm took the German throne in 1888. The 1897 Ottoman successes in a war with the Greeks were in no small measure thanks to them.[6]

The German plan was for the Ottoman Empire to play a major role in the Kaiser's colonial policy of *drang nach osten* – a push toward the east. A key component was for them to build a railroad from Berlin to Baghdad. Meanwhile, Baron von Oppenheim and other Germans explored the countryside, studying language and archeology, but also learning about the geography, water routes and markets. The Kaiser made two lengthy trips to Constantinople.

German technicians built a wireless station. Germany sent in railroad workers, master craftsmen, overseers, workers, truck convoys, war equipment and construction materials. When the Germans sent General Otto Liman van Sanders in December 1913, Russian protests forced him to function not as a general but only as inspector general of the Turkish army. In January 1914 General

Bronssart von Schnellendorf became Chief of Staff of the army. German officers drilled Turkish troops daily.[7]

In November 1914, Enver led a Turkish advance toward Russia. In January his army was completely defeated at Sarikimish, suffering tremendous losses. Berlin demanded to know how this happened, and the Germans doubled down, requisitioning the populace for supplies. Morgenthau called this 'a wholesale looting of the population...destroying the nation's agriculture, and ultimately [leading] to the starvation of hundreds of thousands of people.'[8] By 1915 thousands were dying of starvation; almost all able-bodied men had been drafted and few were left to till the fields. Requisitions had destroyed most businesses. Mediterranean ports had stopped their import and customs dues; the treasury was close to empty.

Yonan[9] has published stunning excerpts from the German archives. These show that before the war the Germans had placed 40 officers, 500 instructors and technicians and 3,000 soldiers in Turkey. By the end of the war, there were 800 German officers and 18,000–20,000 German soldiers. In December 1914, General Colmar Freiherr von de Goltz became the sultan's military adviser, after he had commanded the German mission to the Porte from 1885 to 1895. Later he took charge of the Asia Corps in Mesopotamia. Admiral von Usedom held the chief command of the Straits of the Bosporus and Dardanelles.

General von der Goltz[10] reorganized the Ottoman army and its system of military education, molding the officer corps into a social class loyal to the government, what the Germans called a 'School for the Nation.' Later we will see that this German military training permeated the entire Middle East.

Ambassador Henry Morgenthau served as the American ambassador to the Ottoman Empire during many of the critical war years. Born in Germany to a Jewish family and fluent in German, he maintained a friendly relationship with the German Ambassador Baron von Wangenheim, who talked to him with surprising frankness. Wangenheim freely admitted that he sent regular reports on actions of the Turkish army to Berlin. He also admitted that he considered deportation of 'politically unreliable people' to be legitimate if these people represented a potential internal fifth column.[11]

Yonan writes that the German Protestant missionary Johannes Lepsius was, like Morgenthau, deeply affected by the Armenian Genocide. He collected papers that proved that the Germans knew exactly what was going on during the genocide, and he documented the events extensively. A hero today, he had to dodge the censors at the time.

In the run-up to the war, the Ottoman Empire wanted to maintain neutrality, but Germany made it impossible. On September 27, 1914, Germany closed the Dardanelles, cutting off Russia from its only naval resupply route and blocking the British from entering the Black Sea. Germany sold two warships, the Goeben and the Breslau, to Turkey, and they were renamed the Yavuz and the Medilli. In November 1914, these ships, under the command of the German Admiral Wilhelm A. Souchon, snuck through the Dardanelles to the Black Sea to harass Russia. In a surprise move, they bombarded the port of Odessa, fired on two Russian dreadnaughts, sank a Russian gunboat and a French ship and fired on the town of Odessa. As intended, this caused Russia to declare war on Turkey, putting Turkey in the war on the German side.

The Young Turks had envisioned a secular Turkey, but Morgenthau writes that the German strategy was 'to arouse the whole fanatical Moslem world against the Christians. Germany had planned a real "holy war" as one means of destroying English and French influence in the world.'[12] They expected that if Turkey declared a jihad in 1914 it would begin a domino effect of pan-Islamic uprisings in Persia, the Caucasus, Afghanistan, finally India. Thus Germany would replace the dominance of England and Russia in all these areas.

A rumor started that the Kaiser had converted to Islam. A fatwa appeared calling for all Muslims to declare war against the enemies of Islam – Russia, England and France. Germany, Austria and Hungary were exempt. 'The ceremony of unrolling the prophet's green war flag took place on 29 November in Medina. In Kerbela, center of the Shiites in Mesopotamia, a ceremony serving the same purpose was held , in which Hussein's sword was carried in a procession symbolizing the beginning of the Holy War.'[13] More fatwas appeared, either written by the Germans or helpfully translated by them.[14]

In July 1914 Kaiser Wilhelm II wrote 'Our consuls in Turkey and India, agents etc., must inflame the entire Mohammadan world to a wild uproar against this detested, lying, unscrupulous nation of shopkeepers. If we are to bleed to death, England should lose at least India.'[15] The idea was to trigger Islamic uprisings from Morocco to Egypt and from the Bosporus to India, as outlined in the 'Memorandum on inciting revolution in the Islamic territories of our enemies, by Max Baron von Oppenheim, Imperial Minister-Resident.'

Oppenheim, the most prominent figure in the 'Intelligence Service for the Orient' of the German Foreign Office, was based in Bern, Switzerland. A self-proclaimed expert on the Pan-Islamic movement, he persuaded the Kaiser to back it. While some Germans who knew better urged caution, in the spring of 1915 the Kaiser authorized Oppenheim to set up a German information center in Constantinople. This was followed by over 75 German reading rooms throughout Asia Minor and East Arabia, even in Medina.[16]

The Oriental Propaganda Office in Berlin printed over one thousand publications in 21 Middle Eastern and European languages, and it disseminated three million books, journals, flyers and notices advertising the German alliance with '300 million Mohammadans'. Yonen writes that handbills 'were tossed out of airplanes, aimed at Muslim soldiers, and they included Jihad exhortations, news of victory and reports on the military situation.' Also, 'Between May 21 and December 31, 1915 alone, more than 130,000 Reichsmark were spent, and 300,000 Reichsmark each in 1916 and 1917, mostly for publishing [Holy War] handbills, brochures and books written in numerous Oriental languages and dialects... During 1915 alone, the Imperial Printing Press in Berlin published handbills the Intelligence Service [sic] for a cost of 2.5 million Reichsmark. In all, in the two years from March 1915 the Intelligence Service for the Orient allotted over 800,000 Reichsmark for propaganda to advance the Holy War. A secret pamphlet distributed in the name of the Sultan to India, Egypt, Morocco, Syria and other Muslim countries, in Arabic, called for the assassination and extermination of "all infidels who rule over Islam," and it warned, "Know ye that the blood of infidels in the Islamic lands may be shed with impunity – except those to whom the Moslem power has promised security and who are allied with it."' This meant that the Germans and Austrians were exempt.[17]

No Muslim, ever, had called for such a thing.

During the war, the Germans indoctrinated Muslims who had been captured while fighting for England, France or Russia, reassuring them that they would not retaliate against them. Over nine hundred Muslim prisoners of war were treated to propaganda, courses of Islamic instruction and specially built mosques, all so they would join the jihad when they went home.[18]

Some in the German press did warn of a potential catastrophe, but apologists claimed that modern Turks were more advanced than the Muslims of bygone days; their jihad would 'block an unrestricted development of bloodthirsty fanaticism, which, by the way, is not approved of even in the Shari'a.'[19] This is the same sort of fantasy that wishful thinkers disseminate today.

Yonan comments, 'The extermination and destruction of Christian population which followed shortly thereafter showed that the concept of Holy War was taken quite literally by the Muslim participants, the Turkish gendarmerie and the simple Turkish soldiers, as well as within the Muslim civil population…'

Because of strict censorship, the German press did not report the Ottoman massacres to the German polity, and after the war, the Germans bent over backward to silence the press about the holy war, censoring communications to Europe and other western nations. For the Turks, blocking any acknowledgement or recognition of genocide in their land has been a cornerstone of national policy ever since.

The Christian Genocides of World War I make difficult reading. Descriptions are both gut-wrenching and repetitive, defying the imagination of any normal person. Still, we will go through many of the gory details, because they show what was to come during the Anfal campaign in Iraq and at the hands of ISIS in the twenty-first century. Some things do not change. The Germans made the mistake of believing that mankind had moved on, that jihad would no longer have the same ferocity as it did in medieval times. The world had progressed. People were more civilized. Surely those dark forces either did not exist any longer or were amenable to control, to proper channeling. The behavior of the Nazis themselves belies that thought.

Sadly, what we are about to describe is not new. The world saw this barbarity before World War I, and we see it today. If we leave out any details when we get to ISIS, the reader will be able to imagine them.

GREEK GENOCIDE

The Greeks were the canary in the mine shaft. The Greek word *pontos* means sea. Pontic (Pontus, Pontian) Greeks had lived in Anatolia along the coasts of the Aegean, Bosphorus and Black Sea, speaking their own dialect, since the eighth century BCE. Even after Greeks founded their own state in Europe, the Greeks in the Ottoman Empire lived under a regime that grew increasingly xenophobic. The pretexts were the usual – Greeks were disloyal or they had rebelled. One of my husband's law students, even though she was born in Munich, identifies as a Pontic Greek, because her parents came from Salonika (Thessaloniki), and the family originally was deported from Turkey. She says they always used to hear the refrain: 'Turkey for the Turks.'

It all started just as the Armenian and Assyrian massacres would. Greek conscripts in the Turkish military were disarmed, demoted from the rank of soldier to become manual laborers, and they were worked to death. Official Turkish correspondence reveals that the Turks intended to exterminate the Greek population of Anatolia. They deported the Greeks in forced marches to the interior, and most died along the way through freezing, starvation, or illness. They were given no food. Deportees were forced to sign statements that they left of their own free will. Troops and irregulars who accompanied them were encouraged to commit theft, atrocities, and violence against women, in case they needed encouragement.

Greek persecutions started before 1915. 'In Hellenic sources, there is evidence that mobs committed massacres since 1913. These gangs mercilessly attacked the Greeks, first in Eastern Thrace and then in Western Anatolia, much earlier than any conflict with Greece.'[20] Some 400,000 Greeks were deported from the Aegean Coast and Anatolia before the war. Donef writes 'Bedri Bey, İstanbul Chief of Police, told a secretary of the US Consulate, "The deportation of the Hellenes by the Turks was such an outstanding success; the empire must implement the same method for the other races."'

Deportations and population exchanges began from Smyrna and the islands of the Aegean coast in 1913–14. Morganthau called it a 'peculiar method which German publicists have advocated for dealing with populations that stand in Germany's way. That is by deportation.'[21] Admiral von Usedom told him that it was the Germans 'who urgently made the suggestion that the Greeks be moved from the seashore,' for military reasons. Three years later, von Usedom reassured Morganthau that the Turks had been right in deporting the more than 100,000 Greeks from Smyrna and the Aegean coast. This was the first Turkish deportation of Christians.

Most of the Greek deportations, destruction, and outright murder took place during the Greco-Turkish War of 1919–1922. Prime Minister Eleftherios Venizelos threatened Germany that Greece would abandon its neutrality unless the Turks stopped persecuting the Pontic Greeks. Finally he invaded Smyrna in 1919, enticed by promises of territory if he would join the Allies. From there, the Greeks went on to Anatolia, dreaming of a greater Greece that would include the Pontic Coast of the Black Sea. Ataturk stopped the Greek advance in 1922, but both sides claimed that the other committed murder, ethnic cleansing and atrocities.[22] Donef disclaims Greek atrocities, saying that Greeks differ from Turks, for whom 'the raping of Greek women was almost considered to be a national duty.'[23]

If you talk to the Turkish youth today, you may hear, as I have, that the reason why Turkey had a problem with the Greeks was that they had invaded Turkey.

In 1922–23, Greece and Turkey undertook what history blandly calls an 'exchange of populations.' Turkey only admits to a transfer of Greeks to Thessaloniki and of Muslims from Thessaloniki to Turkey. The truth was that these deportations were as brutal as those of Armenians and Assyrians, with an appalling loss of life. Conveniently, in September 1922 a massive three-day Great Fire of Smyrna (Izmir) destroyed the Christian quarter of that ancient Aegean Coast city. The population of Smyrna had been approximately 270,000, and 140,000 of them were Greeks. Of these, 50,000–100,000 were massacred. Chrysotomos, the Greek metropolitan, was 'torn to pieces' by a mob.[24] Most of the survivors were expelled or deported.

Coincidentally in Greece, the Great Fire of Thessaloniki (Salonika) burned out the entire Jewish section in 1917, clearing the center of the city. Convieniently, this is where they built new housing for the Greeks from Anatolia. On a recent trip, we visited the new Aristotle University of Thessaloniki, part of it built on the old Jewish cemetery.

The Genocide of Pontic Greeks continued until 1923, when Turkey transported the last of their Greeks to Thessaloniki in exchange for 400,000 Muslims from Greece. Over nine years, at least 350,000 died during these deportations, not to mention those who vanished in the interior.[25] Donef tabulates the following mortality figures from 1912–1918: 218,449 from Thrace, 298,449 from Asia Minor and 257,019 from Pontos. That comes to a total of 773,915.[26] Through the spring of 1924, 50,000 more were massacred. According to most estimates, 90,000 to 1.5 million Greeks died, out of a pre-war population of 2.5 million.

ASSYRIAN AND ARMENIAN GENOCIDES

Assyrians call 1914–15 the *Sayfo*, 'The Year of the Sword.' This was a general Christian massacre. 'The Turks made no distinction between Armenians and Syrians. They also killed tens of thousands of Syrian Orthodox, Syrian Catholic and Chaldean Christians, and drove the remainder from their villages…'[27]

'The difference between the Armenian and the Assyrian massacres lies in the fact that in the case of the first every possible step was taken to denounce it, whilst in the second every imaginable precaution has and is being taken to confine, in vain, its sad news to the areas still stained with Assyrian blood,' in the words of Rev. W. A. Wigram, former head of the Assyrian Mission of the Archbishop of Canterbury in Persia.[28]

The Armenian Genocide is well-documented. Most in the general public have not heard about the Greek Genocide or the Assyrian Genocide. The Armenians represented the largest population of the three, and they clearly lost the most, but the percentages lost were staggering for all three groups. In tribute to the scale of the Armenian Genocide, we will not attempt to summarize it. We prefer to pay our respects to their devastating losses and concentrate on a story that is not as widely known, the Assyrian Genocide. In any event, the stories of the Armenians and the Assyrians are interwoven.

Before the war, Assyrians lived peacefully under the sheltering wing of Russia in the villages of the Hakkari Mountains and the northern Iranian plains around Lake Urmia. On August 3, 1914, the Turkish Governor of the Province of Van called upon Patriarch Mar Benjamin Shimon and promised him that if the Assyrians were loyal to the Turks in the coming war they would be rewarded with arms, new schools, and salaries for their religious leadership.[29] This turned out to be disinformation. Persecution of Christians began that month.

In October and November, 1914, 3,000 armed Kurdish horsemen swooped down on Assyrian villages, raiding, murdering and driving villagers out of the Turkish border areas. At first the Russians and Assyrians repulsed them, but then Turkey and Russia went to war in November. By December 1914, the war between Russia and Turkey was raging across the border, spilling into eastern Turkey and northern Persia. This was when Enver decided to drive the Russians back to Russia, and he plunged into the fateful Battle of Sarikamish. Though he had some success in high altitude incursions against Russia at the end of 1914,[30] in the beginning of January, near the town of Sarikamish, it became a debacle. Enver lost at least 60,000 troops, and he had to blame someone. Since the Russians had recruited Armenian volunteer units to fight alongside them, the Ottomans accused the Armenians of treason, and the traitorous Christians had to be punished.

Beside the German-instigated jihad, beside Kurdish aspirations to clear Christians from their future state, beside the old grudges of tribal warfare, and beside the Turkish plan to clear the eastern border for military actions, now there was another reason for the subsequent genocide. Revenge.

The Russians had suffered major losses too at Sarikamish. In the cold of January 1915, the Tsar pulled his troops back to Russia, leaving 45,000 Assyrians stranded in Urmia and Salmas on the western shores of Lake Urmia, now in northwestern Iran. On their way out, the Russians lynched some prominent Muslims for conspiring against them. A flow of Assyrian refugees began immediately, and so did the Turkish attacks on them. Rev. William A. Shedd of the American mission in Urmia documented it in detail, reporting 'The evacuation of Urmia took place on the 2nd January, that of Salmas a day or two later, and that of Tabriz on the 5th.'[31] He testified that 'The Nestorians, except for less than 2,000 in Salmas, all lived in the Urmia district. Including refugees from Turkey and the Armenians, there were in Urmia, at the beginning of 1915, not far from 35,000 Christians.' Of these Christians in Urmia, he estimated that 6,000–7,000 were Armenians, the rest Assyrians or Chaldeans. These numbers may be low.

Most inhabitants ran away from Salmas in the wake of the re-treating Russians, leaving some 800 older people behind. In March 1915, a new disaster struck.[32] Under Djevdet Bey, the blood-thirsty governor of Van, Turks and Kurds herded together the 725 Arme-nian and Assyrian men who still were in Salmas and hacked them to death.[33] There and in neighboring Haftevan, 850 beheaded corpses were found stuffed in wells.[34] A Turkish commander had offered money for every Christian head. Later, 1,175 Christians were killed in Salmas, just three days before Russian troops re-turned. The Persians swooped in too, plundering Christian villages, murdering villagers, and violating girls.

At the end of March, surviving Assyrians from Salmas plus some 8,000–10,000 from Urmia stampeded toward Russia, leaving their cattle, the food they had saved for the winter, everything. Do-nobed[35] writes that more than 27,000 people from more than 100 villages had been killed in the Urmia district by March, 1915, and at least 12,000 refugees fled to Russia. Travis quotes Toynbee's report from the British Foreign Office's 1916 "Blue Book," that said that one fifth of the 30,000 Assyrians from Urmia died, and five-sixths of them were robbed, their houses destroyed.[36] Barely clothed, the escaping refugees suffered tremendous losses from freezing cold and starvation. Counting the thousands of Armenians and other Christians who joined them, the number of refugees may have ris-en to 25,000, perhaps 70,000.

According to Rev. Shedd, approximately 25,000 Christians remained in Urmia and the surrounding villages, and they were subjected to continual assaults and robbery. At least 17,000 found refuge in his American mission in Urmia, and 3,000 in the French mission.[37] Despite the remarkable heroism of Rev. William A. Shedd and his coworkers, at least 4,000 died from the cold, crowd-ed conditions, hunger and typhoid. Another 1000 were killed out-right in raids on the mission. On one case, the Turkish consul kid-napped a bishop and a doctor and demanded ransom. When the Turks kidnapped girls and women, they committed what Rev. Shedd called 'outrages too barbaric to describe.' One woman said 'not a woman or girl above twelve (and some younger) in the vil-lage escaped violation.' Nor were girls younger than seven years old spared, or women over 80.

Shedd's diary reports that in January an American doctor bar-gained with the Kurds to save 3,000 Assyrians packed into a church. By mid-January at least 12,000–14,000 refugees were jammed into the American mission, 2,000 in the hospital and large numbers in the school. The Jewish quarter of Urmia also sheltered some 250 Christians. By February, 700 to 800 refugees, several missionaries and their staff were dead of typhoid or typhus. By March 16, the Americans were feeding 15,000 people a day, largely with bread alone, because resources were so scarce.

The *London Times* published an August 6 letter from a missionary in Urmia: 'Alas! The destruction of life, wealth, and houses was greater than we had imagined. We have lost by death and murder more than 12,000 souls; 150 Christian Nestorian villages have been completely plundered and burned to ashes by Turks and Kurds. I must say that plunder and massacre, and carrying off women and girls...' It continues: 'During the five months of captivity (for 1,500 were shut up in the American Mission) each person could have half a pound of bread in 24 hours. But this bread was made in the city and sold to the Missionaries, and the Persian Governor had taught the bakers to mix fine steel dust, and sometimes lime in the bread.'[38]

On Sunday, May 24, a Russian advance guard entered Urmia, followed by 6,000 Russian troops. The *atour.com* archive contains extensive documentation of what happened. Many Assyrians returned home, only to find their villages utterly devastated. As soon as they began the harvest in August, a rumor circulated that the Russians were going to withdraw again. The Assyrian population panicked, and another 20,000–30,000 streamed toward the Russian border.[39] This was the second evacuation from Urmia. A third of these unfortunates succumbed to illness, starvation, lack of clothing and other privations. Tragically, the rumor was misleading, and a small force of Russians did remain. Again, some Assyrians returned home, and others remained displaced in surrounding villages.[40] The Russians, overwhelmed by the misery, allowed at least 100,000 Assyrians to enter Armenia and Georgia.

Ironically, many Assyrians fled from Urmia over to Salmas, even knowing its history. Meanwhile, in June, many Tiari and Tkhuma tribesmen from Hakkari, pursued by regular Turkish troops and 30,000 Kurds,[41] had either followed their patriarch up into the mountains or run directly to Salmas. Those Assyrians who survived the flight to the mountains ended up back in Salmas anyhow. We soon will learn their fate.

Diyarbakir is in southeast Turkey, about fifty miles northwest of Mardin, and both cities lie west of the Hakkari Mountains. In the Diyarbakir district, the murders began in February. In April, 1915, a large group of Chaldean men from the village of Karabash were murdered while fleeing to Diyarbakir. Some said it was well over 1000. The pretext was that they had attacked Muslims.[42] In May 1915, the Turks began to expel the Armenians, Jacobites, Syrian Orthodox, Syrian Catholics and Chaldeans. As usual, one excuse was that they were loyal to Russia, and another was the need to clear the ground for military purposes. Following the pattern they used with the Greeks, first they disarmed them and then they demoted the soldiers to porters, beasts of burden. After that, the Christians were arrested, held for ransom and deported. Finally a combination of Kurds and Azeris exterminated the Christians of Diyarbakir in a massacre of untold numbers, perhaps as many as 120,000.

Urfa, the ancient city once called Edessa, is situated southwest of Diyarbakir, and before 1915, 5,000 Assyrians lived there. Starting in March, 1915, Armenians and Assyrians were disarmed and the community leaders killed. That month, deportations began. On August 19, 1915, one Armenian in Urfa resisted detention and shot a Turkish gendarme. In the reprisals, 600 were murdered in the Christian quarter. One month later, a German aide-de-camp was seen directing attacks on Christians barricaded in their quarter.[43] When the captives gave in, Turkish troops – supervised by that German aide-de-camp – massacred 5,000 Armenians and Assyrians. Another 15,000, primarily Armenians, were deported, most of them falling dead en route.[44]

Father Rhetore, a French Dominican priest, lived in nearby Mardin. In early June 1915,[45] he reported that 410 Christian men of Mardin had been imprisoned, tortured and sent on a forced march to Diyarbakir. None survived. Later in June, another 266 men were arrested and sent to Diyarbakir. None arrived.

Rhetore reported that successive convoys of Armenians sent to Mardin in June numbered 7,000, 4,000, 2,000 and finally 3,000 starving people. In July alone, 2,700 Armenians were killed in Mardin. In July and August, 1915, even as they were being murdered, Armenians and Assyrians of Mardin were held up for enormous ransoms. In surrounding villages, Kurds killed thousands of Assyrians. Rhetore describes the atrocities as some of the most savage.

According to him, the Mardin region held 8,000–10,000 Armenians before 1915. Of them, 1,500 were left at the end of three waves of massacre in Mardin.[46]

One of the most devastated areas was in Hakkari, the home of the Assyrians, between the Diyarbakir-Mardin area to the west and the Urmia-Salmas area to the east. The *London Times* reported, 'The Russians would occupy a certain area, retreat suddenly, leaving their unfortunate allies to the mercy of the vindictive Turks, who looked on them as renegades, traitors, and, above all, Christians. Then would ensue a series of gruesome massacres, which would continue until such time as the Russian armies again advanced to reoccupy the evacuated territories. The Kurds, who all through the campaign had been intriguing with the Turks, were on all occasions employed by the latter on punitive expeditions against these unfortunate people.'[47]

The Kurds completely surrounded 160,000 mountain Nestorians in 16 villages of the Tiyari district. When the Russians withdrew in the spring of 1915, they promised[48] to arm any Assyrians who would join them, but the Turks threatened to kill the patriarch's brother if they accepted these arms. In an ill-considered move, an assembly of tribal notables pushed Patriarch Shimun XIX Abraham to declare war on the Emir of Hakkari in April, 1915.[49] The Russian vice-consul downplayed the resolution as merely a decision to mobilize.[50] The Assyrians released a statement that 'the Assyrian nation accept the invitation of the Allies and particularly that of England, France, and Russia to join the common cause and to fight to the victorious end as their Smallest Ally.'[51] When the patriarch's brother died, it was said to be of a fever.[52] The Assyrian National Petition makes no bones about saying that the brother was held hostage and that his subsequent death was brutal. At the funeral, the Kurds ambushed and murdered 500 men, took 200 women captive, and exhumed the brother's body in search of gold.[53]

It was the summer of 1915 when the Russians withdrew from the Van province in eastern Turkey.[54] In June, Kochanes, the home of Nestorian patriarchs in Hakkari for centuries, was laid waste. Even today it remains abandoned.

The Assyrians made their last stand in the Hakkari Mountains after Kochanes was destroyed. The Assyrians fought off their assailants on the plains for forty days, after which Patriarch Mar Shimun Benjamin led them to the top of the mountains. There they held out against Kurdish militia, tribal irregulars and Turkish forces for three months, but at elevations of 10,000–14,000 feet, they soon would freeze. And the Kurds were determined to starve them out. There had been a terrible famine since the summer, and the hundreds of thousands of sheep and cows that the Assyrians required for sustenance were gone – stolen by the Kurds. At least 2,000 Assyrians died and over 500 were taken captive[55] while they waited for the promised Russian support, which never materialized.

By September 1915, 25,000 starving Assyrians had gathered in one camp. In the region there once were 100,000 stranded Assyrians, but the Turks had hunted down many of them. By September, 30,000 Turkish regulars and Kurds armed with modern weapons were striking the Nestorian villages of the Hakkari Mountains. Jezirah, on the border with Syria,[56] once had about 2,000 Christians. The Chaldean dioceses had about 5,000. In August and September, all of the adult men were murdered, the women and children locked up in a church, extorted for money, raped and tortured. According to other reports, 4,750 Armenians were killed there, but that number probably is the sum of all the Christians. The Tiyari district was set on fire. From one group of 40 villages, only 17 people escaped.

Finally, 'In two groups, 35,000 mountain Assyrians reached the Salamas plateau in Persia in August and in September/October, 1915.'[57] Thus the patriarch led the mountain Assyrians, destitute and starving, down a perilous route to the plains of Salmas. The Kurds attacked them all the way, and at the end, 15,000–20,000 destitute Armenians and Assyrians made it to Salmas. How many died in the mountains will never be known.

A war correspondent described the flight:[58] 'At the end of September, 25,000 mountain Nestorians from the Tkhuma, Baz and Tiari regions, who had been fighting with the Kurds all summer and had to flee for lack of ammunition, came pouring into the plain led by their Patriarch, Mar Shimun.' The refugees died at a rapid rate from hunger, typhus and dysentery, and in February 1916, the numbers were swelled by the addition of 5,000 to 6,000 more refugees from surrounding villages. An estimated 30,000 Assyrians and Armenians languished in critical condition in Salmas.

We might ask why the patriarch was the one to lead his people to war. Mar Shimun was not just an ecclesiastical leader; he also was the temporal leader of the Assyrians. Like an Old Testament figure, he descended the mountain one night with a few aides to ask the Russians to save his people, and when that failed, he ascended again with one servant[59] knowing he would have to lead the Assyrians down to safety.

How many Assyrians were attacked in eastern Turkey, the Hakkari region and northern Persia in 1915–16? Almost all the towns and villages have heart-breaking stories, but we will try to give a sense of the devastation by focusing on a few. The reader should understand that many, many other towns have an equal claim to be remembered. Several writers, notably Gaunt, have described them, village by village, city by city.

The village of Gulpashan used to be one of the wealthiest in the Persian plain of Urmia. In February a band of Persians invaded the village, chopped the men to pieces, mutilated their bodies and butchered them in the cemetery. Some were tied up with their heads sticking through the rungs of a ladder and decapitated. The women were handed out as gifts to Turks, Kurds and Persians. According to the *New York Times*, 'sixty-five refugees, taken from the French and American missions, have been hanged on gibbets erected in the mission yards.'[60] The United States protested vigorously, but too late.[61]

The Turkish town of Kharput (Harput, Kharpert), located northeast of Urfa and north of Diyarbakir, is on the banks of the Euphrates. One third of its population, 5,000–6,000 people, once was Syrian Orthodox. In 1895–96 over 36,000 Armenians and Assyrians were murdered there, thousands burned and 5,000 raped.[62] In May 1915, the arrests and butchery began again. Starting on the first of June, women, girls and children were forced to leave Kharput, but on the way Arabs and Kurds robbed, stripped, violated and murdered them in an orgy of debauchery. Out of one convoy of 2500, only 600 arrived alive[63] in Der-el-Zor (Deir Ezzor, now in Syria). Other convoys from adjacent villages brought the total number deported to 18,000. Of these, one hundred and fifty women and children reached Aleppo alive.

On July 1, 2,000 Armenian and Assyrian soldiers from the Turkish army were dispatched from Kharput, purportedly to build roads. Every one of them was murdered in cold blood, the bodies thrown in a cave.[64] On July 7, 800–2000 starving soldiers were pushed onto the road from Kharput to Diyarbakir, and soon afterward several hundred more were forced out. In both cases, the

Kurds poured down from the mountains to massacre all of them. Even the Kurdish women attacked them, with butcher knives.[65]

Two Syriac Orthodox villages in Diyarbakir Province, Ain Warda and Azekh, mounted a massive defense. Ain Warda[66] withstood a 52 day siege before surrendering, but all the inhabitants were betrayed and killed in the end. This proved, quotes the author, 'que le traître avec son ruse fait plus que le héros valeureux avec sa force,' meaning, 'the traiter with his ruse does more than the valorous hero with his force.' Azekh fought off the Turks and Kurds from August 1915 to November, when the last attackers withdrew.[67]

During this savagery, Turkish gendarmes ransacked homes and churches, beat priests, stripped women naked, whipped them with branches, and competed among themselves to devise the best means of torture. Sometimes they used bastinado – beating the soles of the feet with a thin rod until it becomes unbearable. From others they pulled out eyebrows, beard, fingernails and toenails. Some they branded with hot irons, horseshoed, even crucified. One Turk told Morgenthau that they searched the records of the Spanish Inquisition for ever more creative methods of torture.[68]

Nothing changes in the Middle East. Things just like this happen today.

Again a forerunner of today, Morgenthau writes that from April to October 1915 the highways of Asia Minor were crowded with unearthly bands of exiles. Over six months some 1,200,000 people moved toward the Syrian Desert. Any gendarmes who accompanied them demanded protection money; each change of guard brought new extortions. Turkish peasants, Kurds, brigands, and the gendarmes all attacked them on the road. When they came to a well, gendarmes often barred them from drinking. An Armenian colleague of my husband sent a translation of the testimony taped by her Armenian grandmother, describing her experiences as a girl. It is chilling.[69]

De Courtois describes the two waves of onslaughts in the Tur Abdin district of Turkey.[70] The first, on the town of Midyat and eight adjacent villages, was in June 1915, at the same time as the attacks on Mardin and Diyarbakir; the next was in 1917, on five villages. The victims were Catholic and Jacobite priests and thousands of Jacobite parishioners, often several hundred per village. The sadism was shocking. People were burned to death in their churches and houses, clergy flayed alive, unspeakable acts committed on women. Small children were abducted and forcibly converted. In 1915, there were 5,693 Syriac Christian houses in the 79 villages of Tur Abdin. In 1987, 1,032 were left. Forty-eight villages had no Christian homes at all by 1987.[71]

The Chaldean town of Seert (Sairt, Siirt) was close to Tur Abdin, not far from to Diyarbakir. It had an archbishop's residence, and it was surrounded by thirty or more Chaldean villages. Rhetore estimated that before the massacres it held over 60,000 Christians: 25,000 Armenians, 20,000 Jacobites and 15,000 Chaldeans, Syriac Catholics or Nestorians. The first Kurdish attack was in April. Between May and June 1915, Djevdjet Bey, the barbarous governor of Van, sent 8,000 soldiers, called 'The Butchers' Battalion,' to Seert and the surrounding villages to exact revenge for the Russian defeat of the Turks at Sarikimash. In a murderous frenzy, they mowed down as many as 7,000–8,000.[72] On one hillside alone, they shot 767 men.[73] One hundred straggled into Mosul, barely alive.

In neighboring Bitlis on June 25, 1915, the Butcher's Battalion massacred thousands inside the town cathedral, along with three priests. One witness wrote that they presented 1000 women and girls to each other.[74] The Kurds repeatedly assaulted them, stripped them and hacked them to death.

From 1916 until the Russian Revolution in October 1917, the Russians maintained an umbrella of protection for the Assyrians and Chaldeans who lived in Persia west of Lake Urmia. Despite his brother's murder when he tried to ally his Assyrians with the Russians in the spring of 1915, in January, 1916 Patriarch Benjamin Shimun XIX met the Tsar, who requested that Assyrian auxiliary battalions help him with a planned advance into Turkey. The Tsar promised to give Russian equipment to 2,000 Assyrians, and that Russian officers would provide them with military training.[75] As a result, between 1916 and 1918, Assyrians participated in fourteen successful expeditions against the Kurds. Even after the revolution, Armenians and Assyrians worked with the Russians. In all, 4,000 Assyrians served in four battalions, under the command of Agha Petros, the patriarch or the patriarch's brother.

After the Russian Revolution, the Russians abandoned any attempt to protect Urmia and Salmas. In 1918, the Assyrians suffered an assault by Turkish divisions from the north, south and west, and to the east their back was up against Lake Urmia. This is when the

British pressured the Assyrians and the Kurdish chief Ismail Agha, known as Simko, to enter into an alliance with them. It also is when the British 'Capt. Gracey undertook to furnish immediately the funds necessary for the payment of the troops and non-commissioned officers. For the future he promised, 'the proclamation of the independence of the Assyrian nation.'[76] To be perfectly clear, the British promised that they would support Assyrian statehood if the Assyrians fought as mercenaries for them against the Muslims. We will see how that worked out at the post-war peace conferences.

In February 1918, the British general Dunsterville arrived in Hamadan, now in northwest Iran. Through an envoy, he promised Assyrians and Armenians support and equipment if they would stay in Urmia to help the British, and he offered to send them a small contingent of British troops. The 25,000 Assyrian soldiers were equipped with leftover Russian arms and ammunition and 20,000 French rifles.[77] That same February, the Persians requested they surrender their arms and attacked them in Urmia. The Assyrians proudly tell how, under Agha Petros, they held out bravely through six major battles. Some observers claimed that what they actually did was savagely pillage Kurdish and Azeri villages. At any rate, until the Brest-Litovsk Treaty ended the war in March 1918, the Assyrians held off Kurds, Germans and two divisions of Turks.

In a chilling example of treachery, on March 16, 1918, Simko invited the Assyrian Patriarch Shemon (Mar Shimun) XIX Benjamin to his home, welcoming the patriarch, his British military escort and a Russian officer with typical Middle Eastern courtesies. As soon as the patriarch walked out of the door, Kurdish sharpshooters assassinated him, along with his bodyguards.[78] In revenge, the Assyrians killed at least 500 Kurds. Meanwhile, 3,500 Assyrians from the Tkhuma tribe had taken shelter in Khoi, where the Kurds went to massacre 2,700 Assyrians and as many Armenians, some of the goriest of all the massacres.[79] In April 1918, the Turks took Van, and the Assyrians under Agha Petros took over 500 Turkish prisoners. By June, Assyrians still were fighting, but the Turks had trapped 50,000 in Urmia.

Armegeddon began in July. With the addition of refugees from Salmas, 70,000 to 80,000 Christians were gathered in Urmia, many dying of cholera, the rest waiting for the British arms that Captain Gracy had promised. Some 10,000 of them had headed to

Russia. Suddenly one day a British plane landed and 'delivered the gladsome news that the British expedition would arrive in Sayen Kala, Persia, within two weeks, with arms of all kinds and abundant ammunition, and that an Assyrian expedition should be dispatched to meet the former and return together to Urmia.' Thus the Assyrians were to rendezvous with the British in Sain Kala (Sayen Kala).[80]

Agha Petros took 1,000 to 2,000 Assyrians with him, but Turks, Kurds and Persians attacked the whole way. He managed to fight his way through to Sain Kala in one week, but by then the British had left. Now the Assyrians and Armenians in Urmia heard that the advance party had been defeated, and they panicked. On July 31, the Turks pounced. The Christians, feeling betrayed by the British and by Agha Petro,[81] plunged into a leaderless flight south, helter-skelter, with Kurds, Turks, and Persians in pursuit. On August 3, they reached Sain Kala and began a fateful 19-day trek to Hamadan.[82]

In an orgy of violence, the Muslim forces took them away in groups to use for target practice. Some had their throats cut just half-way across, others were clubbed, buried alive, dismembered or subjected to other unspeakable tortures. The women were treated fiendishly. One escapee said these surpassed the most harrowing atrocities perpetrated by anyone in Turkey or Persia. At least 15,000 bodies were left unburied, scattered along the way.[83]

Rev. Werda gives a lurid description of what happened in Urmia after this ill-fated exodus. Several thousand Christians sought shelter in the American and the French missions. Amid surging riots, the missions were plundered and the refugees within slaughtered *en masse*. Werda believed that 16,000–17,000 were killed within 48 hours. No more than 300 survived, hiding until the American Consul could transfer them to Tabriz.

Of the 70,000 Assyrians who left Urmia, fewer than 50,000 made the 500 miles to Hamadan, arriving on August 21. The British moved them into a refugee camp in Bakuba, Iraq, and this is where Patriarch Paulus Mar Shimun died, to be replaced by his 13 year old nephew, Ishai Mar Shimun.

British writers admit that their countrymen betrayed the Assyrians, a people they would later call 'Our smallest ally.'[84] This was an ally who stood up valiantly against Turks and Germans on the

Persian frontier between March and July 1918, an ally who the Muslims hated as British agents.

The Nestorians lost their ancestral home in 1918. They had lived in the Hakkari and Urmia regions for a millennium. The site of their patriarchal see now is a wasteland, their abandoned church crumbling. A group of sixteen American bishops said 'the Apostolic Church of the East appeared to have been entirely wiped out... lost altogether by the end of the War about two-thirds of their total number.'[85] In truth, the losses defy any attempt to quantify.

Father Rhetore tabulates census numbers by Christian confession and vilayet.[86] Adding up the columns for Mardin and for the surrounding villages, his table shows a total of 74,705 Christians living in the *sanjak* of Mardin before 1915–16: 10,500 Armenians, 3,850 Syrian Catholics, 7,870 Chaldeans, 51,725 'Jacobites' and 525 Protestants. After 1916, 47,675 disappeared and 26,795 remained. The survivors included 300 Armenians, 22,000 Syrians, 1,070 Chaldeans and 3,150 Syrian Catholics.

Father Rhetore[87] gave the pre-1915 population of the vilayet of Diyarbakir as 174,670: 72,500 Armenians, 84,725 Syriacs (non Catholic or Jacobite), 11,120 Chaldeans and 5,600 Syrian Catholics. After 1915–16, he reports that 30,485 remained: 3,000 Armenians, 24,000 Syriacs, 1,110 Chaldeans and 2,150 Syrian Catholics.

That would mean 69,500 Armenians were murdered, along with 10,010 Chaldeans, 3,450 Syrian Catholics and 60,725 other Syriacs. In the 278 villages of Diyarbakir province, Rhetore estimates that 95% of the Armenians, 90% of the Chaldeans, 71% of the Jacobites and 61% of the Syrian Catholics were killed. The latter two groups are the Assyrians.

Wilmshurst writes that where the Chaldeans lived next to the Armenians in Turkey, two-thirds of the Chaldeans were lost between 1915 and 1916. In northern Iraq they fared better than the Assyrians, but in Van, Diyarbakir, Seert, Gazarta, Mardin and Salmas, their number went from 33,840 Chaldeans in 1913 to only 4,500 left in 1928.[88] Gaunt quotes the numbers submitted to the Paris Peace Conference: 250,000 Assyro-Chaldeans lost in battle or massacred between 1914 and 1919.[89]

An American professor of political science, R. J. Rummel,[90] presents carefully constructed tables, statistical analyses, and calculations of Christians lost before, during and after World War I through genocide. He calculates that before World War I about

5,000 Armenians and Greeks were killed. During the war, between 300,000 and 2,686,000 were killed, the mid-range being 1,404,000. He estimates 84,000 Greeks were killed pre-war. During the war and the genocides of 1915, he calculates that the Young Turks killed 1,883,000 Armenians, Greeks, Nestorians and other Christians. Since he figures that Nestorians represented one fifth of the total, it would mean that 376,600 Nestorians were murdered during the war years, a high number.

Rummel calculates that post-war, 665,000–1,156,000 Armenians and Greeks were murdered, but he does not break out separate numbers for Nestorians. If one again calculates that one-fifth were Nestorian, that means 133,000–231,000 Nestorians (Assyrians) were murdered post-war, but he does not confirm whether he still would use the 1/5 ratio. If so, the totals for the war years and the post-war years would be higher than most estimates. He concludes that in 1894–1923 the Ottoman Empire murdered from 3,500,000 to over 4,300,000 Armenians, Greeks, Nestorians, and other Christians.

Donobed writes that in June 1920, 26,000 Assyrian and 14,000 Armenian refugees were in the British camps in Baquba (Baqubah), now in the Diayala Province of Iraq.[91] Three to five million emigrated to Syria, Lebanon, Europe, North America, South America, Australia or New Zealand, but many did not leave. From 1922 to 1925, trouble came back to Hakkari, the Hakkari Massacres.

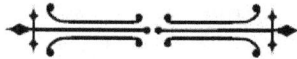

POST-WORLD WAR I

Many nations came to the Paris Peace Conference in Versailles of 1919, all of them cherishing their own hopes and dreams. The Armenians wanted a free, independent Armenia. The Kurds dreamed of a homeland of their own, and so did the Assyro-Chaldeans, both on the same land. The Jews still hoped for the land the Balfour Declaration had promised them on November 2, 1917, and the British promised the Hashemite dynasty a kingdom that would overlap the same land. The French and the British hoped to maintain the spheres of influence they had carved out in the Sykes-Picot Agreement of 1916, but Ataturk intended to keep all of Turkey intact. Meanwhile the British were juggling furiously, because they had promised so many people the same lands, and they knew there was a massive oil field near Mosul, just waiting for them.

WHAT ABOUT AN ASSYRIAN HOMELAND?

The post-war peace conferences should have been an opportunity for the Assyrians and Chaldeans to obtain war reparations, to secure international guarantees of safety for their villages, perhaps even to obtain their own autonomous area in their ancestral homeland. Yet, the politics were against them. Of all the supplicants, they were among the smallest. Of all the areas that anyone wanted to claim, this was the one where the British hoped to strike oil. The claimants for this same land were the British, the Kurds, the nascent state of Iraq and the Turks. What happened to the Assyrians in these conferences would be a forerunner of what would happen repeatedly in the future. We will see the bureaucratic obstacles that were thrown before them, the perfidy of the British and the nonsensical proposals on their behalf that supposedly serious men bandied about.

171

Assyro-Chaldean delegations represented four churches: the Syrian Orthodox, Syrian Catholics, Assyrian Church of the East and Chaldean Catholics. They also were organized regionally. The Iranian (Transcaucasia) delegation never managed to participate. The British blocked them. The Mesopotamian delegation was led by Surma Khanim, sister of the late Patriarch Benyamin Shimun and aunt of the current Patriarch Eshai, but the British stopped her too, detaining her in London until it was too late.

Her presentation would have demanded reparation from the Turks, guarantees of security for Assyrians, release of all Christian captives, punishment of criminals who were responsible for recent atrocities and resettlement of the Assyrians in Hakkari.

Rev. Joel E. Werda led the American Diaspora delegation. They planned to petition for an autonomous Assyrian territory in northern Mesopotamia, which would be north of the Lower Zab River, from Diyarbakir to Armenia, with access to the sea.[1] He never received permission to submit this petition in the name of America, because President Wilson thought it important to maintain the territorial integrity of Turkey.

The Paris Peace Conference created the League of Nations, and it negotiated the Treaty of Versailles, signed in June 28, 1919. This created a British mandate over Iraq, Transjordan and Palestine, a French mandate over Syria and Lebanon, a French sphere of influence over Anatolia and a Greek occupation of Smyrna, resulting in a war in 1920. Armenia had declared its independence in 1918, but it became a Soviet Socialist Republic in 1920.

Since the Assyrians were shut out of the Paris Peace Conference, Agha Petros submitted a series of letters with proposals for an autonomous state. The British connived to have him exiled him to France.

Stafford presents the British take on the proceedings.[2] After the Assyrians were denied audience at the Paris Peace Conference, Mar Shimun wrote a letter requesting that the Assyrians remain under British protection. In the letter he defines the traditional territory of the Assyrians as extending as 'far north in Kurdistan as the line from Bashkala to Bitlis, and as far west as Jezirat Ibn Omar. To the north of this line the Christians are generally Armenian, and to the west of it of the "West Syrian" or "Jacobites" communion.'

Stafford says that during the summer the Assyrians requested a British protectorate within this Mosul-Jezirah-Bashkala-Urmiyah territory, border areas of Turkey, Iraq and Iran. They also asked that the Persian Government guarantee the security of their Assyrian subjects and resettle them around Urmia. They further requested return of the grazing grounds traditionally used by the mountain Assyrians. Stafford points out that this same land was the contemplated home of a future Kurdish nation.

A conference in San Remo, April, 1920, took up the border issue in the context of negotiations about oil. While the Assyrians were struggling to be heard, the British were looking at a 1919 survey that they knew predicted rich oil fields would be found in the Mosul region. The imminent 1921 Report on Palestine and Mesopotamian Oil showed a very high probability of striking oil. Though the oil strike did not come until 1927, at San Remo Britain promised Iraq 25% equity in the future profits of a new Turkish Petroleum Company. In return, Iraq was supposed to detach Mosul from the French sphere of influence, where it was placed in the secret Sykes-Picot agreement of 1917.

In San Remo, Bishop Aphrem Barsoum submitted a memorandum on behalf of the patriarch, requesting that the Assyrians be allowed to settle in their ancestral land in the upper valleys of the Tigris and Euphrates rivers, also in the vilayets of Diyarbakir, Bitlis, Kharput and Urfa in Turkey. He protested against the establishment of an independent Kurdish state in that territory, demanded compensation for Assyrian losses during the war and asked for guarantees of Assyrian safety in the region.

Of importance to the Jews, it was decided at the conference to incorporate the Balfour Declaration into Britain's mandate for Palestine. This meant that Britain was responsible 'for putting into effect the declaration made on the 8th [sic.] November 1917 by the British Government and adopted by the other Allied Powers, in favor of the establishment in Palestine of a national home for the Jewish people; it being clearly understood that nothing should be done which may prejudice the civil and religious rights of existing non-Jewish communities in Palestine, or the rights and political status enjoyed by Jews in any other country.'[3] Especially with many of the Arab suppicants for statehood coming away empty-handed, this set the stage for future resentments and conflict.

On August 10, 1920, the Treaty of Sevres ratified the agreements made at the San Remo Conference. In it, the principal parties paid lip service to the principle of self-determination for Arabs, Armenians and Kurds. Stafford writes that 'The least important were the Assyrians, and they were not accorded autonomy.' The Treaty confirmed the French and British mandates and created the autonomous nations of Syria and Iraq out of the defunct Ottoman Empire. Mosul was awarded to a British Mandate.

Stafford reports that the treaty anticipated an autonomous Kurdistan with 'full safe-guards for the protection of the Assyro-Chaldean and other racial and religious minorities.'[4] This was an empty letter. Mustapha Kemal 'Ataturk' was in power, and nobody was going to cut out a large territory from his country. When the Arab State of Iraq was formally established in 1921, as Stafford drily writes, 'All hopes of an independent Armenia or Kurdistan were clearly at an end.' The Treaty of Sevres was never ratified, and it was replaced by the Treaty of Lausanne.

Throughout all these conferences, Britain remained disingenuous about its interest in oil. As late as January 1923 at the Conference of Lausanne, Lord Curzon claimed 'It is supposed and alleged that the attitude of the British Government to the vilayet of Mosul is affected by the question of oil. The question of the oil of the Mosul vilayet has nothing to do with my argument. I have presented the case on its own merits and quite independently of any natural resources that may be in the country. I do not know how much oil there may be in the neighborhood of Mosul, or whether it can be worked at a profit or whether it may turn out after all to have been a fraud.'[5] Harrumph.

The Lausanne Conference opened in 1922 with vigorous protests from Turkey over losing Mosul. Again the Assyrians were unable to participate directly. Aga Petros was the titular head of an Assyro-Chaldean delegation, but he was barred from participation after the opening ceremony. Instead, he submitted a letter asking for an Assyrian homeland extending from the Tigris to the Zab River, to include Mount Sinjar.[6] The territorial claims that the Assyrians and Chaldeans submitted to these conferences were similar.

The main negotiation at Lausanne was between Britain, France and Turkey, and it was over the Nineveh Plain. This was the plain whose potential oil deposits had no influence on Britain, according to Lord Curzon. A lengthy quote from the report of The

Special Commission of the League of Nations[7] shows that the British had submitted a plan for repatriating the Assyrians, but that Kurdish resistance rendered it impossible. The Commission attributed the poor relations between Assyrians and Muslims to 'the lack of tact displayed by the Assyrians themselves, who are of a warlike temper and...somewhat rough manners.' Indeed. Or maybe they just took offense because the Muslims had killed half to two-thirds of their friends, neighbors and families.

The Treaty of Lausanne was signed on July 24, 1923, setting the borders of modern Turkey and abolishing foreign spheres of influence. Agha Petros, the head of the Assyro-Chaldean delegation, proposed that Turkey grant Hakkari to the Assyrians, and he promised that the Chaldeans living in the Mosul area would ask for Mosul to be annexed to Turkey.[8] In an exchange of cables with Ankara, it was apparent that the Turks did not look with favor on this proposal, nor did they have good memories of their last encounter with Agha Petros when he was the leader of Assyrian fighters in the mountains. The full border dispute was referred to the League of Nations.

A Special Commission of the League of Nations report[9] referenced a May 1924 conference in Constantinople, where Britain had proposed part of northern Iraq for an Assyrian homeland, but would not offer a British protectorate. They did tout 'advantages that Iraq would derive from having on its northern frontier a warlike people united to the Arab state by ties of friendship and gratitude.'[10] Iraq agreed, but the local population was opposed. In September 1924 the Hakkari Massacres would make this matter moot.

The British admitted to the League that the 'small Assyrian people, in the very early days of the Great War, determined to espouse the cause of the Allies and to seize the opportunity to break away from the rule of those whom their past history had led them to regard as their persistent oppressors. They endured great sufferings as the result of this decision.' Nevertheless, 'His Majesty's Government cannot, for various reasons, contemplate so grave an extension of its responsibilities. While therefore, not prepared to respond to their aspirations in full, His Majesty's Government has decided to endeavour to secure a good treaty frontier, which will at the same time admit of the establishment of the Assyrians in a compact community within the limits of the territory in respect of which His Majesty's Government holds a Mandate...'[11] In short, the British admitted their debt to the Assyrians, acknowledged the sacrifices the Assyrians had made, and refused a protectorate.

In a Sept. 5, 1924 memorandum, the Turks complained that a massed settlement of Assyrians along the border could be used aggressively against Kurds and Turks. They asked why the Assyrians could not be settled further south in the Mesopotamian lowlands. The Assyrians furnished the British with the answer – they were used to mountain air. In malarial swamps, the Assyrians experienced a mortality of 30% among adults, 50% among children.[12]

In 1945, Mar Eshai Shimun presented the Assyrian National Petition to the World Security Conference in San Francisco. In it he summarized the arguments that Britain made to the League of Nations in 1925: 'the strongest argument presented by the British in their claim was that since the Assyrian nation had been dispossessed of their homeland by the Turks, they must be recompensed by a similar settlement within the Mosul Vilayet. It was upon this understanding that the League of Nations awarded the Mosul Vilayet to Iraq rather than to Turkey, acting on the advice of the League of Nations 1925 Inquiry Commission.' In other words, Britain used the Assyrian request for a homeland as a tool to get Mosul – and the nearby oil fields – added to the British Mandate in Iraq.

This was despite more than one clear statement of the British obligations to the Assyrians. The Assyrian National Petition quotes a letter written by the British Colonel McCarthy to the Assyrians, admitting that 'your people were definitely promised by me…that they would have their country restored to them and that my orders and only reason for raising the Assyrian contingent in Hamadan in 1918 was to drive the Turk out and reoccupy the country.'

The Petition gives the League of Nations 1925 Inquiry Commission response: 'It is not our duty to enumerate all the conditions that would have to be imposed on the sovereign state for the protection of these minorities. We feel it our duty, however, to point out that the Assyrians should be guaranteed the re-establishment of the ancient privileges which they possessed in practice, if not officially, before the War.' 'Whichever may be the sovereign state, it ought to grant these Assyrians certain local autonomy, recognizing their rights to appoint their own officials and contenting itself with a tribute from them, paid through the agency of their Patriarch.'

The League of Nations appointed a new fact-finding Commission in 1925 to revisit both the British and the Turkish claims for Mosul. By then, Mosul was part of Iraq, and Britain had a 25-year British Mandate over it. As for the Assyrians, the League claimed that the question of settling them north of the vilayet of Mosul was never raised at Lausanne, in flat-footed disregard of the letters from Agha Petros. The League claimed that the matter came up first at Constantinople in 1924. Anyhow, by the time the Commission met, the Turks had begun massacring the Assyrians in Hakkari.

In the end the Commission refused the request for an autonomous Assyrian homeland. Their reasoning reflects Turkey's efforts to conceal the 1915 genocide. Still today, Turkey battles all foreign attempts to call their actions genocide, making strong threats to prevent any act of a parliament or of Congress on the matter. In 1925, their propaganda produced this sadly laughable statement about the Assyrians: 'There is no doubt that this people rose in armed revolt against its lawful government at the instigation of foreigners and without any provocation on the part of the Turkish authorities…Under these circumstances it would hardly be fair to take from Turkey a territory which indisputably belongs to her in order to settle in that territory a people that deliberately took up arms against its sovereign.'[13] Without any provocation?

The last blow to the possibility of a post-war settlement of Assyrians in Hakkari was 'an official communication from the Turkish Consul-General at Baghdad on June 25th, 1928, stating that "the Turkish amnesty law did not cover the Assyrians, who would not be permitted in any circumstances to enter Turkey; [and] that any Assyrians who attempted to enter Turkey would be punished".'[14] Not only did the Turks prevent future Assyrian resettlement by this 1928 edict, they had been trying hard to cleanse their territory of the existing Assyrians since 1924.

THE HAKKARI AND SIMELE MASSACRES

In the absence of practical results from the post-war conferences, many Assyrians simply headed home. Nobody led them. There was no leadership. After Patriarch Mar Shimun (Shimun) died, his brother was not well, and he died at age 30 in 1920. Their successor, an 11 year old nephew, Eshai, became Shimun XXI Eshai in 1920, but he was a child. In lieu of a patriarch, they fell back on

Agha Petros, who once had worked in America as a carpet sales-
man.

In October, 1919, 24,579 Assyrians and 14,612 Armenians
were housed in two Iraqi refugee camps. Two thirds were from
Hakkari, most of the rest from Urmia.[15] When the camps closed in
1921, most of the refugees from Urmia went home. Between 1924
and 1928, about 15,500 refugees moved to Kurdish regions of
northern Iraq.[16] Most of the Tiyari and Tokhuma tribesmen of
Hakkari moved back to their traditional homes, but they would not
stay for long.

In 1918 the British enlisted young men from the Baquba
camp into an Assyrian Army,[17] called the Assyrian Levies, and they
employed these Levies to break a Kurdish rebellion in Amidiye.
Many Assyrians had resettled uneventfully in Hakkari, but the Levies turned the surrounding Turks hostile. By October 1922 some
4,000–6,000 Assyrians had served in either the infantry or the cavalry of the Levies, usually 2,500 at a time.[18] In 1922 they put down
three Kurdish uprisings, earning praise from the British and a reputation for invincibility. When they were disbanded four years later,
the British gave out arms and ammunition, causing the surrounding
population to become even more suspicious.

In his 1945 Assyrian National Petition, the patriarch quoted
Lt. Col. Sir Arnold Wilson on the Assyrian Levies 'By the admission of the then Civil Commissioner in Iraq: It was the Assyrian
force that saved the swamping of our rule in the Arab revolt and it
was they who (as the C.O. in the field, Colonel Cameron, declared)
rolled back the Turkish invasion of Iraq in 1922 and 1923 at a time
when the Iraqi troops were utterly unfit to take the field themselves.'[19] Once again, the British acknowledged their debt to the
Assyrians, even if they never repaid it.

It all started in May 1924 in Kirkuk. Muslim villagers taunted
some Assyrian Levies, and the Levies fired wildly on them.[20] When
Vail Hail Rift Bey, the governor of Hakkari, arrived on an inspec-
tion tour on August 7, 1924, the Assyrians ambushed and wounded
him, also killing part of his escort. In September 1924, the new
president of Turkey, Mustafa Kemal 'Ataturk,' sent in more than
1000 Arabs and irregulars, allegedly to quell a 'Nestorian Assyrian
uprising.' This was the beginning of the Hakkari Massacres.

One of the attackers was Ismail Simko, the same Kurdish
chief who had assassinated Patriarch Mar Shimun so treacherously

in 1918. The carnage and deportations of September 1925 amount-
ed to ethnic cleansing.[21]

When it began, most of the Assyrian fighters were unavailable
to defend their people because 70% of them were working in the
Levies for the British. On September 9, 1924, the Turks mobilized
their regular army.[22] On September 14, English planes bombed
Turkish divisions that had crossed into Iraq. Some Assyrians escaped to Diyarbakir. Others hid in caves. On September 17, army
troops and local tribes killed 600 Assyrians, claiming they had
struck first.

On September 22 and 23, some Assyrians tried to leave their
caves, and a group that went out for water was killed. Some escaped to Amadiye. By September 24, only a handful of women and
children were left. The Turks reported back to headquarters that
500 armed Assyrians had come back from Amadiye to plunder and
burn down villages. In another report this number was inflated to
5,000.

The British issued an ultimatum that Turkish troops must
withdraw from Iraq or else, with no effect. On October 19, 1924
the League of Nations forced Turkey to withdraw, but it would not
be for long.

Donef has assembled extensive documentation of the massacre.[23] In December 1925, a Chaldean priest in Zakho wrote that on
September 26, 1925 a Chaldean priest was arrested; his beard was
torn off, and he was left to die of starvation. Ottoman troops assaulted 20,000 Christians in the mountain villages of the Tiyari dis-
tract, extorted money and deported over 8,000, along with their
cattle, food, and all their belongs. Of these, one quarter escaped to
Zakho. Some 4,000 became refugees in Mosul.

A plague of locusts had ruined the harvest and caused a famine that year. The people who made it to Mosul had been forced to
walk over steep mountains for five days in the cold without food or
drink, some nearly naked. At least a third died on the way. In some
villages they traversed, Christian women were marketed freely and
children were sold for as little as a basket of grapes or a chicken.
Along the way, guards took away the more attractive women at
night and returned them in the morning. The priest writes that they
were 'subjected to despicable acts which I cannot talk about.'

This happened just as the Mosul question came up at the
League of Nations.[24] The September 1925 meeting of the Council

of the League received a commission report describing how Turkish troops attacked Chaldeans 'occupied the villages and obtained delivery of all arms, imposed severe fines, demanded women, pillaged houses, and subjected the inhabitants to atrocious acts of violence, going as far as to massacre.'

The November 23, 1925[25] report said that at least 8,000 Assyrians had been deported, and some 3,000 of them became refugees. The report stated that Turkish soldiers had been extorting money from villagers since March 1925, before they assassinated them. The report continues. From Billo, a village of seventy families, at least 220 people became refugees in Zakho, and 370 were deported to Turkey. Baijo, a village of two hundred houses, once had been one of the richest in the area. By November 1, some 348 of its inhabitants were refugees in Zakho, and 550 had been deported to Turkey. Alto, a village of ten families, was starved for several days, then all of the inhabitants were deported. From Marga, a village of two hundred houses, 970 refugees ended up in Iraq, 860 as deportees in Turkey. The League was perfectly aware of what had happened.

In December 1925, two telegrams from an Estonian envoy to Mosul reported that he found 3,000 Christian refugees from Turkey there, and more arrived each day, 'after shocking atrocities.' Turkish documents blandly reported that all Assyrian villages in the disputed area had been evacuated in response to Nestorian attacks. Donef gives an excerpt from the December 12 meeting of the Turkish National Assembly: 'In any case the Christians in question were spies, brigands, and traitors, and the Nestorians, aided and abetted by the British government had kidnapped the families of Turkish officers.'[26] This was a shameless lie.

Thus, it was with complete knowledge of the facts that, on December 15, 1925, the League voted unanimously to give Mosul to Iraq and not to extend the northern frontier of Iraq into Hakkari to provide the territory the British had requested for an Assyrian homeland.

In 1926–1931 all of northern Iraq and southeast Turkey were heavily populated with Kurds. Despite that, the British again proposed that Turkey cede the territories of the Tiyari, Tkhuma, Baz and Jilu tribes to Iraq for Assyrian resettlement. Since this would not resettle them as a homogenous community, even the Assyrians objected. Stafford claims that the British had placed all but 300 families in new homes, but they kept complaining about the lease arrangements, the malarial lowlands and the British in general.

In September 1929, the British announced that they would terminate their Mandate early. In June, 1932, the remaining Levies mutinied and resigned, fearing their fate in an independent Iraq. The 21-year old Patriarch Mar Shimun brought them back by negotiating an Assyrian National Pact that demanded that Assyrians be recognized as a *millet*, that their Hakkari homes be restored, and that they be given a new national home in Iraq with headquarters in Dohuk. It continued that 'A commission should be formed to provide suitable lands, necessary funds should be provided [and] the lands should be registered in the name of the Assyrians.' This was at a time when 60,000 Kurds and 14,000 Assyrians lived in Mosul province. In October 1932, the Mandate ended, and Mar Shimun took his demands to Geneva. By May, 1933 he was under house arrest in Baghdad.[27]

Meanwhile, King Feisal was in London, and rumors about the Assyrians were rife. 'Officials surmised that a fabricated enemy of alien origin, speaking a barbaric tongue and adhering to an antiquated religion they held in common with the foreign British, could stem Kurdish and Shiite insurgent tendencies and turn their focus to an enemy common to all.'[28] In an angry exchange of letters, the Minister of Interior refused to recognize Mar Shimun as the temporal authority of Assyrians, and Mar Shimun refused to cooperate with a British expert on land settlement. In August he was expelled to Cyprus.

In the Assyrian National Petition, the Patriarch wrote: 'On August 18th, 1933, I was de-nationalized without trial and deported from Iraq to the Island of Cyprus in the Mediterranean. After great efforts I was able to secure a permit from the British Government, which enabled me to proceed to Geneva, and plead the Assyrian case before the League of Nations. My earnest plea for an inquiry commission to be sent to Iraq to investigate the facts leading to the massacre and the existing situation of the Assyrians was ignored.'[29]

The Patriarch explained: 'The climax came during a meeting held in Mosul on the 10th day of July, 1933, when the Mutasarif (Governor) and his British adviser, Col. R. F. Stafford, told the Assyrian leaders to either submit to the policy which the government had decided for them – which was contrary to the letter and spirit of the homogeneous settlement recommended by the League of Nations – or else leave Iraq. The Assyrians did leave Iraq.'[30]

Stafford gives the British view,[31] saying that Tremma Yacu (Yaqo), the son of Malik Ismail of the Upper Tiyari tribe, betrayed the patriarch, gathered a large number of armed retainers and began swaggering about Dohuk. Stafford claims to have held a series of meetings to calm injured feelings on both sides. Donobed gives the Assyrian view – that the British had deliberately provoked friction between the 27,500-strong pro-patriarch faction and the anti-patriarch faction represented by Yacu.

Suddenly in July 14–18, 1933, Yacu and one Malik Loco moved an armed force across the Tigris into Syria, surrendered their arms to the French and requested land in the Khabur basin. According to Stafford, Yacu and Loco sent word to the villages of Dohuk telling them to come to Syria and saying that the French had promised them land free of taxation for five years. They also said that the Iraqi government was about to disarm them. Stafford writes that all this was false.

According to Donabed, Yacu wrote his people to stay home. By the end of July, several hundred Assyrian men had crossed the Tigris, leaving their families in their villages. Iraqi troops who were waiting at the Tigris River were instructed to allow them to return only if they disarmed.

The Patriarch wrote of Yacu and Malik Loco: 'On reaching Fesh Khabur on the Syrian frontier, they wrote informing the Iraqi authorities of their action and assuring them of their peaceful intention and begging that their families and the rest of their compatriots, who may wish to join them, be permitted to do so.'

Stafford points out that nobody was even sure where the border was, since the line just had been redrawn. Rumors flew that the French had instigated this brouhaha to demonstrate why they should not give up their own mandate, or that the British had stirred up the Assyrians as a pretext for reentering Iraq. The French claim they told the Assyrians that they were not welcome in Syria, and they subsequently disarmed them. On August 4 they allowed them to rearm without informing the waiting Iraqi army. Stafford comments, 'The Assyrians are admittedly, a difficult people to handle. They have a veritable genius for irritating even those who are most sympathetic.'[32]

Rumor had it that the Assyrians had an army of 1,600 or more. Word came to Mosul on August 4, 1933 that the Assyrians were returning, armed. When gunshots were heard from one side, it was not clear which, fighting broke out. The Iraqi army of five thousand began shooting at the 800 Assyrians. A group of Assyrians, with Yacu and Loco, crossed the Tigris back to Syria, and the French allowed 1,500 to stay.

Arabs from the other bank of the Tigris crossed over to join the raiding and looting. Stafford writes that the situation was generally under control by August 5; fighting had stopped, and there was no justification for what happened after that. However, the press inundated the country with anti-Assyrian articles. The Ministry of Education raised money to buy a tank to use against the Assyrians. The plan clearly was to exterminate them, thus the Simele Massacre.

Simele once was a town of about 700, lying between Dohuk and Zakho in northern Iraq. Yacu once lived here, but the majority of the inhabitants were not from his tribe. The murderous rampages in August had nothing to do with Simele or with the people who marched to Syria. They just were gratuitous attacks on Assyrians who were quietly returning to their villages and on peaceful Chaldeans. On August 7, Assyrians in Dohuk were machine gunned down in batches of eight or ten, at least eighty in all. The next day, Kurds plundered Tokhuma villages. Some women and children ran to Dohuk, the rest to Simele.

The massacre began on August 8 when the headman of Zakho came to disarm the men of Simele. The next day, the bestial headman (*qaimaqam*) of Dohuk arrived, and he sent for the local priest of Simele. On the way out of town the priest was found 'his male organ having been cut was placed in his mouth, his head had been severed from his body.'[33]

Early on August 11, trucks full of police from Dohuk came to Simele, and 300–500 Assyrians came shortly afterward. The police first disarmed and then began cold-bloodedly shooting all the men in Simele. During their lunch break, neighboring Kurdish tribes stole everything of value, including all grain and foodstuffs. The army came back the next day to bury the dead in shallow graves and to rape women. Donabed relates that 'the killing, raping and pillaging did not cease for a full month.' By official report they buried 305, but that number surely was minimized. Hundreds of wom-

en and children starved over the next six days while smelling their
husbands' bodies decomposing in the summer heat.[34] Stafford
called this 'a massacre which for the black treachery in which it was
conceived and the callousness with which it was carried out, was as
foul a crime as any in the bloodstained annals of the Middle East.'

In Zakho and a neighboring village, 80–100 citizens and three
priests were killed. In one Baz house, 82 men and their families
were slaughtered, after they surrendered. At one village near Dohuk, 'women were killed and mutilated under atrocious circum-
stance.' At least 800 men from the village of Sheikhan fled to Mosul. Of the 64 Assyrian villages, Stafford writes that Kurds, Arabs
and Yazidis looted and burned 60.[35] Donabed lists 121 villages that
were plundered, destroyed or abandoned. Stafford estimates that
600 Assyrians were killed. The highest estimates run from 1,000 to
3,000, most of them murdered by regular army. A refugee camp in
Mosul held about 1,550 women and children, emptying gradually
and closing in 1935. The last inhabitants moved to the Khabur settlement in Syria.

The soldiers who returned from the Assyrian massacre were
hailed with wild enthusiasm in Baghdad. In Mosul, where over
10,000 of the 100,000 residents were Christian, Muslim rejoicing
was tumultuous. The 'Assyrian menace' had been eliminated.
Meanwhile, King Faisal went to Switzerland, where he died in September 1933. His son and successor, Prince Ghazi, was credited
with permitting the Iraqi army to eliminate the 'Assyrian separatists.'

Behind all these massacres lay Turkish fear of the Assyrians,
and a competition between Kurds and Assyrians for land. The
same potential conflict still lurks in the twenty-first century, even as
the Kurds kindly shelter the Christians who have fled ISIS.

WHERE COULD THEY SETTLE?

If conditions permit the Assyrians to settle again in the Middle
East, where can they find a permanent home? The proposals they
presented to the post-WWI conferences delineate the Assyrian
concept of their heartland – actually a maximal version, for the
sake of bargaining. The great powers did not grant them this land,
but these were their aspirations. When we come to the last chapter,
we will see these aspirations scaled down to a minimum achievable

goal, and even that will require a gargantuan effort, plus almost unbelievable luck.

In 1933, Syria allowed the men who had come across the border to stay, and it accepted their women and children. In 1935–1936, another 6,000–9,000 from Iraq settled in the Khabur region of Syria in 34 villages and in the cities of Qamishli, Hassake and Aleppo. They obtained Syrian citizenship in 1941.[36] The patriarch later wrote that about 11,000 Assyrians lived along the Khabur River in Syria in 1937.[37]

Winkler writes that, starting in 1922, about 7,000 Assyrians returned to their previous homes in Urmia and 70 villages in the Urmia region. Some 20,000 also lived in the Caucasus. By 1965, some 25,000 Assyrians had returned to Urmia, and another 15,000 lived in Tehran. In January 1990–91 there was an Iranian pogrom against Armenians and speakers of Armenian in nearby Baku, Azerbaijan, where they once represented over a fifth of the population. By now, over two-thirds of the Armenians have emigrated. As the pogrom was in progress, the family of my Armenian manicurist locked their door, handed the house key to a Muslim neighbor and left everything behind.

When I tell her the name of this book, she says, "Oh yes. When we were in Baku we used to say that we should take care of the Saturday people, because when they finish with the Saturday people, they will come for us."

Stafford believed that 20,000–250,000 Assyrians remained in Iraq in 1933, most of them ready to leave in a minute.

The Council of the League of Nations was assigned the problem of resettling the rest of the Assyrians.[38] Even before the Simele Massacre, in December 1932 the Council had set up a committee of six European representatives, under the chairmanship of one M. Lopez Olivan of Spain, to search for a solution. A local committee, chaired by the British Maj. Thompson, was set up as a liaison to the Assyrian community. Now, in all seriousness, before coming to their senses, these worthies searched as far abroad as southern Brazil and British Guiana for a place to settle the Assyrians. In October 1933 the Committee cast their net as far as Europe, Africa, Turkey and Argentina.

The next brainstorm was to drain a swamp in the valley of the Ghab River, in northwest Syria to the north of Hama. Reclaiming the swamp would require a complex and expensive engineering project, to be supervised by the Public Works Department of the French High Commission. The estimated cost was 62 million French francs, two thirds of which (just over 500,000 pounds sterling) were to be raised by the League. The Council of the League set up an Assyrian Settlement Trustee Board to work on this, and a League publication explains the complicated mechanics they anticipated. Their plan was to begin the transfer in March, 1936. You cannot make this stuff up. It is like a Monte Python sketch of a bureaucratic proposal. Needless to say, this miasma came to nothing.

The man who coined the term *genocide*, Raphael Lemkin, was a Jewish lawyer born in Poland. Affected strongly by large-scale murders in the Ottoman Empire, he made his first presentation on mass murder in October, 1933, immediately after the massacre at Simele. As he wrote later, 'In 1933, at the Fifth International Conference for the Unification of Criminal Law (under the auspices of the Fifth Committee of the League of Nations) the author of the present article introduced a proposal providing for this type of jurisdiction for acts of persecution amounting to what is now called genocide.'[39] Dr. Lemkin provides this definition. 'Genocide is the crime of destroying national, racial or religious groups.' He writes: 'By its very legal, moral and humanitarian nature, it must be considered an international crime.'

Lemkin argues that there is a need to create a legal framework for prosecuting this crime, and there must be an international treaty. Lemkin also wanted to outlaw barbarity, defined as 'the extermination of ethnic, social, and religious groups by pogroms, massacres, or economic discrimination,' and vandalism, 'the destruction of cultural or artistic works which embody the genius of a specific people.'[40] We are still waiting.

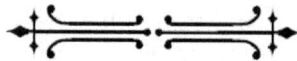

WORLD WAR II THROUGH THE TURN OF THE CENTURY

For over 600 years, from 1299 to 1923, the Ottoman Empire ruled the entire Middle East and part of North Africa. In the twentieth century new countries would emerge from its shards: Iraq, Lebanon, Syria, Jordan and Israel. None of these new nation-states had any experience with self-governance. Not that the Ottoman Empire displayed a genius for governance. It simply collected taxes and tolerated corrupt, often brutal viziers, provincial governors and local officials, winking at them with laissez-faire indulgence. The word *baksheesh*, the universal word for a tip, is Turkish.

ARAB NATIONALISM

The new nations of the Middle East were to be different. Among his fourteen points, President Wilson particularly championed self-determination, the process by which people, usually imbued with a certain degree of national consciousness, form their own state and choose their own government. This presupposes a certain amount of ethnic homogeneity, but the reality of the Middle East was different. People of various ethnic backgrounds and religions had always lived side by side. Sometimes they were at each other's throats; other times they coexisted in harmony. At the same time, they were loyal to their clan, tribe and religion. All attempts to cantonize different peoples who used to live together would unleash latent resentments; when they were lumped together in a newly-formed country, conflict would be inevitable.

What would be the unifying principle for these new nations? Democracy? Dictatorship? Monarchy? Socialism? Theocracy? And, how would they treat minorities?

Up to the eighteenth century, east and west rarely exchanged political ideas. Islamic countries sent emissaries to the west for brief stints and brought them home as soon as possible. In contrast, a number of westerners traveled east, and western countries opened embassies in the Porte. Ottoman Christians and Jews travelled to Europe, but when they returned their annals were not widely shared. Christians usually wrote in Syriac script, and Jews in Hebrew script, so few Muslims read their reports. As a result, while western countries learned a great deal about the east, the Ottoman Empire knew very little about Europe. Then the European missionaries came.

Encouraged by missionaries, Christian Syrian, Palestinian and Lebanese college students went to French universities, where they were exposed to French culture. Coming home from Paris, they founded newspapers and political societies. One of the most influential was in Syria, the Young Arab Society, *al-Fatat*, which began in 1911 to promote equal rights for Arabs in the Ottoman Empire. Later, inspired by the Young Turks and the CUP, their goal became full independence for the Arab provinces of the Ottoman Empire. They were strictly secular, emphasizing the ties of language, culture, territorial continuity and history that bound Arabs together. From this came the Arab Independence Party in 1919. Damascus was the birthplace of Arab nationalism.

Now a real cross-fertilization of ideas began. British military officers spread nationalistic ideas during the mandate. Al-Azhar mosque and Cairo University generated ideas that influenced students from Damascus, and students from Damascus brought radical ideas to Cairo.

The whole Middle East was changing. Information spread via printing presses, books, newspapers, magazines, telegraph, radio, war correspondents, railroads, roads and shipping networks. This interconnectivity has only increased, as television, the internet and social media have further broadened the once-insular world of Islam.

Napoleon is credited with bringing the revolutionary idea of patriotism to the Middle East when he entered Egypt in 1798.[1] In 1804–1815 the Serbs won autonomy, and in 1830 the Greeks created an independent kingdom. This introduced the Ottoman Empire to nationalism. Bernard Lewis draws the following distinction: A patriot lives in a country that already is independent, and he fights for his personal freedom. A nationalist lives in a country that is under external domination, and he fights for his country's political independence. The ethnic groups of the Ottoman Empire became nationalists.[2]

The Tanzimat legislation of 1856 and the first Ottoman constitution fed a revolution of rising expectations. The Young Turks' revolt in 1908 may have been inspired by the west, but when it deteriorated into 'Turkey for the Turks' it devalued the Arab minority and their language, further setting the stage for Arab nationalism.

For generations the Ottoman Empire had authorized the major religious groups in the empire to organize themselves into quasi-nationalist administrative units called *millets*. During the nineteenth century, the Porte expanded this tradition.[3] In a sense a *millet* had local autonomy and acted as a nation within a nation, but it did not have a specific geographic location. The head of the *millet* was granted official authority over civil and family law in accordance with the laws of his religion, as long as he collected taxes for Constantinople, with an allowed deduction for community use. The requirement to pay a *jizya* continued on to the mid-nineteenth century.

There were four *millets*. Constituents of the Muslim *millet* spoke Turkish, Arabic, Kurdish, Albanian and some Balkan languages. The head of the Jewish *millet* was the Chief Rabbi of Constantinople. The Greek Patriarch represented a *millet* of Greeks, Serbians, Bulgarians, Moldavians, Orthodox Albanians, Melkites, Ruthenians and Wallachians. The Armenian Patriarch was the head of a *millet* that represented Armenians, Copts, Jacobites, Georgians, Abyssinians, Syrians, Chaldeans and Nestorians. In the old city of Jerusalem, I noticed an Assyrian Church nestled up against the back gate of the Armenian Quarter, still close to the Armenian Patriarch.

Influenced by novel ideas, the Christian minorities had to decide whether they wanted a change in status. At a minimum they wanted equal status as full citizens of the Ottoman Empire. At most, they hoped for independence. The dilemma was that they did not want to forfeit the autonomy they already had under the *millet* system. Nevertheless, after the wars of 1848, eastern European refugees who escaped to Turkey brought tempting revolutionary ideas.

The Assyrians released a Marxist-influenced Urmia Manifesto in the nineteenth century. One of its theorists, the Soviet writer and physician Dr. Fraidon (Aturaya) Bet-Avraham (house of Abraham in Hebrew), called for a nation of Assyria extending from Tur Abdin and Nisibis to Mosul, including both Hakkari and Urmia.[4] Since it appeared just a few years after the First Zionist Congress in 1897, it should not be surprising that several rabbis and prominent Jews of Urmia supported this Assyrian nationalist movement.[5]

Both the First Arab Conference in Paris of 1913 and the Arab Revolt of 1916–1919 demanded greater autonomy from the Ottoman Empire. Soon they would struggle against secular, military dictatorships in new Arab states that became vile, repressive, socialist regimes. In something of a contradiction, these countries also showed a predilection for hereditary lines, just like monarchies but without the legitimacy. Often the heirs were worse than their fathers. Without the imprimatur of religion, without international support, and without tangible benefits for the people, the governments that Arab nationalism spawned were bound to fail.

Defeat and dissolution of the Ottoman Empire shook the Middle East to the core. Then the 1948 and 1967 wars with Israel shocked an Arab world forced to confront its own impotence. In the 1970s, the Lebanese Civil War tore apart a nation, and the Iraq-Iran war of the 1980s divided Muslim against Muslim. An unaccustomed feeling of inferiority grew within the Arab world. In the heady days of Islamic expansion, Islam's rapid success was taken as proof of its power and truth. Suddenly the west looked stronger. This was disorienting and dispiriting. Some Arabs bgan to emulate western forms of dress, apparently embarrassed about their own traditions. In some ways this new respect for the west made 1850–1950 the 'Golden Age for Christians in the Muslim world.'[6]

Yet other Muslims would turn away from the west. Some Muslims who visited Europe and the U.S. were repelled by the loose morals they found. As they heard intellectuals on the left blame their own countries for the ills of the world, they were happy to agree. The more the western countries floundered in self criticism, the more pride these Muslims felt in their own heritage.

Many advocated a return to the glory days when Islam was pure, true and strong, when it outshone the west and when it was the culture that imparted knowledge to Europe. Now Europe perfidiously overshadowed the world of Islam. Fundamentalists in the

Arab world soon would castigate secular Arab states for their part in the problem.

Ataturk's sin had been his dramatic abolition of the Caliphate in 1924. Foes of the new secularism considered this *bouleversement* equivalent to the hated Mongol overthrow of the Abbasid Caliphate and Hulagu's destruction of Baghdad in 1258, both still fresh in the long memory of the Middle East. One radical Syrian newspaper, *al-Nadhir*,[7] even called Assad's army 'the cohorts of Hulagu.' True believers equated Ataturk with Nasser, Assad and Saddam – agents of Crusaders, imperialism and probably international Judaism.

Pure Islam was under attack. Michel Aflaq, one of the three founders of the Ba'ath Party, was Christian, and one of his co-founders was an Alawite. Traditional protégées of the French, Alawites were regarded as Maronite Crusaders, agents of colonialism. Secular Arab dictators even flirted with the Communists, who were (gasp) atheists. Worst of all, state television brought a profoundly non-Islamic 'hedonism, permissiveness, conspicuous consumption, and greed' directly into the homes of the masses.[8]

Advocates of pure Islam railed against evil rulers and apostates – those who renounce Islam or whose deviant beliefs are considered non-Islamic. Apostasy, a crime and a sin, is considered a form of treason, desertion, betrayal, worse than an infidel. Missionaries, Europeans, communists and capitalists are just infidels. Some of the new Arab organizations that appeared emphasized social education; others flaunted more violent intentions. Most of the Arab radicals of the 1960s were college educated doctors, scientists or engineers. Others were indoctrinated in the harsh prisons of military dictatorships in Egypt, Syria or Iraq. There, inmates made contact with radicals who would help them later.

But Islam was not the only philosophy that influenced Middle Eastern nationalism.

THE NAZI CONNECTION

Germans had reorganized Ottoman military education before World War I, sending the best students to Constantinople where German instructors lectured them on loyalty to state and sultan. The message was not one of liberty or personal freedom; the highest value extolled was patriotism. Emphasizing Ottoman history and pan-Islamism, they created a highly networked, politicized military buoyed by a high *esprit de corps*. The officers who came out of this system would play an important role in post-war Iraq. Most of the early Iraqi prime ministers came from the Ottoman military.

In the interwar period, al-Hajj Amin al-Husseini played an important role in aiding and abetting Nazi Germany. Jeffrey Herf,[9] and Rubin and Schwanitz,[10] describe the profound effect of Nazi propaganda on the Arab world, an influence that has lasted until today.

Al-Hajj Muhammad Amin al-Husseini was born in Jerusalem in 1897 to a family that claimed descent from Muhammad. He attended al-Azhar University in Cairo, where he was taught that a combination of Islamism and nationalism would return Islam to a mythologized era of purity and glory. He began as an officer in the Ottoman army; then he fought against that same army during the Arab Revolt of 1916–1919.[11] He worked with British intelligence to push for a Greater Syria in Damascus in 1918, and later he joined the French against the British.

Al-Husseini once wrote 'Thank goodness al-Hajj Muhammad Hitler has come.'[12] In 1920 he raised funds for the Orient Club, a club that von Oppenheim's propaganda apparatus had organized for Muslims in Germany. Also in Berlin, he helped fund an Islam Institute to train Islamist leaders for the Middle East.

In May, 1921, the British high commissioner for Palestine, Herbert Samuel, appointed al-Husseini Grand Mufti of Jerusalem. Simultaneously president of the General Islamic Congress, president of the Islamic World Congress and of the Arab Higher Committee, Al-Husseini could claim leadership of the entire Muslim world. As such, he set one authoritative test of legitimacy for any Arab organization or government: it must be militant. All who chose moderation were traitors. Diplomacy, pragmatism and compromise were anathema. Later, Yasser Arafat 'concurred with the idea that defeat, no matter how devastating, was never a good reason for altering goals or principles.'[13] This remains the rule among fundamentalists today.

Al-Husseini was not the only Arab under German influence. Hassan al-Banna studied Fascist organization[14] before he founded the Muslim Brotherhood in 1928. The Brotherhood was pro-Axis, pan-Islamic, xenophobic, and it opposed cooperation with Christians or Jews. King Farouk of Egypt was a strong supporter. The slogan was 'The Koran is our constitution.' With some 75,000 members in 1942, it had 500 branches across Egypt. Eventually it spread to Sudan, Palestine, Damascus and Beirut. In 1954, after it made an attempt on his life, Nasser broke it up, jailed many members and put several leaders to death. But the Brotherhood lived on, and so did its leading theoretician, Sayyid Qutb – until he was hanged in 1966.

In his writings, Qutb combined verses from the Koran with Nazi themes.[15] He railed against Arab nationalism, and he advocated the formation of an ideal Islamic community. Islam would be the sole acceptable standard of behavior. After the 1967 war, Qutb's followers became influential opponents of Arab nationalism and advocates for modern Islamist movements.

The Baath party was founded in Syria as a Pan-Arab nationalist party, organized in tight cells like the Nazi party. One member, a Nazi sympathizer, became the father-in-law of Saddam Hussein, and many Ba'athists became part of Saddam's inner circle. Many Iraqi students studied in Germany, and when they returned they founded pro-German social clubs, one patterned after Hitler Youth.

The Middle East had widespread illiteracy, but it did have at least 90,000 shortwave radios. In 1939, German shortwave radio broadcasted Arabic programs for two hours a day. Soon they were on all day. The Department of Radio Policy had 226 employees by 1942–43, and the budget was 6,653,000 Reichmarks. Arabic-speaking Germans wrote the early scripts, but the message was strictly Eurocentric.

Because of the *Farhud*, the pogrom against Jews in Baghdad in June 1941, al-Husseini and Rashid Ali al-Gaylani had to escape from Iraq to Germany. Now the radio station acquired actual Arabs who understood Middle Eastern politics.[16] In their broadcasts they claimed that both Islamists and Nazis wanted to return to their periods of past greatness. Moreover, both Islam and the Nazis believed in a strong leader, an all-powerful state and self-sacrifice as exemplified by jihad. They proclaimed that the common good is more important than individual welfare, and a woman's role is to be a mother. They urged listeners to battle the Jews.

Al-Husseini had a genius for marrying religious arguments and historic Arab political grievances with Nazi propaganda. Nazi racism became Islamist, anti-western, anti-capitalist, anti-imperialist

Arab nationalism. He also melded his own visceral hatred of Jews with verses of the Koran that called for the destruction of Christianity, Buddhism and all other religions. Islam must demonize the British, Americans and Israel. This propaganda influenced Gamal Abdel Nasser, Anwar Sadat, the Baath party, the Muslim Brotherhood, Yasser Arafat, Saddam Hussein, and many twenty-first century radical Islamists.

The programs have been translated into English. Mining the archive, Herf has found common themes: The Jews want to dominate the Arab world. They plan to combine Palestine with Syria and Transjordan to create their national home. The Jews want to destroy Islam. A victory for the Allies would be a victory for the Jews. 'Great Britain is pictured as continually discriminating in favor of her Jewish masters [the Jews were carrying out] a campaign of indiscriminate murder under the eyes of the British, who supply the arms.'[17] The Jews were building an army of 20,000, maybe even 50,000, to use against the Arabs. 'Roosevelt stands behind Churchill as the exponent of world Jewry.'

Because of this propaganda, the Kurdish and the Baghdadi Jews of Iraq ultimately had to leave their homes for Israel. Because of this, Kurdish Jews today no longer speak Aramaic. Because of this, the Christians of the Middle East are the last in the world to speak it, and they risk their lives if they stay at home.

A famous picture taken in November 1941 captures a meeting between Al-Husseini, Ribbentrop and Hitler. Shortly after it was taken, Hitler convened the Wannesee Conference to plan the final solution of the Jewish problem.

In preparation for General Rommel's advance in 1942 the Luftwaffe dropped 3.86 million Arabic leaflets on North Africa, many of them reprints of radio broadcasts from al-Husseini and al-Gaylani. Nazi radio blared that 'a large number of Jews residing in Egypt and a number of Poles, Greeks, Armenians and Free French, have been issued with revolvers and ammunition [to] help them against the Egyptians at the last moment, when Britain is forced to evacuate Egypt.'[18]

They portrayed America, Britain, Russia and France as imperialists. All non-Muslims in the Arab world were traitors, spies and enemies loyal to imperialist nations. Missionaries were the forward troops of western colonization. The Crusades had been forerunners of western imperialism and aggression. Christian nations, ex-

cept Germany, were dominated by Jews. The British were descended from Jews. Roosevelt was Jewish. Jews had always wanted to kill
all Muslims, and so forth. The Middle East was subjected to a daily
drumbeat with this toxic nonsense for over five years, and it has
influenced Islamist ideology ever since.

After World War II, 4,000–7,000 former German officials
found employment in the Middle East, especially in Egypt and Syria.[19] The Palestine Liberation Army hired Saadi Basbous from the
Nazi station in Athens to direct its radio station. Nasser hired the
Nazi propagandist Johann von Leers to assist the Egyptian Ministry of Information with anti-Zionist propaganda. There were many
others.

Not only did former Nazis find work in the post-war Arab
world, but Nazi ideology was recycled as Communist propaganda.
Many of the tropes were virtually unchanged: 'the USSR employed
a host of Nazi trigger words to describe the Israeli defeat of the
Arab 1967 aggression, several of which are still employed on the
Western left today when it comes to Israel, such as "practitioners
of genocide", "racists", "concentration camps", and "*Herrenvolk.*"'[20]

Mahmoud Abbas, Arafat's successor as head of the PLO,
studied in Moscow at the Institute of Oriental Studies of the Academy of Sciences of the USSR. His thesis, *The Other Side: The Secret
Relations between Nazism and the Leadership of the Zionist Movement,* denied the existence of gas chambers. It asserted that a claim that six
million Jews were killed in the Holocaust was 'a fantastic lie,' and it
accused the Jews of collusion. Records show that in 1983 he became a KGB spy. Islamic extremists today use versions of both
Nazi and Communist propaganda in their accusations against both
Jews and Christians.

The Assyro-Chaldean community called four countries home:
Turkey, Iraq, Syria and Iran. The story of Christians in Turkey today is one of near-extinction, but the story of Iraq could become
their future. The plight of Syria fills the newspapers today, but we
have to know what preceded the prolonged war of today. We will
deal with the Syrian Civil War itself when we discuss ISIS. Last, we
will reveal the curious recent history of Christians in Iran. But first,
we need to bring our story up to date.

TURKEY

Turkey has played a seminal role in the birth of Christianity. All the original seven churches of Asia were in Turkey: Ephesus, Smyrna, Pergamum, Thyatira, Sardis, Philadelphia and Laodicea. Two of the five original Christian patriarchates were in Turkey – Constantinople and Antioch. The first seven ecumenical councils were in Turkey, the most notable being the Council of Nicea. Assyrians lived in Tur Abdin, the Mountain of Servants of God, for centuries. Once, countless monasteries dotted these steep mountains. By now, over 95% have receded into history. Before 1915–1923, one third of the Ottoman Empire was Christian. Midyat and other ancient Tur Abdin towns remained majority Christian up to the 1960's.

In 1915 Assyrians were confined to three dozen villages around Midyat and to the mountainous border area around Nusaybin (Nisibis), the heartland of the Syriac Orthodox Church.[21] In the 1950s this population numbered about 50,000. The Assyrian Human Rights Report estimated that over 130,000 Assyrian Christians lived in Turkey in the 1960s, primarily the Syrian (Syriac) Orthodox in the southeast.[22] This number appears to be an outlier. All other estimates are much lower. A 1995[23] study reported that 15,000 Assyrians were left in Turkey, most of them in Istanbul, and, of these, 1,500–3,000 still lived in the southeast. By 1996[24] an estimated 2,000 were in the Tur Abdin town of Midyat and surrounding villages. Most agree now that about 3,000 Assyrians remain in Istanbul.

Again there are parallels with the Jews. Professor Franklin Adler has written[25] 'At the beginning of the Turkish Republic, in 1923, the Jewish population was 81,454. Nevertheless, Turkey's current Jewish population has diminished to 15,000.' The same article cites an attack on Jews in Turkey in 1986, and another more recently 'On November 15, 2003, Islamist Turks and Al-Qaeda sympathizers exploded near-simultaneous car bombs outside two Istanbul synagogues – Neve Shalom and Beth Israel – both filled with worshippers. At least 23 people were murdered, and more than 300 wounded.' Experience has shown that where there are attacks on Jews in the Middle East, there will be attacks on Christians, so this is significant.

The total Assyrian population in Turkey may have been 5,000–15,000 since the mid-1990s, but these numbers are skewed by the Turkish definition of a recognized minority. The Lausanne treaty stipulated: 'Turkish citizens categorized as minorities will benefit from the same political and social rights as Muslims.' But Turkey only recognizes Armenians and Greeks as minorities, not Assyrians. Turkey refers to Assyrians as Turkish Christians or Tur-co-Semites. Thus, since Assyrians are not a recognized minority, they cannot have their own schools, and cannot teach their own language.[26] And Assyrians do not have the rights of the majority either. For example, they cannot be policemen or military officers.

Ever since the 1960's, Kurds have appropriated Assyrian farmland. In 1964, during hostilities between Turkey and Cyprus, rioters attacked Christians in Midyat and Idil. When a Kurdish revolt started in 1984, Christians were caught in the cross-fire between the Kurdish PKK (*Partiya Karkerên Kurdistanê*) and the Turkish government. To suppress the Kurds, Ankara cleared the frontier along the borders of Iraq, Iran and Syria. On the Iraqi side, Saddam was clearing out both the Kurds and the Chaldeans who had lived there for centuries. Some 100–200 villages now lie abandoned in Turkey. Most of the Christians left for Istanbul, Syria and Lebanon.

Those who remained in Tur Abdin suffered harassment, executions and torture at the hands of the *Korucu* – guards supposedly stationed to protect villagers from raids by the PKK. In June 2006, Human Rights Watch (HRW)[27] sent a letter to Ankara calling for the abolition of the *Korucu*, for perpetrating 'murders, rapes, robberies, house destruction, and illegal property occupation, among others.' HRW complained that the Assyrians 'are compelled to join the Turkish government's Kurdish village guards, which provokes violent attacks by the PKK. The Assyrians find themselves attacked from both groups of warring Kurds, the village guards and the PKK.' They further complained that 'the threatening presence of village guards is deterring displaced people from returning to their former homes; village guards occupy displaced persons' houses or land.' Assyrians believe that the government did not intervene for fear of alienating local aghas, village guards or Hizbullah, who are also in the area.

The HRW report continues, 'In February 1993 the State of Emergency Coordination Council decided that outlying settlements which might support the PKK should be evacuated, and in recent

months it appears to have been routine for all or most of the houses in these villages to be burned.'[28]

In 1996 the Assyrian Democratic Organization (ADO) compiled a list of twenty villages that had been burned down in the
previous two years, either by the PKK or the Turkish government,
and they have a long list of murdered Assyrian citizens, with name
and date. They report that 35 citizens had their citizenship revoked,
and since 1980, 20 Assyrian girls were kidnapped. Among many
cases were the following: 'On August 2, 1992, the Assyrian village
of Catalcan was attacked,[29] destroying houses and an Assyrian
graveyard. On January 21, 1993, the village of Izbirak in Midyat
was attacked and four Assyrians were kidnapped.' The priest of
Ogunduk village was kidnapped on January 9, 1994. Altogether,
'since 1975, more than 100,000 Assyro-Chaldeans have left the
country and only 10,000 remain.'

The monasteries of Mardin suffered badly. Deir al-Zafaran,
built in 1397, had been the seat of the Syriac Orthodox Patriarchate
until 1932 when the patriarch moved to Damascus. In 1979 the
Turkish government banned all of its religious instruction and all
classes in the Syriac language, claiming that the children in monastery classes had joined terrorist organizations. When Dalrymple
visited in 1994,[30] both Deir al-Zafaran and the famed fifth century
Mar Gabriel Monastery were no more than rest homes for a few
elderly monks who were waiting to die.

Germany set up a recruiting center in Mardin, which by the
late sixties was funneling Assyrian guest workers (*gastarbeiters*) to
Germany. The Germans knew Turkey. Surely it was no accident
that they set up shop in the middle of the Assyrian heartland. The
result has been a massive transfer of Assyrians from Turkey to
Germany. One Turkish village that once had more than 200 Assyrian families in 1970 was reduced to eight. Ayn Wardo had 300
families in 1970 but only three in 2014. Idil (Azakh) had 3,500 Assyrians in 1964 but no more than 20 in 2014.[31]

In his twenty years as the Middle East reporter for the French
newspaper Figaro, Lorieux interviewed many local political figures,
priests, and laymen. Lorieux reported that only a Turkish citizen
was allowed to be a priest, bishop or patriarch. Foreign priests only
could obtain six month visas, renewable in their embassy or outside
Turkey. Clergy could not wear vestments, such as the long black
robes of the Lebanese church. Christians were not authorized to

build or rebuild schools or churches, and printing presses were not allowed to print in Syriac. Often multiple churches shared one priest, so congregations rotated to different churches each week, regardless of denomination. Their fear was that if they saw a church to be inactive, the authorities would seize it and make it into a museum or a mosque. Still, the churches were almost empty.

Lorieux reported that, while some minimal religious education was permitted in the schools, the ministry required teaching materials to describe the Bible as destroyed by priests who had changed it to their own advantage. The Eastern Orthodox Theological School of Halki closed in 1971, after 127 years of operation. Lorieux called this the 'Waterloo' of Orthodoxy in Asia Minor.[32] In 2001, he reported that since then no Christian community in Turkey dared to train or recruit new clergy.

Christians are still being killed in Turkey.[33] Papers report that, in one publishing house, 'three Christian employees were attacked, severely tortured, then had their hands and feet tied and their throats cut by five Muslims on April 18, 2007.' The perpetrators have been released from their high-security prisons and the matter is back in court. 'On February 5, 2006, Father Andrea Santoro, a 61-year-old Roman Catholic priest, was murdered in the Santa Maria Church in the province of Trabzon.'

The 74-year-old priest who replaced him was stabbed and wounded in July 2006. Then, 'In March, 2007, as the Christian community of Mersin was preparing for the Easter, a young Muslim man with a kebab knife entered the church and [killed the two] priests.' In June, 2010, Bishop Luigi Padovese was murdered by his own driver. All these murders were committed by 'ordinary people,' who faced little in the way of punishment.

Recently, 'In the last four years, more than 100 Christian pastors and other religious officials have been deported from Turkey, and banned from reentering.'[34] American pastors working in Turkey have been arrested, had their passports taken or been deported for 'threatening the national security of Turkey.' Or it might be for 'giving education illegally.' School children only can study about Christianity in approved textbooks. A current textbook teaches 'When Jesus reached 30 years of age, Allah gave him the duty of being a prophet. He then began inviting people to believe in Allah.'" This clearly is not written from a Christian point of view.

In 2015, for the first time in 85 years, Haga Sophia echoed with verses from the Koran. Haga Sophia, once the greatest cathedral in the world, has been a mosque since the Ottomans conquered Istanbul in 1453. In the 1930s, it became a cathedral museum. Now arrangements have been completed to convert Haga Sophia into a mosque, and an imam has been appointed. 'We currently stand next to the Hagia Sophia Mosque… we are looking at a sad Hagia Sophia, but hopefully we will see it smiling again soon,' the deputy prime minister of Turkey Bulent Arinc has said.[35]

According to a 2015 article, only 34 churches and 18 Christian schools are left in Turkey, with fewer than 3,000 students in these schools. Before 1915 an estimated 2,300 Armenian churches and 700 schools were in Turkey, along with many Assyrian and Greek institutions: "The civil war between the Kurdish resistance guerrillas and the Turkish army has resulted in massive destruction in southeastern and eastern Turkey. Most of the buildings in the region have been bombed or burnt by the army and police forces, followed by complete demolition and razing of the damaged buildings." "Entire neighborhoods have disappeared, reduced to rubble. The Surp Giragos Church in Diyarbakır has escaped the fighting relatively intact structurally… But the Turkish security forces have used it as an army base, desecrating the church, burning some of the pews as firewood, with garbage and smell of urine everywhere."[36]

To put it starkly: 'Before the 1915 Christian genocide, the population of the territory that is now Turkey was about 15 million, about 4.5 million of which – nearly a third – was Christian. Today, one can hardly even talk of a Christian minority. Only 0.2 percent of the country's current population is Christian or Jewish.'[37] That means that Christians constitute a smaller percentage of the population in Turkey than they do in neighboring Syria, Iraq or Iran. In short, today there are no more than 120,000 Christians left in Turkey, out of a population of eighty million.

IRAQ

Iraq was cobbled together out of many ethnic groups, none of them happy about sharing the country with any of the others. Still, if Assyrians and Chaldeans ever find a home of their own in the Middle East, it will be in Iraq. Iraq is important to our story, though we will hold some details until we come to the eponymous, and ominous, 'Sunday' of the title.

Of all the new nations created out of the Ottoman Empire, Iraq was the most heterogeneous. King Faisel I began his career as the king of Syria, but in 1921 Britain installed him on the throne of Iraq. His new subjects included Chaldeans, Assyrians, Jews, Yazidis, Kakai, Shabak, Kurds, Turkmen, Arabs, Marsh Arabs, Sunni, Shiite, simple agriculturists in the north and sophisticated urban dwellers in Baghdad.

Faisel abdicated in 1933, and his son succeeded him. In 1958 General Abd al-Karim Qasim led a military coup that deposed the Hashemites, and Ba'athists nearly assassinated him in 1959. One rising star in the Ba'ath party at that time was a young man named Saddam Hussein. When a coup in 1958 failed, Saddam fled to Syria and moved from there to Egypt, where he remained until a Baathist coup in 1963. On his return, Saddam was a leading figure during a definitive coup that brought the Baathists to power in 1968. Saddam became President of Iraq in July, 1979. This chaotic start may have been an omen.

In 1958, the Kurdistan Democratic Party (KDP) had already spread from Iran into Iraq. The important tribal leader Mustafa Barzani, a supporter of the KDP, offered the Assyrians two choices: join the Kurdish fight for independence or leave their ancestral land. As a warning, Barzani's forces killed a group of Assyrians, a bishop and two priests in a village that refused to join him. Throughout the sixties, Kurdish factions fought each other and the government, destroying 70 Assyro-Chaldean villages and 76 Christian religious institutions along the way.[38] The Assyro-Chaldean homeland began to hollow out. Thousands of Assyrians fled south to Baghdad or Basra, and many others found themselves marooned in anonymous collective towns. They saved their lives, but they lost their traditional language and culture.

The Assyrians founded charity organizations, sports clubs and other institutions to represent their interests. The Assyrian Universal Alliance (AUA) began in Paris just before the 1968 Baathist coup, the Bet Nahrain Democratic Party (BNDP) in 1976, and the International Federation of the Assyrian Nation started in 1977. When the Ba'ath party came to power it suppressed them, closed the literary magazines, nationalized the schools, and banned instruction in Syriac.

In the seventies, the Kurds began a new offensive against the Iraqi government, but they were divided into factions. In addition to Barzani's Kurdish Democratic Party (KDP), one offshoot was called the KDP-PL and another was the Patriotic Union of Kurdistan (PUK) led by a rival tribal leader, Jalal Talabani. Now there are even more factions. .

Even though he knew that the Kurds were weak with internal divisions, Saddam decided to suppress them definitively. This was when the Iraqi government began clearing the mountainous region along the Turkish border, also the heartland of the ancient Church of the East. Clearing took place in waves. The final cleared area was thirty kilometers wide, and it displaced 28,000 families. Donabed lists 97 Assyrian villages that were attacked in 1977–78, most in Dohuk province, 41 in the Amediyah district, 17 in the Simele district, 19 in the Zakho district and eight in Telkaif.[39] A third of these were completely destroyed; many of the rest ended up abandoned. Assyrians were scattered to prevent them from concentrating in any one area of Iraq. Their villages are now occupied by Kurds.

Again, the numbers are difficult. Many Assyrians were counted as Christian Arabs or Christian Kurds. In both the 1977 and the 1987 census, they could only check one of two boxes for ethnicity – Arab or Kurdish. All Christians, Yazidis or Turkmen who did not check Arab were counted as Kurdish. This was part of an official Arabization Campaign that started in the 1960s, continued to 1991 and resumed in 1997, when the government handed out 'nationality correction forms,' so minorities could 'correct' their ethnicity by indicating they were Arabs. In fact, 'The Iraqi government also refused to register newborns with non-Arabic ethnic or religious names.'[40] This effort was not entirely new. In 1936 the official Iraqi year book had only listed four ethnic groups: Arab, Kurd, Turkmen and Persian. It did not mention Christians.[41]

A recent Assyrian Human Rights Report lists the restrictions on Christians in Iraq.[42] No new churches may be built, and no old ones repaired without governmental approval. Prayer books cannot be printed without permission. The government must be notified if priests are transferred within the country or out of it. Religious, social and educational programs need official approval. Priests and deacons must serve in the military. They cannot be excused as conscientious objectors. In addition to all this, Christian museum displays and archeological sites have been plundered, and Assyrian artifacts have disappeared until the losses nearly preclude future scholarly or scientific exploration. Perhaps that is the goal, or maybe it is just to sell the artifacts for money.

In 1997, Amnesty International reported that Iraqi prisoners were subjected to appalling psychological and physical torture: beating, electric shocks to tongue or genitalia, hanging from a rotating ceiling fan, skin burned with hot metal or sulphuric acid, and rape.

In September 1980 Saddam declared war against Iran, and the Iraq-Iran War lasted to August 1988. Still the Kurds continued fighting each other and the government, committing what Lorieux calls the classic error of minorities – allying themselves with the enemy of their enemy. In this case the Iraqi Kurds picked the wrong ally, the Iran of Ayatollah Khomeini.[43] Ominously, in 1988 Iranian forces and their Kurdish allies captured an Iraqi border city, Halabja.[44]

Saddam's genocidal retaliation against the Kurds is called the *Anfal*. Notoriously, Saddam sent his cousin Ali Hassan al-Majid (Chemical Ali), the Defense Minister, to exterminate the Kurdish population of Halabja. From February to September, 1988 they dropped chemical weapons, bulldozed villages, salted the earth and dynamited buildings. The BBC reported that 3,200 to 5,000 people were killed and between 7,000 and 10,000 injured. Some Kurdish sources say that the entire Anfal operation, spread over eight campaigns, destroyed close to 4,000 Kurdish villages and killed well over 100,000 people.

A Kurdish center in Halabja reported that 'The regular army, heavy artillery units, aircrafts… several types of Special Forces and Baath party militias…Attacked and bombarded the areas with heavy artillery and chemical poisons. The Iraqi Air Force dropped sarin, VX and tabun chemical agents on the civilian population in the villages and the surrounding areas.'[45] Experts believed that these chemicals also included mustard gas and possibly cyanide. This center reports that the Anfal caused some 185,000 people to disappear through death, deportation or imprisonment.

Assyrian sources reported the loss of 2,000 Assyrians, not counting those who fled to Iran or Turkey. Donobed lists 84 Assyrian villages that were destroyed, suffered population displacements or underwent attacks by chemicals, including napalm. Several ended up transformed into collective towns.

One Assyrian priest told Lorieux that 85 churches and monasteries were destroyed, and 85,000 'agglomerations' of civilians were razed, meaning collections of buildings. He writes that Zakho and the surrounding villages had been 45% Christian before the Anfal, and thirty years later no more than a dozen Christian majority villages were left, struggling to hang on. One priest questioned whether 'The church is not on the way to disappearing in Kurdistan.'

Human Rights Watch[46] charges that there were:

'mass summary executions and mass disappearance of many tens of thousands of non-combatants, including large numbers of women and children, and sometimes the entire population of villages;

'the widespread use of chemical weapons, including mustard gas and the nerve agent GB, or Sarin, against the town of Halabja as well as dozens of Kurdish villages, killing many thousands of people, mainly women and children;

'the wholesale destruction of some 2,000 villages, which are described in government documents as having been "burned," "destroyed," "demolished" and "purified," as well as at least a dozen larger towns and administrative centers (*nahyas* and *qadhas*);

'arbitrary jailing and warehousing for months, in conditions of extreme deprivation, of tens of thousands of women, children and elderly people, without judicial order or any cause other than their presumed sympathies for the Kurdish opposition. Many hundreds of them were allowed to die of malnutrition and disease;' and

'forced displacement of hundreds of thousands of villagers upon the demolition of their homes, their release from jail or return from exile; these civilians were trucked into areas of Kurdistan far from their homes and dumped there by the army with only minimal governmental compensation or none at all for their destroyed property, or any provision for relief, housing, clothing or food, and forbidden to return to their villages of origin on pain of death. In these conditions, many died within a year of their forced displacement.'

They also report on large-scale looting and arbitrary detention in jails where hundreds died of malnutrition or disease. Many of the violent acts described are reminiscent of the Ottoman genocides of 1915. Notably, the 1915 massacres were by Turks and Kurds against Christians, but the Anfal was perpetrated by Arabs against Kurds. Of course, Christians also lived among the Kurds, and Saddam's forces made no more distinction between Kurdish Muslims and Kurdish Christians than the Ottomans made between Assyrians and Armenians.

The reader might well ask how Kurdish Jews could have had a cordial relationship with Iraqi Kurdistan even though Kurds have a history of such savage attacks against these Christians. It is quite simple. The Jews have a homeland of their own. They have no interest in returning to take Kurdish land. The Christians want a homeland exactly where the Kurds are hoping to establish a nation of Kurdistan. For the Kurds, the Christians are in the way.

Perhaps surprisingly, Saddam had another side that looks remarkably pro-Christian. His Minister of Foreign Affairs, later Deputy Prime Minister, Tariq Aziz, was born Mikhail Yuhanna, a Chaldean from Telkaif. Saddam considered the Christian cooks and guards from Tikrit, his home town, to be more trustworthy than Muslims. The founder of his Baath party, Michel Aflak, was born a Christian. The Chaldean Patriarch of Babylon, Patriarch Rafael Bidawid I, maneuvered his way around Saddam so skillfully that he was nicknamed Saddam's monk. Most important, Saddam financed the construction and reconstruction of numerous churches and convents. Lorieux reports that the rebuilt Dominican church of Mosul was so grand that the Muslims complained.

Saddam also restored Christian schools to the community, and he authorized those that were at least 25% Christian to teach the catechism. Norma's family always insisted that Christians were better off under Saddam. They could practice their religion; they just had to play by the rules, keep their heads down, and make no trouble. Of course some of these favorable reviews may have been apologetics, because Saddam offered to finance a new Chaldean church in the Detroit area. On one of Archbishop Garmo's trips back to Southfield from Iraq I asked him how things were there for the Christians. "OK," he said. "We are OK." If only.

The Gulf Wars became a turning point. The first Persian Gulf War started after Saddam invaded Kuwait in August 1990. Immediately after the war ended in February, 1991, the U.S. encouraged civilian uprisings, hoping that a coup would finally get rid of Saddam. The Shiites of southern Iraq rose up in Basra, and Saddam quashed them brutally. He murdered upwards of 100,000, and he

destroyed the great marshes that spread across the southern con-
fluence of the Tigris and Euphrates. The problem was that this was
not only the home of the Marsh Arabs, but opponents of the regime had been using it as a refuge. The marshes were drained, poi-
soned and the Marsh Arabs were expelled, probably never to return. After Saddam was executed and a Shiite administration came
to power in 2003 under Prime Minister Nouri Al-Maliki, the Shiites
would have their revenge.

In the north, the Kurds rebelled, and Saddam quashed them
with maximal violence. The U.S, to its eternal shame, instigated
both uprisings, but then it walked away, leaving the rebels twisting
in the wind. At last, in 1991 the U.S., Britain and France established
no-fly zones over the south and the north to protect the battered
survivors.

Estimated Iraqi military deaths during the war ranged from
8,000 to 100,000. It is impossible to know how many of these were
Christian. Since they were not immune to the draft, some propor-
tion must have been Christian. In the uprisings after the war, the
casualties were uncountable. Victims of the two Iraq wars are buried in more than 200 mass graves.[47] One grave that was found in
2006 held 10,000–15,000, by the admission of the Iraqi Human
Rights Ministry! As many as two million were displaced within the
country or became refugees in Turkey, Syria or Iran. Among the
1990–1991 refugees were 100,000 Assyrians and Chaldeans.[48]

The Second Gulf War began in March 2003, and major com-
bat stopped in May. Saddam was executed in December, 2006.
Even after the war ended, the repercussions have been devastating.
Iraqi Body Count has been tracking monthly civilian deaths from
violence since early 2003. This organization is funded in part by the
conflict-resolution *Institut für Auslandsbeziehungen*, which is funded
by the German government and the government of Bavaria. From
2003 to 2008, they recorded 106,210 civilian casualties.[49] This work
is presented with great specificity, but we can review the gross
numbers. From 2003 through 2015, they meticulously counted
172,059 deaths, with a spike of 37,671 in 2014–2015, attributed to
ISIS. The single month of January 2015 saw 1,431 deaths, and
monthly numbers for the rest of the year are even higher. The year
2016 began with 1,200–1,400 deaths per month.

Since the first no-fly zones were established, the Kurds have
established a provisional state in northern Iraq. Fleeing Christians

have found protection with them, but in many ways Kurdish interests are inimical to those of the Christians. By 1999, the Assyrian Patriotic Party (APP) noted increasing Kurdish violence against the Christians of Iraq.

The Iraq Sustainable Democracy Project[50] documents many abuses. In the January 2005 elections, Christian polling stations were not open, ballot boxes were missing and voters were intimidated. Chaldeans who try to move back to their ancestral homes and villages find them confiscated, along with their lands. Even today, the Kurds who seized them have no intention of giving them back. Chaldeans and Assyrians may have been living there for millenia, but the Kurds want to control the Nineveh Plain. Chaldo-Assyrians have been suppressed ruthlessly. When they tried to train 700 recruits for a police force of their own, the Kurdish Democratic Party threatened them, calling it 'the formation of a "Christian militia."' U.S. Senator Gordon Smith 'had lunch with three soldiers from his state, one of whom had been working with an Iraqi officer training police cadets. That soldier told Smith that when the cadets learned that the Iraqi officer was Catholic, they stoned him to death.'

Right in the midst of ancient Christian artifacts, Aramaic place names and other reminders of the area's Christian history, the Kurds have asserted control by posting signs in Kurdish, displaying the Kurdish flag everywhere and changing place names to Kurdish names. 'The Kurdistan Regional Government's draft constitution indicates that the Nineveh Plain – an area demographically dominated by ChaldoAssyrians, Shabaks and Yazidis – must become part of the Kurdistan region... It specifically names key towns in the Nineveh Plain, such as Tel Kaif, Qara Qosh and Ba'shiqa as areas requiring absorption into the KRG.'[51]

Others have reported that the KDP installs its own people as deputy governors or mayors in villages that are majority Assyrian, even in Dohuk Province, where Assyrians are the second largest ethnic group. Also in Dohuk, they have blocked ChaldoAssyrian representatives from participating in electoral committees.

The Iraqi Democracy Project[52] quotes telling numbers. Some 1.4 million Christians lived in Iraq by the late 1980s, essentially all of them ChaldoAssyrians except for 30,000 Armenians. After Saddam, the number declined to 1.1 million. In 2005, the UN High Commissioner for Refugees found that over 36% of all the refugees were Christian. From 2003 to 2007, the total number of refugees approached 350,000. By 2007, almost a third of the Christians in Iraq were gathered in the Nineveh Province. Just to the north, more than 10,000 internally displaced families were housed in the Dohuk Governate in 2007, over 85% of them Chaldeans and Assyrians.

An Iraqi Christians Advocacy and Empowerment Institute position paper reports that more than 200,000 Christians from the Nineveh Province and Plains have become displaced in Kurdistan, but, 'Christians are targeted by the many and unmarked Radical Armed Sectarian Militias which are roaming free in [the] country...'[53] Meanwhile, they report that since 2014 the Christian community has been subjected to 'crucifying, raping, beheading, torturing, forcibly converting to Islam, driving out every member of the community from their homes, kidnapping children and young girls for sex slavery, annexing their properties, and destroying anything... Christian in the area.'

Donabed writes that ever since the Simele massacre, Ba'athification, and Arabisation have destroyed the culture of the Assyrian community. To that we might add Kurdification. Starting from the first Gulf War, all Assyrian teachers and academics were fired or forced into retirement. Many who had come from Turkey were deported back. Assyrian lands were seized. As their community has become decimated, many Chaldeans and Assyrians have tried to fit into the Iraqi mainstream, but that meant losing their ethnic identification. Many left northern Iraq for Baghdad. There they changed their language to Arabic and they no longer identified as 'rural people wearing funny costumes who speak an obsolete tongue.' Even forty years ago, Chaldeans from Telkaif made it clear to me that Baghdadi Chaldeans were different. They called them Arabs.

The Chaldean Catholic Patriarch Louis Raphael I Sako of Baghdad strongly deplores[54] Chaldean migration into the Diaspora, but the massive exodus has accelerated since the first Gulf War. Now in the area where I live in Michigan, there are over 120,000.[55]

The patriarch pleads 'This is very serious. We are losing our community. If Christian life in Iraq comes to an end, this will be a hiatus in our history.' He told a reporter that Iraqi Christians had numbered 1.2 million before 2003 and dropped to 400,000 by 2014. Two-thirds of these are Chaldeans.[56] The *Guardian* reported that the Assyrian population had decreased to 400,000 even before the civil war, by 2011.[57] Unfortunately, these estimates are out of date. Recent estimates are that no more than 230,000 Christians are left in Iraq.[58]

The impact of the Kurdish referendum of September, 2017 has yet to be felt fully. We will not get into the politics of the vote or the countermeasures taken by the Iraqi government. We do know that it already has led to attacks against Christians who have returned home to a village in Kurdistan. Let us just say that it complicates all calculations about the future of Christians in the area.

The *Guardian* reports that Kurdish authorities responded to questions about violence against Assyrians in Zakho 'by paying lip service to "Kurdish traditions of ethnic and religious coexistence."'

SYRIA AND LEBANON

Syria has traditionally been a land of refuge. Ever since Syriac Christians fled from Iraq to the Syrian shore of the Khabur River, Syria sheltered them in 35 Syriac villages. Syria may not have been their homeland in the same way that the Hakkari Mountains or the Nineveh Plain were, but it gave the Assyrians succor. As Lorieux put it, 'Pour la majorite d'entre elles, la Djezireh ne fut jamais qu'un refuge, bienvenu certes mais ou elles n'avaient pas de racines bien profondes. Tel l'oiseau sur la branche, ells reprirent leur vol quand les circonstances leur furent moins favorable.'[59] In English, 'For the majority, [the shore of the Khabur] never was anything but a refuge, welcome certainly but [where] they never had deep roots. Like the bird on a branch, they would resume their flight when circumstances became less favorable for them.' And in the twenty-first century, they did.

The major cities of Syria used to be heavily Christian and Jewish. Ever since it was a camel stop in a desert oasis, Damascus attracted visiting Jewish traders, later also Christians. Later yet, Sephardic Jews from Spain sought safety and opportunity there.[60] By the mid-nineteenth century travelers reported that 5,000 Jews lived in Syria, all apparently prosperous. This number had reached 6,000 by the time of their exodus to Israel. The Christian community was even larger. Both communities played key roles in the financial affairs of Damascus, Christians perhaps the more important. The French Annales de Geographie[61] counted 478,970 Christians (13% of the population) and 31,000 Jews living in Syria in 1955. Of these,

5,492 were Chaldeans and 11,167 Nestorians. Before the Syrian Civil War, Syria was 5.2–10% Christian. Since the war started, one half to two-thirds of all Christian institutions have been attacked, and the number of Christians killed or kidnapped remains unknown.

The reader will have noted many references to the French. The French have taken a proprietary interest in the Levant – the area of Syria, Lebanon, Israel and Jordan – ever since they arrived in the Holy Land as Crusaders. The Muslims once called all Crusaders Franks. France was the first European country to enter into a trade treaty with the Ottoman Empire, and French missionaries reached the Middle East early in the eighteenth and nineteenth centuries.

Modern French involvement dates back to the Sykes-Picot agreement of 1916, a secret treaty between France and Britain that divided the Ottoman Empire into spheres of influence, to be claimed when the Empire collapsed. After World War I, France received a mandate that was generally in the area of their sphere of influence. Portions of this land became Lebanon in 1943 and the rest Syria in 1945. We will start with Syria.

In history, Damascus was the capital of the Umayyad Caliphate, and today it is the capital of Syria. Damascus still is the patriarchal see of the Greek Catholics (Melkites), the Syriac Orthodox (Jacobites), and the Greek Orthodox Church of Antioch. The Christian quarter, Bab Tuma, once had many beautiful churches, but it is difficult to know their condition today. Damascus has always been the second largest city in Syria, and Aleppo was the largest; however, since Aleppo has suffered such massive destruction in the Syrian Civil War it is difficult to compare their current populations. Both Damascus and Aleppo are among the oldest continuously inhabited cities in the world. Damascus dates back at least to the third millennium BCE, Aleppo to the second millennium BCE.

Aleppo (Halab) is not far from Antioch, the ancient center of Christian Anatolia, and Aleppo has always had the largest number of Christians in Syria. Most of the Christians were Assyrians and Armenians, the rest being Melkites and members of the Eastern Orthodox Church of Antioch. It was the third largest city in the entire Ottoman Empire after Constantinople and Cairo. It too began its long commercial history as a caravan stop on the Silk Route, but archeologists have found artifacts there from even earlier.

After the Suez Canal was built in 1869, trade through Aleppo dropped off. When Syria and Egypt joined to form the United Arab Republics (UAR) and they nationalized industry in the 1950s, trade diminished further. Concomitantly, so did the Christian community. In 1944[62] the Christian population of Aleppo was 112,110, 38% of the population. It dropped to 20% in the 1960s, and by 2012 it was just under 100,000, just 3.5% of Aleppo's population. In 2012 most still said that Christians made up 9–12% of Syria's population, but Ehsani has written that they dropped to 4–5% of the Syrian population. And the Civil War had just begun.

The twenty-first century history of Aleppo is of Civil War and ISIS. As the Syrian Civil War began, the Christian quarter formed militias, fearing the Sunni radicals. Still, already in 2011 and 2015 bombers had started targeting the Christian quarter, seriously damaging all of the city's cathedrals. Further, they blew up the evangelical church and destroyed a major Armenian church.

Aleppo's colorful al-Madina Souk used to be the city's ancient commercial center and a UNESCO World Heritage site. Before the Civil War, a friend sent us gorgeous travel photos of carpets and other exotic merchandise hanging at the entrance to the shops of the covered market, the smiling merchants beckoning to customers. In September 2012, shelling and gunfire set the souk on fire, destroying at least 700–1000 of these shops.[63] In February 2013 the city's Umayyad Mosque caught fire and collapsed. By December, the government was dropping barrel bombs on the city.[64] A March 2016 article reported that the Christian community was down to 50,000.[65] And both the Syriac Orthodox and the Greek Orthodox bishops had been kidnapped.

At this writing, the Battle of Aleppo is over, but the pulverized city will take years to recover. Turkey was involved, either fighting against ISIS, as they claim, or against the Kurds, as the evidence suggests. The Russians, Iranians and Hezbollah were deeply involved on the side of the Syrian government, but each player had their own agenda. America was involved, paradoxically opposing both ISIS and the Syrian government. In both the formerly rebel-controlled eastern zone and the formerly government-controlled western zone, the death and destruction have been sickening.

Until the Civil War, the second largest Christian community in Syria was in Homs, a major pilgrimage destination because of its shrine to St. John the Baptist. Additionally, a fragment of the belt of the Virgin was believed to be kept in Saint Mary's Church of the Holy Girdle, a church built over an underground church that dated to 50 CE. This was the site of the Syriac Orthodox Archbishopric and it was the seat of its patriarchate until the twentieth century. The church was bombed and badly damaged during the Battle of Homs, but it has been rebuilt, its precious relic returned, and it was rededicated in 2014. [66]

Deir Mar Musa, the Monastery of Moses the Abyssinian, is a Syrian Catholic monastery that once sat abandoned in spectacular isolation in the Syrian Desert on a ridge between Homs and Damascus. [67] The Jesuit Father Paolo Dall'Oglio came to this complex in the 1980s, and he was astonished to find the interior covered with remarkable eleventh century frescos. He made it his home, set to work lovingly rebuilding the structure, attracted a religious community and organized an international project to restore the frescos. Father Dall'Oglio was kidnapped and killed in Raqqa in 2013, cutting the very heart out of this monastic community.

Homs is just one of at least ten towns or cities in Syria that once had sizable Christian populations. Another was Latakia, the home of the Alawites. We will have to wait and see if any of these communities survive. There were 4,600 Jews in Syria up to the 1970s, but a dedicated Canadian music teacher has managed to spirit 3,228 out of Damascus, Aleppo and Qamishli, all of them sent to Israel. [68]

Wait, the reader might ask, what happened to Syria the refuge? What changed? For the answer, we have to look back to the time of World War II. After the war, almost immediately after becoming an independent nation, Syria was shaken by coups and counter-coups. By the time of a brutal Ba'ath putsch in 1966, Hafez al-Assad was emerging as a prime mover. He became prime minister and secretary of defense in 1970 in another Baathist coup. Assad became president in 1971, a complete reversal of fortune for his religious group, the Alawites.

Alawites are a syncretic Twelver Shiite sect that combines elements of numerous religions. The Ottomans persecuted them as heretics for hundreds of years. Only the French had a soft spot for them. They regarded Alawites, who combined Shiite Islam with beliefs taken from Christianity, as potential allies. Early in the Mandate period, France created a small Alawite State, which eventually was incorporated into Syria. A minority himself, Assad first was even-handed, but harsh, toward all religions. He ran a police state, but it was nationalist, not Islamic. One diplomat spoke[69] of 'a sort of marriage between Alawites and Christians.' When the Syrian constitution was written, Assad accepted language stipulating that the president must be Muslim, and he promptly obtained a fatwa proclaiming that Alawites are Muslims.

Priests told Lorieux that Assad's spies were everywhere, reporting on everything they said and did. Collelo[70] includes the political sphere, writing that Assad 'brooked no opposition and his control of the Baath Party and the military and security organizations was complete. All political activities continued to be closely monitored by the party and a multiplicity of intelligence and security forces.'

The Assyrian Human Rights Report writes that 'Christians are allowed to convert to Islam but the converse is strictly forbidden.'[71] A Christian man who marries a Muslim woman may be beaten, and the marriage will not be registered. The children must be registered and raised as Muslims or they cannot go to school. Muslim men are free to marry Christian women.

The Assyrian Human Rights Report continues, 'Each Christian religious organization is assigned a member of the Secret Police. The agent's responsibility is to monitor events, programs and people within his assigned Church and report specific information about the congregation. Religious or educational programs are carefully monitored by the State and require approval,' and, to make matters perfectly clear, 'All functions were required to be held in the Church with a secret police official in attendance.'

Meanwhile, the Muslim Brotherhood was actively attacking government institutions. In the 1970s, when Assad came to power, he attempted to suppress them with a series of bloody attacks. This effort failed, but he did weaken them, giving the Christians some respite. That was not the only time he helped Christians. In 1976 at the height of the Lebanese Civil War, he intervened on the side of the Lebanese Christians against the PLO and the Muslim left, to the detriment of his relationships with other Arab countries.

Assad was at his most despicable in his war of extermination in Hama in February 1982. This crushed the Muslim Brotherhood, slaughtered 10,000–25,000 noncombatants, killed 1000 soldiers, and ravaged the center of the old city of Hama. It did break the power of the Muslim Brotherhood in Syria, but their members simply escaped to neighboring countries.

A priest reminded Lorieux that Assad's government was replete with Christians: cabinet ministers, a chief judge of the high court (*cour de cassation*), and a chief of state. Clergy could practice their religion in safety, but sermons had to devote a good word to Assad. Christian schools had been closed, but the Baathists reopened them, with a mandate to implement a Baathist program of instruction. Also the catechism had to incorporate pro-Assad language. Yet, a surprising amount of major new Christian construction took place, more than in the whole previous century, something that would be inconceivable in any other Arab state.

A grand new youth retreat was built near Homs. In the late 1990s the Syriac Orthodox patriarch inaugurated a new monastery near the old Greek Orthodox monastery of Saidnaya,[72] the ancient city of Abilene. This new Mar Ephrem Monastery combined a monastery, university and theological seminary, and it was intended to be a world sanctuary for Syriacs. When Patriarch Ephrem died, he was buried in this monastery, not according to the tradition of burial at the Mar Gabriel in Turkey. 'L'Eglise qui vivait en Turquie revit en Syrie,' a young monk explained. 'The church that lived in Turkey lives again in Syria.'

Yet, Human Rights Watch cites several disturbing cases identified by the Assyrian Democratic Organization (ADO). In one, three Assyrians from the Khabur River area were arrested for raising money for a project to transport water to Assyrian villages. Even worse, they were accused of raising the funds from the Assyrian Diaspora community in the U.S.A. and Australia, apparently a forbidden activity. The other accusation was a scurrilous claim that they had diverted this money for personal use. In the Middle East, accusations of corruption are a common excuse for religious persecution.

Even before the Civil War, Christians left Syria in droves, dreaming of the outside world they saw on television. The young left for more opportunity. Professionals left for better jobs. Families left to give their children a better education, perhaps even to send them to Christian schools. The Christians who remained became ghettoized. Still, in retrospect, the era before the death of Hafez al-Assad in 2000 looks like heaven.

Under Assad, Assyrians kept some political and cultural organizations alive, one of which was the Assyrian Democratic Organization. Founded in Syria in 1957 and in turn a co-founder of the Syrian National Council in October 2011, it aims for 'Constitutional recognition of the Assyrian Chaldean Syriac people as a national community.' In the 1990s it proudly celebrated its fortieth anniversary, though it is hard to believe it can function in Syria today. It has operated underground since its inception, but it takes credit for electing an Assyrian representative, Bashir Saadi, to the Syrian Parliament in 1990. It also was instrumental in 'revival of the Syriac language' and 'in the creation of Western Assyrian music (Turoyo),'[73] music that did not exist before.

Aramaic was not taught under Assad, but it may be taught again in a new educational center in Qamishli, a north-east Syrian city on the Turkish border. The Ourhi Center of Qamishli has announced that it will train teachers in Syriac, which would be the first time Assyrians have taught Syriac in the modern state of Syria.

A few isolated communities north of Damascus still spoke Aramaic on a daily basis until ISIS arose: Maaloula, Jabaadin and Bakha. The latter two converted to Islam in the nineteenth century, probably making them the only Muslim villages in the world to speak Aramaic. Maaloula remained two-thirds Christian until militants occupied it in September 2013, ransacked two convents, decapitated a statue of the Virgin, kidnapped eighteen nuns, and executed three young Christians who refused to convert.[74] In April, 2014, ISIS destroyed St. Sergius, an ancient monastery perched 5,000 feet high on a mountain above Maaloula just as the Syrian army reentered the city. Now Maaloula has begun rebuilding.

Several churches survived the twentieth century only to be occupied by ISIS in the twenty-first. One, in Saidnaya, was the famous Saint Simeon Church that pilgrims used to visit in the fifth century, peering agape up at St. Simeon the Stylite on top of his pillar. Recently Jabhat al-Nusra plundered the church. Yabroud was a site of beautiful historic churches, also occupied and ransacked by Al-Nusra. In Raqqa, ISIS forbade ringing church bells, and forced Christians to pay the *jizya* in gold. But all this occurred in the era of radical Islam, not under Hafez al-Assad.

In short, Christians in the Middle East have done best under nationalist, secular governments with authoritarian dictators. Now though, Syria is broken and at war with itself. Worse, Islamic prophesies have predicted that the final battle against infidels at the great End of Times will take place in al-Sham, or Syria, and jihadis from all over the world have flocked to Syria to take part in this great battle that will herald the Day of Judgement. These apocalyptic predictions threaten the future of Syria.

Nevertheless, the people who hope to live in Syria in the present need to make plans for tomorrow. In a recent article,[75] Nicholson writes: 'The choices in Syria are really only two: 1) keep Syria unified, depose Assad, and let the people draft a new constitution and elect a new government; or 2) move Syria toward federalism or full partition, keep Assad in place as the head of an Alawite province or state along the coast, and empower the other demographic regions of Syria to become self-governing provinces or states of their own.' He goes on to explain how a partition of Syria into provinces – Alawite, Sunni, Kurds and Christians for example – would separate today's warring parties and allow them some autonomy within a federal structure. We will see a similar proposal for Iraq, based on a similar theory – that in the Middle East domination of minorities by any government invariably leads to conflict, especially when the government has an Islamic political agenda.

Lebanon is the only country in the Middle East that was established as a haven for Christians, the Maronite Christians of Mount Lebanon. It also was intended to be non-Islamic, democratic and multicultural, but it has been in turmoil since its inception. We have to wonder whether this is a bellweather of what will happen in any protected area in the Middle East that is set aside for Chaldean and Assyrian Christians.

At first, probably a quarter of the Lebanese population was Maronite Christian, the remaining Christians being Greek Orthodox, Greek Catholics or Armenians. Neither Chaldeans nor Assyrians had a significant presence. In the nineteenth century Maronites spoke Aramaic, and they still use Aramaic as their liturgical language, one of the largest denominations in the world to do so.

Their origin may be in part from Arabia, but they consider themselves to be descendents of Arameans, Assyrians, and other ethnic groups of the Levant. The Maronites first fled to Mt. Lebanon from Byzantine persecution, later, from Muslim persecution. Maronites have had warm relations with France since the Crusades, and they affirmed, or perhaps reaffirmed, their allegiance to the Pope as early as the twelfth century. Many attended Parisian universities, and they brought home a transplanted café culture that helped make Beirut famous as the Paris of the Middle East. Far from the croissants and latte though, their families remained fiercely independent in their mountain redoubts atop Mt. Lebanon.

Another group also escaped to Mt. Lebanon from Muslim persecution – the Druze. Today, Druze villages are scattered in Lebanon, parts of adjacent Israel and Syria. Though their religion is a closely held secret, at least we know it combines Shiite Islam with elements of several other religions. On a visit to a Druze village in northern Israel, they told us that they revere Jethro, the father-in-law of Moses, as their chief prophet.

One might say that the Druze share Mt. Lebanon with the Maronites, but that would gloss over a lot of history. The first war between Maronites and Druze took place in 1840–1860, even before Lebanon became a state. It started in 1845 with a rebellion of Maronite peasants against Druze landowners. The Druze retaliated immediately. The Maronites rebelled again, supported by France, and in 1860 the Druze began to slaughter them on Mt. Lebanon, in neighboring Lebanese cities and finally in Damascus.

On Mt. Lebanon the worst single massacre was at Deir al Qamar, where the Druze killed 2,000 Maronites. Some 3,000 to 6,000 Maronite refugees eventually straggled into Damascus. Relief efforts began, but a small incident set off a series of reactions that drew thousands of Druze pouring into the city. Savagely, they destroyed 1,500–3,000 houses in the Christian quarter of Damascus, as they massacred and butchered Christians. At the end, as many as 10,000 Maronites may have been killed.[76] During this same period, the Druze in Lebanon killed over 20,000 Christians, burned down 380 Maronite villages, destroyed 560 churches and demolished 40 monasteries.[77]

Despite this history between the two major players, sympathetic western powers carved the country of Lebanon out of Syria as a home for Christians. It separated from Syria in 1943, but Syria has continued to have a proprietary feeling about Lebanon. In independent Lebanon, the major political offices were apportioned according to a National Pact, which assumed a population ratio of six Christians to five Muslims, based on a 1932 census. As agreed, the President of Lebanon always is a Maronite Catholic; the Prime Minister a Sunni Muslim and the Speaker of the Parliament is Shiite Muslim. The Deputy Speaker and Deputy Prime Minister are

Greek Orthodox; the Chief of the General Staff Maronite, and the Chief of the Army Staff Druze. Maronites held the offices of Commander-in-chief of the army, President of the Court of Cassation (the Supreme Court), Director-General of Internal security and Intelligence, and Governor of the Central Bank. The Muslims claim that the 1932 census was wrong. Conflict was not long in coming.

In 1970 the Palestine Liberation Organization (PLO) relocated its headquarters to Beirut. Soon the PLO became a state within a state in southern Lebanon, with checkpoints on every road, terrorizing the local Lebanese. Ethnicity determined whether one lived or died. My Arabic teacher, a Shiite Muslim from southern Lebanon, told me that once she was stopped at a checkpoint by guards hostile to Shiites, and she is still alive today only because one of them recognized her from high school, shouting, "Fatme, what are you doing here? Run."

Fatme says that typically the guards would ask a family where they were coming from. If they had been shopping, the guards asked, "For what?" If it was food, the guards would ask what they bought. As soon as they said 'tomatoes', the guards would know whether they were Lebanese or Palestinian. Pronunciation of the Arabic word for 'tomato' is a dead giveaway. And I mean dead.

The Lebanese Civil War broke out in April, 1975, for many reasons. It clearly was sectarian, but, in addition, class and economic differences set rural against urban, poor against rich, leftist against conservative. Muslims identified with the Arab world, but Christians were supported by the West – who armed them just well enough to fight, but not enough to win, as one priest told Lorieux.

Druze, PLO and leftist parties joined to form the Lebanese National Movement. Christians of the Phalange Party joined conservatives to form the Lebanese Front. In 1978 Major Saad Haddad created the Christian South Lebanon Army (SLA). The PLO used South Lebanon as a base for attacking Israel, and, in return, Israel invaded South Lebanon in 1982. Equipped and supported by Israel, the SLA too fought the PLO. Over time the conflict pitted Christians against Muslims, split the Maronite community and set rival Shiite groups against each other.

As Hizbullah grew in the 1980s, the SLA weakened. When Israel pulled out of Lebanon in 2000, the SLA collapsed, its 2,200 soldiers abandoned. Of those who were captured and labelled as traitors for collaborating with Israel, many were sentenced to death, though it is not clear that any were executed. Over 6,500 of the SLA militia[78] escaped to Israel, along with many southern Lebanese civilians. At least 2,000 had returned to Lebanon by 2001, but many settled in northern Israel. Some suggested that they were integrating with difficulty. Still, Arza Haddad, Saad Haddad's daughter, completed her master's degree in aeronautics in 2012 at the prestigious Technion, Haifa, Israel.[79]

Syria, Israel, Iraq and much of the Arab world all have sparred with one other in one small boxing ring – Lebanon – while the U.S., France, the U.N. and the USSR tried to intervene. Rich oil states funded both sides. Fatme says, "They all fought their wars on us."

By 1976, close to 44,000 had died in the Lebanese Civil War,[80] and 180,000 were wounded. Thousands more became homeless or émigrés. By 1991, after 16 years of civil war, more than 100,000 were dead, perhaps 150,000,[81] and 100,000 were left handicapped. Because of Lebanon's ethnic sensitivities, a numerical breakdown of Christian and Muslim mortality may never appear, but at least 900,000 people, up to one-fifth of the pre-war population, were displaced from their homes. One quarter of a million left the Middle East completely.

Christian Lebanese émigrés flocked to South America, West Africa, Canada, Australia and the U.S. Dearborn Michigan acquired the largest Lebanese population in the U.S. There I studied Arabic and took care of their children in my practice of pediatric surgery. In that Dearborn office, one third of my patients were Lebanese.

When the Taif Agreement, known as the National Reconciliation Accord, was signed in Saudi Arabia to formally end the war in October, 1989, it characterized Lebanon as an independent, unified, sovereign, free country with an Arab identity. It proclaimed Lebanon to be a parliamentary democracy with a free economy, and it called for balanced development for the sake of social equity. The parties claimed that their goal was to abolish political sectarianism, but political power remained divided along sectarian lines. Ominously, it transferred away many of the Christian President's powers, distributing them among the Council of Ministers, the Muslim Prime Minister and the Muslim President of the Parliament. It also allocated an equal number of deputies to the Muslims and the Christians. By the end of the 1990s, the Christians in Lebanon only

retained two Christian ministers and 24 Christian members of Parliament. The Christians were losing control of a country that was
created for them.

Shadi Khalloul cautions[82] that 'Saad Hariri, a Sunni Muslim
politician supported by Saudi Arabia, has invited every Lebanese
party to his office to sign a document confirming that Lebanon is
an Arab state.' He writes that the next step could be to amend the
constitution to make it subject to Sharia law. Khalloul writes that
one million Maronite Christians remain in Lebanon along with
700,000 more Christians of other denominations, while eight million Maronites live in the Diaspora. Khalloul points out that at least
95% of the village names in Lebanon reflect their Aramaic Christian heritage, but soon this land will be dominated by Islam.

Khalloul should know. He comes from a Maronite village,
once Lebanese, now in Israel and known as el-Jish. Its villagers
once spoke the Gush Halav dialect of Aramaic. In 1945 the population numbered 1,090, but after the Israeli War of Independence
in 1948, el-Jish and other Arab border villages were depopulated.
Since then, Maronite Christians from the destroyed village of Kafr
Birim moved in, and they have revived Aramaic. Now they have
asked Israel to designate them as Arameans, not Arabs,[83] explaining
that they descend from the indigenous Aramean-Phoenician inhabitants of the land, whose native language was Aramaic. Arabs did
not come to their land until the seventh century, and only after
Arabs reached a majority did the original inhabitants feel con-
strained to speak Arabic. Some remote villages never did. All Maronites maintain Aramaic as their liturgical language. Khalloul has
written extensively that his people are not Arabs, not even Christian Arabs, but Arameans.

Dr. Mordechai Kedar of the Department of Arabic Studies at
Bar-Ilan University writes that Arameans should qualify as a separate group as long as they are members of one of the following
churches: the Maronite Church, the Church of the East, the Greek
Orthodox, the Greek-Catholic or the Syriac-Catholic of Antioch,
and as long as they identify as Aramean.[84] Today many Arameans
volunteer to serve in the Israel Defense Force (IDF). Considering
this to be an Israeli plot to divide the Arabs, some Arabs have
threatened them, but in 2014, despite the opposition of the Arab
members, the Israeli Knesset recognized this group of Israeli Christians as Arameans. In October, 2014, newspapers announced the

first person in Israel to be recognized as an Aramean,[85] Khalloul's son.

IRAN

The borders of Persia have been stable since the time of the Safavi dynasty in 1501–1722. Now the world calls it Iran. To the north, the map shows Armenia and Azerbaijan locked in a (probably uneasy) embrace. Azerbaijan declared its independence after World War I and was promptly absorbed into the USSR, finally becoming an autonomous republic in 1991. The Assyrian presence in Azerbaijan is minimal.

The Assyrian homeland once extended from the Hakkari Mountains of Turkey to Urmia and Salmas in northern Iran. The name Urmia combines the words Ur (city) and *mia*, Aramaic for water. Thus it is the city of water, located on Lake Urmia. Before World War I, some 30,000–35,000 Assyrians lived in 60 Assyrian villages and 60 mixed villages along rivers flowing east from the Zagros Mountains to Lake Urmia.[86] At least 600 lived in the city of Urmia, now in the West Azerbaijan province of Iran. Christians represented about 40% of the population of Urmia in 1900, and the Christian quarter contained their own schools and churches. In 1906, the 201 Christian schools taught 5,084 Assyrian students. The largest schools were in the American, Russian and Catholic missions. Assyrian literacy was 80%. The American Mission produced doctors, teachers, clergy, nurses, and educators, many of them women. The community had its own printing press and four newspapers. From it emerged many works of scholarship.

Before World War I, many Assyrian men left for better paying jobs in Russia, the Caucasus, even the U.S. Right up to the war, the community prospered, its men bringing home generous foreign salaries, building large houses and buying land. All of this was ruined during the war, when 45 Assyrian villages were destroyed, and the Assyrian population dropped from 160,000 to 14,154. By the end of 1918, two-thirds of the original Christian population was gone.

Ishaya[87] quotes a scholar named Paul Bejan: 'By 1918 there was practically nothing left of the Catholic Mission in Persia. After the war, we read, "In 1923 in some places the jungle had returned, full of reptiles, wolves, and savage animals. Churches, schools and houses were in ruin."'

At the northwest end of Lake Urmia, north of the city of Ur-mia, 2500 to 3000 Assyrians had lived in villages around the city of Salmas, and the village of Khosrow Abad (Khusrava) served as the seat of the patriarch of the Church of the East. An inscription in Syriac over the door of Mar Givargis church in Salmas is dated 520 CE.[88] The Facebook page of the Assyrians of Urmia and Salmas has a picture of the church over the following caption: 'Public rela-tions office of the Assyrian Member of the Parliament: Dr. Ghal-ibaf, the mayor of Tehran, visiting Mar Givargis Assyrian Church of the East in Tehran. Wednesday, August 24, 2016.' We hope this is not just public relations.

At the beginning of the twentieth century, 50,000 Jews lived in Iran. By 1948, the number was 100,000–150,000. Of these, 15,000–20,000 lived in Iranian Kurdistan,[89] where Urmia and Salmas are located. Other traditional Jewish centers were Teheran, Hamadan, Shiraz, Isfahan and Tabriz, many of these in northwest Iran. There they lived side by side with the major Christian communities. Ham-adan, the ancient Ecbatana, houses the tomb of Mordechai and Esther, the heroes of the Purim story. An old cemetery next door in Armenia contains Jewish gravestones with Aramaic writing, some engraved with a picture of a menorah or a Star of David. This shows that a flourishing community dated back to the thir-teenth and fourteenth centuries.[90] In 2012 a government census counted 8,756 Jews still left in Iran.[91]

During the genocides of World War I, Assyrians ran for their lives to Urmia as Muslims killed Assyrians in a murderous frenzy. Since then, Iranian Assyrians have almost dwindled out of exist-ence. The population of Iran was 70 million[92] in 2006, less than 1% of them Christians. By some estimates, perhaps 300,000 Armenians remained, and some 32,000 Assyrians,[93] most of them in Teheran, a few in small villages around Lake Urmia. Ishaya's estimated num-bers are the lowest, suggesting that the population was reaching a vanishing point. He believed that fewer than 10,000 Assyrians were left in Iran by 2004, perhaps 20 families left in Urmia.[94]

Oddly, Lorieux wrote that inhabitants of three Syriac-speaking villages near Urmia were believed to be descendants of Mongols who were converted by Assyrian missionaries in the time of Hu-lagu.[95] He reported that at Friday mass they chanted a hymn of Turko-Mongol origin, transcribed into Chaldean.

In the twentieth century, Iran struck oil, which transformed it from an exotic oriental backwater to a world power. In 1925 Reza Khan became shah. His son Muhammad succeeded him, and he was deposed by Ayatollah Khomeini in the Iranian Revolution of 1979. The current Iranian constitution recognizes three minorities: Christianity, Zoroastrianism, and Judaism, not Baha'is. Armenians are allotted two representatives in the Parliament (Majlis) and Assyrians one, a token presence, without power.

Under the shah, Christians could work as doctors, engineers, even ambassadors. After 1979, the doors closed. Before 1979, Christians could produce and sell liquor. After, liquor was driven underground. Now Christians can only drink wine in their homes or outside as part of a religious ceremony. Now, the courts apply Sharia law, and they have reverted to the traditional Muslim practice of ascribing little value to the testimony of a non-Muslim. They also apply penalties more harshly against non-Muslims. Foreign missionaries have been expelled, and foreign-born clergy find it increasingly difficult to obtain long-term visas. Some even have sought Iranian citizenship in order to remain. Christian hospitals and dispensaries have been nationalized.

The election of President Muhammad Khatami raised Christian hopes, only to have them dashed. Christian wives rebelled against the chador. Christian children lost their schools. Many emigrated to the U.S. or Europe. Lorieux reported in 2001 that 85% of the Christians of Iran had left since 1979. Some who became dual citizens, a category that Iran does not recognize, traveled back and forth between Iran and Los Angeles – 'Teherangeles.'

Iran counters that Christians have their own churches, gyms, clubs, and schools. Of course the school director must be Muslim; instructional materials are tightly censored, and any overtly religious imagery is forbidden. All Christian publications are subject to similar censorship, if they are available at all. Lorieux writes that the Christians knew how to play the game, 'the community has always been for and never against the government.' At least they can figure out what is good for them.

The big surprise today is the number of Muslims in Iran who are quietly converting from Islam to Christianity. Of course, since the penalty for apostasy (leaving the Islamic faith) is prison or death, this is dangerous. The 2016 Watch List ranks Iran ninth among the worst persecutors of Christians, but Iran has the fastest growing evangelical Christian population in the world.[96] One source says 'I have talked to an Iranian Christian who called Ayatollah Khomeini, the founder of the Islamic Republic, the greatest Christian missionary in the history of Iran because he established the Islamic Republic which is now pushing people to Christ.'

The Christian population in Iran[97] is growing at a rate of 20% a year, despite innumerable restrictions. Persian language bibles are illegal, cannot be printed in Iran and cannot be imported. Christians are prevented from holding many jobs. They may be denied admission to university, and they may be banned from certain neighborhoods. Wives of converts are pressured to divorce. Children of converts are harassed, or worse. When imprisoned, converts often are tortured.

An Open Doors report exults that there are 450,000 practicing – mostly secret – Christians in Iran, a number far higher than any others available. Some enthuse that as many as a million Iranians may be Christian converts,[98] worshipping clandestinely in what is called the house church movement. For their services, four or five Christians meet in secret locations that change constantly. At least a hundred Christians are in prison, many of them pastors. Since Christianity is legal according to Iran's constitution, the regime charges them with 'actions against national security' if they distribute Bibles in Farsi. The Iranian Bible Society was closed in 1990. Other charges are 'actions against the state,' for preaching to a house church, perhaps 'conspiracy' or being an 'enemy of Allah.'

The modern conversions are to Evangelical Christianity. They do not replenish the ranks of Assyrians that were lost through persecution and emigration, but they do suggest dissatisfaction of the Iranian public with their Ayatollahs.

Lorieux[99] describes the glorious ordination of a Chaldean bishop in Teheran in February, 1999. Hundreds assembled in the church. A great television screen was installed in the courtyard and another out in the street. Clergy gathered in colorful vestments. The chorus was magnificent. The service was stately. And he writes that it was the last ordination in Iran. In fact, it was not. Father Hormoz Aslani of Urmia was ordained on August 10, 2002,[100] with little fanfare.

Also on August 10, 2010, Father Rayan Issa was ordained in Teheran at St. Joseph Chaldean Catholic Church.[101] In September 2010, 'Patriarch Mar Dinkha IV, Patriarch of the Holy Apostolic

Catholic Assyrian Church of the East, chaired the Episcopal ordination of Mar Narsai Benjamin Bishop for Iran in Tehran.' Leading the processional were Mar Dinkha and H.G. Mar Gewargis Sliwa, Metropolitan of the Archdiocese of Iraq, Iran and Russia. With them were bishops from Europe, Syria, Dohuk, Russia, India and several other countries. The ordination, 'according to the ceremonial tradition of the Church of the East, witnessed the largest attendance in Iran's contemporary history from the clergy and faithful members of the Church of the East, our other sister Churches and all the Assyrian people in Iran to participate.' The Iranian media covered the ordination extensively. Altogether, the public record shows that four new priests have been ordained in Iran since the revolution.

To be fair, a German friend recently returned from a trip to Iran, where he attended mass in a church in Urmia. He reports that it was in perfect repair, and congregants told them that their services were unhampered by the authorities. It is hard to know whether this experience was representative.

In 2015, conservative estimates would suggest that there were 80,000–100,000 Christians in Iran.[102] Most of these are Armenians, possibly 6,000 of them Assyrians. Seven churches remain in Tehran – one Armenian, two AssyroChaldean and four Latin. One Assyro-Chaldean church is open in Urmia, another in Hamadan. The AssyroChaldean bishops in Teheran estimate their community to be between 1,500 and 2,000 members.

Meanwhile a steady stream of Christians emigrates from Iran, the numbers increasing during the Iraq-Iran War, in the 1990s and again today. Sunday is coming quickly to the Middle East.

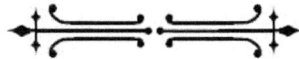

SUNDAY IN THE MIDDLE EAST

The chaos of today's Middle East did not emerge from a vacuum.

After centuries of enjoying well-earned superiority in many fields, the Ottoman Empire began to experience defeat at the hands of the west. In the late seventeenth century, the Ottoman advance into Europe was stopped at Vienna. As a result, they were forced to sign a peace treaty whose terms were dictated to them, not the other way around. In the dozen or so Russo-Turkish Wars from 1568 to 1812, the Ottoman Empire found itself losing more and winning less. When Russia annexed the Crimean Peninsula in 1783 it was a disaster. Imagine infidels taking land that once was Muslim and that still was inhabited by Turkish-speaking Tartars! That is *haram*, forbidden. In the mid-nineteenth century, at the end of the Crimean war, Russia wrested away major Black Sea ports from the Ottomans. By the end of the nineteenth century the Ottomans had lost Greece and most of the Balkans. And this was only the beginning. The next indignities were capitulations, spheres of influence and mandates that powerful western nations obtained in the heart of the Ottoman world.

As the Ottoman Empire faced west it saw Christian nations booming. Europe's industrial revolution led to an explosion of manufacturing, trade, growing financial markets and innovations in communications. Printing, newspapers, radio, telephone, telegraph, electricity, railroads, air travel, everything began in the west, while much of Islam was still measuring the time of day by the number of hours before or after daily prayers.

Bernard Lewis[1] describes this downward trajectory. Finally, he writes, the Empire asked itself: 'What did we do wrong?'

Humiliated, Islam was forced to ask the west for instruction in the new technologies. At the same time, it used the west as scapegoats to blame for its own failures. Surely the fault lay with European colonial powers, the U.S., Israel or the Jews, who were behind everything. The new Arab governments were secular, modern, free of musty religious baggage, but they too proved to be failures. The one apparent success would be the Iranian Revolution, which returned to time-honored fundamentals, to the Koran. Radicalism was rumbling out of the past.

In order to understand contemporary radicalism, we need to start with its roots in the Koran. From there as it grew, it developed branches and off-shoots, and many imperil the indigenous Christians of the Middle East. In the end, we need to be realistic about the Islamic groups that dominate the present before we can help the benighted Christian communities living in the line of fire.

THE ROOTS IN THE KORAN

Certain Koranic verses form the foundation for Islamic extremism. We have quoted several already, but if we concentrate on four,[2] we will understand more about what inspires the fundamentalists of today:

Koran 5:73 declares 'They have certainly disbelieved who say, "Allah is the third of three".' Koran 5:17 says 'They have certainly disbelieved who say that Allah is Christ, the son of Mary.' These target Christians, whose beliefs make them infidels, by definition.

Koran 9:5 says 'And when the sacred months have passed, then kill the polytheists wherever you find them and capture them and besiege them and sit in wait for them at every place of ambush. But if they should repent, establish prayer, and give zakah, let them [go] on their way. Indeed, Allah is Forgiving and Merciful!' This means that all non-Muslims, of any faith, must be killed unless they repent, pay the *jizya* and convert.

Koran 9:29 says 'Fight those who do not believe in Allah or in the Last Day and who do not consider unlawful what Allah and His Messenger have made unlawful and who do not adopt the religion of truth from those who were given the Scripture – [fight] until they give the jizyah willingly while they are humbled.' The word humbled means humiliated, shamed and abased. This verse says that the unbeliever must not only pay the *jizya* but also must be humbled when paying it.

It is true that, throughout history, not all of these injunctions have been followed all the time. In fact, many of them have been honored mostly in the breach, but whenever a reform movement urges its adherents to remember the pure first years of Islam, it returns to these verses, to the payment of the *jizya*, and to a literal injunction to slay non-believers. It is important to recognize that none of these verses say that you *should*, *could* or *ought to* follow them. There are no options here. You must. Moreover, nothing in these or any other verses of the Koran proposes gently educating non-believers, entering into a dialogue with them, compromising with them, loving them in spite of their sins, tolerating their beliefs or forgiving them.

Another concept with roots in the Koran is *dawa*, the practice of religious outreach or proselytizing. While there is nothing unusual about proselytizing, Ayaan Hirsi Ali writes that "dawa aims both to convert non-Muslims to political Islam and to bring about more extreme views among existing Muslims." She says that the goal is to promote sharia law.[3]

One other key concept we hear a lot about is *taqiyya*. The *Shi'ite Encyclopedia*,[4] defines 'al-Taqiyya' as 'Concealing or disguising one's beliefs, convictions, ideas, feelings, opinions, and/or strategies at a time of eminent danger, whether now or later in time, to save oneself from physical and/or mental injury.' In other words, it is strategic dissimulation.

The same encyclopedia quotes a Sunni commentator: 'Qur'anic verse: "Let not the believers take for friends or helpers unbelievers rather than believers: if any do that, (they) shall have no relation left with Allah except by way of precaution ("tat-taqooh"), that ye may guard yourselves ("tooqatan") from them... (3:28).' Ibn Abbas said: 'al-Taqiyya is with the tongue only; he who has been coerced into saying that which angers Allah (SWT), and his heart is comfortable (i.e., his TRUE faith has not been shaken.), then (saying that which he has been coerced to say) will not harm him (at all); (because) al-Taqiyya is with the tongue only, (not the heart).'

In short, it is completely consistent with the Koran for a believer to say whatever seems necessary, whether he actually means these words or not. Thus a Trojan horse is permitted within the company of believers.

THE RADICAL MOVEMENTS

The two best-known radical movements in Islam are Wahhabism and Salafism. Muhammad ibn Abd al-Wahhab (1703–1787), from what is now Saudi Arabia, taught that Islam needed to be purged of the superstitions and modern influences that had corrupted its early purity.[5] It was his alliance with Muhammad ibn Saud in 1745 that brought the House of Saud to power in Saudi Arabia.

Salafism emerged as an intellectual movement in the nineteenth century at al-Azhar in Cairo, notably taught by Mohammad Abduh, Jamal al-Din al-Afghani, and Rashid Rida. Early Salafis wanted to reconcile the beliefs of Islam's 'pious predecessors' with modernism.[6] Many of them were bourgeoisie, neither poor nor deprived, well educated young intellectuals trained in mathematics, medicine or the sciences, inspired by the political theory of Islamism.[7] The name Salafi comes from the Arabic word *salaf*, which means ancestor. Its adherents look wistfully back to the time of Muhammad, the four caliphs who followed him, and the three great empires of Islam: Umayyad, Abbasid, and Ottoman.

Salafists themselves are divided. Some emphasize social reform and education, searching for modernist ideas in the Koran. Others advocate militant struggle and are contemptuous of those who admire the oil-rich sheiks of the Saudi regime more than they do Allah. Some militants, the jihadist-salafis, are committed to jihad against America. The Egyptian writer Sayyid al-Qtub was an early Salafist writer and thinker who, along with Ruhollah Khomeini of Pakistan, advocated for a violent Islamic revolution to establish an Islamic state. In his view, Arab nationalists were ignorant of Islam; admiration for a party, an army or a nation was idolatry. The just ruler is one who governs according to Allah.

Qtub was inspired in part by the Muslim Brotherhood, though his most ardent followers regarded the Brotherhood as too moderate. Their motto was 'The Koran is our constitution.' They viewed Islam as a complete system – religious, social and political. In the early twentieth century, the Jihadist-salafists interpreted the classic Muslim texts in the most literal way, and for them, the enemy within the faith – the infidel secular Muslim ruler – is more pernicious than the enemy without – the infidel nonbeliever.

There are many Islamist movements. We will not go through all of them, but in general we need to know what they advocate, because if they come to power, that is what they plan to do. For instance, one extremist Egyptian group advocates a holy war to regain all lands that ever belonged to Muslims: Palestine, South Yemen, part of the Philippines, the Muslim republics of the USSR, and al-Andalus (Andalusia) in Spain.

Students (Taliban) in the madrassas of Afghanistan first advocated a strict moral code in their own country, but their ideas became more extreme when they came in contact with foreign jihadis. In 1996 they filmed showy executions of sinners and persecutions of women. An Indian group – the Deobandis – started out by promoting Sharia law in India, but their ideas later cross-bred with those of the Taliban. Some of their followers now attack other Muslim groups for being insufficiently faithful to the Koran.

Boko Haram in Nigeria considers it *haram*, meaning forbidden, for Muslims to wear western clothes, vote or receive a western education – especially girls. Yemen has its own AQAP (Al-Qaeda in the Arabian Peninsula), also its Shiite Houthis. Radical groups have formed in many parts of Africa and Asia, many of them franchises of ISIS (the Islamic State in Iraq and Greater Syria), or ISIS wannabes. They all are important, but we will focus now on the ones that concern Chaldeans and Assyrians.

After the 1967 War with Israel, many Arabs believed that their defeat discredited both Nasser and Arab nationalism. Nasser even offered to resign, though he thought better of it. That was a debacle, but the October 1973 Yom Kippur War returned their self-respect. Sixteen years ago, I took a car from Cairo through the eastern Egyptian desert and crossed the Suez Canal at Ismailia. The whole way, my driver and his son could not wait to show me the war memorial to their glorious Egyptian victory in 1973. The memorial turned out to be two captured Israeli bunkers in the Sinai Desert, now in the middle of an Egyptian army camp. When we arrived, two groups of Egyptian school children were just leaving. Each room of the bunker displayed figures of Israeli soldiers dressed in their uniforms of doctor, officer, infantrymen or kitchen staff. The signs were in English, Hebrew and Arabic, as in a museum. An Israeli flag at the entrance was covered with Arabic graffiti that would be best not to translate.

In the 1970s, nationalism was replaced by a rising tide of Islamism. During the 1991 Gulf War, Islamists were horrified when they saw that King Fahd allowed American and international forces to operate from Saudi Arabian soil. And these U.S. forces were accompanied by Christian and Jewish chaplains! Many condemned the king for violating Koranic prohibitions against consorting with infidels, a violation that inflamed Islamists across the Middle East. One of them was a young Saudi named Osama bin Laden.

One of the 54 children of a billionaire Yemeni contractor, he was raised with Saudi princes. Two of his teachers at Abd al-Aziz University in Jeddah were Sayyid Qutb's brother and a future leader of the Afghani jihad, Abdallah Azzam. In 1979, bin Laden moved to Kabul, where he started a guest house for volunteer Arab ji-hadists and Afghani jihadist-salafist veterans of the Soviet-Afghan War. In 1986 he set up training camps for them in Afghanistan, but he needed a database to keep track of their large number. The computer file he created in 1988 was called the (data)base, *al-Qaeda* in Arabic.

Bin Laden maintained a certain plausible ambiguity about his relationship – or lack thereof – with many notorious attacks against America, but they remain associated with his name: the massacre of 18 U.S. marines in Mogadishu in October 1993; the attack on American military barracks at Khobar in Saudi Arabia in June 1996; the explosions at the American embassies in Nairobi, Kenya and in Dar-es-Salaam, Tanzania in August 1998; the strike at the U.S. Cole in Aden on October 12, 2000 and the infamous plane crashes of September 11, 2001. What all these had in common was an intense hostility to the presence of American troops on Arab soil and to what he saw as a 'Zionist-Crusader alliance' against Muslims around the world.

Koran 5:51 teaches: 'O you who believe! Do not take the Jews and the Christians for friends; they are friends of each other; and who-ever amongst you takes them for a friend, then surely he is one of them;'[8]

The 1979 Iranian Revolution dramatically illustrated the revolu-tionary potential of Islam. That same year a group of radicals seized the grand mosque in Mecca, and the Soviet Union's invasion of Afghanistan started a Soviet-Afghan War that would last for ten years. Migrations of war-hardened Afghani jihadists across the Middle East 'excited the enthusiasm of zealots around the globe' and ignited 'the sudden, lightening expansion of radical Islamism in Muslim countries and the West.'[9]

Meanwhile, an Arab oil embargo reaped petrodollars, which the Saudis used to finance mosques and schools all over the world. All this Saudi money attracted Muslim youth to study and work in Saudi Arabia, and they returned home with Wahhabi ideas. Oil-rich nations acquired a reputation for profligate spending and decadent living that might seem incompatible with the Saudi King Abd al-Aziz's title: Custodian of the Two Holy Places – Mecca and Medina. This inconsistency never diminished Saudi prestige though, until the king permitted infidel Americans to sully his land during the 1991 Gulf War.

The Second Persian Gulf War of 2003 caused Islamic fundamentalism to blossom. Abu Musab al-Zarqawi, a Jordanian trained in Afghanistan, was operating in northern Iraq by 2002. There he formed an organization called al-Tawhid wal-Jihad.[10] In 2004 he called his organization AQI (al Qaeda in Iraq) and in 2006 he introduced the term Islamic State. He and Bin Laden had similar, but not identical goals. Zarqawi targeted Israel and Jordan and fought to drive the U.S. out of Iraq, but he also went after the Shiites in Iraq, hoping to create a Sunni-Shiite war.[11] Bin Laden specifically targeted the U.S., and he opposed attacks against Shiites. In June, 2006 Zarqawi was assassinated, and he was succeeded by an Egyptian, Abu Ayub al-Masri. In October, 2006, al-Masri and several other Sunni jihadi groups joined to form what he called the Islamic State in Iraq (ISI). By 2008, the organization had gone into steep decline. Al-Masri was killed in April 2010 – along with Abu Umar al-Baghdadi, the other top leader, and in May 2010 the new leader would be Abu Bakr al-Baghdadi. His assumed name, Abu Bakr al-Baghdadi, honors Abu Bakr, the first caliph after Muhammad. To increase his credibility, he claims descent from the Quraysh tribe, the tribe of Muhammad to which all caliphs must belong.

In May, 2011, Osama Bin Laden was assassinated, and his successor was Ayman al-Zawahiri, a doctor who used to have an office in an upscale neighborhood in the center of Cairo, an area where I once visited the clinic of a surgeon colleague.

The Syrian Civil War started in March 2011. In December, 2011, the American coalition withdrew from Iraq, and the Sunni minority ramped up their opposition to the repressive Shiite government the Americans had left behind. That government was an ideal recruiting tool for Sunni Islamists. Energized jihadi groups in both Iraq and Syria now underwent a rapid series of divisions and mergers. In January 2012 a Sunni opposition group with ties to al-Qaeda appeared in Syria – Jabhat al-Nusra.

In April 2013, al-Baghdadi announced that al-Nusra would unify with ISI and other groups to form ISIS (the Islamic State in Iraq and Greater Syria), also called ISIL (the Islamic State in Iraq and Levant). Soon after he announced that they were loyal to al-Qaeda. Subsequent months saw considerable dispute about whether or not al-Nusra and al-Qaeda were affiliated. To make things more confusing, other Islamic groups, as well as various component organizations of ISIS, did maintain close ties to al-Qaeda. Some of these also formed another coalition, Jaish al-Fath, but all these associations remain murky. Al-Nusra changed its name to Jabhat Fatah al-Sham (Fatah al-Sham), and in July, 2016 it announced it was no longer affiliated with al-Qaeda. This change may have been cosmetic.

From its very beginning, the Islamic State sought a caliphate like the great caliphates of the past. The initial plan was to cover Greater Syria – defined as Syria, Lebanon, Jordan and Israel-Palestine – and it announced that it would fight all Jews, Crusaders – meaning Christians – and all infidel countries, the worst being Russia and the United States. It rejected the division of the former Ottoman Empire into separate states, and it denied the legitimacy of any religion other than Sunni Islam. It decried the western ideas of democracy and nationalism. Moreover, it announced the need for a widespread jihad, because 'the Muslim masses around the world lived in suffering… al-Sham (Greater Syria), Egypt, Iraq, Palestine, the Arabian Peninsula, Tunisia, Libya, Algeria, Morocco, China, India, Somalia, the Caucasus, Afghanistan, Pakistan, the Philippines, Ahvaz [in Iran].'[12]

According to their beliefs, the world is divided into the lands of believers and the lands of apostates (*takfiri*). Apostates include the Shiites, Crusaders and all infidels (*kuffar*). The Koran requires that all of these be destroyed. The ultimate goal is to take over the world, 'and symbolically "the occupation of Rome," the symbol of Christianity.'[13] Strangely, many of these activists once were secular, socialist Baathist officers in Saddam Hussein's army, which suggests that they joined more out of opportunism than religious commitment.

When ISIS burst on the world scene, its splashiest shows featured beheadings. The western world was astonished, though the practice dates back to ancient Nineveh. It also is sanctioned by the Koran. Verse 47:4 says: 'So when you meet those who disbelieve [in battle], strike [their] necks until, when you have inflicted slaughter upon them, then secure their bonds, and either [confer] favor afterwards or ransom them until the war lays down its burdens.' Also, Koran 8:12 warns: 'I will cast terror into the hearts of those who disbelieved, so strike [them] upon the necks and strike from them every fingertip.'

Even today ISIS does not lack for competition. Hundreds of small Islamist groups continue to form, merge and separate again all across Syria and Iraq. In 2014, with major infighting in Syria, some Islamist groups were repelled by ISIS excesses. For example, the Free Syrian Army (FSA), a group of loosely affiliated moderates, actually signed a truce with ISIS in September 2014, but not long after they publicly turned against them.

Both the Taliban and ISIS have destroyed important artifacts of ancient civilizations. Believing that statues are equivalent to idol worship, in 2001 the Taliban dynamited a giant statue of Buddha from a cliffside in Bamiyan, Afghanistan – one of its most infamous acts. ISIS and their fellow Islamists also consider reverence for tombs to be a form of polytheism, which Islam strictly forbids. Thus they destroyed the tombs of Prophet Jonah and Prophet Daniel near Mosul. In Syria, in 2015 the Islamic State bulldozed the 1,500 year old monastery of St. Elian,[14] once a dramatic sight in the desert between Palmyra and Damascus. There, Sufis, Christians and Muslims paid their respects to St. Elian, and there Muslims would celebrate Eid Mar Elian every September.

The Islamic State attacked westerners from the beginning, and since then ISIS has staged, or inspired, attacks all over the world. In June, 2014, ISIS, Daesh to its enemies, declared its own Islamic Caliphate, catapulting into fame with its conquest of Mosul, a city of 'roughly 1.3 million residents…the second or third most populous city in Iraq – many times the size of the caliphate's capital, Raqqa, Syria.'[15] It was not until October, 2016 that a western coalition began the battle to take back Mosul, starting first with the eastern part of the city, then moving on to the ancient western part in March, 2017. On July 9, 2017 the Iraqi government officially declared victory in the Battle of Mosul, but the struggle with ISIS was not over. Hundreds of thousands of Moslawis (Mosul residents) remained in refugee camps, and large swathes of Mosul were destroyed.

By the beginning of 2017, as the Battle of Mosul ended, the Battle of Raqqa, the self-proclaimed capital of ISIS, began. By the end of the year it was all but over, but a large contingent of fighters from Raqqa had moved to more isolated locales in the Syrian Desert, from Deir Ezzor to Abu Kamal. There the battle continued, in the border lands between Syria and Iraq.

While ISIS and its affiliates might be on the run, at this writing they seem far from cornered, and pockets of true believers remain in scattered locations, ready to gather new adherents and rise up again. To understand the recent past and the still-threatening future, we will look at the statistics and some of the most egregious recent attacks on the beleaguered Christians of the Middle East.

ATTACKS AGAINST CHRISTIANS

Today the Christians of the Middle East are a captive population, surrounded by a sea of Islamic radicalism. We have met the Jews who used to live in Mesopotamia. They now live quietly in Israel, out of the line of fire. We have studied the history of Christians in the Middle East, a history that predates the birth of Muhammad by 600 years. We have reviewed verses of the Koran that command Muslims to hate Christians, and we know about the mass slaughter of Christians during World War I. Still, some communities of Christians survived the war in their ancestral villages, few in number, impoverished, their churches and monasteries stripped to the bone, deprived of educated clergy, and gradually losing their youth to emigration. Yet, they were alive, still spoke Aramaic, still maintained their traditions, sang the old songs, and offered up their ancient prayers. Now twenty-first century radical Islam is destroying them.

Several sources have compiled lists of churches destroyed, monasteries ruined, individual people killed, abductions, kidnapping, church bombings and major massacres since 2003. Fredrick Aprim,[16] has culled information from vast numbers of newspaper articles published between 2003 and 2010, and he has created a massive database for AIM, the Assyrian Information Management website. This and other lists have every single incident reported in each time period, with names and exact places. In lieu of reprinting all that, we have counted the gross numbers for each year, and we only will mention the most dramatic incidents. Unless otherwise specified, the next data and examples will be taken from the AIM database. After that, we will cite other databases to take us to the present.

Aprim's list starts in April, 2003, and he records seven Christian deaths for the year 2003.

In 2004, seven churches were bombed, and at Mosul University acid was thrown in the faces of female students who were not wearing veils. That year, at least 110 Christians were killed. By October, an estimated 40,000 Christians had left for Syria and Jordan.

In October, 2005, the executive director for the northern branch of the Iraqi Oil Company told his friends that members of the Kurdistan Democratic Party (KDP) visited him at work, threatened him, demanded that he quit his job and warned he must join their party or else. One day, five armed Kurds knocked at his door, and when he appeared, they killed him. Altogether in 2005, about 40 Christians were murdered and 31 kidnapped. Several of the killers were Kurdish Peshmerga.

The year 2006 started out with six church bombings in January. Over the course of the year, several ancient archaeological sites were vandalized and houses built over them. On October 9, a shopping district in a largely Assyrian Christian neighborhood of Baghdad was bombed, killing 12 people and wounding 56. Four days later, members of the Kurdistan Democratic Party (KDP) attacked the Nineveh headquarters of the Assyrian Democratic Movement TV station. In June, authorities announced that 1,331 families had fled Mosul, an estimated 5,561 people. Altogether, some 100 Chaldeans and Assyrians were killed in 2006 and at least 13 more kidnapped. In October, a boy was crucified. And a priest was beheaded and dismembered.

The most heinous act that October was that 'A toddler was kidnapped. The mother, a Christian, could not pay the ransom and the young child was returned to her, beheaded, roasted, and served on a mound of rice.'

The Iraq Sustainable Democracy Project[17] writes that the excuse for all this mayhem was an accusation that Chaldeans and Assyrians collaborated with their coreligionists in the U.S. In 2007, Christians in the Baghdad neighborhood of Dora were given the following choices: convert, pay the *jizya* plus heavy additional fines, send a daughter or sister to marry a Muslim, leave or die. Dora had

20,000 Christian homes in 2003. By 2007 there were 3,000, many with no man left in the house.

At the Chaldean Church of the Holy Spirit in Mosul, Father Ragheed Aziz Ganni, the pastor, and four subdeacons were killed on June 3, 2007, right after they celebrated mass.

In 2007, attacks escalated in number and severity. ISIS began explicitly threatening students in July. 'A statement by an Islamic group that calls itself the Islamic Emirate of Mosul threatened to kidnap or kill all Christians whether students or employees in Mosul University if they did not leave the university campus in three days. According to the statement that was posted on city streets, the Islamic group threatened as well all Christians living in Mosul to leave the city within three days or the group will behead any Christian who will remain in the city.'

By November 2007, the Kurds too were threatening Assyrian students. The nearly 2,500 students from Assyrian villages of the Nineveh Plain suffered 'continuous acts of violence, threats and harassment, which are exposed on the roads and highways leading to Mosul,' and those who tried to enroll in the colleges of Arbil and Dohuk were 'faced with many hurdles, red tape, unusual local laws and measures which... aren't found in other universities and colleges such as students' hosting and restricted admissions because they're considered not to be part of the so-called Kurdish region.'

In December 2007, female students at Basra University in southern Iraq were threatened if they did not wear the veil and dress of a devout Muslim, and male students were told they needed to grow their beards, under threat of death. Perhaps America's Sunni awakening in Anbar province drove the extremists to Nineveh Province, but in 2007 the number of reported murders and killings rose so steeply that we cannot derive meaningful total statistics from the list. Since so many murders were of an unrecorded number of victims, the best we can say is that there were at least a hundred civilians killed and at least 14 abducted. Surely these numbers are too low.

January 2008 started with the bombing of 11 churches and monasteries. January seems to be the worst month for Christians, perhaps because of the Christmas holidays. In February, right after he celebrated mass, Mar Poulos Faraj Rahho, the bishop of the Chaldean Catholic Church of Mosul, was abducted, his two companions and driver killed. At first the kidnappers demanded a ransom. In March, he was found dead.

In June, 2008, testimony was presented to a Canadian parliamentary committee that since 2003, about 12 Iraqi children had been kidnapped and killed, and that their tormentors 'nailed... makeshift crosses near their homes to terrify and torment their parents. One infant was snatched, decapitated, burned and left on his mother's doorstep.'

On October 11, 2008 the newspapers reported that thirteen Christians had been killed in the past two weeks and thousands of Christians were fleeing Mosul. At least 1,000 people had run away in the past 24 hours, 3,000 in the previous seven days. By October 15, Iraqi officials reported that 1,894 families had left Mosul, generally leaving for villages like Telkaif or Alqosh in the Nineveh Plain. Again it is difficult to count the individual cases, but there were at least 28 murdered and three abducted in 2008.

The dismal list of churches bombed, abductions and Christians murdered continued in 2009. Over July 12–13 alone, eight churches were bombed, notably the Church of Virgin Fatima in Mosul. There were at least 32 reported murders and two abductions, one fatal.

A watershed event occurred on October 31, 2010.[18] During Sunday mass, 120 Christians were besieged for four hours in Our Lady of Salvation Church in Baghdad. At least 58 were slaughtered, along with two priests, and close to a hundred were injured. Now attacks came in close succession, with four abductions or bombings before October 2010 and four bombings or point-blank shootings in November. On December 28, at least four Christian homes were attacked with grenades and bombs, killing two. That month, "Militants left a bomb on the doorstep of the home of an elderly Christian couple and rang the doorbell." When they opened the door, the bomb exploded and killed them, injuring several pedestrians. Christmas services were cancelled in Kirkuk due to al-Qaeda threats, and terrorists broke into another Christian home, where they abducted the daughter.

Clearly, the number of violent acts against Christians was on the rise, and at least 1,000 families left Baghdad and Mosul for Kurdistan. The UN High Commission for Refugees reported that 133 families fled to Syria and 109 individuals fled to Jordan. The Assyrian Church in Beirut received another 450 refugee families.

Church leaders reported that departures increased 213% after the October massacre.[19]

In 2011 a car bomb exploded in Kirkuk outside the Holy Family Syrian Catholic Church, and two weeks later another one exploded near the St. Ephraim Syrian Orthodox Church.

Ibrahim writes[20] that in February, 2012, thirty armed jihadis raided the fourth century Catholic monastery of Mar Musa in Syria, and in two more raids the following summer bandits stole everything they could. A bomb went off in November 2012 near the Orthodox Church of the Annunciation in Raqqa, killing two.[21] The Arabic Evangelical Church of Aleppo was blown up that same month. There were three church attacks in Aleppo that November. In the third, near a Syriac Orthodox Church, the bomb killed between 20 and 80.[22]

To give a sense of how many Christians had left by that time, 'In 2013, the Christian population was estimated at 500,000, half the size estimated in 2003,' and by 2015, Iraqi Christian leaders estimated that only 250,000–300,000 Christians remained in Iraq.[23]

In Mosul, by 2013, IS was making $12 million a month through extortion, and the city had become its 'financial hub in Iraq.' Wealthy and swaggering, it was feeling its oats. While the Iraqi government wanted to control Mosul Province and its oil wells, so did the Kurds. Protecting non-Muslim minorities was low on their priority list. ISIS could attack with impunity.

On June 10, 2014, when ISIS occupied Mosul, a half million inhabitants fled, most of them north to Kurdistan. Archbishop Nikodemis Daoud fled to Erbil, where he issued a warning that ISIS was planning the ethnic cleansing of all Christians in Mosul. That summer, ISIS expanded rapidly in Iraq, sending 3,000–4,500 Yazidis scrambling for safety to the top of Mt. Sinjar. They still managed to kill 500 and divide up the women as spoils of war. By August, of the 300,000 Yazidis who had lived in Sinjar, at least 40,000 were trapped on Mt. Sinjar, and 130,000 had fled to Dohuk or Erbil.[24] The Yazidis, a Kurdish minority, describe it as genocide. At least 20 mass graves have been found so far, and some 3,500 Yazidi women and children were reported to be held as slaves.

The *Assyrian International News Agency* (*AINA News*)[25] lists the 45 Christian institutions in Mosul and writes that 'ISIS has destroyed, occupied, converted to mosques, converted to ISIS headquarters or shuttered' all of them in the less than two months after they took Mosul on June 10, 2014. On March 19, 2015, ISIS blew up the ancient tomb complex of Mar Bahnam and Mart Sarah north of Nimrud Iraq. Dating back to before the Sassanids and the Assyrians, it was revered by the Syriac Orthodox, Syriac Catholics and Yazidis. An article posted in December 2015,[26] lists 11 Syrian churches destroyed by ISIS.

AINA keeps a timeline[27] of ISIS attacks in Iraq, and now we will follow it, starting with the capture of Mosul in June 2014. This was a month of disasters. ISIS cut off water and electricity from the Nineveh Plain. They killed four Christian women in Mosul for not wearing the veil. A nearby battle between the Kurds and ISIS forced 50,000 Assyrians to flee. ISIS seized the house of the Chaldean Patriarchate and of Dr. Tobia, advisor on minority affairs to the Government of Nineveh. ISIS confiscated Christian and non-Sunni Muslim homes, rounded up police and army members and executed them in a mosque.

In July 2014, they declared sharia law, marked Christian homes with an 'N" for Nasrani, and told Christians that they must convert, pay the *jizya*, or leave. Some 2,000 Christians were driven from Mosul. On their way out, they were stopped at checkpoints and relieved of their gold, jewelry and cell phones. On August 2, ISIS looted eight million dollars from Assyrian farms. On August 8, 200,000 Assyrians fled the towns and villages of the Nineveh Plain. That month, 850,000 Assyrians were displaced from their homes.

Saddam had discriminated against the Shiite majority. When Nouri al-Malki became prime minister in 2006, his Shiite government returned the favor by discriminating against the Sunni minority, motivating Sunni extremist groups. Prime Minister Haider al-Abadi replaced him in August 2014 amid high hopes that his regime would calm these groups down. There was little change.

On January 28, 2015, ISIS blew up the walls of ancient Nineveh. On February 26, 2015, ISIS smashed Assyrian artifacts in the Mosul museum. In March 2015, ISIS destroyed ruins of the ancient Assyrian city of Nimrud, the ancient city of Hatra, the ancient Assyrian city of Khorsabad, the St. George Monastery in Mosul, and a fourth century Assyrian monastery in Iraq. On April 12, 2016 in Mosul, ISIS demolished a seventh century BCE Assyrian gate from the time of Sennacherib.[28] In the midde of the great battle to take back Mosul, retreating ISIS terrorists blew up the Grand al-Nuri

Mosque, whose elaborate curved minaret had towered above the city since the 12th century.[29] These are just the highlights.

The United States Commission on International Religious Freedom reports that 'In August 2015, Iraqi Defense Minister, Khaled al-Obeidi reported that ISIL had killed 2,000 Iraqis in the largely Christian Nineveh Plains between January and August 2015, and that more than 125,000 Christians had fled to the KRG for protection.[30] In Kirkuk, ISIL used churches as bases and stormed and desecrated cemeteries; it also demolished Assyrian monasteries. In late January 2016, it was reported that ISIL had destroyed 'the oldest Christian monastery in Iraq, the St. Elijah's Monastery in Erbil...a place of worship for more than 1,400 years; the destruction is believed to have occurred between August and September 2014.'

Another group keeps a list of attacks that reportedly were 'motivated by a sense of Islamic duty,' bringing our story close to the present. The Religion of Peace (TROP)[31] is a non-partisan organization that publishes a daily list culled from news articles about civilian attacks, deaths in battle excluded. They actually caution that their list underreports, 'In 2014, the BBC did a thorough analysis of Islamic terror attacks occurring during the month of November. They found 664 attacks and 5,042 deaths. Our list has only 284 attacks and 2,515 deaths for that month, meaning that we undercounted the true extent of Islamic terror by a significant margin.'

Again, numbers vary. The Assyrian International News Agency[32] lists Assyrians killed and taken hostage in Syria. They count 59 killed and well over 600 abductions in 2015, notably 373 abducted in Hasaka, Syria on February 26 and 250 in Qaryatain, Syria on August 7. Up to June 2016 they report 24 killed in Syria and 81 hostages released. The TROP numbers are considerably lower. Surprisingly, the abduction of 250 hostages in Qaryatain did not make the TROP list, though it was reported by several sources.[33] The large abduction of hostages from Hasaka was reported by different sources, but with widely varying numbers. Early reports started at 90, rose to 150, then 262, and in March 2015, one newspaper reported that there were 373.[34] Possibly this is why TROP just lists 90.

Still, it may be instructive to look through the TROP lists for 2014 through mid-September, 2016. In 2014, TROP lists 101 murders in Syria and 28 in Iraq. In one village massacre, al Nusra and Ansar al Sham killed 80 elderly people, 13 by beheading.

In 2015, TROP lists 106 Christians killed in Syria, plus the episode in which the 90 women and children were taken hostage and dozens injured in Hasaka (and one other village) on February, 23, 2015. Eight Christians were killed in Iraq. In the first three quarters of 2016, there were 46 Christians killed in Syria, one in Iraq, and five by a suicide bomber outside of two ancient churches in Tur Abdin, Turkey.

Several of the murders reported were especially grisly. On February 2, 2015 a priest was beheaded in Mosul. On February 18, 2016, a priest was beheaded in Aleppo. One of the most disgusting attacks was in a village just outside of Aleppo on August 28, 2015, where IS (or ISIS) tortured and murdered twelve Christians. Of these, two women first were raped; eight of the 12 were beheaded; four people were crucified, and, before his crucifixion, the twelve year old son of a Syrian missionary had his fingers chopped off,[35] a punishment prescribed by Koran 8:12, 'I shall put terror into the hearts of those who disbelieved, so strike [them] upon the necks and strike from them every fingertip.'

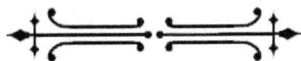

TOMORROW

Chaldeans and Assyrians must decide if they can visualize a future in a Middle East where an ISIS or an al-Qaeda might arise to threaten them again at any time. In both Syria and Iraq, many now have taken shelter among the Kurds. A number have formed militias for self-defense, often working with the Kurds. For others, village life is a thing of the past. They are assimilating in another country and will never go back.

What can be done and what should be done? The highest international priorities in the Middle East today are very basic – fight Islamic extremism, end the Syrian Civil War and deal with Iran. It is impossible to know what Syria will look like after the civil war, so we will not advance any proposals for resettling Christians there. Christians who now live in northern Iran may be willing to stay, but in view of the official attitudes of the government today, the idea of encouraging more Christians to settle there is beyond foolhardy. Turkey today is moving toward a sort of neo-Ottoman Empire, and any attempt to return Christians there right now would be out of sync with the zeitgeist. That leaves us with two credible possibilities: the Diaspora and Iraq. We will look at Turkey and at the Diaspora, but, if it is anywhere, it seems that northern Iraq has the greatest potential for rebuilding tradional Christian communities.

TURKEY AND THE HAKKARI MOUNTAINS

In June, 2001, the Prime Minister of Turkey, Bulent Ecevit, issued a bulletin promising protection for Assyrians who wanted to return to Tur Abdin. The overseas Assyrian community reacted with great excitement, formed development organizations and made plans. An abandoned village, Kafro Tahtayto, became the prototype, and overseas Assyrians returned there in 2004–2006 in a great burst of building activity. Assyrians from Germany renovated ancient monasteries, built new village churches and put up new homes, some of them in palatial style. However, after listening to Erdogan, they were afraid to move into these grand new homes. They started an Aramaic language newspaper. They returned for summer vacations, but even those who were intrepid enough to stay left their wives and children in Europe. Some said that thousands would return if conditions were favorable.

The Justice and Development Party (AKP) came to power in 2002, and it continued to repeat the same invitation. As recently as 2013,[1] Minister of Culture and Tourism Omer Celik called for Assyrians to return home. President Abdullah Gul made the same request on a trip to Sweden, but the Assyrian community viewed it with skepticism.

Abdullah Ocalan and his Kurdish Nationalist Movement (PKK) proposed an alliance with the Assyrians, and they invited them to return.[2] Still, local Kurds never ceased to appropriate Christian land, nor have they stopped intimidating and attacking Christians. Security issues remain serious. A nearby oil pipeline is a magnet for terrorists, and ISIS is too close for comfort. Mt. Sinjar, the scene of recent ISIS onslaughts in Iraq, can be seen from Tur Abdin. General lawlessness, theft and murder completely overwhelm the local police.

In 2016 and 2017, the Turkish government is adding a new complication – a renewed attempt to destroy the remaining Christian and Kurdish heritage of Diyarbakir.[3] Quoting liberally from a 2017 World Heritage Watch report, Uzay Bulut, a Turkish journalist with the Middle East Forum, writes that Christian properties that have survived the Armenian and Assyrian Genocides are being destroyed again today in the ancient center of Diyarbakir, a UNESCO World Heritage Site. Two Kurdish co-mayors of Diyarbakir were arrested in October, 2016 for being 'members of a terrorist organization." Neighborhoods are being destroyed, 'reduced to rubble,' and clashes between the state and Kurdish rebels have killed hundreds.

Even outside of Diyarbakir, land expropriation has been a continuing problem. When the government modernized its land registration records in the late 1990s it treated unoccupied Assyrian homes and villages as abandoned and registered them either to the state or to a third party. They also confiscated farm land that had lain fallow for at least 20 years, even if the owners had left under duress. Nobody who lost Turkish citizenship can register land. Through a tricky legalism, the government has a right to seize any forested land, but all abandoned land eventually grows scrub. Lawsuits over land rights drag on endlessly. As a practical matter, neighboring Kurds normally just move in, squat, and refuse to budge.

The Istanbul Policy Center has a proposal for land restitution where feasible, and, if not, compensation with treasury land with institutional supervision of the restitution/compensation process. In 2008 the Syriac community sued after land belonging to Mar Gabriel Monastery was expropriated. The German parliament debated the issue, and Prime Minister Angela Merkel raised it with Prime Minister Erdogan in 2013. Ultimately the court returned a deed for 12 parcels of land to the Syriac community, but it classified the monastery as an 'occupier.'[4] Another 18 parcels remain in dispute. 'The monastery won the local lawsuits, but the Turkish Supreme Court overturned the rulings [and] the monastery went to the European Court of Human Rights.'[5]

Incidentally, the Istanbul Policy Center warns that, while Germany's interest is heartwarming, direct intervention runs the risk of making the neighbors paranoid. The center suggests that in the future Germany just offer to share its own experience with post-war land restitution and to provide sage advice from its own experts.

Today the door of opportunity may be closing. The older generation that was born in Tur Abdin is dying. They will retire on pensions, but not in Turkey. Grandchildren raised in the west will have no interest in relocating to a land that is foreign to them. Any chance of rebuilding depends on the generation in the middle. Today many of them enjoy summer vacations in Tur Abdin, but as they age they may no longer have the energy for rebuilding. Anyhow, as long as Recep Tayyip Erdogan is Prime Minister or President, this whole discussion may be moot.

THE DIASPORA

The Assyrian-Chaldean exodus has spread all across the world. The Assyrian International News Agency released a set of numbers just before the onslaughts of ISIS.[6] In 2013, other than the U.S., they said the largest populations were in Iraq (150,000), Sweden

(120,000), Lebanon (100,000), Germany (70,000), the Russian Federation (70,000), Syria (70,000), Iran (50,000) and Jordan (44,000). In Turkey, the Assyrians' ancestral home, they only indicated 24,000. These numbers all appear abnormally low. For instance, they quote 40,000 for the United States, but more than that live in southeast Michigan alone. No doubt all these numbers are mere guesses amid civil wars and the associated population shifts of the Middle East today, but it might be worth noting that they only come to about half a million. Even if they are too low by half or more, we still would be left with an estimate of one or two million Assyrian-Chaldeans worldwide in 2013. More recently the Joshua Project has estimated 668,800 worldwide,[7] but the numbers still vary wildly. For instance, this source lists 800 Assyrians in all of Germany, while a German source lists 100,000 Syrian Orthodox (Jacobites) in Germany in 2014 and 10,000 Assyrian Orthodox in 2016.[8]

Then there is the Michigan Chaldean American Chamber of Commerce, which quotes 2.2 million Chaldeans in Syria today. Their website also writes that 300,000 Chaldeans live in the United States outside of Michigan, and 'Metro Detroit area has the world's largest population outside of Iraq with an estimated 150,000 people.'[9] Southeast Michigan has 12 Chaldean parishes, and many eminent clergy have started their careers here. Rev. Sarhad Jammu was a priest at Mother of God Church in Southfield until 1997 when he became Co-Secretary General of the Joint Committee for Unity between the Chaldean Catholic Church and the Assyrian Church of the East. Msgr. George Garmo was consecrated Archbishop when the Pope sent him back to Mosul in 1980. One of my fond personal recollections was of this consecration. Bishops and top level church dignitaries from all over the Middle East took part in the ceremony in their gorgeous vestments, while Chaldeans who came late raucously pounded on the outside doors, trying to get in. We had arrived early.

Today Chaldeans Online[10] lists 19 Chaldean bishops: ten in Iraq, Turkey and Iran, three in the U.S. and one each in Canada, Cairo, Lebanon, Syria, Teheran and Australia/New Zealand. The major Chaldean communities in the United States are: the Detroit area, Chicago, Arizona, and California. The largest in California are San Diego, Los Angeles and Turlock. Only eight monasteries still function in Iraq.

After working for years for reconciliation between the Assyrian and Chaldean churches, in 2008, Mar Bawai Soro of the Assyrian Church of the East brought 1,000 Assyrian families from his California church into full communion with the Chaldean Catholic Church. The churches have approached each other several times recently. In 1994 Pope John Paul II and Patriarch Dinkha IV of the Assyrian Church of the East signed a *Common Christological Declaration,* and on July 20, 2001, they jointly issued: *Guidelines for admission to the Eucharist between the Chaldean Church and the Assyrian Church of the East.* This was the first time another Christian church had recognized the Church of the East. In 1997 the Assyrian and Chaldean Churches agreed to work toward union. The Assyrian Church even attempted to delete from the prayer book language that offended the Jacobites and the Copts, but the Copts opposed the move.

The Holy Apostolic Catholic Assyrian Church of the East[11] maintains dioceses across the United States, Europe, Australia, New Zealand, Lebanon, Syria, Baghdad, Iran and northern Iraq. Large communities exist in California, Chicago and India. India alone has three bishops. Descendents of Assyrian immigrants live in Russia, Georgia and Armenia. In Europe, Assyrians live in Sweden, Netherlands, France, Greece, Britain and in Germany – the descendents of Assyrians from Hakkari who Germany recruited as guest workers.

One of the most established populations of expatriate Assyrians lives in Germany, in communities organized around the Syriac-Orthodox Church. The first bishopric was established in 1971 in Augsburg, Bavaria, and now the seat of the archdiocese is in Warburg, in north Rhine-Westphalia. In one German town, Kirchardt, one third of the 5,500 inhabitants are Syriac.

The Syriac Orthodox Church[12] has its own Diaspora: three archdioceses in Iraq, a Patriarchal Vicarate for Jerusalem and Jordan, three archdioceses for Lebanon, four for Syria and five Patriarchal Vicarates or archdioceses for Turkey. There also is an archdiocese or Patriarchal Vicarate in Australia, New Zealand, South America and Canada. The United States has three. Europe has archdioceses in Austria, Belgium, France, Germany, Sweden, Switzerland and Great Britain.

The Maronite Church may have the largest Diaspora of all. Some estimate over three million, scattered as widely as are the Lebanese themselves – all over North and South America, France and Australia. Aramaic is not their vernacular, but it is their language of prayer.

Members of all these churches, in all the countries where they live, have to pray if they hope to preserve their traditions in the Diaspora. Otherwise, the young generation may only have church classes or such internet sites as learnsurath.blogspot.com, to keep the language of their grandparents alive.

Iraq

Despite the wars that roil the Middle East, some are looking toward a time when the wars will end and Christians can return to their ancestral homes in Iraq. While Chaldeans and Assyrians may dream of having their own land, they will need to feel that their lives, children, jobs and homes are going to be secure. As it happens, they already have been making plans, despite the real problems that they acknowledge.

For example, would the Kurds respect them and give them full citizenship rights in a future Kurdistan? We know the history. For years the Kurds have seen the Assyrians as competitors for the same land. Can this relationship be redefined? But there is much more.

Let us look at some of the complications in the Nineveh Plain. At the beginning of 2017, multiple forces were fighting. In 2016 the Rubin Center (formerly the Global Research in International Affairs Center in Hertzliya, Israel) named 'the Iraqi Security Forces (ISF), the Kurdish Pesh Merga, the Shia militias of the PMF (Popular Mobilization Forces or Hashd al-Sha'abi), the Sunni militiamen of the Hashd al-Watani (National Mobilization) and even the Kurdish PKK, as well of course [the] US-led coalition air power and advisers.'[13]

Here is an expanded version of that thumbnail analysis: Iran is using Shiite militias across the Middle East as proxy forces to establish an arc of Shiite power from Iran through Iraq, Syria and Lebanon to the Mediterranean. The Kurdish Peshmerga do not trust the PKK (the Kurdish Workers Party), believing they are collaborating with Iranian-trained Shiites. Speaking of Shiites, Iran dispatches the Lebanese Hezbullah to fight for its interests whenever it wants. The PKK suspects the KRG (Kurdish Regional Government) of working with Turkey. Turkey, a putative U.S. ally, periodically attacks the Kurdish forces that are fighting with the

U.S. against ISIS, afraid they will link up with the Kurdish separatists who want to create a separate Kurdish state from part of southeast Turkey. The Iraqi government has sponsored the Hashd al-Watani forces – veterans of Saddam's Baathist military, Shiites, Sunni, Christians and Yazidis. The Rubin Center writes that these forces are protected by the Peshmerga and have received training from the Turkish army.

The Kurds want to create their own state out of adjacent Kurdish areas of Syria, Iraq, Iran and Turkey, and they want Mosul. The current government of Turkey wants to reestablish the Ottoman Empire and wants Mosul. The Iraqi government wants Iraq to remain intact, including Mosul. Iran wants to reestablish the Persian Empire. The Arabs want to reconstitute a Muslim Caliphate, with Mosul.

Russia is actively intervening in the Syrian Civil War and in Iraq. The United States has been training, arming and assisting both the Peshmerga and the rebel forces that are fighting the Syrian government. Saudi Arabia and its allies are intervening in ways that are less obvious. Israel usually helps the Kurds. Many local groups will switch sides quickly if a new potential ally makes a good offer.

Got it?

CAN THE ASSYRIANS DEFEND THEMSELVES?

The Assyrians of the Hakkari Mountains have a proud military tradition. In Iraq, Assyrian Levies fought valiantly for the British from 1919 until they were disbanded in 1955. Assyrians formed the bulk of the local forces that successfully defended the Habbaniya Royal Air Force base in Iraq in the 1940–42 Battle for Habbaniya. In 1942, Commanding Air Vice-Marshal HV Champion De Crespigny awarded them the Royal Air Force Red Eagle Badge and commended them: 'your record in this part of the world has been second to none, both in steadfast loyalty to the British Crown, and in your fighting qualities…in contact with the enemy. For the magnificent way in which you fought, and defeated a numerically superior enemy in May of last year…this badge, which has an old history in the Royal Air Force, has been awarded to you.'

More recently, armed Assyrian militias have been defending their own towns and villages in northern Iraq and northeast Syria, and they have been fighting to defend cities with large Assyrian populations: Mosul, Kirkuk and Hasakeh. At various times they have joined forces with Kurds, Turkmans, Armenians, Yazidis, Shabaks, Kawilya, Mandeans, Circassians, Shia Muslim Arabs, Iranians[14] and Kakei[15] to fight ISIS. (The Kakei are an Iraqi minority of some 75,000.) By far their strongest ally is the Kurdish Peshmerga, which is supported by the United States, but there are issues.

Right now there are four 'Christian security forces in the Plains: the Nineveh Plains Protection Units (NPUs), Nineveh Plains Forces (NPFs), Dwekh Nawsha, and the Babylon Brigades, who fight under the Hash'd al-Shaabi.'[16] What they need is training, resources and coordination. In sum, nobody should count the Assyrians out, but they are few in number.

The qustion will be whether the Chaldo-Assyrians can defend themselves when peace does come. Even assuming the physical attacks stop, in their traditional homes they will face the reality of rebuilding their lives in a tough neighborhood. One report, *The Struggle to Exist*, shows how dangerous it will be[17] as the Kurdish Regional Government (KRG) seeks to expand its control over the Nineveh Plain, the traditional home of Assyrians, Yazidis, Shabak, Turkmen and Kakais. One table[18] presents the ethnic make-up of Telkaif in 2010. Out of a population of 155,000, there were 60,000 Sunni Arabs, 30,000 Chaldeans/Assyrians, 5,000 Kurds, 35,000 Yazidis and assorted others.

An article in *al-Monitor* gives the most recent figures and shows the challenge of demographs: "Christians make up about 15% of the Ninevah Plains population, while the Yazidis consist of nearly 40%. The Shabak people represent 25% and Arabs 20%. In addition, there are 65,000 Christian citizens in Qaraqosh, also known as Hamdaniya, alongside 175,000 Shabak and Kurdish people in the Ninevah province."

"There are about 25,000 Christian citizens out of 175,000 people in Tel Keppe district, while there are 7,000 Christians out of 37,000 people in the Shekhan district. Both are in Ninevah."[19]

Despite the large number of other minorities, the Kurdish slogan is 'Kurdistan for the Kurds.' Christian refugees from Turkey would recognize this.

Unfortunately, since 2003 the KRG has become increasingly nationalist, and a Kurdification campaign threatens the existence of indigenous Assyrians. Heavy-handedly, they arrest, detain, torture and intimidate any minorities who resist Kurdish expansionist plans.

So far, the international community has employed very few strategies for protecting the Christians, short of recommending international peacekeepers. A word of caution – Israel has had experience with UN peacekeepers. There is no comparison between what they do and what Israel does for itself. Moreover, many of these peacekeepers seemed to have more swagger than sway. According to the UN job description, they are supposed to 'maintain peace and security, but also to facilitate the political process, protect civilians, assist in the disarmament, demobilization and reintegration of former combatants; support the organization of elections, protect and promote human rights and assist in restoring the rule of law.'[20] Along Israeli border areas, they like to hang out where they can flirt with Israeli girls.

In *Tower of Babble*, Dore Gold writes that 'by 2000, it was clear that UN peacekeepers were spreading AIDS in Cambodia and East Timor. A year later Italian prosecutors were investigating charges that UN troops…monitoring the Ethiopian and Eritrean frontier were involved in a child prostitution racket.'[21] He also writes that UN peacekeepers in Mozambique and in Bosnia had been accused of the same thing.

Gold goes on to point out that UN peacekeepers stood by during massacres in Somalia in 1993, the slaughter of at least 800,000 Tutsis in Rwanda in 1994 and the murder of over 7,000 Muslims in Bosnia the next year. From Bosnia, the conflict spread to Kosovo. From Rwanda, the war moved on to the Congo, eventually involving five African countries, with millions killed. And the UN peacekeepers did nothing.

In theory, the UN can deploy military forces. The UN defines peace enforcement as involving 'the application of a range of coercive measures, including the use of military force.' So if these UN peace enforcers act as a military force, what are their rules of engagement? Are they permitted actual military action? Do they have the strategy, coordination and the accoutrements of a national army? Are they even allowed to protect themselves if the population turns hostile? If not, and without the back-up of an actual army, they are in serious danger. As a practical matter, if their home countries see that their forces are sitting ducks, they generally bring them home.

There are more problems. What is their mandate? If they observe dangerous activity are they authorized to take action against it? Or do they just observe and report on it? And what good is that? If they stay long enough, will they be co-opted? If they serve on short rotations, and they do not know the local language, will they have any idea what is going on right under their noses?

Last, the truth is that international peace-keeping forces have no actual stake in the battle. In contrast, members of an endangered minority have no choice. They will fight to their last breath to save their family and homes. The Christian community has done just that in the past.

THE NINEVEH PLAIN

An impressive number of people and organizations have released plans for resettling Chaldeans and Assyrians in the Nineveh Plain. While the plans differ in some respects, they have many elements in common. All are based on a concept of federalism, and almost all tie a proposed federal structure directly to the national government of Iraq. Few envision a protectorate within a future Kurdistan. Though they seek improved relationships with the Kurds, they do not put all their eggs in a Kurdish basket.

Many federalist proposals have been discussed. One is to create an Assyrian self-administered zone north of Mosul, extending north to Dohuk and from there to the northeast. This has been called the Nineveh Plain Administrative Area for Assyrian/Chaldean/ Syriacs. Knowing what the Assyrians and Chaldeans asked for in the post-WWI conferences, the reader will recognize how scaled down today's dreams are. Yet today the Assyrians and Chaldeans would be happy to get this much.

The proposed Nineveh Plain Solution is based on Article 125 of the Iraqi Constitution, which says 'This constitution shall guarantee the administrative, political, cultural and educational rights of the various nationalities, such as Turkmen, Chaldeans, Assyrians, and all other constituents, and this shall be regulated by the law.' The goal of this proposal is to stem the tide of emigration and to attract current émigrés to return to Iraq. Its proponents argue that 'This population provides the United States a powerful ally in disseminating ideas and political solutions that seek to mitigate more pernicious ethnic and sectarian trends in Iraqi politics. This opportunity is being lost with the departure of every Iraqi ChaldoAssyrian family.'[22]

What is the proposal? The Iraq Sustainable Democracy Project is a policy research body that is working to help Assyrian political and civil societies in Iraq to achieve what they characterize as 'an administrative area.'[23] Others have proposed an Autonomous Assyrian Region or, alternatively, an Assyrian Province.

Michael Youash of the Iraq Sustainable Democracy Project argues against the concept of an Autonomous Assyrian Region, saying that according to the Iraqi constitution, 'To establish a region, like the Kurdistan Region, you must get 30 percent of each Governorate Council or 10 percent of registered voters in the governorates you want, to request a referendum to create a region. Then you must win a majority of over 50 percent approving the creation of the region in the referendum.' He sees that as politically problematic.

He also argues against the idea of an Assyrian Province because the current Iraqi constitution makes no provision for putting together portions of adjacent governates or for combining governates. Of course, a constitution can be changed. In fact, a resolution[24] before the 2016 U.S. Congress said, 'Iraq's Council of Ministers on January 21, 2014, "agreed, in principle, to turn the districts of Tuz Khurmato, Fallujah and the Nineveh Plains into provinces..." And that same resolution asked Congress to support the Iraqi Government in creating a 'Nineveh Plain Province in accordance with the Government of Iraq Cabinet decision of January 21, 2014.' We will come back to that.

Youash writes that an 'Administrative Area will have an elected Governing Authority and also an elected legislature. There would also be district and sub-district elected officials to manage purely local affairs, along with town and village mayors and councils. This would be just as is done for any federal unit... directly linked to the federal government... It would be responsible for health (pharmacies, primary health care centers, district-level hospitals,); primary, secondary and tertiary education, as well as special cultural, technical and vocational education programs; various judicial matters; economic development planning (rural and urban); social welfare; agriculture; sanitation; local policing; along with special powers regarding archeology and tourism, among others. It would have the power to tax based on its functions and therefore would also have treasury and revenue agencies.'

How would the Nineveh Plains Solution work? The Iraq Sustainable Democracy Project (ISDP) explains the Nineveh Plain Province Solution in *At the Tipping Point: A Nineveh Plain Province and Related Solutions to Iraq's Indigenous Minority Crisis.* In this paper, Youash,[25] writes that after the murder of 58 Assyrians on October 31, 2010 at evening mass of All Saints Day in Baghdad, the years 2011–2012 were the 'the tipping point.' This is the point at which the number of people coming to the Nineveh Plain equaled the number leaving. The Project lays out the Nineveh Plain Province Solution in three sections: *Governance, Development* and *Security.*

Governance would be in a form of federalism tied to the Iraqi government, not Kurdistan. Preparation would start with community dialogue. From there it would move on to 'Training and Capacity Building for 'Get Out the Vote' campaigns and referenda, and finally to 'Government Capacity Building for Nineveh Plain Province Representatives and Administrators.'

Development would have as its centerpiece the creation of a Nineveh Plain University and a Nineveh Plain Provincial Hospital, along with basic infrastructure development, promotion of large-scale industry, development of small and medium size enterprises, and eventually promotion of economic and trade relations with the U.S.

Security would be taken over by some 5,000 local minority recruits to a Nineveh Plains Police Force (NPPF) and Special Forces, which would have local officers from the Nineveh Plain. These would need sustained training and support. The report also envisions the recruitment and training of chief magistrates. The first phase would cost $128 million, and the whole plan would require over $300 million.

The report explains that currently 'One primary means by which the NPPF is consistently undermined in terms of operational effectiveness is because its officer corps and commanders are foreign to the NP and drawn from other communities. As with the police officers themselves, the Officer Corps/Commanders should also be drawn from the demographics in the NP, who have local legitimacy and local interests central to their mission.' Not only have 'the Kurds opposed the NPPF, their Peshmerga, while purportedly offering temporary security [has] now become an occupation force.'

In fact, he writes, 'The Kurdistan Regional Government [KRG] is the primary impediment to the creation of the NPPF. The KRG understands that once the NPPF is functional, it will remove the basis for their continued occupation of the NP. The KRG has been so determined in this respect that while blocking any attempt to establish the NPPF, they also established an informal Christian Militia paid for by the KRG Ministry of Finance, rather than allow for the fulfillment of the Government of Iraq order to establish the NPPF.'[26]

Fifteen Assyrian political parties and national institutions have signed a declaration in support of the Nineveh Plain Province proposal: the Assyrian Democratic Movement, Chaldean Syriac Assyrian Popular Council, Assyrian Democratic Organization, Chaldean Democratic Forum, Assyrian Universal Alliance, Syriac Independent Assembly, Bet-Nahrain Democratic Party, Chaldean Democratic Party, Chaldean National Council, Assyrian General Conference, Bet-Nahrain National Union, Assyrian American National Federation, Chaldean Culture Society, Assyrian Patriotic Party and the ChaldoAshur Organization of the Communist Party of Kurdistan.

What would be the source of financing? The Nineveh Project is an economic development fund[27] set up for the benefit of Assyrians, Chaldeans and Syriacs who are members of the Holy Apostolic Assyrian Church of the East, the Ancient Church of the East, the Chaldean Catholic Church, the Syriac Orthodox Church, the Syriac Catholic Church or the Maronite Syriac Church, and who live in or are willing to relocate to the Nineveh Plain. This too 'directly evolved from the Black Marches that took place throughout the world after the attack on Our Lady of Salvation Syriac Catholic Church in Baghdad, Iraq, on October 31, 2010.'

This Nineveh Project emphasizes that 'We have maybe a decade, perhaps less, to stop this flight and stabilize our population in Iraq.' They hope to generate 'an economic development of $10 million per year to invest in the Nineveh Plain' through an internet pledge drive. Their calculation is 'at $250 per person, we would need 40,000 people to get $10 million.' They consider that goal to be 'completely within reach. We have one million people or more in Diaspora.'

They propose that 'A qualified but democratically elected Board of Directors from across the Diaspora will oversee a paid, professional Executive Staff... The Nineveh Project is all about hiring a team of talented people to take the resources of the Diaspora with accountability, transparency, and genuine oversight; and then use these resources to save our people and our culture from extinction by investing concertedly in smart, sustainable development in collaboration with our people on the ground who are desperate for this hope from the Diaspora.'

As of the spring of 2017, 'church leaders in northern Iraq say they need $262 million for a Marshall Plan-style reconstruction of Christian-majority villages devastated by the occupation of ISIS. The Catholic Bishop's Emergency Committee, which spends $1.2 million a month to help displaced families in Iraq, in mid-May said it hopes to raise funds from a variety of government and non-state organizations in Europe and the U.S.'[28]

What do other organizations propose? The Nineveh Center for Research and Development (NCRD) and Alliance of Iraqi Minorities identify[29] possible international interventions: military action, trade and economic sanctions, imposition of a safe haven or no-fly zone, humanitarian aid, UN peacekeepers, fact-finding committees and crime tribunals. They request American pressure on the Iraqi and Kurdish governments, military action against ISIS, and U.S. pressure on the UN for humanitarian aid. They also ask that the Security Council expand the mandate and functions of UNAMI, the UN mission to help Iraq. Finally, they request a safe zone in northern Iraq, possibly under the auspices of the UN.

The Restore Nineveh Now Foundation,[30] jointly established by the American Mesopotamian Organization, the Iraqi Christian Relief Council and the Seyfo Center, concurs with the need for a self-governing Nineveh Plain Province defended by Nineveh Plain Protection Units. In addition, in May 2016, they appealed to the UN Human Rights Council in Geneva in an unprecedented 300-page Human Rights Complaint against both the Kurdish Regional Government and the Iraqi government.

The Assyria Council of Europe and the Hammurabi Human Rights Organization present a long list of recommendations directed to the Kurdistan Regional Government, the Iraqi Government, the U.S., the UN and international human rights organizations.[31] They request the Kurds to legally recognize minority populations; they also want Kurds to allow minorities to self-identify, to allow minorities to remain in their homes and to stop replacing them with Kurds. They want the Kurds to cease their repression, to allow minorities to participate fully in civil society, to permit non-Kurdish schools and to recognize the Nineveh Province's March 2003 boundaries.

To put teeth into their recommendations, they ask the U.S. and the international community to 'not cooperate with the Kurdish Regional Government until the Kurdish authorities stop the suppression of other indigenous Iraqi communities, abandon claims to lands inhabited mainly by nonKurds, and abandon the use of militias, intimidation and violence.' They request investigation of and remedies for a long litany of human rights abuses: electoral fraud, discriminatory resource and service allocations, tortures and outright killings.

The two organizations ask for an amendment to the Iraqi constitution 'so that it ensures protection of minority groups' linguistic and cultural rights, removes discrimination between the ethnic communities in Iraqi society, improves the access of ethnic communities to education in their own mother tongue, and prevents the publication of immense Iraqi state documentation in Kurdish.' Further, they request the government to 'Look into the establishment of an area where indigenous minority communities can prosper, progress and protect themselves within the framework of a united and free Iraq.' Finally they too call for 'Local recruitment into Nineveh's security forces and especially integration of members of diverse ethnic groups in security forces deployed in disputed territories.'

Two requests, the Nineveh Plains Police Force and a protected area, or safe haven for settlement, seem to be unanimous. Lately, three Syriac bishops – one Syriac Catholic and two Syriac-Orthodox – have proposed[32] that this protected area be put under international protection.

Joseph Kassab, the former Executive Director of the Chaldean Federation of America, is the founder and president of the Iraqi Christians Advocacy and Empowerment Institute (ICEA). Its headquarters are in suburban Detroit, the home of one of the largest Chaldean communities in the Diaspora. He has made presentations to the White House, to many other entities, and on May 31, 2017 to the Pope. When he went to the Vatican he brought a letter that asked for relief and protection for immigrants and refugees, plus assistance with voluntary repatriation. It asked for help in increasing the representation of Christians at all levels of government, ensuring their constitutional rights in Iraq, promoting laws that would give the community a voice, addressing their humanitarian concerns, and preserving their cultural heritage.

Other ICAE publications request reforms within Iraq.[33] They want the Iraqi constitution to ensure universal civil rights and freedom of religion, and they want an independent Iraqi National Reconciliation process for political parties, tribes, religions and ethnic groups. They want to dissolve both the sectarian Popular Mobilization Forces and the Sectarian Armed Militias, in favor of American-trained Iraqi armed forces, police, and security forces. They call for Americans to mediate between the Iraqi government and Kurds, and they ask the U.S. to maintain its bases in Iraq. Significantly, they ask for an international conference, sponsored by the UN, EU and U.S., that would pledge support for reconstruction, using money from the sale of Iraqi oil and administered by the US.

Many have missed it, but Iraq made the following announcement on January 2014:[34] 'The Iraqi cabinet made big headlines today with a shock decision to form three brand new provinces. Supposedly, there will be new governorates in Tuz Khormato (a Turkmen-dominated area currently in Salahaddin province), the Nineveh plains (a Christian-dominated part of Nineveh province) and Falluja (centre of the current Sunni-led uprising in Anbar province).' It may have been met with scepticism because 'agreement on the formation of these new decisions was made "in principle", to be completed after the necessary formalities "had been completed."' However, 'The largest seven Assyrian, Syriac and Chaldean political organizations in Iraq made a historic unified appeal to Prime Minister Haider Al-Abadi on Tuesday, March 7, [2017] demanding the creation of a Nineveh Plain Province to serve as a home for Iraq's long-targeted minorities.'

The Iraqi Christian Relief Council[35] has 'demanded that a future Nineveh Plain Province be excluded from all political and military conflicts, and that its borders be considered a green demarcation line, politically and militarily neutral...The people of the [Nineveh Plain] region should be granted their constitutional right to administer their areas, and should be enabled to defend themselves and protect their properties with the integration of all private security forces formed by minorities under Iraqi federal forces and local police.'

Will any of this happen? Even the geography is problematic. The Kurds might like to annex Christian and other minority areas, but nobody really expects a future Kurdistan to reach as far south as Telkaif, certainly not to Mosul. The mountains of the 36th parallel form the natural northern border of the Nineveh Plains, but this would limit the Nineveh Plains area to only a fraction of northern Iraq. Certainly a Nineveh Plains province split between Kurdistan and the government of Iraq would be untenable.

Some have suggested forming a federation with the Kurdistan Regional Government, but recent experience is not encouraging. The Assyrian Human Rights Project[36] has published 12 categories of Kurdish abuses against Assyrians: religious persecution and regulation, political persecution and executions, attacks against Assyrian civilians, disenfranchisement of the Assyrians, displacement and land expropriation, Kurdification policies, Islamist attacks, abduction and forced conversion to Islam, lynchings of Assyrians, churches attacked, restricted humanitarian aid to Assyrians, and plundering of historic artifacts/erasing Assyrian Heritage.

The report emphasizes 'The authority to distribute humanitarian aid ought not to be left in the hands of those who have fostered an environment of conflict, violence and anarchy.'

On June 28, the European Union sponsored a conference in Brussels. Since many of the participants were avowedly pro-Kurdish, many mainstream Chaldean and Assyrian organizations boycotted it. Early reports of the conference seem to validate their concerns. One of the few written in English[37] expresses the concerns of the writer: 'First, on security, it contemplates the KRG and Peshmerga having control over the unified security force. The KRG had primary responsibility for the security of the Nineveh Plain. They disarmed us and abandoned us. If the intent is for security to be by the people of the Nineveh Plain, then whatever security apparatus is developed should not be under the supervision of the KRG.'

He continues: 'Then what follows is totally curious: a reference to Article 35 of the KRG constitution (an article which has yet to be implemented for any group) followed by a plea for the Government of Iraq to work in this spirit. The only reason to include this reference to Article 35 in this context is to imply a refer-

endum be held to join the KRG and become a "region" within the
KRG.' Continuing, 'The second reference to a referendum is for
the international coalition to work with the KRG and GoI to recognize the Interim Nineveh Plain Council and plan a referendum.'
He concludes: 'If the goal was to have the people of the Nineveh
Plain decide their fate on their own terms with their decisional autonomy and integrity intact, this policy document falls short of that
mark.'

WHAT DOES THE WEST NEED TO DO?

Chaldeans, Assyrians and Syriacs will only return to their homelands if their families can live there in peace and security. In Syria,
they must wait until the Syrian Civil War ends. In Iraq, they need
guarantees of basic human rights, civil rights and a constitution that
gives them political representation. Wherever they go, Chalde-
ans/Assyrians/Syriacs need their own well trained security forces
with their own officers. To achieve these goals, they will need help
from the international community, principally the United States.

That raises a matter of conscience for the countries of the
west. What is our responsibility? What can Europe and the United
States do to help save the first and last Christians of the Middle
East? Can we prevent or reverse the loss of their communities,
their traditions, and their ancient language? Will our geopolitical
imperatives blind us to our humanitarian obligations? Will we act at
all? Will it help?

Some who are intimately familiar with the region consider
themselves realists. Joseph Kassab of the Michigan-based Iraqi
Christians Advocacy and Empowerment Institute ICAE) fears that
neither the Iraqi government nor a future Kurdish state can ever
protect returning Iraqi Christians securely from Islamic extremists,
and he questions whether even the most valiant Christian troops
can do the job. In his opinion, only international forces can offer
them adequate protection.[38] He writes: 'The Iraqi government did
not provide them protection and security, therefore they do not
trust it anymore…There is nothing to return for; their homes,
properties and places of business are seized, looted, and destroyed,
[and] their neighbors, the local Arab-Muslims [betrayed] them
when they helped identify for ISIS their vacant homes and properties by marking [them] with the letter N, meaning the property belongs to [a] Nazereth person, i.e. Christian.' While he acknowledges

that ISIS is on the run today, he believes that its remnants simply will mutate later, perhaps to an even more threatening form. He says that ISIS cannot be eliminated by military means, only by a change in their philosophy, but their philosophy comes from the Koran, which is immutable. He acknowledges that moderate Muslims may quietly urge some extremists toward a milder form of Islam, but he basically sees the future of his people, their families and their children in the Diaspora.

Some are more optimistic about a future in Iraq. Robert Nicholson of the New York-based Philos Project has articulated a vision that would be a model for the entire Middle East. He writes[39] that a consensus is emerging in favor of: 'The creation of a safe haven for Iraq's three largest minority groups in the northern part of the country.' Yazidis would settle in their traditional homeland, the Sinjar District of northwestern Iraq. The Turkmen would go to their historic land just north of Sinjar, the Tal Afar District. The Assyrians would settle north and east of Mosu, the Nineveh Plain. These three areas are contiguous. Together they could form one province, or they could become a group of provinces under an amended constitution of a federal Republic of Iraq.

Several attempts have been made to pass a bill through Congress. Rep. Juan Vargas (D-CA) introduced House Resolution 683 to the 113th Congress on July 24, 2014, under the title 'Expressing the sense of the House of Representatives on the current situation in Iraq and the urgent need to protect religious minorities from persecution from the Sunni Islamist insurgent and terrorist group the Islamic State in Iraq and Levant (ISIL) as it expands its control over areas in northwestern Iraq.' This requested the U.S. to support safe havens for those who claim amnesty in Iraq. It passed the House, but it never reached the president's desk.

Representatives Anna Eshoo (D-CA), Jan Schakowsky (D-IL), and Sen. Gary Peters (D-MI) put forward a legislative proposal called 'The Nineveh Plain Province Solution.'[40] This was consistent with language supported by the Religious Minorities in the Middle East Caucus, under the Co-Chairmanship of former Rep. Frank Wolf (R-VA) and Rep. Anna Eshoo (D-CA).[41]

On March 17, 2016, Secretary of State Kerry declared that the systematic murder of minorities in Iraq by ISIS is genocide. On that day Sen. Cotton introduced his own bill, 'The Religious Persecution Relief Act,' saying that it 'would grant religious minorities fleeing persecution at the hands of ISIS and other groups in Syria priority status so they can apply directly to the U.S. resettlement program without going through the U.N. And it will set aside 10,000 resettlement slots annually that must be devoted to religious minorities.'

In his address to the Senate, Sen. Tom Cotton (R-AR) testified that 'while 13 percent of Syria's pre-war population consisted of religious minorities, only 2.3 percent of the refugees that make it to the U.S. are religious minorities.'

He pointed out that "The priority status – known as "P-2 status" – will allow religious minorities to skip the U.N. referral process and it will fast-track the process by which we confirm that they are the targets of persecution and genocide." As S. 2708, the bill was referred to the Senate Judiciary Committee.

Cotton says the idea is not entirely new: 'And in 2007, the late Senator from Massachusetts, Ted Kennedy, passed a bill that granted priority status to certain Iraqi religious minority members.' It is devoutly to be hoped that this recent bill will have more impact.

On September 8, 2016, Rep. Anna Eshoo (D-CA) Rep. Chris Smith (R-NJ), co-sponsors Rep. Jeff Fortenberry (R-NE) and Rep. Trent Franks (R-AZ) introduced H.R. 5961, the Iraq and Syria Genocide Relief and Accountability Act of 2016. The purpose of the bill was 'To provide for relief of victims of genocide, crimes against humanity, and war crimes in Iraq and Syria, for accountability for perpetrators of these crimes, and for other purposes.' This passed the House and, as HR 390, in June, 2017 it was referred to the Senate Committee on Foreign Relations. The bill requests $1.3 billion for refugee services, a portion of which would be provided to affected minorities in Iraq. This money would be allocated by the Secretary of State and the USAID administrator to groups that can be shown to be providing aid effectively.

Rep. Fortenberry (R-NE) introduced H. Con. Res. 152 to the House of Representatives on September 9, 2016 under the title 'Resolution on a Nineveh Plain Province in Iraq.'[42] This too was referred to the House Committee on Foreign Affairs. On September 12, more than 50 members of Congress attended a three-day rally in Washington in support of this legislation.

This resolution seeking a safe haven in the Nineveh Plain[43] had the support of several organizations, including: In defense of

Christians (IDC), the Philos Project, and the Institute for Global Engagement. It had 11 co-sponsors, and it was referred to the House Foreign Affairs Committee. The bill requested that return of the indigenous people of the Nineveh Plain be a policy priority for the United States. It asked for them to have their 'have their fundamental human rights fully restored,' and it emphasized their 'right to security and self-determination within the federal structure of the Republic of Iraq. That is important to note – the *federal structure*.

It called upon the United States, the international community, the Government of Iraq and the Kurdish Regional Government to commit to the economic revitalization of the Nineveh Plain, to maintaining its territorial integrity and to promoting 'a sustainable security settlement.'

This resolution combined elements from a number of proposals, and it offers a road map for the United States as it tries to navigate the tangled byways of Iraq in the future. It no doubt will undergo some changes, but it gives a sense of what the parties believe is important. The reader will note the emphasis on proactive action, not on seeking redress or vengeance. Those who crafted this resolution are not pushing to right all past wrongs; they simply want the Christians to be able to come home and live in safety.

Advocates for the Christian community in the Middle East continue to press for action, but not always focusing on the community in the Middle East. The most recent effort was designed to help those who are trying to immigrate to the U.S. HR 565 was introduced to the U.S. House of Representatives on January 13, 2017, under the title 'Save Christians from Genocide Act.' Among the sponsors were Rep. Dana Rohrabacher (R-CA) and Mike Bishop (R-MI). The text of the bill 'recognizes that Christians and Yazidis in Iraq, Syria, Pakistan, Iran and Libya are targets of genocide' and asks for 'priority and expedited processing' for those who are 'seeking admission to the United States as an immigrant' under a specific subsection of the Immigration and Nationality Act.

The resolution will go to the House Judiciary Committee and the Foreign Affairs Committee. Its first referral was to the Subcommittee on Immigration and Border Security.

Robert Nicholson explains 'We believe that they need: safe passage to return to their homeland; administrative autonomy; training and equipment to field their local police and security forces; protection from an international Rapid Deployment Force; first priority for economic aid and development; legal protections for their language and culture [and] greater political participation.'[44]

Others think it is important to right past wrongs. Naomi Kikoler serves as the Deputy Director of the U.S. Holocaust Center's Simon-Skjodt Center, which 'is dedicated to stimulating timely global action to prevent genocide and to catalyze an international response when it occurs.' In September 2015, she visited Iraq in a Bearing Witness trip, to investigate[45] the persecution of minorities in Nineveh Province. She reported that ISIS has 'perpetrated crimes against humanity, ethnic cleansing, and war crimes against Christian, Yezidi, Turkmen, Shabak, Sabaean-Mandaean, and Kaka'i people in Ninewa province between June and August. Also, ISIS 'has been and is perpetrating genocide against the Yazidi people.'

Since we still are fighting extremists, , the Holocaust Center warns that 'winning the war but failing to prevent atrocities and provide adequate security to ALL Iraqis will likely fuel future grievances, a proliferation of armed actors, and continued conflict.' Moreover, 'When done effectively, both counterterrorism and atrocity prevention advance core US national security interests.'

The most significant point that Kikoler and other responsible parties make is that the international community must: 'Revoke or withhold foreign military assistance for any forces committing gross human rights violations.'

Some of the Holocaust Center recommendations for the international community are:

'1. International assistance to the Iraqi government, the Kurdistan Regional Government, and local civil society organizations to systematically document, gather, and preserve evidence of atrocities – including genocide, crimes against humanity, and war crimes – perpetrated by IS.

2. Identifying, with the assistance of coalition satellite imagery if needed, the location of mass graves, their excavation and protection, and the preservation of forensic material.

3. Iraq's accession to the Rome Statute of the International Criminal Court (ICC) and acceptance of the exercise of jurisdiction by the ICC.

4. Referral of the situation to the ICC by the UN Security Council.

5. Prosecution of foreign nationals who have fought for IS by their governments for the commission of atrocity crimes.

6. Assistance to the Iraqi government to document and investigate [sic] reports of missing persons.'

The Center asks the Iraqi government to abide 'by its obligations as a party to the United Nations Convention on the Prevention and Punishment of the Crime of Genocide, including by enacting comprehensive legislation criminalizing genocide and by pursuing prosecutions for alleged perpetrators that adhere to internationally recognized legal standards.'

Kikoler also calls for international donations to help Kurdistan with the costs of housing, social services and education for refugees, because Kurdistan's budget has been strained by a 28% increase in population. That sounds logical, but, while the refugees certainly need help, experience to date does not support the assumption that all this donor money will be spent on behalf of Assyrians. On the other hand, since Kurds have been serving as important 'boots on the ground' fighting ISIS on behalf of the international coalition, they both deserve and require a subsidy for that activity. As always, the calculation is complicated.

A high-powered United States Commission on International Religious Freedom[46] also calls for punishment for crimes committed. The Chairman is Dr. Robert P. George. Dr. M. Zuhdi Jasser and Hon. Eric P. Schwartz are the Vice-Chairs. Their report on Syria focuses on the civil war and its refugees. It too asks the International Criminal Court to investigate the crimes of ISIS (ISIL) and of the Assad regime. Their report on Iraq asks the U.N. Security Council to refer ISIS (ISIL) to the International Criminal Court.

One recommendation has teeth. Financial assistance should be conditioned on good behavior: 'Include in all military or security assistance to the Iraqi and Iraqi Kurdistan governments a requirement that security forces are integrated to reflect the country's religious and ethnic diversity, and provide training for recipient units on universal human rights standards and how to treat civilians, particularly religious minorities.'

They recommend the United States 'Include in the Fiscal Year 2017 Department of State, Foreign Operations, and Related Programs Appropriations Bill, or in another appropriate vehicle, a provision that would permit the U.S. government to appropriate or allocate funds for in-kind assistance to genocide, crimes against humanity, or war crimes cases at the ICC on a case-by-case basis and when in the national interest to provide such assistance.'

Some Chaldo-Assyrian groups have focused on war crimes. Both the Assyria Council of Europe and the Hammurabi Human Rights Organization[47] have asked the United States to pressure the Kurdish government to investigate Kurdish and Arab violations of human rights, and to remedy injustices that have resulted from altering the demographics of the Nineveh Plain. They asked the U.S. to 'Assist relevant Iraqi parties to reach the necessary compromises in Nineveh, primarily by: a) pressing the Iraqi government to reintegrate certain members of the Baath party and the insurgency in local civilian and security institutions; b) pressuring local allies that rely heavily on the U.S., notably tribal forces, to promote a power- and security-sharing agreement; and c) insisting on the necessary protection of the diverse indigenous ethnic groups.' They also ask for an Iraqi government investigation into several lethal attacks in Mosul, as well as into beatings and torture of minorities.

They caution the U.S.: 'Do not cooperate with the Kurdish Regional Government until the Kurdish authorities stop the suppression of other indigenous Iraqi communities, abandon claims to lands inhabited mainly by non-Kurds, and abandon the use of militias, intimidation and violence.'

These recommendations come directly from the locals and should not be taken lightly. They ask for investigation of human rights violations, giving political suggestions for Iraq that reflect a deep understanding of the ethnic realities in that complex nation. Their points are consistent with proposed legislation, but they have specifics.

One eloquent plea for help is based on human and religious values. The Melkite Bishop Jean-Clemont Jeanbart wrote from Aleppo on June 11, 2015: 'In Syria, my country, Christians are caught in the middle of a civil war and they are enduring the rage of an extremist jihad. And it is unjust for the West to ignore the persecutions these Christian communities are experiencing...Syrian Christians are in grave danger; we may disappear soon...'

The bishop emphasizes: 'Christians must be able to count on the US and its allies for continued, long-term military protection…To ensure political stability, it is essential that Christian leaders, both lay and religious, are given a voice and presence at the negotiating table. Christians can act as bridge-builders between Shiites and Sunnis, and they can help develop a political system that ensures the rights of all citizens.' In practical terms, 'Last but not least, Christians – like other people whose lives have been overturned by years of fighting – need practical, financial help to rebuild their lives, especially their professional lives. If Christians are not given the means to earn a living, there is no way they can remain in Syria or Iraq. The hierarchy's lamenting of mass emigration can do little good if the Churches do not give their flock concrete means to rebuild their lives.'[48]

On January 19, 2017, Telkaif was liberated by the Iraqi army. It had shrunken from a city of 3000 families, 500 of them Christian, to 700 families, few if any Christian. According to some reports, since then, 18,594 inhabitants have returned.[49] In the week after liberation though, observers[50] saw a few frightened survivers rise from the ruins and small groups of Christians driving over from Kurdistan. They found ruined houses, a few shops reopening, and a destroyed church. They then drove back.

Why is it in the interest of the United States to create safe havens for Christions in northern Iraq? Nicholson[51] has summarized the reasons. He points out that lawless regions and failed states are in nobody's interest: 'Creation of a safe haven will weaken ISIS and its offshoots; it will establish a zone of stability in a lawless region; and it will protect disputed lands against a post-ISIS vacuum.' Returning these districts to their indigenous populations will make it clear that these lands are not part of a caliphate and it is not 'disputed territory' between the Kurds and the central government, as it often is characterized.

Politically, 'The creation of a safe haven will help move Iraq toward greater federalism; it will allow minority communities greater political participation; it will diversify Iraq's political landscape and strengthen the cohesiveness of the country; and it will reinforce Iraqi military capabilities in the country's vulnerable northern reaches.' Once this land is in the hands of its original owners, they will defend it.

Given the ethnically diverse nature and the size of Iraq, it always has been difficult to rule. The strategy of creating new provinces for each of these three safe havens would turn Iraq into a federal nation in which each nation would maintain its own language and identity but be self-governing within its own state. The model is that of the European Union, not of the United States concept of a melting pot. The argument for minority representation is that: 'Bringing a sizable non-Arab, non-Sunni bloc into parliament will diversify political voices, break stalemates, and set up opportunities for mediating between opposing viewpoints.'[52]

The last argument is that 'The creation of a safe haven will increase regional stability by blocking expansionist foreign powers; it will provide an example for other Middle Eastern countries moving toward federalism; and it will demonstrate in microcosm that coexistence and good governance is possible in the region.'

The United States alone cannot create a federal system in northern Iraq. This can only come about through a joint effort between the Government of Iraq and the concerned minority groups. Yet, the Middle East has no experience with federalism. All parties will need leadership and operational guidance from the United States as they work toward this goal.

After meeting the Chaldeans and Assyrians of the Middle East and learning their history, the reader will agree that they deserve a better future than to vanish into the Diaspora. After learning about the historical and religious importance of the Aramaic language, the reader surely will understand that we cannot let it die now. After reading the newspapers and seeing shocking pictures of killing and torture, the reader will realize that we must deny extremists their own country. It should be clear that the only way to do this is for the original inhabitants of the region to return to their own homes, rebuild, flourish, and defend their own territory. And, for this to happen, we in the west have an obligation to help.

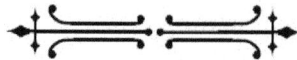

FURTHER READING

Ahituv, Shmuel, *Echoes From the Past* (Jerusalem: Carta, 2008)

Bacall, Jacob, *Chaldeans in Detroit* (Charleston: Arcadia Publishing, 2014)

Badger, Reverend George Percy, *The Nestorians and their Rituals with the Narrative of a Mission to Mesopotamia and Coordistan in 1842 to 1844, Part Two* (London: Joseph Masters, 1852)

Baum, Wilhelm and Winkler, Dietmar W., *The Church of the East: A concise history* (Oxon: Routledge Curzon, 2003)

Bat Ye'or, *The Dhimmi: Jews and Christians under Islam* (London: Associated University Press, trans, 1985)

Beyer, Klaus, *The Aramaic Language: Its Distribution and Subdivisions* (Gottingen: Vandenhoeck and Ruprecht, 1986), Trans. By John F. Healey

Ben Yaakov, Avraham, *Kurdistan's Jewish Community* (Jerusalem: Institute Ben Zvi Hebrew University, 1961) ‏קהילות יהודי כורדיסתאן‎

Benjamin, The Travels of Benjamin of Tudela, 1173 CE, http://www.sacred-texts.com/jud/mhl/mhl20.htm

Black, Edwin, *The Farhud: Roots of the Ara-Nazi Alliance in the Holocaust* (Washington, D.C.: Dialog Press, 2010)

Black, Ian and Morris, Benny, *Israel's Secret Wars* (New York: Grove Press, 1991)

Brauer, Erich and Patai, Raphael, *The Jews of Kurdistan* (Detroit: Wayne State University Press, 1993)

Budge, Wallis E.A., "The Monks of Kublai Khan Emperor of China or The History of the Life and Travels of Rabban Sawma, Envoy and Plenipotentiary of the Mongol Khans to the Kings of Europe, and Markos who as Mar Yahbhallaha III Became Patriarch of the Nestorian Church in Asia," (London: The Religious Tract Society, 1928) http://www.nestorian.org/history_of_rabban_bar_sawma_1.html

Chaldean Diocese in the United States of America, Chaldean Directory 1998 (Eastpointe: Cal Press, 1998)

Dalrymple, William, *From the Holy Mountain* (New York: Henry Holt and Co., 1977)

De Courtois, Sebastien, *The Forgotten Genocide: Eastern Christians, The Last Arameans* (New Jersey: Gorgias Press, 2004)

Donabed, Sargon George, *Reforging a Forgotten History: Iraq and the Assyrians in the Twentieth Century* (Edinburgh: Edinburgh University Press, 2015)

Donef, Racho, *Assyrians post-Nineveh: identity, fragmentation, conflict and survival (672 BC – 1920), A study of Assyrogenous Communities* (Sydney: Tatavla Publishing Mesopotamia Series 1, 2012)

Donef, Racho, *The Hakkari Massacres: Ethnic cleansing by Turkey 1924–25* (Sydney: Tatavla Publishing, 2009, reprinted 2014)

Emhardt, William Chauncey and Lamsa, George M. Lamsa, *The Oldest Christian People: A brief account of the history and traditions of the Assyrian people and the fateful history of the Nestorian Church* (Eugene: Wipf and Stock Publishers, 2012), first published by Macmillan, 1926

Etz Hayim (New York: Jewish Publication Society, 2001)

Fitzhugh, William W, Rossabi, Morris, Honeychurch, William, *Genghis Khan and the Mongol Empire* (Arctic Studies Center, Smithsonian Institution: W.W. Norton & Co., 2013)

Fitzmyer, Joseph A., *A Wandering Aramean: Collected Aramaic Essays*, republished in *The Semitic Background of the New Testament* (Cambridge: William B. Eerdmans Publishing Co., 1997)

Frykenberg, Robert Eric, *Christianity in India: From Beginning to Present* (Oxford: Oxford University Press, 2008)

Gaunt, David, *Massacres, Resistance, Protectors: Muslim-Christian Relations in Eastern Anatolia During World War I* (Piscataway: Gorgias Press, 2006)

Gaunt, David, 'The Assyrian Genocide of 1915,' *Seyfo Center*, April 18, 2009. https://blu169.mail.live.com/mail/ViewOffice

Preview.aspx?messageid=mgIxCqjqO-5RGiaAAiZMIHSg2&folderid=flinbox&attindex=1&cp=-1&attdepth=1&n=12264205

Gavish, Haya, *Unwitting Zionists* (Detroit: Wayne State University Press, 2010)

Godspeed, George, 'International World History Project, History of the World: Assyrians, parts one through sixteen,' (*History World International* 2004) http://history-world.org/assyrians.htm

Gold, Dore, *Tower of Babble* (New York: Three Rivers Press, 2004)

Goldenberg, Gideon, *Semitic Languages, Features, Structures, Relations, Processes* (Oxford: Oxford University Press, 2013)

Grayzel, Solomon, *A History of the Jews – From the Babylonian Exile to the Present 5728–1968* (New York: Penguin Group, 1947, 1968)

Hetzron, Robert, *The Semitic Languages* (Oxon: Routledge, 1997)

Hinton, Alexander Laban, La Pointe Thomas and Irvin-Erickson, Douglas, Ed. *Hidden Genocides: Power, Knowledge, Memory* (New Brunswick: Rutgers University Press, 2013)

Herf, Jeffrey, *Nazi Propaganda for the Arab World* (New Haven: Yale University Press, 2009)

Ibrahim, Raymond, *Crucified Again: Exposing Islam's New War on Christians* (Washington D.C.: Regnery Publishing, Inc., 2013)

ISIS: Portrait of a Jihadi Terrorist Organization, Meir Amit Intelligence and Terrorism Information Center at the Israeli Intelligence and Heritage Information Center, November 2014, http://www.crethiplethi.com/files/cp_0115.pdf

Jammo, Mar Sarhad Y. and Younan, Fr. Andrew, *Chaldean Grammar* (San Diego: Chaldean Media Center, 2014)

Jammo, Fr. Sarhad and Najar, Basil, *Chaldean Epic of Mary* (Detroit, 1992)

Kaltner, John and McKenzie, Steven, Eds., *Beyond Babel: A Handbook for Biblical Hebrew and Related Languages* (Leiden: Society of Biblical Literature, 2002)

Kaufman, Stephen A., 'The Akkadian Influences on Aramaic,' *The Oriental Institute of the University of Chicago, Assyriological Studies No. 19*, The University of Chicago Press, Chicago and Lon-

don, 1974 https://oi.uchicago.edu/sites/oi.uchicago.edu/
files/uploads/shared/docs/as19.pdf

Kepel, Gilles, *Jihad: The Trail of Political Islam* (Cambridge: Harvard University Press 2002)

Rashid Khalidi, Lisa Anderson, Muhammad Muslih and Reeva S. Simon eds., *The Origins of Arab Nationalism* (New York: Columbia University Press, 1991)

Kinross, Lord, *Ataturk: A Biography of Mustafa Kemal* (New York: William Morrow and Company, 1978)

Kinross, Lord, *The Ottoman Centuries: The Rise and Fall of the Turkish Empire* (New York: Morrow Quill Publishers, 1977)

Layard, Austen Henry, *Nineveh and Its Remains, Volume 1* (Cambridge: Cambridge University Press, 1849)

Layard, Sir Austen Henry, *Nineveh and Its Remains, Volume 2* (London: John Murray, Albemarle Street 1849)

Layard, Austen Henry, *Discoveries in the Ruins of Nineveh and Babylon, Part 1* (London: John Murray, 1853)

Layard, Austen Henry, *Discoveries in the Ruins of Nineveh and Babylon, Part 2* (London: John Murray, 1853)

Lewis, Bernard, *The Middle East: A Brief History of the Last 2,000 Years* (New York: Scribner, 1995)

Lewis, Bernard, *The Jews of Islam* (Princeton: Princeton University Press, 1984)

Lewis, Bernard, *What Went Wrong? The Clash Between Islam and Modernity in the Middle East* (New York: HarperCollins, 2002)

Lipinski, Edward, *The Aramaeans, Their Ancient History, Culture, Religion* (Leuven: Peeters Publishers and Department of Oriental Studies Bondgenotenlaan, 2000)

Lorieux, Claude, *Chretiens d'Orient en terres d'islam* (Saint-Amand-Montrond (Cher) France: Editions Perrin, 2001)

Manz, Beatrice Forbes, *The Rise and Rule of Tamerlane* (Cambridge: Cambridge University Press, 1989)

McCants, William, *ISIS: Apocalypse, The History, Strategy, and Doomsday Vision of the Islamic State* (New York: St. Martins Press, 2015),

Mazower, Mark, *Salonica, City of Ghosts: Christians, Muslims and Jews 1430–1950* (London: Harper Perennial, 2005)

Morgenthau, Henry, *Ambassador Morgenthau's Story* (reprinted in New York: Cosimo Classics, 2010), First published in 1918

Morris, Benny, *The Birth of the Palestinian Refugee Problem Revisited* (Cambridge: Cambridge University Press, 2004)

Patai, Raphael, *The Vanished Worlds of Jewry* (New York: Macmillan Publishing Co., Inc., 1980)

Polo, Marco, *The Travels of Marco Polo, a Venetian, in the Thirteenth Century: Being a Description … of Remarkable Places and Things in the Eastern Parts of the World,* trans. William Marsden (London, 1819)

Polo, Marco, *The Travels of Marco Polo* (New York: Dover Publications, 1903), reprinted 1993, revised and annotated by Henri Cordier

Pereltsvaig, Asya, *Languages of the World, An Introduction* (Cambridge: Cambridge University Press, 2012)

Raphael, Chaim, *The Road from Babylon: The Story of Sephardi and Oriental Jews* (New York: Harper & Row, 1985)

Rhetore, Jacques, *Les Chretiens aux Betes* (Paris: Les Editions du Cerf, 2005)

Rollston, Christopher, *Writing and Literacy in the World of Ancient Israel: Epigraphic Evidence from the Iron Age* (Atlanta: Society of Biblical Literature, 2010)

Rosenthal, Franz ed., *An Aramaic Handbook, Part I* (Wiesbaden: Otto Harrassowitz, Porta Linguarum Orientum, 1967)

Ruben, Barry and Schwanitz, Wolfgang G., *Nazis, Islamists, and the Making of the Modern Middle East* (New Haven: Yale University Press, 2014)

Rueda, Ulises Casab, *Los Cristianos del Iraq en Mexica* (Mexico, 2009)

Sabar, Yona, *The Folk Literature of the Kurdistan Jews* (New Haven and London: Yale University Press, 1982)

Sabar, Ariel, *My Father's Paradise* (Chapel Hill: Algonquin Books of Chapel Hill, 2008)

Raymond P. Scheindlin, *A Short History of the Jewish People from Legendary Times to Modern Statehood* (New York: Oxford University Press, 1998)

Sivan Emmanuel, *Radical Islam: Medieval Theology and Modern Politics* (New Haven: Yale University Press, 1985)

Stafford, R.S., *The Tragedy of the Assyrians* (Piscataway: Gorgias Press, 2006), originally published by George Allen & Unwin Ltd, USA

Soro, Mar Bawai, *The Church of the East: Apostolic and Orthodox* (San Jose: Adiabene Publications, 2007)

Vukosabovic, Filip, *By the Rivers of Babylon* (Jerusalem: Bible Lands Museum, 2015)

Wace, Henry and Percy, William Coleman, *Dictionary of Christian Biography and Literature to the End of the Sixth Century* (London: John Murphy, 1911)

Warda, William, *Assyrians beyond the Fall of Nineveh, A 2,624 Years Journey* (Lexington: 2014)

Weatherford, Jack, *Genghis Khan and the Making of the Modern World* (New York: Crown Publishers, 2004)

Werda, Rev. Joel E., *The Flickering Light of Asia* (Assyrian International News Agency Books Online: 1924).

Whitehorn, Alan, *The Armenian Genocide: The essential reference guide* (Santa Barbara: ABC-CLIO, LLC, 2015)

Wilmshurst, David, *The Martyred Church: A History of the Church of the East* (London: East & West Publishing Ltd., 2011)

Yang Sen-Fu, *A History of Nestorian Christianity in China* (Taiwan: Commercial Press, Ltd., 1969), Trans: Herbert J Hatcher, 2007.

Yona, Mordechai, *Those Who Perish in the Land of Assyria: The Jews of Kurdistan and Zakho* וזאכו כורדיסתאן יהודי אשור: בארץ האוכדים (Jerusalem: Bialak, 1989)

Yonan, Gabriele, *Lest We Perish: A forgotten Holocaust, The Extermination of the Christian Assyrians in Turkey and Assyria*, http://www.aina.org/books/lwp.pdf, 1996, accessed June 2016; http://www.syriacstudies.com/2011/04/06/lest-we-perish-a-forgotten-holocaust-the-extermination-of-the-

christian-assyrians-in-turkey-and-persiagabriele-
yonan/ accessed May 2017,

Zadok, Ron, *On West Semites in Babylonia during the Chaldean and Achaemenian Periods: An Onomastic Study* (Jerusalem: HJ&Z Wanaarta and Tel Aviv University, 1977)

NOTES

Introduction
[1] Christophe Neff, "Bientôt le souvenir de l'église catholique chaldéenne et des églises syriaques (orthodoxes & catholiques) sera plus qu'un souffle de vent chaud dans le désert," *Paysages*, accessed June, 2016 https://tinyurl.com/ybbggeg3.

What is at Stake
[1] B.C. "The Christians of Iraq and Syria" *The Economist*, August 19, 2014, accessed August 2016, https://tinyurl.com/ycax9dbx.

[2] Janine Di Giovanni and Conor Gaffey, "The New Exodus: Christians Flee ISIS in the Middle East," *Newsweek*, March 22, 2016, accessed August 2016, https://tinyurl.com/q429w2b.

[3] Knights of Columbus, and In Defense of Christians, "Genocide Against Christians in the Middle East," *Stop The Christian Genocide*, March 9, 2016, 219, accessed July 2016, https://tinyurl.com/ybn629kg.

[4] B.C. "The Christians of Iraq and Syria."

[5] Knights of Columbus, and In Defense of Christians, "Genocide Against Christians in the Middle East," 223.

[6] Ibid., 80.

[7] Ibid., 194–99.

[8] European Parliament, "Joint Motion for a Resolution: On Recent Attacks and Abductions by Da'esh in the Middle East, Notably of Assyrians," November 3, 2015, accessed July 2016, https://tinyurl.com/y6vrg4le.

[9] Raphael Ahren, "'Thank God, There are Almost No Jews in Syria Now,' says the woman who rescued most of them," *The Times of Israel*, August 17, 2012, accessed July 2016, https://tinyurl.com/d9eue2n.

[10] Austen Henry Layard. *Nineveh and Its Remains, Vol. 1 and 2* (Cambridge: Cambridge University Press, 1849).

[11] William Warda, *Assyrians Beyond the Fall of Nineveh: A 2,624 Years Journey* (Lexington: printed by author, 2013).
[12] William Chauncey Emhardt and George M. Lamsa, *The Oldest Christian People: A Brief Account of the History and Traditions of the Assyrian People and the Fateful History of the Nestorian Church* (1926; Eugene, OR: Wipf & Stock Publishers, 2013), 23.

Norma
[1] Ulises Casab Rueda, *Los Cristianos del Iraq en Mexica* (Oaxaca, Mexico: Compañía Editorial Comersa, 2009), as well as personal communication.

Arameans and Aramaic
[1] David L. Lieber, ed., *Etz Hayim* (New York: Jewish Publication Society, 2001), 62.
[2] Mar Sarhad Y. Jammo and Fr. Andrew Younan, *Chaldean Grammar* (San Diego: Chaldean Media Center, 2014).
[3] Stephen A. Kaufman, "The Akkadian Influences on Aramaic," *The Oriental Institute of the University of Chicago: Assyriological Studies,* no. 19 (Chicago and London: The University of Chicago Press 1974): 107, https://tinyurl.com/ybrghben.
[4] John Kaltner, ed. and Steven L. McKenzie, ed., *Beyond Babel* (Atlanta: Society of Biblical Literature, 2002), 7–30; Robert Hetzron, *The Semitic Languages* (Oxon: Routledge, 1997); and Kaufman, "The Akkadian Influences on Aramaic," for the Akkadian words. I translated several of the words into Hebrew and Arabic with help from Fatima Fawaz; Norma Hakim helped with Chaldean.
[5] Jammo and Younan, *Chaldean Grammar,* 238.
[6] Joseph A. Fitzmeyer, "A Wandering Aramean," in *The Semitic Background of the New Testament,* ed. Joseph A. Fitzmeyer (Cambridge: William B. Eerdmans Publishing Co., 1997), 46.
[7] Jastrow, quote in Hetzron, *The Semitic Languages,* 347–8.
[8] Anthony Woodbury, "What is an Endangered Language?" Linguistic Society of America, 2012, https://tinyurl.com/9g8zfy2.
[9] Karin Wiecha, "New Estimates on the Rate of Language Loss," *The Rosetta Blog,* March 28, 2013, https://tinyurl.com/kogkmgw.
[10] Elizabeth Malone, "Endangered Languages," National Science Foundation, accessed June 2016, https://tinyurl.com/yc7p6wfm.
[11] UNESCO, "UNESCO Atlas of the World's Languages in Danger," 2010, accessed June 2016, https://tinyurl.com/yaxxjnel.

The Jews and the Church

[1] Charles F. Home, "The Kurash Prism: Cyrus the Great; The decree of return for the Jews, 539 BCE," Iran Chamber Society, April 7, 2016, accessed July 2016, https://tinyurl.com/ycskksrg.

[2] Dietmar Winkler, "The Age of the Sassanians," in *The Church of the East: A Concise History*, ed. Wilhelm Baum and Dietmar W. Winkler (Oxon: Routledge Curzon, 2003), 7–9.

[3] Chaim Raphael, *The Road from Babylon: The Story of Sephardi and Oriental Jews* (New York: Harper & Row, 1985), 33–37.

[4] Elias J. Bickerman, "Persia," in *Encyclopedia Judaica*, Cecil Roth and Geoffrey Wigoder, eds. (Jerusalem: Keter Publishing House, 1973-1991), 307.

[5] Raphael, *The Road from Babylon*, 63.

[6] Bernard Lewis, *The Jews of Islam* (Princeton: Princeton University Press, 1984), 118.

[7] Mar Bawai Soro, *The Church of the East: Apostolic and Orthodox* (San Jose: Adiabene Publications, 2007), 45–101.

[8] William Chauncey Emhardt and George M. Lamsa, *The Oldest Christian People: A Brief Account of the History and Traditions of the Assyrian People and the Fateful History of the Nestorian Church* (1926; Eugene, OR: Wipf & Stock Publishers, 2013), 21.

[9] Ibid., 58.

[10] Roberta R. Ervine, ed., *Worship Traditions in Armenia and the Neighboring Christian East: An International Symposium in Honor of the 40th Anniversary of the St. Nersess Armenian Seminary (Avant)* (New York: St Vladimir's Seminary Press, 2006), 142–5.

[11] Emhardt and Lamsa, *The Oldest Christian People*, 21.

[12] William Dalrymple, *From the Holy Mountain* (New York: Henry Holt and Co., 1977), 149.

[13] David Wilmshurst, *The Martyred Church: A History of the Church of the East* (London: East & West Publishing, 2011), 150.

[14] Ibid., 359–61.

The Churches of the East

[1] "Statistic on Christians in the Middle East," United States Conference of Catholic Bishops, accessed July 2016, https://tinyurl.com/ycmc76az.

[2] "The Syrian Orthodox Church," The Syriac Orthodox Church Worldwide, last revised 2005, accessed July 2016, http://www.syrianorthodoxchurch.net.

[3] *The Catholic Encyclopedia, New Advent*, s.v. "Eastern Churches," ed. Kevin Knight, accessed September 2016, http://www.newadvent.org/cathen/05230a.htm.
[4] "Nestorian Church," *Nestorian.org*, accessed September 2016, http://www.nestorian.org/nestorian_church.html.
[5] "The Holy Apostolic Catholic Assyrian Church of the East," World Council of Churches, accessed July 2016, https://tinyurl.com/ybjaxkvs.
[6] "The Syro-Malabar Church: An overview," *Syro-Malabar Church*, accessed August 2016, https://tinyurl.com/yca4hurj.
[7] "Statistic of Christians in the Middle East," U.S. Conference of Catholic Bishops, accessed October 2016.
[8] Ibid.
[9] William Chauncey Emhardt and George M. Lamsa, *The Oldest Christian People: A Brief Account of the History and Traditions of the Assyrian People and the Fateful History of the Nestorian Church* (1926; Eugene, OR: Wipf & Stock Publishers, 2013), 28–36.
[10] Mar Bawai Soro, *The Church of the East: Apostolic and Orthodox* (San Jose: Adiabene Publications, 2007), 37–42, 137–142.
[11] *Merriam Webster*, s.v. "Gnosticism," accessed July 2016, http://www.merriam-webster.com/dictionary/gnosticism.
[12] Jammo and Younan, *Chaldean Grammar*, Dictionary in Appendix, as well as personal communication with Norma Hakim.
[13] "Mandaean Statement about the Current Situation in Iraq," Mandaean Associations Union, July 27, 2014, https://tinyurl.com/yajlmbdn.
[14] Emhardt, and Lamsa, *The Oldest Christian People*, 50.
[15] *Papal Encyclicals Online*, s.v. "First Council of Nicaea - 325 AD" accessed August 2016, https://tinyurl.com/y8asv8hh.
[16] Soro, *The Church of the East*, 233–34.
[17] Soro, *The Church of the East*, 233–43.
[18] Soro, *The Church of the East*, 179–83.
[19] Wilhelm Baum and Dietmar W. Winkler, *The Church of the East: A Concise History* (Oxon: Routledge Curzon, 2003), 29.
[20] David Wilmshurst, *The Martyred Church: A History of the Church of the East* (London: East & West Publishing, 2011), 54–55.
[21] *LookLex Encyclopedia*, s.v. "Babai the Great," accessed October 2016, http://i-cias.com/e.o/babai_the_great.htm.

Islam arrives
[1] Bat Ye'or, *The Dhimmi: Jews and Christians under Islam*, rev. ed., trans. David Maisel (London: Associated University Press, 1985), 44.

[2] Mohamad Jebara, "Myth of the Medina Massacre," *The Times of Israel*, June 14, 2016, accessed June 2016, https://tinyurl.com/y7sb2nuz.

[3] Sahih International translation, in *Quranic Arabic Corpus*, Kais Dukes, ed. (copyright 2009-2011), accessed October 2016, http://corpus.quran.com/translation.jsp. This is an open source website with seven parallel translations in English for each verse of the Koran, and it is the source of the translations in this chapter. The Sahih International translation is used unless otherwise noted.

[4] Raymond Ibrahim, *Crucified Again: Exposing Islam's New War on Christians* (Washington D.C.: Regnery Publishing, 2013), 95–115.

[5] Ibrahim, *Crucified Again*, 187.

[6] Bernard Lewis, *The Jews of Islam* (Princeton: Princeton University Press, 1984), 25.

[7] Ibrahim, *Crucified Again*, 24.

[8] Lord Kinross, *The Ottoman Centuries* (New York: Morrow Quill Paperbacks, 1977), 614.

[9] Lewis, *The Jews of Islam*, 63–64.

Learned Men, Patriarchs and Schisms
[1] Wilhelm Baum and Dietmar W. Winkler, *The Church of the East: A Concise History* (Oxon: Routledge Curzon, 2003), 66–67.

[2] J. B. Abbeloos and T. J. Lamy, *Bar Hebraeus, Chronicon Ecclesiasticum*, 3 vols (Paris: 1877); J. A. Assemani, *De Catholicis seu Patriarchis Chaldaeorum et Nestorianorum* (Rome, 1775).

[3] "Account of Mari," quoted at length in wikipedia.org/wiki/Surin_(Nestorian_patriarch)

[4] David Wilmshurst, *The Martyred Church: A History of the Church of the East* (London: East & West Publishing, 2011), 140–145.

Mongols and Turks
[1] Jack Weatherford, *Genghis Khan and the Making of the Modern World* (New York: Crown Publishers, 2004), xviii.

[2] Ibid., 114–118.

[3] Ibid., 170–3.

[4] David Morgan, "Rashi al-Din," in *Genghis Khan and the Mongol Empire*, eds. William Fitzhugh, Morris Rossabi, and William Honeychurch (Arctic Studies Center, Smithsonian Institution: W.W. Norton & Co., 2013), 170–1.

[5] David Wilmshurst, *The Martyred Church: A History of the Church of the East* (London: East & West Publishing, 2011), 245–6.

[6] Morris Rossabi, "Rabban Sauma and Marco Polo," in *Genghis Khan and the Mongol Empire*, eds. William Fitzhugh, Morris Rossabi, and William Honeychurch (Arctic Studies Center, Smithsonian Institution: W.W. Norton & Co., 2013), 217–219.

[7] Wilmshurst, *The Martyred Church*, 256.

[8] "Chapter XVII, The Massacre of the Christians at Arbil," *The History of the Life and Travels of Rabban Bar Sawma*, reprinted by *Nestorian.org*, accessed August 2016, https://tinyurl.com/yb6jqfse.

[9] Gerard Chaliand and Arnaud Blin, *The History of Terrorism: From Antiquity to Al Qaeda* (CA: University of California Press, 2007), 87.

Unification with the Catholic Church

[1] *Encyclopaedia Britannica*, s.v. "Andrew of Longjumeau", vol. 1 (1911), accessed July 2016, https://tinyurl.com/y7qo36ky.

[2] *Papal Encyclicals Online*, s.v. "The Council of Basel-Ferrara-Florence, 1431-45 A.D.," see "Session 14 7 August 1445: Bull of union with the Chaldeans and the Maronites of Cyprus," accessed October 2016, https://tinyurl.com/pvu42cm.

[3] David Wilmshurst, *The Martyred Church: A History of the Church of the East* (London: East & West Publishing, 2011), 297–99, 317–21.

[4] Heleen H.L. Murre-Van Den Berg, "The Patriarchs of the Church of the East from the Fifteenth to the Eighteenth Centuries," *Hugoye: Journal of Syriac Studies*, vol. 2.2, 235–264.

[5] Wilmshurst, *The Martyred Church*, 322–339.

The Church spreads across Asia

[1] Yang Sen-Fu, *A History of Nestorian Christianity in China*, trans. Herbert J Hatcher (1969; Taiwan: printed by author, 2007), 3–4.

[2] Ibid., 11.

[3] John M.L. Young, *By Foot to China: Mission of The Church of the East, to 1400* (*Assyrian International News Agency: Books Online*, 1984), ch. 3, accessed October 2016, http://www.aina.org/books/bftc/bftc.htm#c4.

[4] Ibid.

[5] Bernard Lewis, *The Middle East: A Brief History of the Last 2,000 Years* (New York: Scribner, 1995), 46.

[6] Sam Lieu and Ken Parry, "Manichaean and (Nestorian) Christian Remains in Zayton (Quanzhou, South China) ARC DP0557098," (Australia: Macquarie University), accessed July 2016, https://tinyurl.com/yas5obqf.

[7] Yang Sen-Fu, *A History of Nestorian Christianity*, 29.

[8] Ibid., 35.

[9] David Wilmshurst, *The Martyred Church: A History of the Church of the East* (London: East & West Publishing, 2011), 222.

[10] Wilhelm Baum and Dietmar W. Winkler, *The Church of the East: A Concise History* (Oxon: Routledge Curzon, 2003), 82.

[11] Marco Polo, *The Travels of Marco Polo*, revised and annotated by Henri Cordier (1903; reprinted by New York: Dover Publications, 1993), 231–237.

[12] Baum and Winkler, *The Church of the East*, 89.

[13] Jack Weatherford, *Genghis Khan and the Making of the Modern World* (New York: Crown Publishers, 2004), xviii–xix.

[14] Young, *By Foot to China*, ch. 4.

[15] Polo, *The Travels of Marco Polo*, 348–9.

[16] Baum and Winkler, *The Church of the East*, 101.

[17] "Nestorian Crosses of the Yuan Dynasty," *Asian Art*, May 11, 2016, http://www.asianartnewspaper.com/?p=585.

[18] Yang Sen-Fu, *A History of Nestorian Christianity*, 4.

[19] Baum and Winkler, *The Church of the East*, 73–74.

[20] Glen L. Thompson, "Christ on the Silk Road," *Touchstone*, April 2007, accessed October 2016, https://tinyurl.com/6z6vfe.

[21] Baum and Winkler, *The Church of the East*, 49.

[22] Robert Eric Frykenberg, *Christianity in India: From Beginning to Present* (Oxford: Oxford University Press, 2008), 93–99.

[23] I am indebted to Mr. George Mammen, an Assyrian Christian, for many of the local details in this section.

[24] Leonard Pinto, "A Brief History of Christianity in Sri Lanka," *Columbo Telegraph*, Sept. 20, 2013 (summary of a paper presented to the Ceylon Society of Australia, Sydney August 25, 2013), https://tinyurl.com/ybt6q6bu.

[25] Many of the observations about Kerala and the comments on the caste system come from my own travels and research there, acquired over more than 40 years of travels in India.

[26] Robert Eric Frykenberg, "Thomas Christians," in *Encyclopaedia Britannica*, accessed October 2016, https://tinyurl.com/ybdhvl6k.

[27] Robert Eric Frykenberg, *Christianity in India*, 108–113.

[28] Baum and Winkler, *The Church of the East*, 62.

[29] Henri Hosten, *Antiquities from San Thome and Mylapore* (San Thome, Mylapore, Madras: The Diocese of Mylapore, 1936).

[30] Frykenberg, *Christianity in India*, 138.

[31] Personal communication.

[32] Baum and Winkler, *The Church of the East*, 53–7.

[33] Ibid., 107–109.
[34] Frykenberg, *Christianity in India*, 124.
[35] Ibid., 132–135.
[36] *Indian Church History*, Alpha Institute of Theology and Science (Thalassery, Kerala, India: Alpha Institute of the Theology and Science, 2014), https://tinyurl.com/y8f6q56l, 20-24.
[37] H. E. Dr. Mar Aprem Metropolitan, "Assyrian Church of the East in India," *Nestorian.org*, accessed October 2016, http://www.nestorian.org/church_of_the_east_in_india.html.
[38] Frykenberg, *Christianity in India*, 366.
[39] Malankara Mar Thoma Syrian Church website, http://marthoma.in.
[40] Syriac Orthodox Church of Antioch: Archdiocese for the Eastern United States website, http://syrianorthodoxchurch.org.
[41] Wilmshurst, *The Martyred Church*, 342–3.

The Jews of Kurdistan
[1] Erich Brauer and Raphael Patai, *The Jews of Kurdistan* (Detroit: Wayne State University Press, 1993), 251.
[2] Rabbi Benjamin, *The Travels of Benjamin of Tudela*, 1173 CE, e-book, accessed October 2016, https://tinyurl.com/yb9a8g6r.
[3] Benjamin of Tudela, *Travels*, in Yona Sabar, *The Folk Literature of the Kurdistan Jews* (New Haven and London: Yale University Press, 1982), 94–100.
[4] Brauer and Patai, *The Jews of Kurdistan*, 66.
[5] Yona Sabar, "Introduction," in *Folk Literature*, xxv.
[6] Haya Gavish, *Unwitting Zionists* (Detroit: Wayne State University Press, 2010), 269.
[7] Ibid, 330.
[8] Brauer and Patai, *The Jews of Kurdistan* – all of his incomparable research will not be cited by specific page.
[9] Ibid., 251.
[10] Mordechai Yona, *Those Who Perish in the Land of Assyria: The Jews of Kurdistan and Zakho*, האוכדים בארץ אשור: יהודי כורדיסתאן וזאכו (Jerusalem: Bialak, 1989).
[11] Avraham Ben Yaakov, *Kurdistan's Jewish Community* (Jerusalem: Institute Ben Zvi Hebrew University, 1961).
[12] Mordechai Yona, *Those Who Perish*, 19–30.
[13] Ariel Sabar, *My Father's Paradise* (Chapel Hill: Algonquin Books of Chapel Hill, 2008).
[14] Gavish, *Unwitting Zionists*, 59–65.

[15] Allen Cone, "Jewish Officials Seek to Save Ancient Nahum tomb," *United Press International.com*, August 3, 2016, accessed October 2016, https://tinyurl.com/yabepgqh.

[16] Edwin Black, *The Farhud: Roots of the Ara-Nazi Alliance in the Holocaust* (Washington, D.C.: Dialog Press, 2010), 293–306.

[17] Black, *Farhud*, 297–9.

[18] Esther Meir-Glitzenstein, "The Farhud," in *Holocaust Encyclopedia*, United States Holocaust Memorial Museum website, 2016, https://www.ushmm.org/wlc/en/article.php?ModuleId=10007277.

[19] Bernard Lewis, *The Jews of Islam* (Princeton: Princeton University Press, 1984), 156.

[20] Edwin Black, "Jews in Islamic Countries, The Sudden End of Iraqi Jewry," in *Jewish Virtual Library*, accessed August 2016, https://tinyurl.com/ycey7qm5.

[21] Edwin Black, "The Expulsion that Backfired: When Iraq Kicked Out its Jews," *The Times of Israel*, May 31, 2016, https://tinyurl.com/ybdm6mnm.

[22] Meir-Glitzenstein, "The Farhud."

[23] Patai, "Preface," in Brauer and Patai, *The Jews of Kurdistan*, 16.

[24] Personal interviews; with additions from Gavish, *Unwitting Zionists*, as corrected by Batia Aloni.

[25] Ari Greenspan and Ari Z. Zivotofsky, "An Old World Treasure," *The Jerusalem Post*, April 24, 2008, https://tinyurl.com/ycbjgsyw.

[26] Jay Bushinsky, "The Passion of Aramaic-Kurdish Jews Brought Aramaic to Israel," *Ekurd Daily*, April 15, 2005, http://ekurd.net/mismas/articles/misc2005/4/kurdisrael1.htm.

[27] Ibid.

[28] Brauer and Patai, *The Jews of Kurdistan*, 294.

[29] Lazar Berman, "Cultural Pride, and Unlikely Guests, at Kurdish Jewish festival," *The Times of Israel*, September 30, 2013, https://tinyurl.com/y9p6o6hw.

[30] Dov Lieber, "After Declaring Autonomy, Syrian Kurds 'Open to Ties with Israel,'" *The Times of Israel*, March 18, 2016, https://tinyurl.com/y7rxxxyk.

[31] David Sheppard et al, "Israel Turns to Kurds for Three-quarters of its Oil Supplies," *Financial Times*, August 23, 2015, https://www.ft.com/content/150f00cc-472c-11e5-af2f-4d6e0e5eda22.

32 Dov Lieber, "Iraqi Kurdistan Sees a Jewish Revival, Thanks to the Islamic State," *The Times of Israel*, March 15, 2016, https://tinyurl.com/y73pofdw.

33 Ibid.

[34] Almut Nebel et al, "The Y Chromosome Pool of Jews as Part of the Genetic Landscape of the Middle East," *American Journal of Human Genetics*, vol. 69, no. 5 (November 2001): 1095–1112, published online Sep 25, 2001, https://tinyurl.com/y75zuj62.

[35] Ian Black and Benny Morris, *Israel's Secret Wars* (New York: Grove Press, 1991), 521–2, 184.

[36] *The International Jerusalem Post*, October 7–13, 2016, 8.

[37] Idan Pink-Avidani, "Why Israel Must Help the Kurds in Iraq," *+972*, Sept. 1, 2014, accessed July 2016, https://tinyurl.com/y8uoacob.

The Nineteenth Century and Persecutions

[1] Sebastien De Courtois, *The Forgotten Genocide: Eastern Christians, The Last Arameans* (New Jersey: Gorgias Press, 2004), 3–9.

[2] Edward Irving Carlyle, "Ainsworth, William Francis," in *Dictionary of National Biography, 1901 Supplement*, accessed July 2016, https://en.wikisource.org/wiki/Ainsworth,_William_Francis_(DNB01).

[3] Rev. George Percy Badger, *The Nestorians and Their Rituals with a Narrative of a Mission to Mesopatamia and Coordistan in 1842 to 1844, Part Two* (London: Joseph Masters, 1852).

[4] Layard, Austen Henry, *Nineveh and Its Remains, Volumes 1 and 2* (Cambridge: Cambridge University Press, 1849). All his books are fascinating reading.

[5] Wilhelm Baum and Dietmar W. Winkler, *The Church of the East: A Concise History* (Oxon: Routledge Curzon, 2003), 128.

[6] "Archbishop of Canterbury's Mission to the Assyrian Christians," *The London Times*, July 23, 1889.

[7] David Wilmshurst, *The Martyred Church: A History of the Church of the East* (London: East & West Publishing, 2011), 328.

[8] Layard, *Nineveh and Its Remains*.

[9] Baum and Winkler, *The Church of the East*, 127.

[10] Wilmshurst, *The Martyred Church*, 383–4, 402–3.

[11] William Dalrymple, *From the Holy Mountain* (New York: Henry Holt and Co., 1977), 91–7.

[12] Marco Polo, *The Travels of Marco Polo*, revised and annotated by Henri Cordier (1903; reprinted by New York: Dover Publications, 1993), 60–62.

[13] *Draft Constitution of the Iraqi Kurdistan Region*, Iraq-Kurdistan Parliment, prepared by The Committee for Revising the Draft Constitution of the Iraqi Kurdistan Region (Utah: University of Utah / Global Justice Project: Iraq, 2009), https://tinyurl.com/yc2tglgn.

[14] Wilmshurst, *The Martyred Church*, 373–5.

[15] Sargon George Donabed, *Reforging a Forgotten History: Iraq and the Assyrians in the Twentieth Century* (Edinburgh: Edinburgh University Press, 2015), 55.

[16] "Massacre of the Nestorian Christians," *The London Times*, Sept. 6, 1843.

[17] Wilmshurst, *The Martyred Church*, 378, 397–400.

[18] De Courtois, *The Forgotten Genocide*, 76.

[19] Donabed, *Reforging a Forgotten History*, 59–61.

[20] Hannibal Travis, *Genocide in the Middle East: The Ottoman Empire, Iraq and Sudan* (Durham, NC: Carolina Academic Press, 2010) 273.

[21] R.S. Stafford, *The Tragedy of the Assyrians* (1935; repr. Piscataway: Gorgias Press, 2006), 21.

[22] David Gaunt, *Massacres, Resistance, Protectors: Muslim-Christian Relations in Eastern Anatolia During World War I* (Piscataway: Gorgias Press, 2006), 18–28.

[23] David Gaunt, *Massacres, Resistance, Protectors*, 405–28.

[24] Cyril Nelson Barkley, "Helmuth von Moltke, German General (1800–1891)," in *Encyclopaedia Britannica*, 2016, http://www.britannica.com/biography/Helmuth-von-Moltke.

[25] Lord Kinross, *The Ottoman Centuries* (New York: Morrow Quill Paperbacks, 1977), 566.

[26] De Courtois, *The Forgotten Genocide*, 17.

[27] Ibid., 99–121.

[28] Kinross, *The Ottoman Centuries*, 558.

[29] DeCourtois, *The Forgotten Genocide*, 110–18.

[30] Ibid., 111–2.

[31] Hannibal Travis, "'Native Christians Massacred': The Ottoman Genocide of the Assyrians during World War I," *Genocide Studies and Prevention: An International Journal*, vol. 1, no. 3, article 8, 2006, accessed July 2016, https://tinyurl.com/yclo8cfr.

[32] William Warda, *Assyrians Beyond the Fall of Nineveh: A 2,624 Years Journey* (Lexington: printed by author, 2013), 226.

[33] DeCourtois, *The Forgotten Genocide*, 128–9.

[34] Kincross, *The Ottoman Centuries*, 560–62.

[35] Henry Morgenthau, *Ambassador Morgenthau's Story* (1918; repr. New York: Cosimo Classics, 2010), 199–201.

The Twentieth Century and Genocide

[1] David Gaunt, *Massacres, Resistance, Protectors: Muslim-Christian Relations in Eastern Anatolia During World War I* (Piscataway: Gorgias Press, 2006), 22–25.

[2] Lord Kinross, *The Ottoman Centuries* (New York: Morrow Quill Paperbacks, 1977), 572–4.

[3] Claude Lorieux, *Chretiens D'Orient en terres d'islam* (Saint-Amand-Montrond (Cher) France: Editions Perrin, 2001), 84.

[4] Gaunt, *Massacres, Resistance, Protectors*, 44–5.

[5] Kinross, *The Ottoman Centuries*, 598.

[6] Ibid., 568.

[7] Gabriele Yonan, *Lest We Perish: A Forgotten Holocaust, The Extermination of the Christian Assyrians in Turkey and Assyria*, 1996, Syriac Studies, accessed May 2017, https://tinyurl.com/ybqwmnra, 79–82.

[8] Henry Morgenthau, *Ambassador Morgenthau's Story* (1918; repr. New York: Cosimo Classics, 2010), 45.

[9] Yonan, *Lest We Perish*, 79.

[10] Reeva S. Simon, *The Origins of Arab Nationalism*, eds. Rashid Khalidi, Lisa Anderson, Muhammad Muslih, and Reeva S. Simon (New York: Columbia University Press, 1991), 155.

[11] Yonan, *Lest We Perish*, 81.

[12] Morganthau, *Ambassador Morgenthau's Story*, 111.

[13] Yonan, *Lest We Perish*, 86–93.

[14] Barry Ruben and Wolfgang G. Schwanitz, *Nazis, Islamists, and the Making of the Modern Middle East* (New Haven: Yale University Press, 2014), 40–41.

[15] Yonan, *Lest We Perish*, 88.

[16] Ibid., 88–93.

[17] Morganthau, *Ambassador Morgenthau's Story*, 113–114.

[18] Ruben and Schwanitz, *Nazis, Islamists*, 40.

[19] Yonan, *Lest We Perish*, 87.

[20] Racho Donef, "The Pontian Massacre: The continuous cycle of violence and massacres," *Assyrian Information Management*, August 7, 2015, http://www.atour.com/~aahgn/news/20150807a.html.

[21] Morganthau, *Ambassador Morgenthau's Story*, 34.

[22] Daniel Blatt, review of *Paris 1919*, by Margaret McMillan, *Futurecasts Online Magazine*, vol. 10, no. 10, pt. 2, November 1, 2008, http://www.futurecasts.com/book%20review%2010-4A.htm.

[23] Donef, "The Pontian Massacre."

[24] Constantine G. Hatzidimitriou, "Smyrna, 1922 Destruction of," in *The Armenian Genocide: The essential reference guide*, ed. Whitehorn (Santa Barbara: ABC-CLIO, LLC, 2015), 237–239.

[25] Paul G. Pierpaoli, "Pontic Greek Genocide," in *The Armenian Genocide*, ed. Whitehorn, 217–19.

[26] Donef, "The Pontian Massacre."

[27] David Wilmshurst, *The Martyred Church: A History of the Church of the East* (London: East & West Publishing, 2011), 412.

[28] Rev. Dr. W. A. Wigram, in *Royal Central Asian Journal.* vol. 21, January 1934, pt. 1, p. 41, quoted in Yonan, *Lest We Perish*, 103.

[29] Surma d-Bet Mar Shimun, sister of Patriarch Mar Shimun Benyamin, "The Expulsion of the Assyrians of Hakkari (Kurdistan) 1914 – 1915," quoted in Yonan, *Lest We Perish*, 91.

[30] Gaunt, *Massacres, Resistance, Protectors*, 59–60.

[31] William A. Shedd, "1915: Urmia : Statement By The Rev. William A. Shedd, D.D., of The American (Presbyterian) Mission Station at Urmia; Communicated by The Board of Foreign Missions of The Presbyterian Church in The U.S.A.," *Assyrian Information Management*, posted July 18, 2000, http://www.atour.com/history/1900/20000718a.html.

[32] "1915: Rev. Robert M. Labaree, Tabriz, Persia, The Jihad Rampant in Persia," *The New York Times*, July, 1915, in *Assyrian Information Management*, http://www.atour.com/history/ny-times/20041016a.html. Rev. Labaree was subsequently murdered by Kurds.

[33] Paul Shimmon, "Massacres of Syrian Christians in N.W. Persia and Kurdistan," London, November 1915, quoted in Yonan, *Lest We Perish*, pt. 2, Document 16, 13–20.

[34] Anna Friedeman, "Account of director of German Orphanage in Urmia," quoted in Yonan, *Lest We Perish*, pt. 2, Document 26, 83–84.

[35] Sargon George Donabed, *Reforging a Forgotten History: Iraq and the Assyrians in the Twentieth Century* (Edinburgh: Edinburgh University Press, 2015), 62.

[36] Hannibel Travis, "'Native Christians Massacred:' The Ottoman Massacre of the Assyrians during World War I," *Genocide Studies and Prevention: An International Journal*, vol. 1, no. 3, art. 8 (2006): 331–3, https://tinyurl.com/yclo8cfr.

[37] Shedd, "1915: Urmia."

[38] "Urumiah Massacres Death of 12,000 Nestorian Christians," *The London Times* (London: October 9, 1915), in *Assyrian Information Management*, accessed June 2016, https://tinyurl.com/yd4lr7xf.

[39] Rugo A. Müller, "1915: The Second Exodus from Urmia: Letter from Mr. Rugo A. Muller (Treasurer of the American Mission Station at Urmia)," *Assyrian Information Management*, August 20, 1915, accessed October 2016, http://www.atour.com/history/1900/20000718t.html.

[40] Wife of the Rev. David Jacob, of Urmia, "Second Exodus From Urmia: Narrative Of A Nestorian Victim," *Ararat* (London: January, 1916).

[41] Paul Shimmon, "Urmia, Salmas and Hakkiari," *Ararat* (London: November, 1915), in *Assyrian Information Management*, accessed July 2016, http://www.atour.com/history/1900/20000718n.html.

[42] Gaunt, *Massacres, Resistance, Protectors*, 152, 245–6.

[43] Ibid., 265–267.

[44] Joseph Naayem, "Eyewitness Reports on the Massacre of the Assyro-Chaldeans in Urfa, Seert, Kharput and Diyarbakir," quoted in Yonan, *Lest We Perish*, pt. 2, Document 37, 30-34.

[45] Jacques Rhetore, *Les Chretienes aux Betes* (Paris: Les Editions du Cerf, 2005), 116.

[46] Sebastien De Courtois, *The Forgotten Genocide: Eastern Christians, The Last Arameans* (New Jersey: Gorgias Press, 2004), 195.

[47] "Training the Assyrians. Refugee Camp at Bakuba," *The London Times* (London: April 24, 1920), in *Assyrian Information Management*, accessed July 2016, https://tinyurl.com/y9mmg8oz.

[48] Donabed, *Reforging a Forgotten History*, 61–63.

[49] Surma d-Bet Mar Shimun, sister of Patriarch Mar Shimun Benyamin, "The Expulsion of the Assyrians of Hakkari (Kurdistan) 1914–1915," quoted in Yonan, *Lest We Perish*, pt. 2, Document 2, 93.

[50] Gaunt, *Massacres, Resistance, Protectors*, 140.

[51] Mar Eshai Shimun, "The Assyrian National Petition" (New Jersey: Kimball Press, 1946), presented to the World Security Conference in San Francisco, California, May 7, 1945, in *Assyrian Information Management*, accessed October 2016, http://www.atour.com/Assyrian_Nation.shtml.

[52] Paul Shimmon, "Hakkari: Further Statement by Mr. Paul Shimmon," quoted in Yonan, *Lest We Perish*, pt. 2, Document 49, 74.

[53] Mr. Shlemon, of Berwar, "Mar Shimun's Highlanders and Their Fight for Life," quoted in Yonan, *Lest We Perish*, pt. 2, Document 29, 108–9.

[54] Wilhelm Baum and Dietmar W. Winkler, *The Church of the East: A Concise History* (Oxon: Routledge Curzon, 2003), 137.

[55] Mr. Shlemon, of Berwar, "Mar Shimun's Highlanders," quoted in Yonan, *Lest We Perish*, 109.

[56] Gaunt, *Massacres, Resistance, Protectors*, 227–230.

[57] Yonan, "Assyrian Refugees in Persia," *Lest We Perish*, pt. 2, 51.

[58] M. Philips Price, "Azerbaijan: Statement, dated Tiflis, 22nd February, 1916, by Mr. M. Philips Price, War Correspondent for Various British and American Newspapers on the Caucasian Front; Communicated to Aneurin Williams, Esq., M.P., and Published in the Armenian Journal "Ararat," of London, March, 1916," in Viscount Bryce, *The Treatment of the Armeni-*

ans in the Ottoman Empire: 1915-16 (London: Sir Joseph Causton and Sons, 1916), accessed October 2016, https://tinyurl.com/y9clcy9n.

[59] Surma d-Bet Mar Shimun, sister of Patriarch Mar Shimun Benyamin, "The Expulsion of the Assyrians of Hakkari (Kurdistan) 1914 – 1915," quoted in Yonan, *Lest We Perish*, pt. 2, Document 27, 91-95.

[60] "Turks Continue Urumiah Slaying," *New York Times*, March 27, 1915, in *Assyrian Information Management*, accessed July 2016, http://www.atour.com/history/ny-times/20001125o.html.

[61] Paul Shimmon, "Massacres of Syrian Christians," quoted in Yonan, *Lest We Perish*, 13–20.

[62] Sargon Donabed and Shamiran Mako, "Harput Turkey to Massachusetts: Immigration of Jacobite Christians," (Bristol, RI: Fernstein College of Arts and Sciences, 2011), online pdf, 20, accessed October 2016, http://docs.rwu.edu/cgi/viewcontent.cgi?article=1053&context=fcas_fp.

[63] Anonymous source, "Aleppo Memorandum by a Foreign Witness from Aleppo Communicated by the American Committee for Armenian and Syrian Relief," in Viscount Bryce, *The Treatment of the Armenians in the Ottoman Empire: 1915-16* (London: Sir Joseph Causton and Sons, 1916), accessed October 2016, https://tinyurl.com/y6uy4and.

[64] Morganthau, *Ambassador Morgenthau's Story*, 208.

[65] "Consul Leslie Davis on the Conditions in Harpout, July 1915,"in *The Armenian Genocide*, ed. Whitehorn, 321–323.

[66] Yves Ternon, "Les cinq-deux jours d'Ain Warda (La Source de la Rose)," in *Mardin*, 1915, http://www.imprescriptible.fr/rhac/tome4/l1-p4-ch2.

[67] Gaunt, *Massacres, Resistance, Protectors*, 202, 275–279, 348–363.

[68] Morganthau, *Ambassador Morganthau's Story*, 210–11.

[69] Prof. Susan Karamanian, personal communication.

[70] De Courtois, *The Forgotten Genocide*, 184–189.

[71] Ibid., 75–81.

[72] Gaunt, *Massacres, Resistance, Protectors*, 250–56.

[73] Abbé Joseph Tfinkdji, "Report from a Chaldean priest," Conveyed by the managing director of the French Consulate in Basra to the French Minister for Foreign Affairs, St. Pichon, January 16, 1918, quoted in Yonan, *Lest We Perish*, Document 43, 48.

[74] Hannibal Travis, "'Native Christians Massacred," 333.

[75] Yonan, "The Assyrians as the 'Smallest Ally' in the First World War," *Lest We Perish*, 89–90.

[76] Shimun, "Assyrian National Petition," 1945.

[77] Donabed, *Reforging a Forgotten History*, 63.

[78] Shlemon d-Malik Ismail, "War diary, The murder of the Assyrian patriarch by the Kurd Simko Agha on March 16, 1918 in Kohin Shahir," quoted in Yonan, *Lest We Perish*, Document 56, 97–100.

[79] Rev. Joel E. Werda, *The Flickering Light of Asia* (*Assyrian International News Agency: Books Online*: 1924), accessed October 2016, http://www.aina.org/books/fla/fla.htm#c26.

[80] Shimun, "Assyrian National Petition," 1945.

[81] R.S. Stafford, *The Tragedy of the Assyrians* (1935; repr. Piscataway: Gorgias Press, 2006), 24–5.

[82] Yonan, "'The Assyrians as the 'Smallest Ally,'" *Lest We Perish*, 92–96.

[83] Werda, *The Flickering Light of Asia*, 176–77.

[84] Yonan, "The Assyrians as the 'Smallest Ally,'" *Lest We Perish*, 87.

[85] Travis, "Native Christians Massacred," 334.

[86] De Courtois, *The Forgotten Genocide*, 195.

[87] Rhetore, *Les Chretiens aux bêtes*, 136–8.

[88] Wilmshurst, *The Martyred Church*, 436–44, 397–400.

[89] Gaunt, *Massacres, Resistance, Protectors*, 300.

[90] R.J. Rummel, "Statistics of Turkey's Democide, Estimates, Calculations and Sources," *Hellenic Resources Network*, accessed September 2016, http://www.hri.org/docs/Democide.

[91] Donabed, *Reforging a Forgotten History*, 73.

Post-World War I

[1] Fred Aprim, "Assyrians in the World War I Treaties: Paris, Sevres and Lausanne, Assyrian Star," *Assyrian Star*, vol. 58, no. 1 (2006), 6/16/2006, in *Assyrian International News Agency*, accessed July 2016, http://www.aina.org/news/20060616121030.htm.

[2] R.S. Stafford, *The Tragedy of the Assyrians* (1935; repr. Piscataway: Gorgias Press, 2006), 70.

[3] *The Jewish Virtual Library*, s.v. "Pre-State Israel: The San Remo Conference," https://tinyurl.com/yazctmbh.

[4] Stafford, *The Tragedy of the Assyrians*, 76.

[5] Peter Sluglett, *Britain in Iraq* (London: Ithaca Press, 1976), in "The Primacy of Oil in Britain's Iraq Policy," Global Policy Forum, 2016, accessed August 2016, https://tinyurl.com/ybuu884s.

[6] Aprim, "Assyrians in the World War I Treaties," *Assyrian Star*.

[7] William Chauncey Emhardt and George M. Lamsa, *The Oldest Christian People: A Brief Account of the History and Traditions of the Assyrian People and the Fateful History of the Nestorian Church* (1926; Eugene, OR: Wipf & Stock Publishers, 2013), 117.

[8] Racho Donef, *The Hakkari Massacres: Ethnic Cleansing by Turkey 1924–25* (Sydney: Tatavla Publishing, 2009, reprinted 2014), 23–25.

[9] League of Nations, "1935: League of Nations – The Settlement of the Assyrians, a Work of Humanity and Appeasement," in *Assyrian Information Management*, posted April 4, 2004, https://tinyurl.com/y7u7l2lv.

[10] Emhardt and Lamsa, *The Oldest Christian People*, 122.

[11] Stafford, *The Tragedy of the Assyrians*, 80, 84.

[12] Mar Eshai Shimun, "The Assyrian National Petition" (New Jersey: Kimball Press, 1946), presented to the World Security Conference in San Francisco, California, May 7, 1945, in *Assyrian Information Management*, accessed October 2016, http://www.atour.com/Assyrian_Nation.shtml.

[13] Emhardt and Lamsa, *The Oldest Christian People*, 128.

[14] League of Nations, *Settlement of the Assyrians of Iraq: Report of the Committee of the Council on the Settlement of the Assyrians of Iraq in the Region of the Ghab (French Mandated Territories of the Levant)*, Communicated to the Council Official No.: C. 352. M. 179. 1935. VII. and the Members of the League (Geneva, September 12, 1935), *Assyrian International News Agency: Books Online*, accessed October 2016, https://tinyurl.com/yd7dew62.

[15] Stafford, *The Tragedy of the Assyrians*, 34.

[16] Sargon George Donabed, *Reforging a Forgotten History: Iraq and the Assyrians in the Twentieth Century* (Edinburgh: Edinburgh University Press, 2015), 78–79.

[17] Shimun, "Assyrian National Petition," 1945.

[18] Stafford, *The Tragedy of the Assyrians*, 60–67.

[19] Shimun, "Assyrian National Petition," 1945.

[20] Stafford, *The Tragedy of the Assyrians*, 62.

[21] Donef, *The Hakkari Massacres*, 162.

[22] Ibid., 92–113.

[23] Donef, *The Hakkari Massacres*, 137–144.

[24] Emhardt and Lamsa, *The Oldest Christian People*, 131.

[25] Donef, *The Hakkari Massacres*, 198.

[26] Ibid., 37.

[27] Stafford, *The Tragedy of the Assyrians*, 105–122. The British story of the massacre starts here and continues.

[28] Donabed, *Reforging a Forgotten History*, 99–22.

[29] Shimun, "Assyrian National Petition," 1945.

[30] Ibid.

[31] Stafford, *The Tragedy of the Assyrians*, 123–165.

[32] Ibid., 142.

[33] Donabed, *Reforging a Forgotten History*, 108.

[34] Stafford, *The Tragedy of the Assyrians*, 160–3.

[35] Ibid., 164–8.

[36] Wilhelm Baum and Dietmar W. Winkler, *The Church of the East: A Concise History* (Oxon: Routledge Curzon, 2003), 145.

[37] Shimun, "Assyrian National Petition," 1945.

[38] League of Nations, *The Settlement of the Assyrians: A Work of Humanity and Appeasement* (Geneva, 1935), posted April 4, 2004 in *Assyrian Information Management*, accessed July 2016, https://tinyurl.com/y7u7l2lv.

[39]Raphael Lemkin, "Genocide," *American Scholar*, vol. 15, no. 2 (April 1946): 227–230, accessed July 2016, https://tinyurl.com/6my5onv.

[40] Donobed, *Reforging a Forgotten History*, 123.

World War II through the Turn of the Century

[1] Lord Kinross, *The Ottoman Centuries* (New York: Morrow Quill Paperbacks, 1977), 424, 440.

[2] Bernard Lewis, *The Middle East: A Brief History of the Last 2,000 Years* (New York: Scribner, 1995), 329.

[3] Bernard Lewis, *The Jews of Islam* (Princeton: Princeton University Press, 1984), 125–6.

[4] Sargon George Donabed, *Reforging a Forgotten History: Iraq and the Assyrians in the Twentieth Century* (Edinburgh: Edinburgh University Press, 2015), 75.

[5] Sargis G. Osipov, "Dr. Fraidoon Atturaya," *Melta Magazine*, vol. 1, no. 1, 4 (Moscow, 1995), accessed Aug. 2016, http://aina.org/aol/fraydon.htm.

[6] Raymond Ibrahim, *Crucified Again: Exposing Islam's New War on Christians* (Washington D.C.: Regnery Publishing, 2013), 13.

[7] Emmanuel Sivan, *Radical Islam: Medieval Theology and Modern Politics* (New Haven: Yale University Press, 1985), 56–57, 104.

[8] Sivan, *Radical Islam*, 121.

[9] Jeffrey Herf, *Nazi Propaganda for the Arab World* (New Haven: Yale University Press, 2009).

[10] Barry Ruben and Wolfgang G. Schwanitz, *Nazis, Islamists, and the Making of the Modern Middle East* (New Haven: Yale University Press, 2014).

[11] Rubin and Schwanitz, *Nazis, Islamists*, 63.

[12] Ibid., 4.

[13] Ibid., 241.

[14] Herf, *Nazi Propaganda*, 225.

[15] "Sayyid Qutb, Radical leader of the Muslim Brotherhood," *The Muslim Brotherhood*, a website created for Vincent Ferraro's World Politics class at Mount Holyoke College, accessed August 2016, https://tinyurl.com/ydebkasn.

[16] Herf, *Nazi Propaganda*, 9, 37–39.

[17] Ibid., 33.

[18] Ibid., 125.

[19] Rubin and Schwanitz, *Nazis, Islamists*, 209–223.

[20] Judith Bergman, "The Soviet-Palestinian Lie," *Gatestone Institute: International Policy Council*, October 16, 2016, accessed October 2016, https://www.gatestoneinstitute.org/9090/soviet-union-palestinians.

[21] Susanne Gusten, "Istanbul Policy Center-Mercator Policy Brief: The Syriac Property Issue in Tur Abdin," Istanbul Policy Center (Istanbul: Sabanci University, 2015), 1, accessed October 2016, http://www.aina.org/reports/apita.pdf.

[22] "Assyrian Human Rights Report," *Assyrian International News Agency*, last updated 2016, accessed September 2016, http://www.aina.org/reports/ahrr.htm.

[23] Minority Rights Group International, "World Directory of Minorities and Indigenous Peoples – Turkey: Assyrians" (2008), accessed September, 2016, http://www.refworld.org/docid/49749c9837.html.

[24] "Turkey destroys Assyrian villages," *Turkish Daily News*, August 29, 1996, accessed September 2016, https://tinyurl.com/yd874q3q.

[25] Robert Jones, "Jews Die, Turks Celebrate," *Gatestone Institute: International Policy Council*, Nov. 1, 2016, https://tinyurl.com/yd8x2c2z.

[26] "Turkey destroys Assyrian villages," *Turkish Daily News*.

[27] Holly Cartner, "Turkey: Letter to Minister Aksu calling for the abolition of the village guards," *Human Rights Watch*, June 8, 2006, accessed August 2016, https://tinyurl.com/ydy4q7em.

[28] "Assyrian Human Rights Report," *Assyrian International News Agency*, last updated 2016, accessed September 2016, http://www.aina.org/reports/ahrr.htm.

[29] "Turkey destroys Assyrian villages," *Turkish Daily News*.

[30] William Dalrymple, *From the Holy Mountain* (New York: Henry Holt and Co., 1977), 88–99.

[31] Gusten, "Istanbul Policy Center-Mercator Policy Brief: The Syriac Property Issue in Tur Abdin," 4.

[32] Claude Lorieux, *Chretiens D'Orient en terres d'islam* (Saint-Amand-Montrond (Cher) France: Editions Perrin, 2001), 92–97.

[33] Robert Jones, "Turkey's Tradition of Murdering Christians," *Gatestone Institute: International Policy Council*, July 31, 2016, accessed November 2016, https://tinyurl.com/z7eye3q.

[34] Robert Jones, "Turkey Target Christians," *Gatestone Institute: International Policy Council*, October 23, 2016, accessed October 2016, https://www.gatestoneinstitute.org/9130/turkey-targets-christians.

[35] Robert Jones, "Turkey Converts Hagia Sophia to Mosque," *Gatestone Institute: International Policy Council*, November 9, 2016, accessed November 2016, https://tinyurl.com/nfvly8o.

[36] Uzay Bulut, "Turkey's Mass Persecution of Chrisians and Kurds," *Gatestone Institute: International Policy Council*, September 4, 2017, https://tinyurl.com/y9wdfel7.

[37] Uzay Bulut, "Is Turkey Becoming Another Iran?" *Gatestone Institute: International Policy Council*, July 20, 2017, https://www.gatestoneinstitute.org/10622/turkey-another-iran.

[38] Donabed, *Reforging a Forgotten History*, 155–7.

[39] Ibid., 178–86.

[40] "Iraq: The Struggle to Exist," Assyria Council of Europe and Hammurabi Human Rights Organization, February 2010, 16, accessed October 2016, http://www.aina.org/reports/acetste.pdf.

[41] Donabed, *Reforging a Forgotten History*, 233.

[42] Assyrian Human Rights Report," *Assyrian International News Agency*, last updated 2016, accessed September 2016, http://www.aina.org/reports/ahrr.htm.

[43] Lorieux, *Chretiens D'Orient*, 58–67.

[44] "1988: Thousands Die in Halabja Gas Attack," *BBC News: On This Day*, accessed Sept, 2016, https://tinyurl.com/j4d3b.

[45] Shakhawan Shorsh, *'Anfal': the Iraqi State's Genocide Against the Kurds* (Center of Halabja against Anfalization and Genocide of the Kurds, February 2007), 28–33, accessed October 2016, https://tinyurl.com/y73vedjw.

[46] "Genocide in Iraq," *The Anfal Campaign Against the Kurds* (New York: Human Rights Watch, 1993), accessed August 2016, https://www.hrw.org/reports/1993/iraqanfal/ANFALINT.htm.

[47] John Burns, "Uncovering Iraq's Horrors in Forgotten Graves, *The New York Times*, June 5, 2006, accessed August 2016, https://tinyurl.com/y8fyuavo.

[48] Donobed, *Reforging a Forgotten History*, 212–214.

[49] "Documented Civilian Deaths from Violence," *Iraq Body Count*, copyright 2003–16, accessed September 2016, https://www.iraqbodycount.org/database.

[50] "Preventing the De-Christianization of Iraq: How to Stop the Exodus of Iraq's Indigenous ChaldoAssyrians Christians," Iraq Democracy Project, September 2007, accessed October 2016, https://tinyurl.com/y8zp572m.

[51] "Preventing the De-Christianization of Iraq," Iraq Democracy Project, 13.

[52] Ibid., 5–8.

[53] Joseph Kassab, *Proposed Strategic Initiatives*, Iraqi Christians Advocacy and Empowerment Institute, July 2017.

[54] Loraine Cabellero, "Church Should Not Encourage Christian Exodus from Iraq, Bishop Says," *Christian Daily*, April 17, 2016, accessed July 2016, https://tinyurl.com/yavr6cv2.

[55] "Chaldean Americans at a Glance," Chaldean American Chamber of Commerce, accessed October, 2016, https://tinyurl.com/y7lotbcf.

[56] John Pontifex and Oliver Maksan, "Christian Exodus from Iraq Accelerating – Two-thirds have left since 2003," *Christian Today*, July 2, 2014, accessed October 2016, https://tinyurl.com/l8oczg7.

[57] Mardean Isaac, "The Desperate Plight of Iraq's Assyrians and Other Communities," *The Guardian*, December 24, 2011, accessed October 2016, https://tinyurl.com/y8flcut4.

[58] Kate Mansfield, "End of Christianity in Iraq? Priest sees NO FUTURE for the religion in Middle Eastern city," *The Express*, February 11, 2017, https://tinyurl.com/y7pwc6lg.

[59] Lorieux, *Chretiens D'Orient*, 144.

[60] *Virtual Jewish World*, s.v. "Damascus, Syria," accessed September 2016, http://www.jewishvirtuallibrary.org/jsource/vjw/Damascus.html.

[61] Etienne de Vaumas, "La Structure Confessionelle de la Population Syrienne," Annales de Geographie, 1955, vol. 64, no. 341, 74–76, accessed September 2016, https://tinyurl.com/yabha96o.

[62] Ehsani, "The Declining number of Christians in Aleppo, Syria," *Syria Comment*, Feb. 16, 2012, accessed October 2016, https://tinyurl.com/yasn2g35.

[63] "Souk Burns as Aleppo Fight Rages," *The Irish Times*, September 29, 2012, accessed September 2016, https://tinyurl.com/ybtagqde.

[64] Shireen Qabbani, "Syria: Intense Aleppo Offensive Prompts Mass Exodus," *Asharq Al-Awsat English Archive*, December 26, 2013, accessed September 2016, https://tinyurl.com/y8vr3k4q.

[65] Lochon, "ISIS and the Threat to the Christian Architectural Heritage," *Oasis: Christians and Muslims in the Global World*, March 21, 2016, accessed September 2016, https://tinyurl.com/y9uh8scf.

[66] "Holy Belt of Virgin Mary Returned to Un Az-Zinnar Church in Homs," *SANA: Syrian Arab News Agency*, August 16, 2014, accessed September 2016, http://sana.sy/en/?p=10227.

[67] Alisar Iram, "Der Mar Mousa – The Story of Father Paolo Dall'Oglio and the Picturesque Deir Mar Mousa," *The Why.com*, May 29, 2014, accessed September 2016.

[68] Raphael Ahren, "'Thank God, There are Almost No Jews in Syria Now,' says the woman who rescued most of them," *The Times of Israel*, August 17, 2012, accessed July 2016, https://tinyurl.com/d9eue2n.
[69] Lorieux, *Chretiens D'Orient*, 135.
[70] Thomas Collelo, ed., "The Assad Era," in *Syria: A Country Study* (Washington: GPO for the Library of Congress, 1987).
[71] "Assyrian Human Rights Report," *Assyrian International News Agency*, accessed September 2016, http://www.aina.org/reports/ahrr.htm.
[72] Lorieux, *Chretiens D'Orient*, 145–7.
[73] Abdulmesih BarAbrahem, "A National School: A Brief Review on the 40th Anniversary of ADO," Assyrian Democratic Organization, 1997, accessed October 2016, http://www.atour.com/~ado/docs/ns.html.
[74] Lochon, "ISIS and the Threat to the Christian Architectural Heritage."
[75] Robert Nicholson, "Why the Best Solution for Syria is Partition," *The Federalist*, June 21, 2017, https://tinyurl.com/y877yb6f.
[76] Leila Tarazi Fawaz, *An Occasion For War: Civil Conflict In Lebanon And Damascus in 1860* (Berkeley and Los Angeles: University of California Press, 1994), e-book, 132–3, accessed on October 2016, https://tinyurl.com/ybw5o555.
[77] Vladimir Borisovich Lutsky, "Chapter IX: Lebanon, Syria and Palestine in the Period of the Tanzimats (1840–80)," in *Modern History of the Arab Countries*, ed. Robert Daglish, trans. Lika Nasser (Progress Publishers, Moscow for the USSR Academy of Sciences, Institute of the Peoples of Asia, 1969), on *Marxist Internet Archive*, transcribed for marxists.org by Sam Benner, 2008, accessed September 2016, https://www.marxists.org/subject/arab-world/lutsky/ch09.htm.
[78] United States Bureau of Citizen and Immigration Services, "Lebanon Information on South Lebanese Army (SLA) members and their families after the Israeli withdrawal from Southern Lebanon in May 2000," February 21, 2002, LBN02001.SND, accessed September 2016, http://www.refworld.org/docid/3f51fb0f4.html.
[79] "From Lebanese Refugee to Israeli Rocket Scientist," *The Times of Israel*, June 6, 2012, accessed October 2016, https://tinyurl.com/y8a2m3jn.
[80] "Lebanon: (Civil War 1975–1991)," *GlobalSecurity.org*, 2000–2016, accessed September 2016, https://tinyurl.com/cpy2nhf.
[81] Martha Wenger, "Primer: Lebanon's 15–year War 1975–1990," Middle East Research and Information Project, accessed September, 2016, https://tinyurl.com/ya8zvb63.
[82] Shadi Khalloul, "Lebanon, Christians, Under Islamic Threat," *Egret News*, April 24, 2016, accessed September 2016, http://egretnews.com/2017/?p=1239.

[83] Shadi Khalloul, "Israel's Christian Minority," *Jerusalem Post*, April, 6, 2016, accessed October 2016, https://tinyurl.com/y9gngx3k.

[84] Mordechai Kedar, "Op-Ed: Is there Really an Aramaean Nation?," *Arutz Sheva*, September 27, 2014, accessed October 2016, https://tinyurl.com/yacdcqwe.

[85] "History Made as Israeli Christian Child Registered as 'Aramaen,'" *Israel Today*, October 21, 2014, accessed September 2016, https://tinyurl.com/ycwhrbh3.

[86] Arianne Ishaya, "From Contributions to Diaspora: Assyrians in the History of Urmia, Iran," *Journal of Assyrian Academic Studies*, vol. 16, no. 1, 2002, originally presented as a paper in the Middle East Studies Association (MESA) Conference, San Francisco, 2001, accessed September 2016, https://tinyurl.com/y9xnbau4.

[87] Arianne Ishaya, "Settling into Diaspora: A History of Urmia Assyrians in the United States," *Journal of Assyrian Academic Studies*, vol. 20, no. 1, 2006: 27, accessed September 2016, https://tinyurl.com/y9gre975.

[88] "St. George (Mar Givargis) Church in Khusrow Abad (Khusrava) Iran," in *Ancient and Modern Assyrians*, ed. George V Yana (2009), e-book, accessed September 2016, https://tinyurl.com/ybzgfpp9.

[89] *Jewish Virtual Library*, s.v. "Iran," last update 2016, http://www.jewishvirtuallibrary.org/jsource/vjw/Iran.html.

[90] Robert Evans, "Gravestones showed mystery Jewish community flourished in medieval Armenia," *Ecumenical News*, December 1, 2015 accessed September 2016, https://tinyurl.com/y98qaadb.

[91] Ilan Ben Zion, "Jewish Woman Brutally Murdered in Iran over Property Dispute," *Times of Israel*, November 28, 2012, accessed October 2016, https://tinyurl.com/y9gjk5d5.

[92] Glenn E. Curtis and Eric Hoogland ed., *Iran: A Country Study* (Washington D.C.: Federal Research Division Library of Congress, 2008), 66, accessed September 2016, https://tinyurl.com/y8q69xw6.

[93] Ibid., 128–9.

[94] Arianne Ishaya, "Settling into Diaspora."

[95] Lorieux, *Chretiens d'Orient*, 268.

[96] Angie Chui, "Underground churches thriving in Iran despite persecution," *Christian Today*, April 7, 2016, accessed September 2016, https://tinyurl.com/y882kopx.

[97] Sofiamo, "Why is Christianity Growing So Fast in Iran?," *Daily Kos*, February 2, 2015, accessed September 2016, https://tinyurl.com/yd2fwl6u.

[98] "Iran's Secret Christian Movement Grows, With Help from Abroad," *Fox News*, March 7, 2016, accessed September 2016, https://tinyurl.com/zfjacel.

[99] Lorieux, *Chretiens D'Orient*, 285.

[100] "About Us" on Assyro-Chaldean Catholic Archdiocese Urmia-Salmas website, accessed September 2016, https://tinyurl.com/y7vs9re3.

[101] Paul Caldan, "Ordination of Priest Rayan Issa in Iran," *Kaldaya.net*, August 23, 2010, accessed September 2016, https://tinyurl.com/yc32rp3f.

[102] "Christians in Iran," *Oasis: Christians and Muslims in the Global World*, November 6, 2015, accessed September 2016, https://tinyurl.com/ybkdxrks.

Sunday in the Middle East

[1] Bernard Lewis, *What Went Wrong? The Clash Between Islam and Modernity in the Middle East* (New York: HarperCollins, 2002).

[2] Raymond Ibrahim, *Crucified Again: Exposing Islam's New War on Christians* (Washington D.C.: Regnery Publishing, 2013), 18–31, 96–104.

[3] Judith Bergman, "Dawa: Sowing the Seeds of Hate," *Gatestone Institute: International Policy Council*, November 4, 2017, https://www.gatestoneinstitute.org/11283/islamic-dawa-hate.

[4] "Al-Taqiyya, Dissimulation Part I," *Al-Islam.org*, https://tinyurl.com/y89bldyw.

[5] Gilles Kepel, *Jihad: The Trail of Political Islam* (Cambridge: Harvard University Press, 2002), 50.

[6] Trevor Stanley, "Understanding the Origins of Wahhabism and Salafism," *Terrorism Monitor*, vol. 3 no. 4, July 15, 2005, on *The Jamestown Foundation*, accessed September 2016, https://tinyurl.com/ya4yxn4d.

[7] Kepel, *Jihad: The Trail of Political Islam*, 6.

[8] Shakir translation, *Quranic Arabic Corpus*.

[9] Kepel, *Jihad: The Trail of Political Islam*, 299.

[10] "The Islamic State," *Mapping Militant Organizations*, Stanford University, April 4, 2016, accessed September 2016, https://tinyurl.com/mvbqokg.

[11] "ISIS: Portrait of a Jihadi Terrorist Organization," Meir Amit Intelligence and Terrorism Information Center at the Israeli Intelligence and Heritage Information Center, November 2014, 24, accessed September 2016, http://www.crethiplethi.com/files/cp_0115.pdf.

[12] "ISIS," Meir Amit Intelligence and Terrorism Information Center, 46.

[13] Ibid., 45

[14] Kanishk Tharoor, "Life Among the Ruins," *The New York Times*, March 19, 2016, accessed September 2016, https://tinyurl.com/hqxex3h.

[15] James Verini, "The Living and the Dead," *The New York Times Magazine*, July 19, 2017, https://tinyurl.com/y9yj7ql4.

[16] Frederick A. Aprim, "Assyrians Face Religious Persecution and Ethnic Genocide: Assyrians Face Oppression, Harassment, Intimidation and Murder in Iraq with the Rise of Arab Islamists and Kurdish Regional Power," *Assyrian Information Management*, accessed October 2016, December 31, 2010, http://www.atour.com/news/assyria/20100424a.html.

[17] "Preventing the De-Christianization of Iraq: How to Stop the Exodus of Iraq's Indigenous ChaldoAssyrians Christians," Iraq Democracy Project, September 2007, accessed October 2016, https://tinyurl.com/y8zp572m.

[18] Ibrahim, *Crucified Again*, 68–69.

[19] Martin Chulov, "Iraqi Christians Flee Baghdad after Cathedral massacre," *The Guardian*, accessed September 2016, https://tinyurl.com/y8t4yrqo.

[20] Ibrahim, *Crucified Again*, 84.

[21] Raymond Ibrahim, "Muslim persecution of Christians: November, 2012," *Gatestone Institute: International Policy Council*, February 1, 2013, accessed September 2016, https://tinyurl.com/ycpkprdt.

[22] "Third Attack in New Assyrian Quarter in Aleppo, Scores Injured and Killed," *Assyrian International News Agency (AINA)*, November 20, 2012, accessed September 2016, https://tinyurl.com/y98gyaya.

[23] Katrina Lantos Swett, chair, "United States Commision on International Religious Freedom: Annual Report 2015," Washington D.C., 2015, 95, https://tinyurl.com/qaapjmu.

[24] Martin Chulov, "40,000 Iraqis stranded on mountain as ISIS jihadists threaten death," *The Guardian*, August 6, 2014, accessed September 2016, https://tinyurl.com/y7gzqrts.

[25] "All Christian Institutions in Mosul Destroyed or Occupied by ISIS," *Assyrian International News Agency (AINA)*, July 29, 2014, accessed September 2016, http://www.aina.org/news/20140729100528.htm.

[26] "List of Assyrian and other Churches Destroyed in Syria," *Assyrian International News Agency (AINA)*, December 13, 2015, accessed September 2016, http://www.aina.org/news/20151212211531.htm.

[27] "Timeline of ISIS in Iraq," *Assyrian International News Agency (AINA)*, last updated July 2016, accessed September 2016, http://www.aina.org/news/20140729115702.htm.

[28] Sozbin Celeng, "ISIS Destroys Assyrian Archeological Gate in Mosul," *Assyrian International News Agency (AINA)*, April 12, 2016, accessed October 2016, http://www.aina.org/news/20160412012359.htm.

[29] Hamdi Alkhshali et al, "U.S., Iraq Say ISIS Blows Up Famous Mosul Mosque," *CNN*, June 23, 2017, https://tinyurl.com/ybyrxaa4.

[30] Robert P. George, chair, "United States Commission on International Religious Freedom: 2016 Annual Report," Washington D.C., 2016, accessed September 2016, http://www.aina.org/reports/uscirf2016.pdf.

[31] "Islamic Terror on Christians," *The Religion of Peace*, last updated September 2016, https://tinyurl.com/h4mncda.

[32] "Attacks on Assyrians in Syria by ISIS and Other Muslim Groups," *Assyrian International News Agency (AINA)*, accessed September 2016, http://www.aina.org/releases/20150226225711.htm.

[33] Gianlucca Mezzofiore, "Syria: ISIS Releases 22 Assyrians Abducted in February," *International Business Times*, August 11, 2015, accessed October 2016, https://tinyurl.com/ycmbtlyn.

[34] "Up to 373 Assyrians captured by ISIS, executions have begun," *Orthodox Christianity*, March 17, 2015, accessed October 2016, http://www.pravoslavie.ru/english/77640.htm.

[35] Vincent Funaro, "ISIS Militants Rape, Torture and Crucify 12 Christians Who Refuse to Deny Jesus Christ," *Christian Post*, October 5, 2015, accessed October 2016, https://tinyurl.com/y93bcoxs.

Tomorrow

[1] Enis Tayman, "Turkey Invites Wary Minorities to Return from Exile" *Al-Monitor*, March 2013, accessed September 2016, https://tinyurl.com/y85sydfh.

[2] Susanne Gusten, "Istanbul Policy Center-Mercator Policy Brief: The Syriac Property Issue in Tur Abdin," Istanbul Policy Center (Istanbul: Sabanci University, 2015), accessed September 2016, http://www.aina.org/reports/apita.pdf.

[3] Uzay Bulut, "Turkey's Mass Persecution of Christians and Kurds," *Gatestone Institute: International Policy Coucil*, September 4, 2017, https://tinyurl.com/y9wdfel7.

[4] Okan Konuralp, "Syriac Community Receives Deed for Lands of Mor Gabriel Monastery," *Hurriyet Daily News*, February 27, 2014, accessed September 2016, https://tinyurl.com/ycmk3epn.

[5] Robert Jones, "Turkey targets oldest Syriac monastery," *Gatestone Institute: International Policy Coucil*, November 16, 2016, accessed November 2016, https://www.gatestoneinstitute.org/9326/turkey-syriac-monastery.

[6] Peter BetBasoo, "Brief History of Assyrians," *Assyrian International News Agency (AINA)*, November 1, 2013, accessed September 2016, http://www.aina.org/brief.html.

[7] *The Joshua Project*, s.v. "Assyrian," accessed June 28, 2017, https://joshuaproject.net/people_groups/10464.

[8] "Christentum: Orthodoxe, Orientalische und Unierte Kirchen," *REMID*, accessed June 28, 2017, https://tinyurl.com/yd6x6jhq.

[9] "Community Overview," Chaldean American Chamber of Commerce, accessed October 2016, https://tinyurl.com/ydb5kmjt.

[10] "History of the Chaldean Catholic Church," *Chaldeans On Line*, accessed September 2016, http://www.chaldeansonline.org/church.html.

[11] Holy Apostolic Catholic Assyrian Church of the East Official News Website, accessed September 2016, http://news.assyrianchurch.org/category/diocese.

[12] "The Syrian Orthodox Church," Syriac Orthodox Church Worldwide, 2004, accessed September 2016, https://tinyurl.com/ycsh65sv.

[13] Jonathan Speyer, "Beyond Mosul," Rubin Center Research in International Affairs, September 25, 2016, accessed September 2016, http://www.rubincenter.org/2016/09/beyond-mosul.

[14] *Everything Explained Today*, s.v. "Chaldean Catholic Church Explained," accessed September 2016, https://tinyurl.com/y8f86j2t.

[15] Seth J. Frantzman, "Why the Kurds Should Fascinate Western Liberals," *The Tower Magazine*, September 2016, no. 42, accessed September 2016, https://tinyurl.com/yapvsvrv.

[16] Yousif Kailan, "The Nineveh Plains and the Future of Minorities in Iraq," *Rudaw*, February 15, 2017, https://tinyurl.com/y7skw54n.

[17] "Iraq: The Struggle to Exist," Assyria Council of Europe and Hammurabi Human Rights Organization, February 2010, accessed October 2016, http://www.aina.org/reports/acetste.pdf.

[18] Ibid., 12.

[19] Omar Sattar, "Iraq's Christians Ponder Future in Wake of Kurdish Independence Vote," *Al-Monitor*, October 24, 2017, https://tinyurl.com/ya3rp2um.

[20] "What is Peace-keeping?" *United Nations Peacekeeping*, accessed October 2016, https://peacekeeping.un.org/en/what-is-peacekeeping.

[21] Dore Gold, *Tower of Babble* (New York: Three Rivers Press, 2004), 6–10.

[22] "Preventing the De-Christianization of Iraq: How to Stop the Exodus of Iraq's Indigenous ChaldoAssyrians Christians," Iraq Democracy Project, September 2007, accessed October 2016, https://tinyurl.com/y8zp572m, 15.

[23] Micael Youash, "What Does the Nineveh Plains Administrative Area Mean?," *Assyrian International News Agency*, June 8, 2007, accessed October 2016, http://www.aina.org/news/20070608121220.htm.

[24] H. Con. Res. 152, 114th Cong. (2015-2016).

[25] Michael Youash, "At the Tipping Point: A Nineveh Plain Province and Related Solutions to Iraq's Indigenous Minority Crisis," Iraq Sustainable Democracy Project, accessed October 2016, https://tinyurl.com/y8v29eqt.

[26] Youash, "The Tipping Point," 12.

[27] "The Nineveh Project,"*Assyrian Information Management*, May 09, 2012, accessed September, 2016, https://tinyurl.com/y7rrou3y.

[28] Susan Crabtree, "Activists and Religious Leaders Urge Protection for Religious Minorities," *The Washington Free Beacon*, May 31, 2017, https://tinyurl.com/y7f4lx26.

[29] Mikhael Benjamin, "The Minorities of Nineveh Plain and the Demand for a Safe Haven and International Protection: A vision For Implementation," *Assyrian International News Agency*, August 7, 2014, accessed October 2016, http://www.aina.org/reports/mnpdsh.pdf.

[30] Restore Nineveh Now, accessed October 2016, http://www.restoreninevehnow.org.

[31] "Iraq: The Struggle to Exist," Assyria Council of Europe and Hammurabi Human Rights Organization, February 2010, 24-27, accessed October 2016, http://www.aina.org/reports/acetste.pdf.

[32] "Bishops ask for International Protection for Christians in Iraq, Chaldean Patriarch Disagrees," *Assyrian International News Agency*, May 15, 2017, http://www.aina.org/news/20170515172959.htm.

[33] Joseph Kassab, "Proposed Strategic Initiatives," *Iraqi Christians Advocacy and Empowerment Institute*, July 2017.

[34] Reidar Visser, "The Iraqi Cabinet Decides to Form Three New Governorates," Iraq and Gulf Analysis, January 22, 2014, https://tinyurl.com/ybcj6j3h.

[35] Kelsey Wendelberger, "Historic Demand from Christian (Assyrian, Syriac, Chaldean) Political Parties to Prime Minister Al-Abadi for Creation of Nineveh Plain Province," press release from the Iraqi Christian Relief Council, March 8, 2017, https://tinyurl.com/ybzs38vk.

[36] "Assyrian Human Rights Report," *Assyrian International News Agency*, http://www.aina.org/reports/ahrr.htm.

[37] Elmer Abbo, "Preconditions for a Free and Fair Future for the Nineveh Plain," *ankawa.com*, July 2, 2017, https://tinyurl.com/ydyxh56d.

[38] Joseph Kassab, "The Grim Plight of Iraq's Christians; Strategies and Durable Solutions To Rise From Ashes: A White Paper," *The Iraqi Christians Advocacy and Empowerment Institute*, July 2016, personal communication.

[39] Robert Nicholson, "The Strategic Case for a Safe Haven in Northern Iraq," Philos Project, accessed October 2016, https://philosproject.org/strategic-case-safe-haven-northern-iraq.

[40] "Prevent the Ethno-Religious Extermination of Iraq's Indigenous, Christian Assyrians: The 'Nineveh Plain Province Solution' – A Legislative Proposal," Iraq Sustainable Democracy Project, accessed September, 2016, https://tinyurl.com/ya8ccqor.

[41] "State Department Inaction Must End," Assyrian American National Coalition, September 2016, accessed October 2016, http://aancoalition.rallycongress.com/4655/the-state-department.

[42] "More than 50 Members of Congress Attended IDC's Convention to Address the Persecution of Christians, Other Minorities in the Middle East," *In Defense of Christians*, September 12, 2015, accessed October 2016, http://www.prweb.com/releases/2016/09/prweb13678104.htm.

[43] "House Resolution Introduced to Create Safe Haven for Persecuted Minorities in Iraq," *The Algemeiner*, September 15, 2016, accessed October 2016, https://tinyurl.com/ydenf4vj.

[44] Patrick Goodenough, "ISIS Genocide Brings Fresh Calls for a Semi-Autonomous Haven for Christians in Iraq," *Assyrian International News Agency*, September 13, 2016, accessed October 2016, http://www.aina.org/news/20160913143759.htm.

[45] Naomi Kikoler, "Our Generation is Gone: The Islamic State's Targeting of Iraqi Minorities in Ninewa," *Bearing News Trip Report*, The United States Holocaust Memorial Museum, 2014, 10, accessed September 2016, http://www.aina.org/reports/nhmreport.pdf.

[46] Robert P. George, chair, "United States Commission on International Religious Freedom: 2016 Annual Report," Washington D.C., 2016, accessed September 2016, http://www.aina.org/reports/uscirf2016.pdf.

[47] "Iraq: The Struggle to Exist," Assyria Council of Europe and Hammurabi Human Rights Organization, February 2010, 26-27, accessed October 2016, http://www.aina.org/reports/acetste.pdf.

[48] "Syrian Christians are Caught Between Civil War and Islamist Terrorism," *Oasis: Christians and Muslims in the Global World*, accessed October 2016, https://tinyurl.com/yad9znvf.

[49] "Are Christians Beginning to Return Home In Iraq?" *Solidarity with the Persecuted Church (SPC)*, https://tinyurl.com/yaucf3gy.

[50] "Fear and Renewal; a Town is liberated From ISIS," *Free Burma Ranger*, February 22, 2017, https://tinyurl.com/y8ljmr7f.

[51] Robert Nicholson, "The Strategic Case for a Safe Haven in Northern Iraq," The Philos Project, accessed October 2016, https://philosproject.org/strategic-case-safe-haven-northern-iraq.
[52] Robert Nicholson, "The Right Way to Liberate Mosul," *Providence*, August 19, 2016, accessed October 2016, https://tinyurl.com/y8szl49v.

www.ingramcontent.com/pod-product-compliance
Lightning Source LLC
Chambersburg PA
CBHW060327100426
42812CB00003B/907